The Politics of Privacy, Computers, and Criminal Justice Records

Controlling the Social Costs of Technological Change

DONALD A. MARCHAND
*ASSOCIATE DIRECTOR, BUREAU OF GOVERNMENTAL
RESEARCH AND SERVICE
AND
ASSISTANT PROFESSOR, DEPARTMENT OF
GOVERNMENT AND INTERNATIONAL STUDIES
UNIVERSITY OF SOUTH CAROLINA*

INFORMATION
RESOURCES PRESS
Arlington, Virginia   1980

Available from
Information Resources Press
1700 North Moore Street
Arlington, Virginia 22209

Library of Congress Catalog Card Number 80-80675

ISBN 0-87815-030-7

To My Parents

Adelard F. and Laurette D. Marchand

Foreword

For several decades, we have been in the midst of a technological revolution variously known as "the computer age," "the technetronic society," and the "age of information." Enthusiasts see this as the opening of a data-rich civilization. For the first time in history, they believe, we could provide the breadth of information that a truly rational society needs to make objective and fair judgments about the access of individuals to benefits, rights, and opportunities in an organizational world; to design, operate, and evaluate governmental policies and business affairs; and to allow students of society and its institutions to analyze its behavior in newly sophisticated and insightful ways. This is, indeed, the modern alchemist's dream: to turn base data into golden insights.

But there are those who view the dawning of the electronic age with less than Aquarian joy. The creation of powerful data banks, filled with sensitive personal information, raises serious issues of privacy and due process. The "mechanization of judgment" and "machining of decisions" could skew the policymaking processes of government and business into overly quantifiable approaches that neglect the human and social aspects of events and problems. And, as more judgments are made by a new priesthood of technicians and administrators relying upon high-technology approaches, we could further erode the citizen participation and individual involvement on which a healthy democratic system depends.

These competing visions—one looking at the potential advantages of new information technology and the other stressing its potential dangers—present a host of questions for society and its leaders. For the serious student of society pursuing both the improvement of knowledge and the possible value of scholarly insights to public decisions, analyzing the arrival of information technology calls for an orderly and disciplined strategy.

The first step, I believe, is to adopt the proper theoretical perspective: that information technology is an immensely powerful tool but still a variable in the larger social and political process, and not vice versa. It seems clear that no previous new technology—the printing press, the internal combustion engine, and so on—can be compared to the combination of sheer technological power contained in the post World War II package of television, computers, and telecommunications. But, although awesome in its magnitude and in potential ways it might alter our society, information technology remains a tool or process that will be used according to social choice. Despite the cautionary science-fiction stories of machines that think for themselves and take over the management of society from fumbling mortals, how information technology is used in the real world is and will remain a matter of human will. Therefore, serious analysis of information technology should be understood as an examination of a variable in the social process.

Second, the serious analyst must construct a model of the technology-reception process that takes into account the complex set of forces that control the decisions about such issues. One way to conceptualize this is to visualize a new technology as a physical object moving into a steel web that represents society's rules and arrangements. Technology never breaks through this social web, which is an extremely dense intertwining of economic, legal, organizational, social, and cultural constraints. Rather, a new technology makes a slow and gradual passage through the web. In the process, both the technology is shaped in its forms of application and accepted capabilities and the strands of the web are altered. Sometimes, the strands open fairly widely to accommodate new forms of technological use; sometimes, they hold firm to block certain uses of the technology or substantially alter its application.

Following this image, the task of the scholar is to identify the nature, characteristics, and potential of the new technology and the uses proposed by its own developers and those forces in society that endorse such uses. With the technology thus launched into the social web, the analyst then tries to trace each forward passage, studying the forces propelling, repelling, and modifying the passage. At each stage, the analyst tries to identify how the technology's development and uses are altered and how, in turn, the technology is affecting society—in its culture, politics, economics, inter alia.

Third, the analyst must understand that the process of technological passage is inescapably a *political* one, using political in the broader, nonperjorative sense of that term. Although new technologies may be socially "neutral" in an abstract sense ("a gun don't make a killer, ma'am, it's the man what uses it..."), the fact is that, which groups in society get to use a new technology and to what social ends its capabilities are directed, are preeminently political questions. In the case of information technology, the fact that computer and telecommunication systems began as very costly machinery, requiring very expensive technological staffs to operate them and very expensive installations to house and power them, meant that this technology would be available in its first decades only to large, powerful organizations: corporations, government, unions, and so on. To make a very rough comparison, the handgun was a power-distributing technology; it could be made with limited capital and skills, and, once made, it was cheaply available to masses of individuals. The Molotov cocktail (fuel, wick, and bottle) was a similar power-distributing tool. But information technology is a power-enhancing tool; its costs of production and operation guaranteed that it would go to the organizational establishment of each nation.

But, once this overarching political fact is recognized, there are a host of political factors to analyze: Which organizations within the establishment adopted the new technology and how was the adoption accomplished? What effects has the adoption had on organizational performance of goals, programs, and procedures? At what point does the use of information technology by business, a government agency, or private organization become a matter of public debate, political decision, or legal intervention?

At this stage in the historical development of information technology applications, the accumulation of detailed case studies is probably the prime requirement for intellectual progress. What we need is an accurate reconstruction of events, motives, and decisions: the analysis of interests pursued and accommodations arranged; the role of legal rules, institutional processes, and organizational factors; the perceptions of problems, possible solutions, obstacles to be overcome, and cost-benefit analyses conducted; and, finally, the interplay of this area of policy with the larger political trends and social forces that make up the total environment.

My objective in sketching these elements of a scholarly analysis of information technology's impact on contemporary society is not to provide a detailed catalog but only to note the major elements, and to explain my conviction that we have reached the moment at which such serious studies can and should be conducted. Enough time has passed since the arrival of information technology in the organizational world in the late 1950s and enough experience with technology-reception has been accumulated that such studies can be attempted.

This is precisely what Professor Marchand has done in this excellent work assessing the use of information technology in criminal justice recordkeeping and examining its impact on one particular social value—privacy. He has applied the political scientist's "politics of..."

approach—"the politics of revenue-sharing," "the politics of federal aid to education," "the politics of gun-control"—to the uses of computer systems by law enforcement agencies, and has done it with great skill. It is, first of all, an extremely valuable descriptive analysis, tracing two decades of debates, actions, and effects of computer use in the criminal justice field in a careful manner that tells the reader what has happened and why. Professor Marchand then goes on to offer the judgment that our existing, pluralist model of the policymaking process has failed to weigh adequately the social costs of using automated criminal justice records against the social benefits of such action. He believes that major changes are needed in the way we operate our social web of technology-reception if the public interest of a democratic society is to be well served. His blend of theoretical clarity, re-creation of the organizational and political actions, and proposals for real-world improvement of the policy process offer a model that could be followed in dozens of other areas in which information technology has been employed. It is just the kind of work that social scientists should make a major priority of the 1980s.

January 1980   ALAN F. WESTIN
                                                                    Professor of Public Law
                                                                       in Government
                                                                    Columbia University

Preface

This study examines the social costs of the computerized information systems used by criminal justice agencies in the United States and the problems of identifying and controlling these costs. Social costs are defined as uncompensated costs to individuals or groups in society, arising from the activities of public organizations that result in significant infringements or denials of individual rights, such as privacy and due process, or that restrict social, political, or economic opportunities. The central question of the analysis is the extent to which the social costs arising from the introduction of technological innovations in public organizations have been reduced through the existing public policymaking process or can be reduced with proposed changes in that process. This is perceived as the means through which the costs and benefits associated with particular technological applications are distributed. The study focuses on the processes of participation and representation related to reducing the social costs of criminal justice records and on the political costs and benefits of choosing various regulatory arrangements.

The principal finding of this study is that the prevailing policymaking process does not ensure that the social costs of criminal justice records will be significantly reduced and weighed against the interests of criminal justice agencies that use computerized information systems. The problem of the social costs of criminal justice records provides a direct challenge to the basic assumptions of the pluralist model of politics. Not only are there significant constraints on the prospects for collective action on the part of those affected by the social costs of criminal justice records, but there also are significant limitations on the successful reduction of the social costs of criminal justice records in the policymaking process by relevant interest groups, entrepreneurs, and public officials at various levels of government.

Criminal justice agencies—the primary producers of social costs—also have an important role in the decision-making process to reduce these costs. The extent to which agencies have taken action to reduce such social costs, however, generally has depended on agency perceptions that, if privacy and security safeguards were not provided, significant curtailments in the development of large-scale computerized information networks and systems might be demanded by the public. This study analyzes a number of limitations on the capabilities of public officials, interest groups, and individuals to influence criminal justice agency decisions and activities. In addition, the prospects for reduction of social costs through proposed changes in regulatory arrangements are assessed, and eight proposals for a national policy concerning criminal justice information systems and the use of criminal justice records are examined.

This study suggests that the relationship between technology and politics has mutually interacting variables, since technology does not operate autonomously. The introduction of computers in criminal justice recordkeeping has made the uses of records and recordkeeping systems a public issue where the stakes and trade-offs are very high for the principal actors involved. Thus, whether technological innovations are used for good or bad purposes is integrally linked with the existing policymaking process because the use of such innovations is influenced by political choices. The problem of social costs, then, is connected with the political context in terms of how such costs are identified and the manner in which information about social costs is used by participants in the policymaking process.

If technological changes bring on high social costs, they will be imposed by men on men and not by machines on men: Many of the problems associated with the introduction of new technology existed prior to the development of the technology. What to some apparently are the inevitable results of technology are largely the consequences of political and organizational structures and processes biased in favor of nonrecognition, or only limited recognition, of social costs and the need for their identification and control.

This book is divided into three parts. Part I deals with the practical and conceptual concerns that guided the research effort; Part II presents the case study and responds to the problems and issues suggested in Part I; and Part III assesses the political and administrative implications of the social costs of technological change in public organizations in a democratic society.

The materials and documents for the research were collected between 1972 and 1978. I began working on this topic in 1972 while a research associate at the Institute on Law and Urban Studies at Loyola University Law School in Los Angeles and a graduate student in the Department of Political Science at the University of California at Los Angeles. What began as a review of the role of the Law Enforcement Assistance Administration in supporting the use of information technology in criminal justice agencies in California, gradually, over a period of several years, developed into a consuming and intense interest in the social and political effects of such innovations, especially their impacts on individual rights and on disadvantaged people. From 1973 to 1976, interviews were conducted and materials assembled for the writing of the doctoral dissertation on which this book is based. During the summer of 1978, the dissertation was updated, a new round of interviews with key participants was conducted, and more recent materials were collected.

The motivation for completing the book was enhanced significantly in 1977 and 1978 by an appointment to serve on the Federal Data Processing Reorganization Study of the President's Reorganization Project. The extensive field experience provided through the project during the winter of 1977–1978 confirmed that I was pursuing a topic that needed clarification and that the problems and issues raised in this book were common to government recordkeeping activities in areas other than criminal justice.

During 1979, as a principal contractor for the history, use, and social impacts studies on the Assessment of the National Crime Information Center and Computerized Criminal History Program, I was provided a unique and significant opportunity to deepen and extend the research on which this book is based. The program was conducted by the Office of Technology Assessment of the U.S. Congress as part of OTA's project on Societal Impacts of National Information Systems. At the time of this writing, OTA is preparing a report to Congress on its assessment of the National Crime Information Center, which promises to significantly broaden and extend the policy debates on the benefits and costs of law enforcement and criminal justice information systems in the United States.

A number of individuals have provided encouragement, advice, and friendship during this book's evolution and deserve special mention: Stan Bachrack, Eva Bogan, John Bollens, Lynne Cooper, Steve Doyle, Robert Gerstein, Steve Hays, Lance Hoffman, Marcia Mac-Naughton, Ed Merrow, John Stucker, and Mark Tompkins. Support and administrative assistance to complete the book were provided by the Bureau of Governmental Research and Service and the Department of Government and International Studies at the University of South Carolina. I would like to thank Dr. Charlie B. Tyer, Director of the Bureau, and Dr. James Kuhlman, Chairman of the Department, for their assistance and encouragement. A special thanks to Saul Herner, editor-in-chief, and Gene Allen, publisher, of Information Resources Press for their initial concern and willingness to encourage work in a new direction, and to Susan Heylman and Margaret Emmitt, editors, for their patience, perseverance, and constant assurances that everything would turn out all right. Finally, my love and gratitude to my wife, Joyce, and my sons, David and Todd, for providing the encouragement, caring atmosphere, and stimulation to pursue the project to its conclusion.

Any errors in fact or judgment are, of course, my responsibility.

January 1980

Acronyms and Abbreviations

ACLU	American Civil Liberties Union
AIDS	Automated Fingerprint Identification Systems
FBI	Federal Bureau of Investigation
CCH	Computerized Criminal History
CCM	Crime Control Model
CHRI	Criminal History Record Information
CJIS	Criminal Justice Information Systems
CDS	Comprehensive Data System
CJIC	Criminal Justice Information Control
CORI	Criminal Offender Record Information
CSR	Central State Repositories
DPA	Delegation of Procurement Authority
DPM	Due Process Model
DOJ	Department of Justice
EFT	Electronic Funds Transfer
GSA	General Services Administration
IOCI	Interstate Organized Crime Index
LEAA	Law Enforcement Assistance Administration
LETS	Law Enforcement Teletype System
NASIS	National Association of State Information Systems
NCIC	National Crime Information Center
NLETS	National Law Enforcement Telecommunications System
NYSIIS	New York State Identification and Intelligence System
OBTS	Offender-based Transaction Statistics
OLEA	Office of Law Enforcement Assistance
OMB	Office of Management and Budget
OTA	Office of Technology Assessment
OTP	Office of Telecommunications Policy
PDM	Presidential Decision Memorandum
RFP	Request for Proposal
RM	Rehabilitative Model
SEARCH	System for Electronic Analysis and Retrieval of Criminal Histories
SGI	Search Group, Inc.
SPA	State Planning Agency
SIPI	Scientists' Institute for Public Information
SSRC	Social Science Research Council

Contents

PART I

1

Technology Assessment and Control—Problems of Public Choice

Americans have always delighted in the discovery and use of new technology. Our fascination with gadgetry, enthusiasm for new machines, pursuit of progress, and taking on vast technological challenges, such as the Apollo space program, have both amazed and dismayed observers of our society. At various times in our history, technology has been closely linked to the pursuit of political and administrative reforms. Beginning with the Progressive movement around the turn of the century and continuing to the present period, a variety of reform groups and activists have promoted the dual concepts of technological innovation and managerial efficiency as ways of transforming what they perceive as an inefficient, ineffective, or even corrupt governmental system into one that is responsive to the needs of the community and the imperatives of economic and technological change.

As the negative consequences of the technology that has pervaded every aspect of our lives have become apparent, Americans have become less and less willing to consider technological and scientific discoveries as "irresistible forces bringing unquestioned technical advantages and intrinsically containing the seeds of economic and social progress."[1] The passage of air and water pollution legislation in the 1960s, the creation of the Environmental Protection Agency in 1970, the decision by Congress against development of a supersonic transport (SST) aircraft, and the public debates over nuclear power, the "limits of growth," and the use of "appropriate technologies," all reflect a new direction in the attitudes of the public and of the intellec-

[1] Francois Hetman. *Society and the Assessment of Technology*. Paris, Organization for Economic Cooperation and Development, 1973, p. 19.

3

tual and scholarly community toward science and technology. Moreover, the recognition that technology can have both beneficial and undesirable consequences gives rise to questions about the effectiveness of governmental processes and structures in responding to the need to properly identify, monitor, and manage the adverse effects of complex and new technologies.

In recent years, changes in public attitudes have required the government to begin accounting for and controlling its negative effects on the public and on individuals. The increasing size and complexity of government agencies and the proliferation of government programs also have caused a growing uneasiness among elected officials, managerial executives, and the public about the abilities of governing agencies to account for the consequences of their actions. Americans also have become increasingly dissatisfied with their everyday contacts with government as well as with paperwork and reporting burdens. Concern and fear about the ability of government agencies to manipulate individual lives have been accompanied by pervasive doubts about the capabilities of the public policymaking processes to bring government institutions under effective control and, at the same time, to enhance their performance.

The past two decades have witnessed rapid development in computer technology, as well as numerous ideas, in both private industry and government institutions, for application of this technology. This book focuses on the applications of technological innovations by public organizations in the 1960s and 1970s and the capabilities of the public policymaking process to identify, monitor, and control the adverse consequences of these technological innovations. The improved capabilities and flexibility of information technology, coupled with its use at all levels of government, have raised serious questions about whether the adverse consequences of these technologies are being appropriately considered by the government.

Since the advent of computers, bureaucracy and technology have merged to create information-processing systems, which operate in a symbiotic way, that pose a substantial challenge to prevailing concepts of how a democratic government should work. Moreover, because these innovations have occurred in the context of large, complex organizations, the resultant political and governmental issues have been obscured. Despite the difficulty of identifying these issues, the consequences for millions of individuals and for democratic government are very real and dramatic. A more complete picture of precisely how technological innovations and their consequences are considered in government agencies and the extent to which the interests and concerns of those individuals affected by government information-processing systems are represented in the public policy process also is discussed.

ASSESSING THE EFFECTS OF TECHNOLOGICAL CHANGE

The movement to identify, monitor, and control the negative consequences of technological innovations has led to the development of a class of policy studies called "technology assessments," which attempt to "systematically examine the effects that may occur when a technology is introduced, extended, or modified with special emphasis on those consequences that are unintended, indirect, or delayed."[2] Technology assessments aim at identifying the secondary or tertiary consequences of new technology rather than the primary (intended) effects, because

1. In the long run, the unintended and indirect effects may be most significant;
2. Undesirable secondary consequences often are unnecessary and may be prevented by proper planning;
3. First-order impacts usually are subject to extensive study in the planning stage.[3]

Thus, technology assessments focus "on the question of what *else* may happen when the technology is introduced."[4]

While advocates of technology assessment studies recognize that the introduction of technology may have second-order consequences, they do suggest that, given the complex and pervasive qualities of new technology, it is more difficult to anticipate secondary consequences

---

[2] Joseph F. Coates. "Technology Assessment: The Benefits ... the Costs ... the Consequences." *Futurist*, 5:225, December 1971. For a general history of technology assessment and a review of its developments, see Hetman, *Society and the Assessment of Technology*; Derek Medford, *Environmental Harassment or Technology Assessment?*, New York, Elsevier, 1973; Organization for Economic Cooperation and Development, *Methodological Guidelines for Social Assessment of Technology*, Paris, 1975; U.S. Congress, House, Committee on Science and Astronautics, Subcommittee on Science, Research, and Development, *Technical Information for Congress*, 92d Congress, 1st Session, April 15, 1971; and National Academy of Sciences, *Technology Assessment: Processes of Assessment and Choice*, Report to Committee on Science and Astronautics, House, U.S. Congress, 1969.

[3] Coates. "Technology Assessment: The Benefits," p. 225.

[4] *Ibid.*

than primary consequences. Proponents of this approach to policy analysis emphasize the need to evaluate second-order consequences of technologies, especially adverse consequences, and to include their costs in the public policymaking process.

Technology assessment, then, is perceived as a method for mapping out policy and technological options. Two general modes of performing assessments have been developed: problem-oriented assessments and technology-oriented assessments.[5] In the former case, the widespread effects of a technology, such as air pollution caused by automobiles or congested air traffic, are analyzed with the intention of pinpointing the causes and seeking possible solutions. In the latter case, the future consequences of a new technology, for example, space satellites, lasers, or digital computers, are identified to determine whether and what technological developments might be favored or discouraged. In recent years, technology assessments have been completed in five major areas: monitoring negative side effects of existing technologies; maintaining environmental quality; recycling resources; screening scientific knowledge and research; and assessing desirable new technologies.[6] Common to technology assessment in these areas is the twofold problem of reducing uncertainty concerning the secondary effects of technological change and redirecting the public policymaking process to respond to the goals and information provided by technology assessments.

Technology assessments aim at improving the quality of decision making about technological developments and of information about the causal relationships between technological innovations and their manifold effects, as well as the significant constraints on the development and use of such information in the public policymaking process. In addition, they question the adequacy of the public policymaking process for coping with the tasks of assessing and planning technological developments amidst changing social demands and changes of growing complexity in the technology itself.

To what extent are the present policy-making patterns obsolete? In the face of a rapidly increasing rate of technological change, the obsolescence of sociopolitical processes is accelerated through the rigidity of existing institutions.

Institutions seem to have an in-built tendency to stick to their first or initial purposes and to erect a wall against changes and external influences. They end up by concentrating on the defense of their existence and perenniality instead of modifying their functioning or yielding to new forms of action.[7]

---

[5] See Hetman, *Society and the Assessment of Technology*, pp. 61, 63.
[6] *Ibid.*, pp. 263–330.
[7] *Ibid.*, p. 333.

Thus, the proponents of technology assessment recognize that, ultimately, the extent of control over technological change requires a political decision. They emphasize that "the existing policy-making process implies no guarantee that a balance would be achieved between the benefits to society and (a) the economic and social costs to the various groups affected by the technology; (b) the costs of controlling the damage; and (c) the cost to various groups of limiting the use of the technology."[8] Indeed, the production of information concerning the negative effects of technological innovations is not an indication that government has attempted to or would act. Advocates of technology assessment are quick to point out that governmental institutions generally have not sought evidence of or acted on the potential hazards of technological change but, rather, that government usually has reacted only when hazards have been shown to exist or when sufficient public attention or distress has been focused on such hazards.[9]

The concern with technology assessment, therefore, has led to exploration of the interaction between technology and politics and, in particular, to concentration on participation and representation in the political process. Attention to the dynamics of the existing policymaking process has arisen from the perceived inability or limitation of that process to anticipate or monitor the adverse consequences of technological innovation. Specific emphasis on the problems of participation and representation has resulted from the concern that adverse consequences of technologies affect various public groups who have not been included in decisions to design, extend, or modify technologies or their applications.[10] Participation and representation in the existing policymaking process have been limited, to a great degree, to those directly responsible for and/or benefiting from the uses of the technology.

The approach of technology assessment, therefore, has suggested the need for an analysis of the existing policymaking process and its capabilities in responding to the problems brought on by the use of various technologies. What form or forms such analysis should take, however, has not yet been specified, other than demands to make the process "more pluralistic" or "more open."[11] Proponents of technol-

[8] *Ibid.*, p. 335.

[9] *Ibid.*, pp. 335–336.

[10] See Erasmas H. Kloman, "Public Participation in Technology Assessment," *Public Administration Review, 34*:52–61, January–February 1974; and Erasmas H. Kloman, ed., "A Mini-Symposium on Public Participation in Technology Assessment," *Public Administration Review, 35*:67–82, January–February 1975.

[11] See Kloman, "Mini-Symposium on Public Participation," pp. 67–82.

ogy assessment highlight the need for consideration of the negative consequences of technological change and the problems of participation and representation of interests promoting the reduction of these negative consequences; nevertheless, technology assessments tend to concentrate on the normative aspects of political action and government intervention rather than on explaining how that intervention actually takes place.[12] The actual dynamics of the public policymaking process and the effects of existing structures, processes, goals, and distribution of resources on the identification and control of the adverse consequences of technological innovations and applications have received relatively little attention.[13]

THE POLITICAL IMPLICATIONS OF TECHNOLOGY ASSESSMENT

The central objective of this study is to define the relationship between the negative consequences of technological innovation and the response of the public policymaking process to these consequences. The study focuses on two principal problems of analysis:

1. Defining the nature and significance of social costs and their relationship to problems of information and collective action
2. Exploring the dynamics of information production and use relative to the social costs of technological innovation and the politics of public policy formation

In the first problem of analysis, the conditions under which collective action or inaction—in response to the existence of social costs—is a rational alternative for those affected by or bearing such costs will be identified. This analysis seeks to question the pluralist, or what has been called "the hydraulic thesis," [14] of the public policymaking process in the context of three dimensions of the social costs problem:

1. The incentives of individuals affected by social costs not to reveal their true preferences concerning the reduction of social costs

[12] Much of the political effort of the technology assessment movement has been oriented to establishing and maintaining an Office of Technology Assessment in Congress. See Medford, *Environmental Harassment*, pp. 15–91.

[13] See Todd R. LaPorte, "The Context of Technology Assessment: A Changing Perspective for Public Organization," *Public Administration Review*, *31*:63–73, January–February 1971.

[14] Nicholas Henry. "Bureaucracy, Technology, and Knowledge Management." *Public Administration Review*, *35*:572, November–December 1975.

2. The high level of uncertainty associated with social costs, which gives rise to problems of their identification and control

3. The reciprocal nature of social costs, which produces problems of strategic interaction and transaction costs related to efforts to provide for the reduction of social costs on the part of some individuals, groups, and organizations and efforts to promote technological developments and uses on the part of organizational innovators who are trying to protect their efforts.

To understand the second problem of analysis, the relationship between the social costs of technological innovations and the politics of public policy formation will be defined. First, the study will focus on how social costs are identified as public issues as opposed to private concerns. Under what conditions are some negative external effects of technological change identified as social costs requiring or demanding some public action while others are not? Second, how a public issue is expanded and the costs of participation and representation in the policy formation process will be examined. Third, the role of political and legal symbols in the policy formation process will be described, particularly in reference to activity of the mass media in the development of an issue. Fourth, patterns of agenda access of a public policy issue and the effects of access on the choice of regulatory arrangements for the control of social costs by the participants in the policy formation process will be identified.

Each of the problems of analysis is presented in Chapters 2 and 3, followed by an empirical investigation of the social costs of criminal justice information systems and the politics of information policy formation.

SELECTION OF THE CASE STUDY

It has become somewhat commonplace to suggest that our society is in the midst of an information-processing revolution. The development of modern digital computers notwithstanding, contemporary American society has witnessed an enormous expansion of information gathering and recordkeeping. According to Westin, "As our industrialized system has grown more complex, as government regulatory functions have increased, as large bureaucratic organizations have become the model in our private sector, and as social science has committed itself heavily to data-collection and analysis, we have become the greatest data-generating society in human history."[15] Indeed, with the growing scale of organization throughout society, the need for information has become crucial. In the midst of this expanding need for information and the recognition of the limits of human action without it, the computer emerged with the promise of providing previously unimagined potential for greater speed of calculation in handling data. With speed of calculation, man has the key for new capabilities; however, as noted by Laudon, "Speed for its own sake is hardly impressive. Speed is important because it allows men to do things they otherwise would not have done, for lack of will, time, or energy. The development of computers signifies not just an increase in speed of calculation, but offers as well a quantum leap in the amount and kinds of things that can be done within a human framework."[16]

The computer has been perceived as a great source of promise, but it also has been considered a serious threat. In the 1960s, this concern developed into what came to be known as the "privacy and computers" debate. Third-generation computers, with the capability of storing on-line (i.e., instantly available to users) very large information files with random access, created the potential for information networks connecting geographically distant users (frequently organizations or organizational subunits). Much public attention and political debate focused on the development of information policy by which records stored in information systems could be safeguarded and the social costs of such technology minimized. Prominent among the record-keeping uses and problems cited are those in the areas of law enforcement and the administration of criminal justice.

Due to the sensitivity and nature of criminal records, law enforcement and the administration of criminal justice have often been the focal point of public debate and controversy concerning the development of computers and the uses of automated criminal justice records. In large measure, this is because criminal justice agencies at federal, state, and local levels, with the aid of federal funds provided by the Law Enforcement Assistance Administration of the Department of Justice, have been rapidly applying advancements in information technology to the tasks of crime control and the processing of individuals through and among criminal justice agencies. In response to such developments, public concern has centered on the use of indi-

---

[15] Alan F. Westin. *Privacy and Freedom.* New York, Atheneum, 1970, pp. 158–159.
[16] Kenneth C. Laudon. *Computers and Bureaucratic Reform.* New York, Wiley, 1974, p. 6.

vidual record information in state and local criminal justice information systems, as well as on a developing nationwide interstate criminal history system operated as part of the Federal Bureau of Investigation's National Crime Information Center. In particular, the problems arising from the use of individual record information—such as arrest records and criminal history records—for purposes other than law enforcement and criminal justice administration have resulted in reassessments of criminal justice information policy at the local, state, and federal levels. Various approaches to the control and reduction of social costs through the use of computers in criminal justice agencies also have been developed.

This case study of criminal justice information policy and information systems development thus represents an important aspect of the more general concern about the control of the social costs of computers in American society. In addition, the difficulties of identifying and controlling social costs based on the widespread use of criminal justice records and the political problems of representing such interests in the existing public policymaking process are reviewed.

TECHNOLOGY AND POLITICS—CHOOSING A POINT OF DEPARTURE

A primary concern about the direction and effects of technological innovation is the problem of understanding the relationship between technological innovations and the structures, processes, and end results of human choice. Technology, it is asserted, is nothing new. What *is* new is the major role of technology in modern society. The ubiquity of technology in modern affairs has tended to cast substantial doubts on the efficacy of governmental institutions and political processes in using or controlling technological innovations.

In response to this situation, several divergent points of view on the relationship between technology and politics have evolved. The differences between these perspectives have had an important bearing on scholarly and public debates on the public policy implications of these developments. Since this study focuses on the relationship between information technology and political-administrative structures, processes, and goals, it is important to clarify at the outset which of these perspectives this study uses as its point of departure.[17]

[17] While there has been, in recent years, a great deal of interest on the part of the public and the intellectual community concerning the relationship between technology

Technology as a Determining Variable

A great deal of contemporary thinking about the relationship of technology and politics has been formed by what Manfred Stanley has called "the technicist projection."[18] This view is based on the assumption of some form of technological domination. Technology is considered to be autonomous and to constitute an end in itself and not a means, and the effects of technology are perceived as inevitable. Thus, the realm of human freedom and public choice in technological society is severely restricted, if not impossible.

The technicist projection includes two very different attitudes. One exhibits a profound pessimism about the prospects of technological change. In *The Technological Society*,[19] Jacques Ellul suggests that technology is no longer a means by which we achieve our ends in modern society but, rather, that technology has become an end in itself, an end that dominates and obfuscates all other ends (such as the traditional values of society). Technical rationality informs all choices in a technological society and thus *legislates* those choices that it deems appropriate, rejecting the rest.

Herbert Marcuse, moreover, has argued that, not only is the tyranny of technological society a reality, but that most Americans are happy with it.[20] Although pluralism exists in American society, it is ineffective in counteracting the more fundamental effects of technology. Americans already are one-dimensional persons controlled by technocrats and false consciousness.

A second attitude toward change represented by the technicist projection is one of profound hope. A substantial commitment to science and technology is viewed as the first step in expanding the limits of

---

and politics, political scientists, in contrast to sociologists, psychologists, legal scholars, and social philosophers, have made only limited contributions. A notable exception is the work of Victor C. Ferkiss, who deals with this problem directly. See Victor C. Ferkiss, *Technological Man: The Myth and the Reality*, New York, New American Library, 1969, as well as his significant literature review entitled "Man's Tools and Man's Choices: The Confrontation of Technology and Political Science," *American Political Science Review*, 67:973–980, September 1973. The present analysis is indebted to Ferkiss's theoretical insights developed in the latter article.

[18] See Emmanuel G. Mesthene's review of Professor Manfred Stanley's analysis in Harvard University, *Program on Technology and Society, 1964–1972, A Final Review*, Cambridge, Mass., Harvard University Press, 1972, pp. 225–231.

[19] Jacques Ellul. *The Technological Society*. New York, Vintage, 1964.

[20] See Herbert Marcuse, *One-Dimensional Man*, Boston, Mass., Beacon Press, 1964.

society. While not all manifestations of technology are viewed as unalloyed blessings, a substantial faith persists in the efficacy of technology in helping man deal with social problems. Indeed, it has been argued that a "technological fix" can be applied to many pressing social problems.[21]

Common to both points of view concerning technological change is an important fundamental assumption. Jack Douglas observed that "both sides have already assumed the necessity of some form of tyranny and the impossibility of human freedom. Their main dispute is simply over which kind is better."[22] Both sides are significantly influenced by historical forces, and both assume some form of historical necessity, leading either in the direction of men making no choice or exercising the "right" choices regarding their future in a technological society. In both cases, whatever choices are made in a technological society would be dominated by the dictates of instrumental rationality and not by a consideration of human purposes, priorities, and the traditional values and concerns of society. As noted by Ferkiss, "This viewpoint is embodied in the belief that whatever man can do he will do. Politics and culture are relegated thereby to the role of purely dependent variables. In technological determinism not only is technology an unexcused, unwilled cause which causes other things, but technological change is the sole and irresistible cause of all changes in all other fields of human activity."[23] In attempting to explain the relationship between technology and politics, this approach assumes that technology is a completely independent or determining variable which changes and conditions political structures, processes, goals, traditions, and resources (see Figure 1). Neither the positive nor negative consequences of technological change are influenced by politics, since politics itself is transformed by technology; rather, the political variable is shaped by the positive or negative consequences of technological change. As such, the significance of politics derives not from its mediating or filtering effect on the consequences of technology, but from the fact that it simply represents another arena of human activity, such as ethics, religion, and culture, where the technological factor can dominate.

[21] See Alvin M. Weinberg, "Can Technology Replace Social Engineering?," in: *Technology and Man's Future*, edited by Albert H. Teich, New York, St. Martin's Press, 1972, pp. 27–34.

[22] Jack D. Douglas, ed. *Freedom and Tyranny: Social Problems in a Technological Society.* New York, Knopf, 1970, p. 13.

[23] Ferkiss. "Man's Tools and Man's Choices," p. 974.

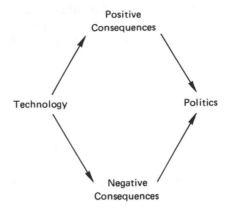

FIGURE 1   Technology as a determining variable.

Technology as a Conditioning Variable

An alternative approach to understanding the relationship between technology and politics is reflected in the perspective of Emmanuel Mesthene, director of the Harvard University Program on Technology and Society.[24] In summarizing what was learned from the program about the implications of technological change for society, Mesthene states that technology influences social and political change in two ways: Technology creates new opportunities and also generates new problems for men and society. "It has both positive and negative effects, and it usually has the two *at the same time and in virtue of one another.*"[25] This two-sided result stems from the following series of events: Technological innovation provides a new opportunity to achieve a desired goal, but this requires social organizations to change in order to take advantage of the new opportunity, thus interfering with the functions of existing social structures. As a result, other goals that were attained before the social structure changed are now inadequately met. One type of problem arises when society is unable to take advantage of technological opportunities because of inadequacies in the social structure and institutions. Another type of problem arises when negative side effects of new technologies are not controlled because existing institutions have been unwilling to respond to the

[24] See Emmanuel G. Mesthene, *Technological Change*, New York, New American Library, 1970, and Harvard University, *Program on Technology and Society*, pp. 225–231.
[25] Mesthene. *Technological Change*, p. 26.

problems or because "it has not been anybody's explicit business to foresee and anticipate them."[26]

While technology cannot be fully understood without comprehending its effects on social and individual values, in the final analysis, technology creates problems that, according to Mesthene, must be considered political: "The strains that technology places on our values and beliefs, finally, are reflected in economic, political, and ideological conflict. That is, they raise questions about the proper goals of society and about the proper ways of pursuing those goals."[27] Thus, "in the end...the problems that technology poses (and the opportunities it offers) will be resolved (and realized) in the political arena..." Mesthene suggests that we "need to develop new institutional forms and new mechanisms to replace established ones that can no longer deal effectively with the new kinds of problems with which we are faced."[28] Agreeing with Manfred Stanley, he concludes that the problem is "how to organize society so as to free the possibility of (human) choice and how to control our technology wisely in order to minimize its negative consequences."[29]

For Mesthene, technology is neutral in value: Technology is developed and can be used for good or bad purposes. Admitting that technologies have necessary consequences about which differing value judgments can be made and that changes in technology can affect changes in the values of society, he nevertheless tends to perceive technology as what McDermott has termed a largely "self-correcting system."[30] Mesthene, therefore, treats technology as a conditioning variable whose effects he largely approves (see Figure 2). Ferkiss states that technology is "one among many factors exogenous in its origins to the political process having necessary, significant and definable effects on political ideas, institutions, and actions." Moreover, technology is considered to be more important than other historical and social variables since "it is usually regarded as monolithic in its nature and social consequences and unidirectional in its development."[31] Thus, like the first approach, this approach assumes that politics is affected

[26] Emmanuel G. Mesthene. "The Role of Technology in Society." In: *Technology and Man's Future*, pp. 130–131, 134.

[27] *Ibid.*, p. 148.

[28] *Ibid.*, pp. viii, 148.

[29] Mesthene. *Technological Change*, p. 24.

[30] See John McDermott, "Technology: The Opiate of the Intellectuals," in: *Technology and Man's Future*, pp. 151–178.

[31] Ferkiss. "Man's Tools and Man's Choices," p. 974.

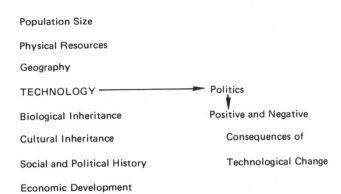

FIGURE 2 Technology as a conditioning variable.

by technology in a single direction, with the former largely giving way to or being conditioned by the latter. The second approach, which considers technology as a conditioning variable, differs from the first approach, which considers technology as a determining variable, in that it recognizes that the effects of technology may be limited or mediated by political and social factors. Nevertheless, for the most part, technology is perceived as existing independently of any social or political decisions and as having second-order consequences that are, to a great degree, irresistible and necessary.

Technology and Politics as Mutually Interacting Variables

A third approach to the interface between technology and politics assumes that the two variables are mutually interacting.[32] This is illustrated in Figure 3. Unlike the first and second approaches, this approach does not assume that technology impacts on politics "like two ships colliding at sea."[33] Rather, political structures, processes, and goals influence and condition the development and use of technological innovations, and, at the same time, technological innovations influence political structures, processes, and goals. The basic assumption of this approach is that technological innovation is a political process. New technologies present opportunities for individuals, groups, and organizations to bring about particular changes. At the same time, demands and strategies for change are influenced by the

---

[32] *Ibid.*
[33] Laudon. *Computers and Bureaucratic Reform*, p. 30.

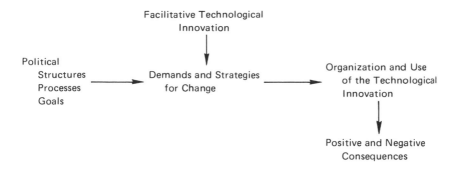

FIGURE 3   Technology and politics as mutually interacting variables.

preexisting political structures, processes, and goals. The latter influence the development and use of technological innovations and, in turn, produce both good and bad consequences. Thus, technological innovations are filtered through or mediated by the preexisting political structures, processes, traditions, and patterns of resource distribution.

This study investigates how the policymaking processes, structures, and goals influence the development of information policy to deal with the negative consequences of those changes on individuals in the United States who are affected by criminal justice recordkeeping. Since it is assumed that the benefits and costs associated with technological change are distributed through the existing policymaking process, the burden of the study will be to indicate how existing collective choice processes respond to the problem of developing and controlling technological innovations and to clarify the consequences of such processes for groups and individuals in our society who are adversely affected by political-technological change.

Most studies of technology and politics have tended to treat technology as one unit and the political system as another unit; however, as Jack Douglas has pointed out, neither the political system nor technology is monolithic.[34] In terms of enhancing understanding of the relationship between technological change and politics, it is by no means clear that exclusive attention to "macro" perspectives on such matters provides more understanding of the interaction of technology and politics than specific analysis of particular types of applications of technological innovations and their subsystem politics. Indeed, as Ferkiss points out,

[34] See Douglas, *Freedom and Tyranny*, pp. 3–32.

the most clear-cut recognition of the technology-politics relationship as one of mutual causation is usually to be found in case studies of particular problems, where the intertwining of cause and effect, necessities and alternatives become evident from a consideration of the empirical data and the political and social history of a particular problem.[35]

The need for case studies such as this one, to explore the relationship between technology and politics, is well-stated by Ferkiss:

Much more needs to be done to create a body of empirical studies of the interface between technology and politics for two reasons: (1) to expand our understanding of the limits of political choice in relation to technological possibilities; and (2) to provide the raw material for a synthetic literature on which to base the study of technology as a crucial variable affecting modern politics.[36]

This study explores the public policy implications of a relatively new application of a technology, which is particularly suited to such a task.

---

[35] Ferkiss. "Man's Tools and Man's Choices," p. 979.
[36] *Ibid.*, p. 980.

2

The Political Economy of Social Costs

The consequences of technological innovation and economic growth have, in recent years, led to an increasing awareness of the interdependence of human actions and the unaccounted and often unanticipated benefits and costs of individual choices (e.g., problems as mundane as an argument over the effects of smoke from a neighbor's fireplace and as significant as air, water, and noise pollution and the effects of such technological innovations as new drugs, nuclear reactors, SSTs, computers, and telecommunications). Social complexity and interdependence have highlighted a central feature of modern society: that the operations of firms and public organizations and the actions of individuals have effects that they do not and need not account for. When such consequences involve benefits to others, there is little cause for concern; however, when such consequences involve costs to others, there are significant theoretical and practical problems of accounting for such costs and reducing them.

Economists, among others, have used a variety of labels in addressing these negative consequences, namely, negative externalities, negative side effects, "spillover" costs, external costs, "private or public bads," and social costs.[1] The variety of terms and concepts used to explain this class of phenomena has in part betrayed the considerable ambiguity in the purposes and levels of analysis.[2] While it has been

---

[1] See, for example, John G. Head, *Public Goods and Public Welfare,* Durham, N.C., Duke University Press, 1974, Chapter 9, "Externality and Public Policy," pp. 184–213; and Robert J. Staaf and Francis X. Tannian, eds., *Externalities: Theoretical Dimensions of Political Economy,* Port Washington, N.Y., Dunellen, 1973.

[2] See Kenneth J. Arrow, "Political and Economic Evaluation of Social Effects and Externalities," in: *The Analysis of Public Output,* edited by Julius Margolis, New York,

suggested that such categories are residual at best for a discipline whose main emphasis lies elsewhere,[3] there has been increasing emphasis on the use of such notions as externality, public and private goods (or bads), and social costs as genuine theoretical tools when discussing these problems. Also, the use of such concepts has not been confined to the normative concerns of welfare economists in examining various compensation principles and social welfare functions. Rather, political scientists and economists interested in explaining the political dimensions of such problems and assessing the benefits and costs of various institutional arrangements for allocating private or public goods and services have begun to use these concepts as analytical tools.[4]

In this chapter, the problem of social costs will be defined and related to three concerns: the conditions under which organizations will provide for the reduction of social costs resulting from their productive activities; the conditions under which collective action or inaction by those individuals bearing social costs can be expected; and the conditions under which representation of the interest in reducing social costs by entrepreneurs and interest groups are likely to lead to a reduction in such costs. As suggested in Chapter 1, the aim of this analysis will be to set forth the pluralist thesis of the public policy-making process as it applies to the social costs of technological innovations in public organizations. (In Chapter 3, a more appropriate approach to social costs and the politics of public policy formation will be presented.) In the context of "the administrative state"[5]—that is, a public policy process increasingly influenced and, oftentimes, dominated by public organizations—the pluralist thesis concerning the capabilities of the political process to counteract, through individual and group action, the social costs of public organizations is seriously deficient. Only under limited conditions is the pluralist thesis helpful as an analytical guide to the interactions of the public policy process in response to the social costs of public organizations.

National Bureau of Economic Research, 1970, pp. 1–3; K. William Kapp, "On the Nature and Significance of Social Costs," in: *Externalities*, pp. 3–17; and K. William Kapp, *The Social Costs of Private Enterprise*, New York, Schocken Books, 1950, pp. 1–46.

[3] See Sherman Krupp, "Analytic Economics and the Logic of External Effects," in: *Externalities*, pp. 19–24.

[4] See Head, *Public Goods;* Margolis, *Analysis of Public Output;* and Richard A. Musgrave and Peggy B. Musgrave, *Public Finance in Theory and Practice*, New York, McGraw-Hill, 1973, pp. 51–82.

[5] See Emmette S. Redford, *Democracy in the Administrative State*, New York, Oxford University Press, 1969.

DEFINING THE PROBLEM OF SOCIAL COSTS

The concept of social costs originated with the efforts of economists to account for the problems or losses to society arising from private productive activities in a competitive economic system. Two approaches to the problem of social costs evolved: the Pigovian approach and the Paretian approach.[6]

The Pigovian approach is derived from the work of A. C. Pigou, who sought to integrate the phenomenon of social costs into the conceptual system of neoclassical equilibrium economics. Pigou's central thesis is based on a comparison of the "marginal social net product" with the "marginal private net product." The marginal social product includes the "total net product of physical things or objective services due to the marginal increment of resources in any given use or place, no matter to whom any part of this product may accrue." Since the investment of more resources may throw costs "upon people not directly concerned through, say, uncompensated damage done to surrounding woods by sparks from railway engines," the marginal social net product of a given unit of investment may diverge and, indeed, be considerably smaller than the marginal private net product. Marginal private net product is "that part of the total net product of physical things or objective services due to the marginal increment of resources in any given use or place which accrues in the first instance—i.e., prior to sale—to the person responsible for investing resources there."[7]

This distinction between private net product and social net product enabled Pigou to trace cases in which the private product was greater than the social product, that is, where private productive activities tended to give rise to social losses of various kinds. Pigou believed that such divergencies, caused by private production activities, could be remedied by appropriate government intervention and thus could maintain the market system as well as maximize total social welfare.

In an effort to move away from the neoclassical approach of Pigou, a second approach, based on the work of Vilfredo Pareto, points to the structural limitations and costs of institutional arrangements, including the competitive market system. To examine the problems of social costs, the approach relies on a model of an ideally functioning market system and explains the conditions under which resources are allocated efficiently or in an optimal manner.

All institutional arrangements—like an economic system—provide a

[6] See Mark Blaug, *Economic Theory in Retrospect*, Homewood, Ill., Richard D. Irwin, 1968, pp. 574–614.

[7] A. C. Pigou. *The Economics of Welfare*. London, Macmillan, 1932, pp. 134–135.

framework for making choices. The necessity for making choices stems from scarcity. There are three primary choices to be made: *what* goods and services are to be produced, *how* they will be produced, and *who* will enjoy the use of society's production (*for whom* are the goods produced).[8] The need for choice is clear, as no set of political and economic arrangements can produce everything for everyone. The choice of what kind of institutional arrangements shall guide society's allocation of resources is in large measure a choice of what group or groups in society will make the three choices noted. The decentralized, competitive market system for resource allocation and choice is based on the assumption "that the personal wants of the individuals in the society should guide the use of resources in production, distribution, and exchange; and that the individuals themselves are the best judges of their wants and preferences and best able to act accordingly."[9]

In the Paretian approach, the ideally functioning market system has four characteristics. First, all markets are competitive. No particular firm or individual can affect any market price by increasing or decreasing the supply of goods and services offered. All firms and individuals are price takers rather than price makers. In each market, price and quantity will be determined by the intersection of the supply and demand curves. At this price, individuals' marginal willingness to pay will just equal the marginal costs of production. Second, all participants in the market are fully informed as to the qualitative characteristics of goods and services and the terms of exchange or prices among all commodities and services. Third, all decision makers in this system are rational and self-interested. Fourth, all resources are individually owned and individuals can shift their resources freely from one use to another and capture all the benefits of ownership.[10] It is assumed, then, that there are no positive or negative externalities. (Externalities are the effects of one individual's consumption or production of a good on another individual.)

An economic system having these characteristics would produce an allocation of resources that could be called efficient or optimal. In Paretian terms, this means that no other allocation would make at least one person better off without making someone else worse off. Although the competitive market system outlined here results in an

---

[8] A. Myrich Freeman III, R. H. Haveman, and Allen V. Kneese. *The Economics of Environmental Policy.* New York, Wiley, 1973, p. 66.

[9] *Ibid.*

[10] For a qualification of this fourth assumption, see Arrow, "Political and Economic Evaluation," pp. 14–15.

efficient allocation of resources, it has clear limitations. First, there is the rather narrow criterion of desirability.[11] The Paretian definition of efficiency ignores the question of equity or the distribution of the output. The initial distribution of resources is taken for granted in such an arrangement, no matter how unequal it may be. Second, there are the limitations that derive from the unrealistic character of the model. The four characteristics of the model are not often met in the real world: Not all markets are competitive, information may be imperfect and costly, men may act irrationally, and significant external costs and benefits may be present. Such limitations in the Paretian model point to sources of market failure. Of primary importance for this analysis is the case of market failure resulting from externalities and the existence of social costs.

As previously noted, there has been some confusion in the literature concerning the meaning of the terms *externality* and *social cost*. Some analysts have suggested that there is no appreciable difference between negative externalities and social costs, while others have observed that social costs are not synonymous with external costs or negative externalities.[12] In the context of this analysis, there are two reasons why social costs are not the same as negative externalities. First, social costs represent the sum of external and internal costs. Attention, therefore, must be given not only to the problem of reducing external costs but to the total costs of change, that is, the costs of regulation as well as the reduction of external costs. Second, the specific case treated in this study, concerning the social costs of public organizations, is (as will be discussed in the next section) distinguishable in important ways from social costs arising from the activities of private individuals or firms in the market system.

The social costs of public organizations, then, can be defined as the uncompensated costs arising from the productive activities of public organizations which are (at least initially) both outside the control of the individual suffering the effect and of no direct consequence to the producer.[13] Such costs usually exhibit jointness of supply that may be either completely nonexcludable or excludable at a high cost. In addition, due to the conditions of nonexclusion or the high costs of exclusion, such costs also are characterized by high levels of uncertainty. Also, the social costs of public organizations are reciprocal. These characteristics, in turn, pose significant problems for reducing social

---

[11] Freeman, Haveman, and Kneese. *Economics of Environmental Policy*, p. 70.

[12] Compare, for example, Kapp, *Social Costs of Private Enterprise*, with A. J. Culyer, *The Economics of Social Policy*, Port Washington, N.Y., Dunellen, 1974, pp. 25–30.

[13] See E. J. Mishan, *Economics for Social Decisions*, New York, Praeger, 1972, pp. 85–90.

costs, because social costs, at least initially, are costly to identify and communicate information about; social costs are either completely nonexcludable or excludable at a high cost, creating incentives for individuals to either not reveal their true preferences about or to forego completely attempts to provide for reductions in social costs; the reciprocal character of social costs creates problems of collective action, especially in the context of significant inequalities in influence and resources between individuals and interest groups on the one hand and public organizations on the other; and public (or private) actions aimed at reducing social costs tend to be associated with social costs of their own.

Like externalities in general, a basic feature of social costs is that they are uncompensated costs.[14] Social costs are, at least initially, outside the control of the individuals affected and of no direct consequence to the producer. Two important implications can be derived from this definition. First, public organizations that impose social costs on individuals in the society must be induced to perceive that they are responsible for such costs and that they should do something about them. Second, this latter activity in itself is a costly process for those individuals affected by social costs or for those representing the interest in reducing social costs.

Unlike externalities in general, which can be both private and public, social costs are characterized by their public good or, more appropriately, public "bad" nature. A public good (or bad), once supplied to one individual, is by definition freely available to all.[15] A public good can be characterized in terms of "jointness of supply." In contrast to a private good, which is excludable in terms of *A* paying a price to consume and *B* not paying a price to consume all of the good, a pure public good is nonexcludable: "Extension of the supply of a given unit to one individual facilitates its extension to all." A second defining characteristic of a public good is that it gives rise to external economies, or, in the case of a public bad, diseconomies.[16] A pure public good exhibits nonexclusion to an extreme degree. It is this characteristic that accounts for the failure of the market mechanism to reveal true preferences. Samuelson observed that: "It will pay for each rational man to dissemble"[17] or to give "false signals, to pretend to

[14] Head. *Public Goods*, p. 185.

[15] For the best-known exposition of the concept of public goods, see Paul A. Samuelson, "Pure Theory of Public Expenditure" and "Aspects of Public Expenditure Theories," in: *Externalities*, pp. 89–92 and 93–104, respectively.

[16] Head. *Public Goods*, pp. 167, 169.

[17] Samuelson. "Aspects of Public Expenditure Theories," p. 97.

have less interest in a given collective consumption activity than he really has."[18] Thus, rational individuals in a public good or public bad situation will have incentives to act as "free riders"; that is, they do not want to bear the costs of consuming such a good or alleviating a bad.

Most public goods and bads do not conform completely to the theoretical definition. In the case of mixed goods or bads, such as open lands or polluted air, it is equally costly in terms of transaction costs to add characteristics to a particular good or bad in terms of information or exclusion as, for example, it is to apply the allocation mechanism of the market system.[19] In this context, market failure is not absolute: "It is better to consider a broader category, that of transaction costs, which in general impede and in particular cases completely block the formation of markets." Transaction costs are the costs of "running the market" as well as the costs of running any institutional arrangement.[20] They may include the costs of exclusion, the costs of information, and the costs of communication. They also may include the costs of participation and representation in the political process. What makes transaction costs significant is that they help focus attention on the limitations of institutional arrangements in moving to a condition where social costs or public bads can be minimized.

A third aspect of social costs is the uncertainty attached to their identification and reduction. Because social costs exhibit jointness of supply, there is a significant political problem in getting people to reveal their desires for the provision of a good or the reduction of a bad. In addition, there are the problems of the information and communication costs involved in identifying social costs, as well as what Kapp terms an "inevitable residuum of indeterminacy" that is tied to the difficulty of delineating social costs in any precise manner and measuring their incidence or dollar impact.[21] Because it is costly to become informed about social costs, it is rational for various individuals, groups, and organizations in the political process to refrain from seeking information about the identification of such costs and how to reduce them.

A final aspect of social costs is that they are reciprocal.[22] They represent the sum of internal and external costs, that is, not only the

[18] Samuelson. "Pure Theory of Public Expenditure," p. 92.
[19] P. H. M. Ruys. *Public Goods and Decentralization.* The Netherlands, Tilbury University Press, 1974, pp. 65–66.
[20] Arrow. "Political and Economic Evaluation," p. 17.
[21] Kapp. "On the Nature and Significance of Social Costs," p. 14.
[22] See R. H. Coase, "The Problem of Social Costs," in: *Externalities,* p. 119.

external costs of a decision or action that falls beyond the boundaries of an individual's purview or an organization's interest but also the internal costs of the producer. Reducing social costs, then, implies the achievement of a more appropriate balance between internal and external costs. One of the main difficulties in doing so is the cost of changing institutional arrangements and operating new arrangements to reduce social costs. Rather than simply correcting the "divergence between internal and external costs," as Pigou proposes, Coase suggests that it is necessary to have regard for the "total effect":

> Analysis in terms of divergencies between private and social products concentrates attention on particular deficiencies in the system and tends to nourish the belief that any measure which will remove the deficiency is necessarily desirable. It diverts attention from those other changes in the system which are inevitably associated with the corrective measure, changes which may well produce more harm than the original deficiency.[23]

The analysis of the divergence between internal and external costs also tends to disregard the characteristics of social costs, which make efficient reduction of such costs more or less costly in terms of transaction costs. As Samuelson concludes, "given sufficient knowledge the optimal decisions can always be found by scanning over all attainable states of the world and selecting the one which according to the postulated ethical welfare function is best. The solution 'exists'; the problem is how to 'find' it."[24]

In the absence of any omniscient observer, finding the solution to the problem of social costs entails attention to the costs of interaction in the political process as well as the biases and inequalities of resources inherent in that process.

SOCIAL COSTS, TRANSACTION COSTS, AND PUBLIC ORGANIZATIONS

Providing for the reduction of social costs as a public policy issue poses some significant problems of political action, both for those organizations or individuals generating external costs and for those bearing such costs. This study focuses on the social costs of technological innovations in public organizations, which, in terms of the transaction costs involved, differ substantially from the problems of social costs

---

[23] *Ibid.*, pp. 156–157.
[24] Samuelson. "Pure Theory of Public Expenditure," p. 192.

that arise between private individuals. This difference is due to the nature of organizational rationality in general and the characteristics of public agencies in particular, which can have an effect on raising the costs of interaction between public agencies and individuals in society who incur external costs.

According to James D. Thompson, because organizations are "expected to produce results, their actions are expected to be reasonable or rational. The concepts of rationality brought to bear on organizations establish limits within which organizational action must take place."[25] Coping with uncertainty is a major challenge to organizations. This challenge arises from many sources; however, the basic sources of uncertainty for organizations are their technologies and environments. It is assumed that organizations seek to reduce these sources of indeterminateness by seeking rational courses of action.

Organizations are expected to operate technologies that are impossible or impractical for individuals to operate. Technologies in organizations exhibit the characteristics of technical rationality; however, there are limits to the operation of a closed system of logic in most organizations. Although technology emphasizes the need for desired outcomes, knowledge of cause/effect relationships, and control over all resources and variables necessary for the operation of the technology, environmental influences make it difficult for an organization to "seal off (its) technology." Organizational rationality, therefore, is more than technical rationality. It has an important political component linked to the need of organizations to protect their technical cores from environmental influences. In addition, where organizations cannot buffer or smooth their transactions with the environment, they will seek to predict and adapt to changes in the environment. The problem that organizations must avoid is being controlled by elements of the environment. According to Thompson, "under norms of rationality, organizations seek to minimize the power of the task-environment elements over them."[26] Organizations are constantly seeking to attain a "viable domain" in which they can operate without becoming overly dependent on their environment; thus, they exhibit a "bias toward certainty" in regard to their technologies and environments which tends to control the processes of organizational search and change.

In organizations, search (i.e., information seeking) is closely related to change: "both organizations and individuals need additional infor-

[25] James D. Thompson. *Organizations in Action.* New York, McGraw-Hill, 1967, p. 1.
[26] *Ibid.*

mation most when they are in relatively new and unfamiliar situations."[27] According to Anthony Downs, since individuals in organizations are utility maximizers, they

are always willing to adopt a new course of action if it promises to make them better off, even if they are relatively happy at present. However, they cannot search for new courses of action without expending resources. Since the supply of these is limited, they tend to avoid further search whenever the likely rewards seem small *a priori* (that is, the expected marginal payoff seems smaller than the expected marginal cost). This is the case whenever their current behavior seems quite satisfactory in light of their recent experience.[28]

One constraint on the willingness of an individual or official to change are the "sunk costs of established behavior patterns"; organizations, in particular, become centered on their usual levels of performance, and deviation from such customary actions, rules, structures, and purposes can impose consequences of varying depths and costs. Downs notes that "it is usually more rational for them to continue their behavior patterns while conducting an intensive search to see whether the old *status quo ante* will return."[29] When the organization cannot expect to return to the *status quo ante,* it will

maintain intensified search while seeking to find the most effective response to this change. Other things being equal, it will select the response that involves the least profound change in its structure. Thus, it will prefer responses requiring it to change only its behavior to those requiring alterations in its rules, and it will prefer the latter to those that necessitate shifts in institutional structure. Only in the most drastic situations will it alter its fundamental purposes.[30]

Organizational change in response to environmental influences is integrally linked with the need to reduce uncertainty and dependence and to minimize change in established behavior patterns: "The greater the 'sunk costs' that must be duplicated or replaced by any innovation, the greater the incentives to avoid innovation."[31]

Organizations do change their behavior, rules, and structures, however, and performance gaps between actual performance and expected performance do arise, either as a result of internal turnover

---

[27] Anthony Downs. *Inside Bureaucracy.* Boston, Mass., Little, Brown, 1967, p. 167.
[28] *Ibid.,* p. 168.
[29] *Ibid.,* pp. 173, 174.
[30] *Ibid.*
[31] *Ibid.* See also James G. March and Herbert A. Simon, *Organizations,* New York, Wiley, 1958, pp. 173–182.

in personnel or changes in technology, external changes in the organization's environment, or repercussions to an organization's performance. Although the organization may not take any action to reduce the gap, it may respond to external influence and change its behavior; it may influence external individuals to change their expectations or demands; it may redefine its functions to exclude the problem under consideration; or it may claim that there is no gap, since the desired change corresponds with what it is already doing. In any event, the organization will either be motivated to retain its status quo or to change its behavior. As noted, the organization's action or nonaction will depend on its assessment of the marginal gains to be derived from its response minus its marginal costs. Because of the pervasive nature of "sunk costs," "the larger the costs of getting the organization to change its established behavior pattern, the greater will be the organization's resistance to it, other things being equal." This is true because adopting new behavior patterns means that an organization must incur some of the "sunk costs" again. Thus, "it can rationally adopt new patterns only if their benefits exceed both the benefits derived from existing behavior and the costs of shifting to the new patterns."[32]

Clearly, organizations will work for reductions in social costs only under limited conditions; they generally will not have incentives to reduce the external costs of their productive processes or to search for and identify the depth and extent of external costs being borne by individuals. Neither are organizations likely to respond favorably to efforts to alter their behavior, rules, and/or structures when such changes imply increases in marginal costs that exceed any corresponding increases in marginal benefits.

In addition, the transaction costs incurred between individuals and public organizations are likely to be higher under conditions of inequality of resources and influence than under conditions of relative equality of resources and influence. This is true for three reasons. First, under conditions of inequality of influence and resources, the public agency as a provider of a public good or service will be relatively free to induce savings in production costs by increasing external costs to individuals in society. Also, because exclusion is very costly or impossible, each individual will have little choice but to take whatever is provided.[33] Second, individuals incurring external costs may not have sufficient resources or influence to identify the relevant costs involved

---

[32] Downs. *Inside Bureaucracy,* pp. 191–193, 195, 196.

[33] See Vincent Ostrom, *The Intellectual Crisis in American Public Administration,* University, Ala., University of Alabama Press, 1973, pp. 61–62.

and to organize to reduce the performance gap between the internal costs to the public agency and the external costs to individuals. In this situation, organizational responses will tend to maintain the status quo or to minimize the effects of demands for change on the organization's behavior, rules, structures, and purposes. Third, the outcome of the interaction between public organizations and individuals in society is likely to be regressive: "The citizens with the greatest needs are granted relief only to the extent that such relief is equally beneficial to all citizens."[34] In other words, individuals in the lower socioeconomic levels of the community, who may be in most need of relief, may have their needs met only when individuals in the higher socioeconomic levels can benefit in some way. Individuals in the lower socioeconomic categories must bear comparatively higher transaction costs in seeking relief from the external effects of public agency activities than individuals in the higher socioeconomic categories. This suggests that the problem of individuals bearing external costs will be considered by a public organization only to the extent that the organization is exposed to the demands and preferences of both groups of individuals and that these influences can overcome the incentives of organizations to buffer or redirect demands for change to return to the *status quo ante*. When such outside influence is not generated through some form of collective action, there is no rationale for an organization to increase its internal costs to effect a reduction of external costs to individuals in society.

THE PROBLEM OF COLLECTIVE ACTION AND INACTION—A CHALLENGE TO THE PLURALIST THESIS

The central concern about the social costs of public organizations is the problem of collective action—that is, an examination of the conditions under which collective action or inaction by individuals bearing external costs can be expected and the conditions under which the allocation of internal and external costs will be changed by entrepreneurs and interest groups concerned with reducing external costs.

A realistic discussion of the social costs of technological innovation and the capacities of the public policymaking process to reduce such costs has to confront, at some point, the prevailing theory of the

[34] Mark V. Nadel. *The Politics of Consumer Protection.* New York, Bobbs-Merrill, 1971, p. 223.

American political process—interest-group politics or pluralism. Although this theory has been severely criticized in recent years as both a descriptive guide to and a normative model of American politics, interest-group pluralism remains the dominant paradigm of the public policymaking process in both public and scholarly debate. With regard to the interaction of bureaucracy and politics, relatively little attention has been given to the ways in which the pluralist thesis is deficient as an analytical model of collective action in the public policymaking process.[35]

The pluralist thesis of the political process rests on the notion that organized and effective group pressures will emerge, when necessary, to counteract suffering, dislocation, and disturbances experienced by individuals in society.[36] This thesis is based on several related propositions concerning the dynamics of collective action:

1. All publics affected by particular policy questions are, or will easily become, aware that the resolution of such questions will affect them and that such publics have a reasonable understanding of the issues involved.

2. The costs of collective action and organization for affected publics will not be so high as to make such action impractical.

3. There are no systematic constraints on the organization and mobilization of new publics.

4. The preexisting biases and inequalities of resources in the political process are not so great as to preclude access to the decision-making channels at some point.

These propositions represent the basis on which the "hydraulic thesis" of the political process is constructed. This thesis has been characterized by some of its advocates as a theory of dynamic equilibrium, which corresponds to equivalent notions of market equilibrium in economics. Irrespective of the merits of this comparison, it will be argued that this thesis is not appropriate with respect to the social costs of public organizations. The defining characteristics of social costs diverge in whole or in part from the supporting propositions of the pluralist thesis and, in turn, make this theory of collective action ineffective as an analytical tool for understanding the problems

[35] Nicholas Henry. "Bureaucracy, Technology, and Knowledge Management." *Public Administration Review*, 35:573, November–December 1975.

[36] See, for example, Robert A. Dahl, *A Preface to Democratic Theory*, Chicago, University of Chicago Press, 1956; and David B. Truman, *The Governmental Process*, New York, Knopf, 1951.

of collective action or inaction related to the social costs of public organizations.

The first proposition of the pluralist thesis assumes that a high level of information is or will become available to individuals that bear external costs of technological innovation in public organizations at a relatively low cost in resources expended. In contrast, political decision making in this context is characterized by relatively high levels of uncertainty about the existence and nature of social costs, and such information is costly to obtain.

Because social costs are uncompensated, those agencies that impose external costs on individuals are not responsible for the losses they inflict. Thus, attendant to the identification of activities of public agencies that generate external costs for a particular public is uncertainty concerning the causal relationship between agency activities and negative consequences to individuals in society. External costs may arise in different ways, and it often is difficult to attribute a direct causal connection between the activities of public agencies and the losses sustained by individuals.[37] Some external costs clearly have their origins in particular organizational acts or decisions; others arise from the processes and structures of sets of organizations involved in related productive activities. In some cases, external costs are felt immediately; in other instances, they remain hidden for considerable periods of time, so that affected persons do not become immediately aware of them. Certain losses affect only a limited group, whereas other losses may be felt by all members of society. Indeed, some damages may be distributed so widely that any one person individually will sustain only a relatively small loss. With regard to social costs of public organizations, the fact that such costs are uncompensated suggests that affected publics cannot easily become aware of these costs and how they are caused by the behavior, rules, processes, and structures of public agencies. In addition, obtaining such information or, as Downs notes, "becoming informed," is itself a costly process. "To make rational decisions, a man must know (1) what his goals are, (2) what alternative ways of reaching these goals are open to him, and (3) the probable consequences of choosing each alternative. The knowledge he requires is contextual knowledge as well as information, both of which are usually necessary for each of the above aspects of decision-making."[38] Acquiring both information and contextual knowledge is costly. Downs notes that the primary costs of gathering

---

[37] See Kapp, *Social Costs of Private Enterprise*, pp. 229–232.

[38] Anthony Downs. *An Economic Theory of Democracy*. New York, Harper and Row, 1957, pp. 207, 210.

and transmitting information (and contextual knowledge) include two major classes: transferable costs—those costs that can be shifted from the individual to someone else—and nontransferable costs—those costs that must be borne by the individual himself. Transferable costs include procurement costs (the costs of gathering, selecting, and transmitting data), analysis costs (the costs of making factual analysis of data), and evaluative costs (the costs of relating data or factual analysis to specific goals). Nontransferable costs include the costs in time and other resources of assimilating information and deciding what, if anything, the individual can or wishes to do.[39]

Each individual decides how much information to acquire by using the marginal cost-return principle:

The marginal return from information is computed by first weighing the importance of a right instead of a wrong decision. To this value is applied the probability that the bit of information being considered will be useful in making this decision. The marginal cost is the opportunity cost of acquiring this bit of information. Much of this cost can be shifted from the decision-maker to others, but the time for assimilation is a nontransferable cost. The decision-maker continues to acquire information until the marginal return equals the marginal costs to him.[40]

Although individuals will rationally seek to reduce information costs by taking advantage of society's "free information stream"[41] and by delegating the responsibility for information production and transmission to information providers in the political process, such as interest groups, professional data gatherers and publishers, government officials, and other individuals, not all people involved in the political process can be equally well informed. Inequality in resources such as education, money, and time will mean that the relevant amount of information individuals receive and their ability to use it will differ. The costs of acquiring information about the external costs of public agency activities and what to do about such costs is likely to be higher for lower socioeconomic groups than for higher socioeconomic groups.[42] In addition, where information providers perceive a low return from collecting and transmitting information about social costs, they will not adequately inform the publics affected by these costs about the problems and the feasible action alternatives available.

Related to the problem of becoming informed about social costs and

[39] *Ibid.*, p. 210.
[40] *Ibid.*, p. 219.
[41] *Ibid.*, pp. 221–225.
[42] *Ibid.*, pp. 226–227, 234–236, 253–258.

the questioning of the first proposition in the pluralist thesis is the public goods character of social costs and the questioning of the second proposition. Social costs exhibit jointness of supply and may be completely nonexcludable or excludable at a high initial cost. Two points are important to emphasize: that providing for reductions in social costs is very costly to the individuals involved and that such reductions, as a rule, must be supplied by political arrangements and not by market mechanisms.

Political action to secure reductions in social costs is a collective good.[43] Like the problem of public goods in general, providing for a reduction in social costs involves the problem of the "free rider." Individuals may withhold their support and resources in hopes that others will move to provide the good, and, because of its collective nature, individuals will receive the good even if they do not contribute to its supply. If social costs are to be controlled, collective political action requires that this free-rider problem be overcome or circumvented.

Political action will be used in society when some individuals find it profitable to do so; that is, when the various transaction costs involved do not outweigh the marginal benefits to be derived from political action. Political action involves strategic interaction: "Each member of the group will find that his sense of personal efficacy (or inefficacy) concerning contributions for the supply of the collective good will be predicated upon expectations regarding the behavior of others."[44] Thus, when all members of a group or public "feel inefficacious with respect to their contributions, expect the others to feel the same way, and do not expect that a donation on their part would change the feelings of the others,"[45] it is likely that "collective inaction" will result.[46] On the other hand, some individuals may conclude that "it is worthwhile to contribute toward the supply of a collective good. . . . Nevertheless, such contributions are likely to remain very limited unless some mechanism is established to allow the members of the group to share the marginal costs of purchasing units of the good."[47]

According to Frohlich, Oppenheimer, and Young, collective action

---

[43] See Norman Frohlich and Joe A. Oppenheimer, "I Get By with a Little Help from My Friends," *World Politics, 23:*104–120, October 1970; and Mancur Olsen, *The Logic of Collective Action,* Cambridge, Mass., Harvard University Press, 1965, p. 15.

[44] Norman Frohlich, Joe A. Oppenheimer, and Oran R. Young. *Political Leadership and Collective Goods.* Princeton, N.J., Princeton University Press, 1971, p. 20.

[45] *Ibid.,* p. 21.

[46] See Olsen, *Logic of Collective Action,* pp. 5–52.

[47] Frohlich, Oppenheimer, and Young. *Political Leadership,* p. 22.

in large or small groups is dependent on mechanisms for coordinating expectations and pooling resources. Political entrepreneurs, for example, act as mechanisms for coordination and pooling of resources. In the absence of such mechanisms, "it is highly likely that the members of the group will act in such a way as to fail to supply themselves with meaningful amounts of the collective good."[48] Thus, it is by no means obvious that the second proposition of the pluralist thesis is valid in the context of the social costs of public organizations, without close examination of the transaction costs that must be borne by individuals in the political process and the presence or absence of mechanisms for coordination and pooling of resources.

Finally, the adequacy of propositions three and four of the pluralist thesis is questioned by the reciprocal character of social costs and the significant disparities of resources between many individuals and public organizations in the political process. As suggested, reducing social costs implies some change in the allocation of internal and external costs. Achieving such change in the allocation of costs through the political process involves problems of strategic interaction between public organizations and individuals, groups, and entrepreneurs. The marginal costs of such interaction by individuals, groups, and entrepreneurs must be outweighed by the marginal benefits to be derived from political competition and conflict. In this regard, the "sunk costs" of public organizations in present structures, processes, rules, and plans weigh heavily on the process of change by raising the costs of political action. The existing biases and inequalities in the political process will tend to work for limited and controlled change that generally is favorable to public organizations, rather than work for change that is beneficial for individuals bearing external costs.[49]

In addition, public policy usually is not made by individual citizens directly. It is developed and formulated by representatives, which raises the principal-agent problem. As Kenneth Arrow has noted, "this means that the link between individual utility functions and social action is tenuous, though by no means completely absent. Representatives are no more a random sample of their constituents than physicians are of their patients."[50] There is no assurance that the representation of publics who are not organized by entrepreneurs, interest groups, and public officials will work to the benefit of the

[48] *Ibid.*, p. 24.

[49] See Louis C. Gawthrop, *Administrative Politics and Social Change*, New York, St. Martin's Press, 1971, pp. 41–56.

[50] Arrow. "Political and Economic Evaluation," p. 19. See also Hanna F. Pitkin, *The Concept of Representation*, Berkeley, University of California Press, 1972.

unorganized publics. In some situations, the motivations of entrepreneurs, interest groups, and public officials to represent unorganized
interests will not work to the benefit of the unorganized publics and
may be more symbolic than real, obscuring more immediate benefits
to the representatives rather than the represented. [51]

In summary, it cannot be assumed a priori that the pluralist thesis
is an adequate analytical model of the dynamics of the public policy
process in responding to the social costs of public organizations. Only
under limited conditions will such assumptions hold, and, as the next
chapter and the case study will suggest, such conditions have not been
present in the context of the social costs of criminal justice information
policy formation.

[51] See Murray Edelman, *The Symbolic Uses of Politics,* Urbana, Ill., University of Illinois
Press, 1964.

3

Social Costs and
the Politics of
Public Policy Formation

Chapter 2 defined the concept of social costs and suggested the implications of that concept for understanding the public policymaking process. More specifically, it proposed that the defined characteristics of social costs cast substantial doubt on the assumptions of the pluralist model of the policymaking process and raise serious questions about the possibility of effectively reducing social costs.

In this chapter, a more dynamic and developmental view of the public policymaking process, in relation to the problem of social costs, will be presented. The aim is to integrate the assumptions and the analytical view developed earlier into a policy process approach to public policymaking.[1] The policy process approach focuses on the study of the political process by examining specific public problems: how public problems get to be defined as such, how they get on the agenda of government decision makers, how they are acted on, and what the consequences and costs of adopted regulatory solutions are. This approach assumes that a significant factor in the working of the political process is the definition of the problem that reaches government decision makers. While the policy process approach covers each stage of policymaking through implementation and evaluation, it places particular emphasis on the first stage in the policy development process—the stage of policy formation. In recent years, this approach has highlighted the dynamics of problem identification and agenda building in the public policy process, which have been ignored or

---

[1] See Charles O. Jones, *An Introduction to the Study of Public Policy*, Belmont, Calif., Duxbury Press, 1970, pp. 1–5.

overlooked by analysts focusing on institutional politics or group interactions.[2]

In this chapter, the politics of public policy formation will be discussed in relation to the problem of social costs. In particular, the dynamics of issue creation and agenda building will be explored in the context of the characteristics of social costs as a public policy issue and the prospects for political action to reduce such costs. As Figure 4 indicates, a causal model of the policy formation process will be devel-

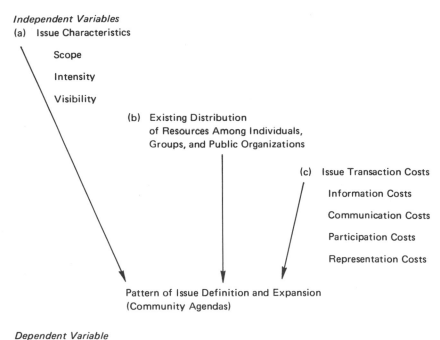

Independent Variables
(a)   Issue Characteristics

Scope

Intensity

Visibility

(b)   Existing Distribution
of Resources Among Individuals,
Groups, and Public Organizations

(c)   Issue Transaction Costs

Information Costs

Communication Costs

Participation Costs

Representation Costs

Pattern of Issue Definition and Expansion
(Community Agendas)

Dependent Variable
Entrance and Treatment on Formal Decision-Making Agendas

Probable Reduction
(or Nonreduction)
in Social Costs

FIGURE 4   A causal diagram of public policy formation.

[2] *Ibid.*, pp. 2–3. See also Roger W. Cobb and Charles D. Elder, *Participation in American Politics: The Dynamics of Agenda-Building*, Boston, Mass., Allyn and Bacon, 1972, pp. 1–35.

oped to explain the political implications and costs of issue formation and adoption in the American political process.

SOCIAL COSTS AS A PUBLIC PROBLEM: THE POLITICS OF ISSUE IDENTIFICATION

Economists and other analysts who are concerned with the problem of social costs have sometimes taken it for granted that the adverse consequences of the actions of organizations present problems involving social cost considerations, and they tend to obscure the evaluative element implicit in the term social cost. Not all negative consequences of organizational conduct are characterized as social costs; thus, implicit in an analyst's consideration of particular negative consequences of organizational activities as external or social costs is the human value judgment concerning the significance of treating only *some* negative consequences in such a manner. This is more than a definitional problem: What justification is used to identify certain activities or consequences of human conduct as significant and deserving of specific attention and not others?

A somewhat similar problem arises in the public policymaking process. Not all human needs, deprivations, dissatisfactions, and negative consequences of organizational conduct are identified as public problems deserving of some relief. As Charles O. Jones has noted: "There are needs and needs."[3] What, then, is a public problem? John Dewey has suggested that the difference between a public and private problem is as follows:

We take. . .our point of departure from the objective fact that human acts have consequences upon others, that some of these consequences are perceived, and that their perception leads to subsequent effort to control action so as to secure some consequences and avoid others. Following this clew, we are led to remark that the consequences are of two kinds, those which affect the persons directly engaged in a transaction, and those which affect others beyond those immediately concerned.[4]

Dewey associated a public concern with what economists call an externality and suggested that, when such consequences are *perceived* by

[3] Jones. *Introduction to the Study of Public Policy*, p. 18. See also James E. Anderson, *Public Policy-Making*, New York, Praeger, 1975, pp. 55–58.

[4] John Dewey. *The Public and Its Problems*. Chicago, Swallow Press, 1927, p. 12.

others and considered to be *significant enough* to be controlled, a public problem as well as a public was born.[5]

The identification or creation of a public problem, then, is a process of focusing on particular individual needs and preferences as politically significant. The manner in which a public problem is identified will, in turn, influence the way that problem is or is not dealt with in the policymaking process. More specifically, the process of problem identification becomes integrally linked with the process by which certain public problems achieve agenda status and others do not.[6]

The policy agenda represents "those demands that policy-makers either do choose or feel compelled to act upon."[7] Cobb and Elder identified two basic types of policy agendas in the political system: the community or systemic agenda and the governmental or formal agenda. The community agenda "consists of all issues that are commonly perceived by members of the political community as meriting public attention and as involving matters within the legitimate jurisdiction of existing governmental authority."[8] A community agenda exists in every local, state, and national political community; it is essentially a discussion agenda. For public problems or issues to reach community agenda status, three prerequisites must be fulfilled: "(1) widespread attention or at least awareness; (2) shared concern of a sizeable portion of the public that some type of action is required; and (3) a shared perception that the matter is an appropriate concern of some governmental unit and falls within the bounds of its authority."[9] Issues that reach community agenda status usually are stated in abstract rather than concrete terms and are related in some way to the dominant opinions, values, and ideology of the community.

The second type of agenda, the governmental or formal agenda, is defined as "that set of items explicitly up for the active and serious consideration of authoritative decisionmakers."[10] Although the community agenda is comprised of many general concerns and problems,

---

[5] Dewey defines a "public" as "all those who are affected by the indirect consequences of transactions to such an extent that it is deemed necessary to have those consequences systematically cared for" (*Ibid.*, pp. 15–16). Thus, there is no one public in the political process; rather, there are as many publics as there are public problems.

[6] See David G. Smith, "Pragmatism and the Group Theory of Politics," *American Political Science Review*, 58:600–610, September 1964.

[7] Anderson. *Public Policy-Making*, p. 59.

[8] Cobb and Elder. *Participation in American Politics*, p. 85.

[9] *Ibid.*, p. 86.

[10] *Ibid.*

the formal agenda has fewer, but more specific and significant, items. Not all items on the community agenda are subsequently treated on the formal agenda.

Putting items on the two agendas is a costly process. The content of both the community and formal agendas usually will reflect the structural and preferential biases within the existing system. Throughout the policy formation stage, public officials—legislators, administrators, and judges—are active participants in the agenda-building process. Their strategic location in controlling formal agendas means that they can choose or influence the choice of items that enter the formal agenda and influence the appearance of concerns on the community agenda.[11] Thus, the access that individuals, groups, and entrepreneurs have to public officials in various functional capacities at all levels of government is an important factor in translating private demands into agenda items.

There is likely to be differential access to these policymakers due to inequalities in resources, influence, and what Cobb and Elder refer to as "differential legitimacy" or standing accorded to different publics, groups, and entrepreneurs in the policy process. Because of such inequalities, it will be costly, in terms of transaction costs, for the various actors in the policymaking process to engage in political action for the purpose of identifying various consequences of public organizational activity as social costs that require status on the community and/or governmental agendas of the policy process and recognition by public officials.

ISSUE DEVELOPMENT AND POLITICAL TRANSACTION COSTS

Different issues have different characteristics that affect the manner in which they are developed or expanded in the public policymaking process. The focus here is not on the specific content of issues but, rather, on the nature of the political conflict or competition that arises. The three basic dimensions of issues include scope, intensity, and visibility (see Figure 4).

Scope of the issue refers to the number of individuals or groups

---

[11] For a discussion of strategic individuals in the policy formation process as "leverage points," see Kenneth J. Gergen, "Assessing the Leverage Points in the Process of Policy Formation," in: *The Study of Policy Formation*, edited by Raymond A. Bauer and Kenneth J. Gergen, New York, Free Press, 1968, pp. 181–203.

affected by the problem. Some issues affect only a limited number of individuals or groups, while others, such as air pollution, have a more diffuse impact on many or all people in a community. The scope of the issue has a direct bearing on what Cobb and Elder define as the social significance of an issue or what Gergen calls its impact.

Intensity of the issue refers to how strongly individuals or groups feel about an issue. One measure of intensity is the amount of resources that individuals or groups are willing to use in seeking a favorable resolution of the issue. Those who expend a large proportion of their resources on an issue are likely to feel more intense about that issue than those who use only a small proportion of their resources for political action. The intensity of an issue and the degree to which resources will be used will vary, depending on how relevant or salient that issue is to a particular public. Not all publics will be similarly concerned about an issue: Some issues may be limited to specific publics or "identification groups," some may come within the purview of "attention groups" or attentive publics, and others may reach the general public.[12] The nature of the groups or publics involved in a controversy will indicate the relative strength of the contending parties as well as the visibility (or lack thereof) of the issue.

Visibility, the third dimension, refers to the extent an issue is perceived as significant by individuals, groups, and public officials not directly affected by the problem. Several factors affect visibility. First, how the issue is defined affects its development: whether the problem and demands can be stated specifically or only abstractly; whether the issue is complex or readily understandable; whether the issue has limited, immediate relevance or is more enduring and fundamental; and whether the issue is new or has an established history and clear precedents.[13] Second, the relationship of the issue to other issues and to the dominant community ideology may affect its placement and treatment on policy agendas. Third, the available means of publicizing the issue and generating information will affect its development. Whether the issue is reported on favorably or unfavorably in the mass media will have a direct bearing on its "life chances."[14] In addition, the extent to which individuals or groups bear the costs of generating information about a public problem and communicating that information as widely as possible will affect both the definition of the issue and its visibility.

[12] Cobb and Elder. *Participation in American Politics*, pp. 105–108.

[13] *Ibid.*, pp. 96–102.

[14] Matthew A. Crenson. *The Un-Politics of Air Pollution*. Baltimore, Md., Johns Hopkins Press, 1971, p. 156.

At the heart of the policy process then are the problems of issue definition and expansion. Both problems are closely linked with the characteristics of public problems. In turn, issue characteristics influence the costs of transactions for individuals, groups, and public organizations by either developing the issue and getting it on the community and formal agendas or containing its development by preventing it from achieving agenda status or controlling how the issue is dealt with on the community and formal agendas.

There are four major types of transaction costs for individuals, groups, and public officials involved in the policy process: information costs, communication costs, participation costs, and representation costs. They will vary with both the particular characteristics of an issue and the distribution of resources among individuals, groups, and public officials.

If issue expansion is fundamental to the political process, then information generation and collection is crucial to issue expansion and success in achieving agenda status. As noted in Chapter 2, information is costly; thus, the visibility of an issue will be directly affected by the costs of information about a public problem. Such costs include policy information costs and strategy information costs. Policy information costs are those "incurred in the search, purchase, analysis, and understanding of information" regarding a public problem and the available alternatives to deal with it. Strategy information costs are those incurred in determining what other individuals or groups will do in relation to the public problem and the choice of policy alternatives.[15]

As suggested in Chapter 2, some information costs are transferable and some are not. Assimilating both types of information is a nontransferable cost. All other costs of information are transferable and, therefore, may be provided by various information suppliers.

A second category of transaction costs closely related to information costs are the costs of communication: "Every message involves the expenditure of time to decide what to send, time to compose the message, the resource-cost of transmitting the message (which may consist of time, or money, or both), and time spent in receiving the message."[16] Since time and money of individuals are limited, the more time and money an individual spends in searching or communicating, the less he has for other kinds of activities. In addition, the capacity of an individual for absorbing and using information is limited in terms

---

[15] Wayne L. Francis. *American Politics: Analysis of Choice*. Pacific Palisades, Calif., Goodyear, 1976, p. 38.

[16] Anthony Downs. *Inside Bureaucracy*. Boston, Mass., Little, Brown, 1967, p. 112.

of available resources and already acquired contextual knowledge. While an individual may receive information through society's free stream of political information about an issue and cut some communication costs, generally, the cost of communication will depend on his position in society: "If he (the citizen) happens to be Vice-President of the United States, it will be low; if he is a laborer in a mining town, it may be very high."[17]

Participation costs, a third category of transaction costs, are the costs of coordination and pooling of resources involved in collective action. Participation costs will vary with the presence or absence of entrepreneurs and groups that will undertake the efforts needed for coordination of expectations and the pooling of resources. Individuals will engage in collective action only if the expected benefits exceed the costs of membership and involvement in joint efforts.

The fourth category of costs in the policy process are the costs of representation. As noted in Chapter 2, the utility preferences of representatives and represented may, for a variety of reasons, differ considerably. This divergence may impose costs for individuals affected by a public problem. Like the other three types of transaction costs, the costs of representation are likely to vary with the position of the citizen in society, the resources the citizen can use to influence, either directly or indirectly, the choices of the representative, and the probability of a favorable outcome. Even if representation and delegation may generally reduce information, communication, and participation costs by transferring the decision-making responsibility to public officials, the transaction costs of specific issues may be higher when the preferences of representatives and public officials differ from the preferences and needs of individuals affected by the issue.

Since public problems differ in scope, intensity, and visibility, transaction costs may vary as well. Diffuse, low-intensity, and low-visibility issues are likely to be more costly to expand and place on the community and formal agendas than nondiffuse, high-intensity, and highly visible issues. In addition, transaction costs will vary with the relative distribution of resources among individuals, groups, and organizations and the strategies used by opponents of issue expansion to contain the development of an issue.

The containment of political conflict and competition is an integral aspect of the political process. It arises because political change is a costly process. Public officials, for example, are likely to use various

[17] Anthony Downs. *An Economic Theory of Democracy.* New York, Harper and Row, 1957, p. 252.

strategies of conflict containment to minimize the depth and cost of changes to their organizations. Cobb and Elder identified two general categories of strategies used for conflict containment: group-oriented strategies and issue-oriented strategies. Groups can be attacked in several ways. Either the group itself or the leaders of the group may be discredited, or the group's base of support may be reduced by co-opting the leaders or by appealing to the members of the group rather than to the leaders.[18] Issues may be attacked directly by creating a new organizational unit to deal with the problem, by anticipating the issue before public mobilization, or by co-opting the symbols of the opponents. Issues also may be attacked indirectly by postponing the treatment of the issue, by feigning constraint of an individual or organizational kind, by providing symbolic rewards or assurances, or by showcasing or tokenism.[19] Such strategies of containment raise transaction costs in the expansion of public issues and place constraints on the definition of public problems and their treatment on policy agendas.

SYMBOL UTILIZATION, THE MEDIA, AND ISSUE EXPANSION

An important aspect of the information used to define public issues in the political process is the type of language used. Public issues, as Murray Edelman has observed, have both a substantive and a symbolic character.[20] Symbols are used in the political process to expand or constrict the scope of conflict and competition. With respect to various public issues, such symbols as liberty, justice, free enterprise, and communism have a certain "potency" or "weight":

> Symbol potency, or *symbol weight*, is influenced by the situation and by the people using it. The symbol must be appropriate for each instance and must appear to be the right type of language for a leader to utter at that time. The situation will depend on two elements: the nature of the combatants and the nature of the audience that might be added to either camp. Thus, language must be correct, not only for followers, but also for potential supporters. All of these elements are relevant when determining the impact of a series of symbols on a developing issue dispute.[21]

[18] Cobb and Elder. *Participation in American Politics*, pp. 125–127.

[19] *Ibid.*, pp. 127–129.

[20] Murray Edelman. *The Symbolic Uses of Politics*. Urbana, University of Illinois Press, 1964, p. 43.

[21] Cobb and Elder. *Participation in American Politics*, p. 131.

An essential aspect of symbols that affects their potency is their historical background.[22] Certain types of symbols will have a particular meaning for the political community. Some symbols, such as justice, liberty, and due process, may evoke a positive response; others, such as communism, fascism, *1984*, and *Brave New World*, may evoke a negative response. Symbols may gain or lose potency with the passage of time.[23] They can vary in their scope and the intensity of the reaction they evoke. In the late 1960s, the phrase "law and order" was identified with a number of issues involved with the control of crime and administration of criminal justice and evoked intense reactions, both pro and con, from various publics. In recent years, the term "automation" has evoked progressively negative reactions from various publics; in the past, it was associated with the leading edge of social and economic progress.

The use of symbols in the political process cuts the costs of communication and information: Symbols are the shorthand of politics. They can be used to expand or contain the scope and depth of political conflict. A phrase such as "the expanding role of the Federal Government" has been a cue both for government interference in private affairs and for government attention to serious social problems. In the 1960s, it was used by groups and public officials to promote social reform and, in the 1970s, to restrict the activities of the Federal Government in social services delivery.

Apart from their substantive content, symbols are used in various contexts as cues for either expanding or constricting the scope and depth of political conflict and competition. Although at times certain symbols may be overworked or used inappropriately,[24] generally, symbols, either singly or in combination, are used to mobilize support for or against issues and policy alternatives and, thus, they play a significant role in the development of political strategies. Symbols play this role largely through the communications media, who act as important information providers and symbol users in the political process. As Michael Lipsky has noted: "In granting or withholding publicity, in determining what information most people will have on most issues, and what alternatives they will consider in response to issues, the media truly, as Norton Long has put it, 'set the civic agenda.'"[25] The communications media set the limits of conflict expansion by empha-

---

[22] *Ibid.*, p. 132.

[23] *Ibid.*, p. 133.

[24] *Ibid.*, pp. 133–135.

[25] Michael Lipsky. *Protest in City Politics: Rent Strikes, Housing, and the Power of the Poor.* Chicago, Rand McNally, 1970, p. 169.

sizing symbols and issues. Symbols cannot be used for arousal, provocation, dissuasion, demonstration of commitment, or affirmation without the communications media playing its integral intermediary role.[26] Whether symbols are used to influence onlookers and important decision makers or to encourage group commitment or resolve to bear the costs of fighting for a particular cause, the communications media may emphasize or ignore issues and political actions. This may increase or decrease the costs of information and communication in the political process. In the context of specific issues, the communications media may provide favorable or unfavorable coverage of events and decisions and significantly affect the marginal cost-return principle of individuals, groups, and public officials in the political process.

In addition, the communications media will have a differential impact in two ways. First, not all communications media report "news" or generate information in the same way. Television may select for broadcast only very brief portions of a news conference or may present a report with a minimum of background or explanatory material.[27] Newspapers and magazines may give more complete accounts of the same event or report. A still more comprehensive account may be found in books and articles written by intellectuals and professionals in the field. Also, public officials may publish materials pertinent to an issue that will provide more background material and analysis. Thus, not all the communications media will cover an issue in the same manner, either substantively or with respect to its "politics."

Second, the assimilation of information communicated to citizens by the various communications media will vary. It will depend, as Anthony Downs has suggested, primarily on three factors: "(1) the time he (the citizen) can afford to spend assimilating it, (2) the kind of contextual knowledge he has, and (3) the homogeneity of the selection principles."[28] Because there are significant differences among citizens in a society with respect to each factor, the use of information derived from the communications media in political action will differ. Individuals with higher socioeconomic status generally will be able to better afford to procure and use information derived from the communications media than individuals with low socioeconomic status.[29]

As part of the information component in political activity, symbols have a direct effect on the definition of issues and their chances in the political process. Coupled with the filtering effect of the various com-

---

[26] See Cobb and Elder, *Participation in American Politics,* pp. 142–150.
[27] See Edward Jay Epstein, *News from Nowhere,* New York, Random House, 1973.
[28] Downs. *Economic Theory of Democracy,* p. 234.
[29] *Ibid.,* p. 236.

munications media on the dissemination of information, the use of symbols has a major impact on the cost of transactions in the political process.

AGENDA ACCESS AND THE POLITICS AND COSTS OF REGULATION

Depending on the process and the costs of issue definition and expansion to various individuals, groups, and public officials, issues will have different patterns of placement and treatment on the community and on formal agendas. Not all issues may achieve community agenda status; some issues may achieve agenda status only indirectly by inclusion in broader community concerns. Some issues may achieve community agenda status but may not be assigned to the formal agenda of public decision makers. Particularly in cases where the costs of change are likely to be high, there may be a decision by public officials to make no decision concerning an issue—what Bachrach and Baratz define as a "nondecision."[30]

One point is clear concerning the formal agendas of public decision makers: "Policy-makers are not faced with a *given* problem."[31] Formal agendas are made up of numerous issues competing for various degrees of attention. Thus, the expansion of an issue will determine the manner in which it achieves recognition. Cobb and Elder suggest that "the larger the public to which an issue has been expanded, the greater the likelihood of the conflict being placed on the docket."[32] They observe that issues that cannot be expanded beyond their identification group will face great difficulty in gaining the attention of public officials. On the other hand, issues expanded to attentive publics or even to the mass public are more likely to gain the attention of public decision makers. The way in which an issue is brought to the attention of public officials will, in turn, depend on the extent to which it is made visible to various publics.

The problem, of course, is that expansion of various issues is a costly process. Depending on the cost of altering the status quo, some issues may meet the active resistance of public officials, agencies, and private

[30] Peter Bachrach and M. S. Baratz. *Power and Poverty*, London, Oxford University Press, 1970. See also their earlier article, "Two Faces of Power," *American Political Science Review*, 56(52):947–952, 1962.

[31] Charles E. Lindblom. *The Policy-Making Process*. Englewood Cliffs, N.J., Prentice-Hall, 1968, p. 13.

[32] Cobb and Elder. *Participation in American Politics*, p. 152.

groups intent on maintaining their present situation and controlling rather carefully the direction, pace, and depth of change. The existing distribution of resources among groups and individuals in the political process and the costs of overcoming strategies to contain conflict will determine whether particular issues gain formal agenda status as well as their subsequent treatment on that agenda.

Treatment on the formal agenda refers to the way in which public decision makers respond to an agenda item. Every item that reaches the formal agenda implies some conflict over the distribution of rights and resources. Public decision makers are involved in the process of formulating courses of action to deal with such conflict and choosing whether or not to alter the existing distribution of benefits and costs among individuals, groups, and public organizations. Public officials, in responding to specific agenda items, will find it more or less costly to support various proposals for change. The visibility of an issue and the expected or anticipated distribution of benefits and costs of the policy change will determine how an issue will be treated on the formal agenda.[33]

The stage of public policy formation is of crucial importance to the public policy process, since it is at this point that the business of politics is defined. Out of the many potential problems and issues in modern society, only a few become significant: "Political conflict is not like an intercollegiate debate in which the opponents agree in advance on a definition of the issues. As a matter of fact, *the definition of the alternatives is the supreme instrument of power.*"[34]

For this reason, it is suggested that studying the politics of public policy formation, in relation to the social costs of technological innovation in public organization, will provide important insight into how technology and politics interact. How the problem of social costs is defined and expanded as a political issue and treated on community and formal agendas is the key to understanding what the ultimate benefits and costs of technological change to American society will be.

---

[33] See Crenson, *Un-Politics of Air Pollution*, pp. 120, 139–140; and James Q. Wilson, *Political Organizations*, New York, Basic Books, 1973, pp. 327–346.

[34] E. E. Schattschneider. *The Semisovereign People*. New York, Holt, Rinehart and Winston, 1960, p. 68.

PART II

Introduction

The principal concern of this study is to understand the relationship between the social costs of information technology in public organizations and the response of the public policymaking process to control and regulate these costs. Part I of the study attempted to clarify the nature and significance of social costs and their relationship to problems of collective action and public policy formation. In Part II, a case study of criminal justice information systems and information policy will be presented to illustrate the application of the theoretical perspective developed in Part I.

Chapter 4 sets the stage for the case study by reviewing the history of the development of criminal justice information systems since 1965 from the perspective of developers of such systems, who were interested in more effective law enforcement and administration of criminal justice through the widespread use and application of the new technology.

Chapter 5 aims at defining social costs related to the use of criminal justice records. The identification of social costs is analyzed as a problem of collective action and inaction in relation to the public affected.

Chapter 6 examines the patterns of governmental response to the reduction of social costs associated with criminal justice information usage beginning with the precomputer period and proceeding to the early period of information system development. This chapter focuses on the emergence of the social costs of criminal justice records as a public policy issue.

Chapter 7 reviews the legislative history of attempts to develop a national criminal justice information policy and why these efforts failed (during 1974 and 1975).

Chapter 8 focuses on organizational conflicts and problems that, in recent years, have led to a cycle of congressional/executive branch interactions and conflicts which have contributed only marginally, if at all, to the resolution of the political, technical, and moral issues involved in reducing the social costs of criminal justice records.

In Chapter 9, representation of the interest in reducing the social costs of criminal justice records is analyzed. Particular attention is

53

given to the conditions for and limitations on the successful representation of such a nonintense, low-visibility, diffuse interest.

Chapter 10 reviews the approaches to regulation that have been
proposed or used during development of the debate over a national
criminal justice information policy in terms of the anticipated costs
and benefits involved in the choice of available regulatory options for
various participants and affected publics in the public policy process.

4

Criminal Justice
Information Systems
and the Reform of the
Criminal Justice System

Since it is assumed throughout this study that technological innovation is a political process, it is essential that efforts to develop computerized criminal justice information systems be placed in their appropriate historical and political context. How was the movement for the development of such systems initiated? How has it been justified and supported by legal, fiscal, and organizational resources? What have been the principal results of efforts to develop criminal justice information systems? How widespread have these efforts been? What have the developers of such systems envisioned as a design strategy for their use in law enforcement and administration of criminal justice in the United States?

CRIMINAL JUSTICE REFORM AND MODERNIZATION: THE EMPHASIS ON INFORMATION AND COMPUTERS

In his March 8, 1965 message to Congress, President Lyndon B. Johnson announced the establishment of a President's Commission on Law Enforcement and Administration of Justice to investigate the causes of crime and to recommend ways to improve crime prevention and control.[1] In 1967, the commission issued a series of reports on

---

[1] "Crime, Its Prevalence and Measures of Prevention." President's Message to the Congress, March 8, 1965. *1965 Congressional Quarterly Almanac*. Washington, D.C., Congressional Quarterly Service, 1965, pp. 1396–1397.

crime in American society,[2] including a specific analysis of the principal problems and deficiencies in law enforcement and the administration of criminal justice. A detailed strategy was presented for the reform and modernization of the criminal justice system in America that highlighted the use of computer technology and emphasized scientific methods of management and control.

The president's commission identified three principal problems: First, the process of criminal justice administration could not be called a "system," because the process suffered from extreme decentralization, fragmentation, and general lack of coordination among the agencies involved.

The system of criminal justice America uses to deal with those crimes it cannot deter is not a monolithic, or even a consistent, system. It was not designed or built in one piece at one time. Its philosophic core is that a person may be punished by the Government if, and only if, it has been proved by an impartial and deliberate process that he has violated a specific law. Around that core, layer upon layer of institutions and procedures, some carefully constructed and some improvised, some inspired by principle and some by expediency, have accumulated. Parts of the system—magistrates' courts, trial by jury, bail—are of great antiquity. Other parts—juvenile courts, probation and parole, professional policemen—are relatively new. The entire system represents an adaptation of the English common law to America's peculiar structure of government, which allows each local community to construct institutions to fill its special needs. Every village, town, county, city, and State has its own criminal justice system, and there is a Federal one as well. All of them operate somewhat alike. No two of them operate precisely alike.[3]

The second problem was that the process was overburdened.[4] The incidence of crime had been continuously rising, both in relative and absolute terms, for many years. Also, there had been a general tendency towards over-criminalization, that is, to prescribe criminal justice solutions to what were essentially social and moral problems.

Third, there were serious deficiencies in information about crime and criminals and how the "system" of criminal justice worked. Available information and statistics were perceived as seriously deficient:

[2] See President's Commission on Law Enforcement and Administration of Justice. *The Challenge of Crime in a Free Society; Task Force Report: Assessment of Crime; Task Force Report: Corrections; Task Force Report: Courts; Task Force Report: Juvenile Delinquency; Task Force Report: Organized Crime; Task Force Report: Police*; and *Task Force Report: Science and Technology.* Washington, D.C., U.S. Government Printing Office, 1967.
[3] President's Commission on Law Enforcement. *Challenge of Crime*, p. 7.
[4] *Ibid.*, pp. 7, 10.

It has been possible to identify many specific inadequacies in the published data concerning crime and the criminal justice system. These deficiencies fall under two main headings. First, much of the published data are incomplete, inconsistent, and inaccurate. For example, different criminal justice agencies report their operations in inconsistent units: The police report "arrests", the courts report "cases", and correction agencies "offenders". Information from different jurisdictions often has different underlying interpretations. In some jurisdictions, stealing from parking meters is a burglary, while in others it is larceny.

The second class of deficiencies in existing data includes the vast number of instances in which no data at all are available. We know much too little about how various actions of the criminal justice system affect the number and types of crimes committed by different classes of offenders.[5]

In response to these significant problems with the administration of criminal justice, the commission looked to science and technology as a key to modernizing and increasing the capabilities of criminal justice agencies. The commission focused on two important areas. First, it suggested that better and more timely information could be provided by the use of recent advancements in information technology, especially computers.

Modern information technology now permits a massive assault on these (information) problems at a level never before conceived. Computers have been used to solve related problems in such diverse fields as continental air defense, production scheduling, airline reservations, and corporate management. Modern computer and communications technology permits many users, each sitting in his own office, to have immediate remote access to large computer-based central data banks. Each user can add information to a central data bank. Each user can add information to a central file to be shared by the others. Access can be restricted so that only specified users can get certain information.

Criminal justice could benefit dramatically from computer-based information systems, and development of a network designed specifically for its operations could start immediately.[6]

In addition, the administration of criminal justice could be improved by adapting the new methods of scientific analysis and management, such as systems analysis, to the requirements of criminal justice agencies.

Because of the enormous range of research and development possibilities,

[5] *Ibid.*, p. 266.
[6] *Ibid.*

it is essential to begin not with the technology but with the problem. Technological efforts can then be concentrated in the areas most likely to be productive. Systems analysis is a valuable method for matching the technology to the need. It uses mathematical models of real-life systems to compare various ways of designing and using these systems to achieve specified objectives at minimum cost.

These same techniques of systems analysis can often be helpful when applied to the design of some of the operations in police, courts, and corrections agencies, and to relating these parts to the overall criminal justice system.[7]

The commission's emphasis on the use of science and technology to reform the operations of criminal justice agencies represented a political strategy of administrative reform. By equating reform with modernization and by equating modernization with the adaptation of science and technology to criminal justice purposes, the commission effectively interpreted the crisis in public policy and administration to be a crisis in information and technology. Thus, the reform of the criminal justice system was characterized not in terms of fundamental political change but in terms of modernization and the need for "technology transfer."[8] The goal was to update the operations of the criminal justice system by involving in the tasks of criminal justice the manpower and know-how that had been developed, for example, by working on military and space matters.[9]

The natural sciences and technology have long helped the police to solve specific crimes. Scientists and engineers have had very little impact, however, on the overall operations of the criminal justice system and its principal components: police, courts, and corrections. More than 200,000 scientists and engineers have applied themselves to solving military problems and hundreds of thousands more to innovations in other areas of modern life, but only a handful are working to control the crimes that injure or frighten millions of Americans each year. Yet, the two communities have much to offer each other: science and technology is a valuable source of knowledge and techniques for combating crime; the criminal justice system represents a vast area of challenging problems.[10]

Amidst the many recommendations of the commission was con-

[7] President's Commission on Law Enforcement. *Task Force Report: Science and Technology*, p. 3.

[8] See Kenneth C. Laudon, *Computers and Bureaucratic Reform*, New York, Wiley, 1974, pp. 35–56.

[9] See Ida R. Hoos, *Systems Analysis in Public Policy*, Berkeley, University of California Press, 1972, pp. 82–112.

[10] President's Commission on Law Enforcement. *Task Force Report: Science and Technology*, p. 1.

tinual emphasis on the rationality and political viability of reforming the administration of criminal justice through advanced scientific techniques and technology. At the heart of this effort of modernization, the commission felt, was the "need to know much more about crime. A national strategy against crime must be in large part a strategy of search."[11] Supporting this strategy of search was the development of computerized information systems to collect, maintain, and disseminate information about crime, criminals, and the operations of the criminal justice system: "Modern information technology now permits an assault on these problems at a level never before conceivable."[12]

By focusing on modernizing and reforming criminal justice administration through new scientific techniques of analysis and management and computerized information systems, the commission set the formal agenda for subsequent legislative initiatives and organizational and technological changes. Its national strategy provided significant support to developing efforts for applying new resources and capabilities to criminal justice agencies.

THE OMNIBUS CRIME CONTROL AND SAFE STREETS ACT AND THE LAW ENFORCEMENT ASSISTANCE ADMINISTRATION

The approach of the commission to reform and modernization in criminal justice represented an extension of the trend of the 1960s: a more significant federal role in the administration of criminal justice in the United States. In the late 1960s, the definition of this expanded federal role led to the passage of the Omnibus Crime Control and Safe Streets Act and the establishment of the Law Enforcement Assistance Administration (LEAA). LEAA became the conduit for federal monies to state and local criminal justice agencies for reform and modernization, including the widespread development of computerized criminal justice information systems. The passage of the "safe streets" legislation and the funding of LEAA represented significant extensions of prior efforts reflecting enhanced presidential support of the "war on crime" or "law and order" issues.

---

[11] President's Commission on Law Enforcement. *Challenge of Crime*, p. 279.
[12] President's Commission on Law Enforcement. *Task Force Report: Science and Technology*, p. 68.

Office of Law Enforcement Assistance (OLEA): A Precursor

In the same message to Congress that established the President's Commission on Law Enforcement and Administration of Justice, President Johnson proposed, on March 8, 1965, the Law Enforcement Assistance Act as the first federal grant-in-aid program designed solely for the purpose of enhancing state and local crime reduction responsibilities.[13] Six months later, Congress enacted the Law Enforcement Assistance Act of 1965.[14]

The basic thrust of this legislation was to generate new approaches and techniques and to upgrade existing practices, resources, and capabilities for dealing with the problems of crime. The attorney general was authorized to make grants to public and private nonprofit organizations for projects intended to improve law enforcement and correctional personnel, to increase the ability of state and local agencies to protect persons and property from lawlessness, and to instill greater public respect for the law. The attorney general administered the program through the Justice Department's Office of Law Enforcement Assistance (OLEA). The program was intended to spearhead the Federal Government's war on crime, but it was funded at only a demonstration or experimental level. Actual appropriations for the three years of its existence amounted to approximately $22 million: $7.249 million in 1966, $7.25 million in 1967, and $7.5 million in 1968.[15]

The OLEA program was a pioneering attempt by the Federal Government to assist state and local jurisdictions with their law enforcement and criminal justice operations and to undertake new programs through funding a variety of research and demonstration projects. It initiated what President Johnson conceived to be a "creative federal partnership" in the fight against crime.[16]

Because the OLEA program generally was considered successful, support mounted in the Congress and the Johnson administration for a greater federal commitment to reduce crime in the nation. Subsequently, a Safe Streets and Crime Control Act was proposed by Presi-

[13] "Crime, Its Prevalence and Measures of Prevention." pp. 1396–1397.

[14] For a more complete legislative history of this act, see Advisory Commission on Intergovernmental Relations, *Making the Safe Streets Act Work: An Intergovernmental Challenge*, Washington, D.C., U.S. Government Printing Office, 1968, pp. 8–10.

[15] *Ibid.*, p. 9.

[16] U.S. Department of Justice, Office of Law Enforcement Assistance. *Third Annual Report to the President and the Congress on Activities Under the Law Enforcement Assistance Act of 1965*. Washington, D.C., U.S. Government Printing Office, 1968, p. 1.

dent Johnson in his February 6, 1967 message to Congress on crime. This bill was intended to build on the efforts initiated by OLEA.

The Omnibus Crime Control and Safe Streets Act of 1968

As noted earlier, the Johnson administration proposed the Safe Streets and Crime Control Act of 1967 to implement many of the recommendations advanced by the President's Commission on Law Enforcement and Administration of Justice. The commission concluded that greater resources should be made available to support new approaches for improving all components of the law enforcement and criminal justice system at the federal, state, and local levels. The commission recognized that prevention and control of crime was basically a state and local responsibility, but it urged that crime reduction also should be considered a national problem requiring help from the Federal Government. Similarly, President Johnson characterized the Federal Government's overall role in this intergovernmental crime reduction effort as involving stimulation and support rather than control and coercion.

After extended debate, the bill was passed by the House and the Senate, and signed into law by President Johnson as the Omnibus Crime Control and Safe Streets Act of 1968.[17] Title I of the act represented the Federal Government's first comprehensive grant-in-aid program for reform and modernization of the criminal justice system as well as a new type of block grant approach to funding. In contrast to the direct federalism of the OLEA program, which had largely bypassed state governments in an effort to deliver federal funds to local agencies, the 1968 act placed heavy reliance on state governments as planners, administrators, coordinators, and innovators.[18] The states were assigned the major share of administrative responsibility for the programs. Each state's overall role was to act as a catalyst in bringing together previously isolated components of the law enforcement and criminal justice system and to coordinate, direct, and support their efforts in a comprehensive crime program.

[17] For a more complete legislative history of this act, see Advisory Commission on Intergovernmental Relations, *Making the Safe Streets Act Work*, pp. 10–18; and U.S. Department of Justice, Law Enforcement Assistance Administration, Office of the General Counsel, *Index to the Legislative History of the Omnibus Crime Control and Safe Streets Act of 1968*, Washington, D.C., 1973. For a discussion of the political context and history of this act, see John T. Elliff, *Crime, Dissent, and the Attorney General*, Beverly Hills, Calif., Sage Publications, 1971, pp. 50–78.

[18] See Advisory Commission on Intergovernmental Relations, *Making the Safe Streets Act Work*, pp. 18–19.

In turn, the Federal Government had important responsibilities to fulfill under the act. The Law Enforcement Assistance Administration was established within the Department of Justice to ensure that the federal funds were properly spent, but its structure did not rely extensively on the conditions that served as the normal instruments of federal control in grant programs.[19] LEAA was intended to encourage and assist state criminal justice planning agencies by establishing broad program guidelines, by approving comprehensive plans, and by stimulating innovation and experimentation.

Law Enforcement Assistance Administration

LEAA's role was perceived as that of a partner with states and localities in strengthening and improving criminal justice administration at every level.[20] While the LEAA program originated during President Johnson's term, it also was supported by the Nixon administration as the forerunner of the New Federalism and as the cutting edge in that administration's effort to restore law and order in the nation.[21] Local responsibility with federal support was seen as the essence of both the New Federalism and LEAA.[22] From an original appropriation of approximately $60 million in fiscal year 1969, LEAA's appropriations increased sharply each year: between 1969 and 1974, for example, LEAA was allocated a total of $3.2 billion.[23] Since 1974, LEAA's budget allocations have increased at a slower pace, and, in 1979, have declined significantly.

LEAA's primary focus of activity has been the administration of block action grants to the states: "These are called block grants because they are allocated to the states on the basis of population. They are action grants because they are designed to implement the plans which states have already made."[24] With LEAA funds, each state established a state

---

[19] *Ibid.*, p. 19.

[20] U.S. Department of Justice, Law Enforcement Assistance Administration. *5th Annual Report of the Law Enforcement Assistance Administration, Fiscal Year 1973*. Washington, D.C., U.S. Government Printing Office, 1973, p. 1.

[21] See Richard Harris, *Justice*, New York, Avon Books, 1969, pp. 35–41.

[22] Advisory Commission on Intergovernmental Relations. *Making the Safe Streets Act Work*, p. 19.

[23] U.S. Department of Justice, Law Enforcement Assistance Administration. *6th Annual Report of the LEAA, Fiscal Year 1974*. Washington, D.C., U.S. Government Printing Office, 1974, p. 4.

[24] U.S. Department of Justice, Law Enforcement Assistance Administration. *2nd Annual Report of the LEAA, Fiscal Year 1970*. Washington, D.C., U.S. Government Printing Office, 1970, p. 1.

TABLE 1   Basic Programs Supported by LEAA Funds

Comprehensive State planning for law enforcement improvement
Action programs to reduce crime and enhance the capabilities of criminal justice agencies
Technical assistance to build state and local expertise
Special grants to modernize and reform the corrections system and strengthen offender rehabilitation efforts
Education and training for criminal justice personnel
Research into the causes of criminal behavior and development of innovative techniques to prevent and control crime
Development of reliable statistics on crime, offenders, and the operations of the criminal justice system

Source: U.S. Department of Justice, Law Enforcement Assistance Administration. *5th Annual Report of the Law Enforcement Assistance Administration, Fiscal Year 1973*. Washington, D.C., U.S. Government Printing Office, 1973, p. 1.

planning agency (SPA) to develop a state comprehensive plan. Once the state plan is approved by LEAA, the state receives its block action grant.

LEAA also was authorized to make discretionary grants[25] to states, cities, or other organizations for innovative or demonstration projects and to provide funds for academic assistance and for research and development in the criminal justice field (see Table 1).

Table 2 indicates how these funds were distributed among LEAA's program categories over the first five years of the agency's existence. Following the recommendations of the president's commission, relatively high priority was given to the development of information and statistical systems for the states as well as to the application of new technology.[26] In the remaining sections of this chapter, the effects of these expenditures on information systems development in federal, state, and local criminal justice agencies will be discussed.

---

[25] *Ibid.*

[26] Much more money has been spent on information systems than Table 2 indicates. In addition to the monies that were specifically allocated for "Data Systems and Statistical Assistance," many states have allocated large portions of their action grants for such purposes, and LEAA has allocated a number of discretionary grants to support information systems research and development. See, for example, Lawyer's Committee for Civil Rights Under Law, and Urban Coalition, *Law and Disorder III*, Washington, D.C., Special Projects Office, Lawyer's Committee for Civil Rights Under Law, 1972, pp. 59–104 (Chapter 4, "The Story of the States").

THE DEVELOPMENT OF CRIMINAL JUSTICE INFORMATION SYSTEMS—FEDERAL LEVEL

Three developments at the federal level influenced the growth and use of computerized criminal justice information systems. Two of these developments were initiated and developed by LEAA; the third, under the direction of the Federal Bureau of Investigation (FBI).

Project SEARCH (System for Electronic Analysis and Retrieval of Criminal Histories)

Early in calendar year 1967, LEAA began to receive a number of grant applications from states seeking funds to develop state criminal justice information systems. At that time, a decision had to be made concerning future development of such systems. As Richard Velde, associate administrator for LEAA, stated in 1970:

> The need for such systems—both from LEAA's viewpoint and that of the states—was great. But there were problems. First, each application or proposal dealt with only one state. If a number of states were given funds, then there could be a number of state systems. But each state might go off in its own direction, leaving us with a bewildering complex of independent and incompatible programs. Then, there was the matter of the amount of money available to support such projects.
>
> In fiscal year 1969 out of that $63 million budget, only $4 million was available in action funds, which LEAA could give at its own discretion. One state wanted $300,000 for its own criminal justice information project. Other requests were comparably large. It quickly became clear that only one project could be started. It would have to be defined precisely. It would have to embrace a number of states. It was also clear that the system would have to be compatible not only among participating states, but would utilize a format in which other states could eventually fit so that a true nationwide system could be developed.[27]

After LEAA completed an informal survey to determine those states with the greatest promise for becoming participants in the project, Project SEARCH was established, with a $600,000 discretionary grant. Originally, there were six grantee states—Arizona, California, Maryland, Michigan, Minnesota, and New York—and four observer states—Connecticut, Florida, Texas, and Washington. California was named as coordinator.[28]

---

[27] Richard W. Velde. "Keynote Address." In: *Proceedings of the National Symposium on Criminal Justice Information and Statistics Systems*. Edited by Project SEARCH. Sacramento, California Crime Technological Research Foundation, 1970, p. 10.
[28] *Ibid.*

TABLE 2 Distribution of LEAA Funds—Fiscal Years 1969–1974 (in thousands)

	1969	1970	1971	1972	1973	1974
Comprehensive plans	$19,000	$ 21,000	$ 26,000	$ 35,000	$ 50,000	$ 50,000
Action grants	24,650	182,750	340,000	413,695	480,250	480,250
Discretionary grants	4,350	32,000	70,000	73,000	88,750	88,750
Aid for correctional institutions and programs			47,500	97,500	113,000	113,000
Manpower development	6,500	18,000	22,500	31,000	45,000	45,000
National Institute of Law Enforcement and Criminal Justice	3,000	7,500	7,500	21,000	31,598	40,098
Data systems and statistical assistance		1,000	4,000	9,700	21,200	24,000
Technical assistance		1,200	4,000	6,000	10,000	12,000
Administration	2,500	4,487	7,454	11,823	15,568	17,577
TOTAL	$60,000	$267,937	$528,954	$698,718	$855,366*	$870,675

*Excludes $14.2 million that was transferred to the Department of Justice.
Source: Adapted from U.S. Department of Justice, Law Enforcement Assistance Administration. *6th Annual Report of the LEAA, Fiscal Year 1974*. Washington, D.C., U.S. Government Printing Office, 1974, p. 2.

A project group (the policymaking group), or board, was organized, containing one representative from each of the original six states and the four observer states. The latter subsequently were added to the project as grantee states. The project was scheduled to run for 14 months, from July 1, 1969 through August 31, 1970, and had two principal objectives:

(1) to develop and demonstrate that a computerized criminal offender file, containing data from all segments of criminal justice, can be standardized and exchanged between states on a timely basis, and
(2) to computerize statistical records by exploring the feasibility of develop-

ing various statistical series and meaningful research data directly from computerized offender files.[29]

Within 14 months, and with substantial grants from LEAA, the Project SEARCH group assembled its working committees, developed a "rap sheet" format, and completed an on-line demonstration of the exchange of criminal history records between six states, with a central index computer in the Michigan State Police Headquarters.[30]

When the initial mission of the Project SEARCH group was completed, LEAA decided to expand the group to a national organization containing representatives from all 50 states. The new role of Project SEARCH was to apply advanced technologies to criminal justice—in particular, to develop and test prototype systems having multistate utility in criminal justice and to provide LEAA with recommendations for implementing whatever resulted from the prototype tests.[31]

Project SEARCH was conceived as a research and development group to study the application of computer and other technologies to criminal justice. After successfully testing a prototype interstate criminal history exchange system, the Federal Bureau of Investigation assumed responsibility for the operation of the system within its own National Crime Information Center (NCIC). The existence of Project SEARCH did not end at this point: In 1974, the original SEARCH organization became a private, nonprofit corporation called SEARCH Group, Inc. It has developed as a mechanism to assist state and local governments in the application of technology to criminal justice administration and as an active representative of state and local government interests in the field of criminal justice information policy.

National Crime Information Center (NCIC)

The FBI has a long history of providing services to police agencies throughout the United States (see Table 3). In September 1965, the FBI undertook development of the National Crime Information Center with an initial grant from OLEA. The NCIC system is a computerized, national law enforcement information system that links more

[29] Project SEARCH. *Newsletter*, *1*(1):1. Sacramento, California Crime Technological Research Foundation, 1969.

[30] See Paul K. Wormeli, "Project SEARCH—System for Electronic Analysis and Retrieval of Criminal Histories," in: *Proceedings of the National Symposium on Criminal Justice Information*, pp. 17–25.

[31] Paul K. Wormeli. "Developments in Criminal Justice Technology." In: *Proceedings of the International Symposium on Criminal Justice Information and Statistics Systems*. Edited by Project SEARCH. Sacramento, California Crime Technological Research Foundation, 1972, pp. 9–14.

TABLE 3 Types of FBI Assistance to State and Local Criminal Justice Agencies

National fingerprint identification and arrest record services—Identification Division

Fast response service for wanted persons and property—National Crime Information Center

Training for law enforcement—National Academy Program

Uniform crime reports

National Criminal Laboratory

than 4,000 police agencies through the use of some 104 terminals in the 50 states, Washington, D.C., and Canada (see Figure 5). Table 4 lists the nine basic record files in the NCIC computer system. In 1978, there were more than 6 million records computerized in the NCIC system (see Figure 6). By January 1978, these records were accessed an average 256,546 times daily (see Figure 7).

In December 1970, the responsibility for operating the Project SEARCH computerized criminal history file was placed under the NCIC system. Since 1924, the FBI had served as the national clearinghouse for fingerprint cards and criminal identification records, such as arrest records, which include fingerprints. Two files evolved that serve various purposes (see Figure 8). The first, called the Civil File, was composed of fingerprint cards "submitted on Federal Government employees and applicants, Armed Forces personnel, civilian em-

TABLE 4 Chronology of Information Bases for NCIC Computer

Information Bases	Date Operational
Stolen motor vehicles	1967
Stolen articles	1967
Stolen, missing, or recovered guns	1967
Stolen license plates	1967
Wanted persons	1967
Stolen securities	1968
Stolen boats	1969
Computerized Criminal History (CCH)	1971
Missing persons	1975

68

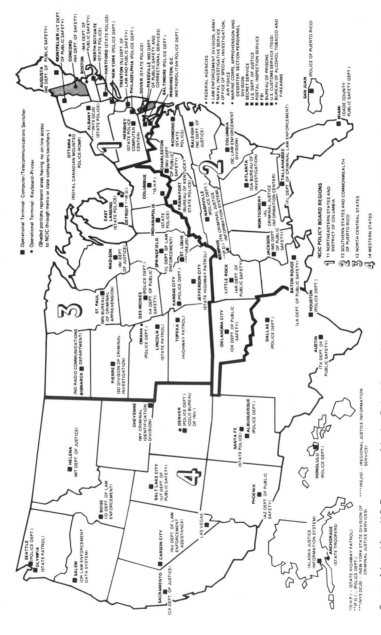

Source: Adapted from U.S. Department of Justice, Federal Bureau of Investigation. *Appropriation Request 1979, Testimony of William H. Webster, Director, Federal Bureau of Investigation, Before the House Subcommittee on Appropriations, on March 16, 1978.* Washington, D.C., 1978, p. 46.

FIGURE 5 The NCIC network (February 1978).

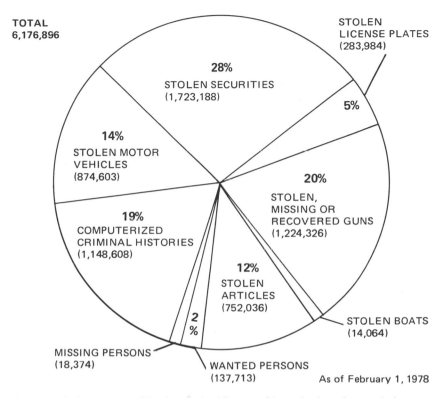

TOTAL
6,176,896

STOLEN
LICENSE PLATES
(283,984)

28%
STOLEN SECURITIES
(1,723,188)

5%

14%
STOLEN MOTOR
VEHICLES
(874,603)

20%
STOLEN,
MISSING OR
RECOVERED GUNS
(1,224,326)

19%
COMPUTERIZED
CRIMINAL HISTORIES
(1,148,608)

12%
STOLEN
ARTICLES
(752,036)

2
%

STOLEN BOATS
(14,064)

MISSING PERSONS
(18,374)

WANTED PERSONS
(137,713)

As of February 1, 1978

Source: U.S. Department of Justice, Federal Bureau of Investigation. *Appropriation Request 1979*, p. 47.

FIGURE 6   Breakdown of records in NCIC computer.

ployees in National Defense industries, aliens and persons desiring to have their fingerprints placed on file for personal identification purposes."[32] This file has been retained for individuals who either are designated by a public agency to need or want, for their own purposes, the positive identification that only fingerprints can provide.

The second, called the Criminal File, contains fingerprint cards submitted to the FBI by local, state, and federal law enforcement agencies, including penal institutions. These identification records and

[32] U.S. Department of Justice. "FBI Fingerprint and Criminal Identification Record Files." In: *Federal Data Banks and Constitutional Rights*. Vol. 4. U.S. Congress, Senate, Committee on the Judiciary, Subcommittee on Constitutional Rights. 92d Congress, 2d Session, 1974, p. 2,247.

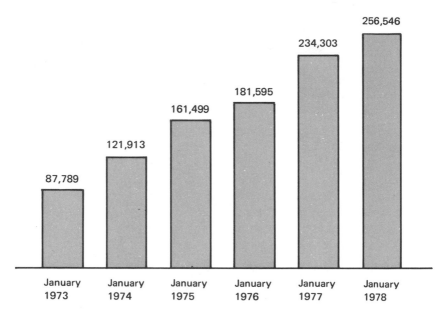

Source: U.S. Department of Justice, Federal Bureau of Investigation. *Appropriation Request 1979,* p. 47.

FIGURE 7   National Crime Information Center average daily transactions.

arrest records have been retained manually and disseminated through the mail.

The Computerized Criminal History (CCH) program of NCIC includes most of the records on arrests entering the FBI from local and state agencies. CCH produces the Criminal History Record, which is a summary of the formal decisions made about an individual in the courts, probation departments, and penal institutions—that is, all formal decisions made about an individual as he proceeds through the criminal justice process [33] (see Table 5).

The CCH segment of NCIC is not intended to eliminate local and state systems for handling such information; rather, it is viewed as the top of a three-level pyramid. On the local level, there exists a very broad base of data with items of interest to any local agencies, such as parking tickets and reports of minor crimes. At the state level, there is a

[33] U.S. Department of Justice, Federal Bureau of Investigation, National Crime Information Center, Advisory Policy Board. *National Crime Information Center (NCIC), Computerized Criminal History Program, Background, Concept and Policy.* Washington, D.C., 1972, p. 10.

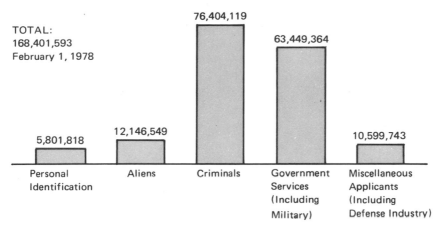

ESTIMATED PERSONS REPRESENTED:
For the 76,404,119 prints in the criminal file   22,034,985
For the remaining prints totaling 91,997,474 all of which are in the civil file   41,853,915

TOTAL ESTIMATED PERSONS REPRESENTED   63,888,900

Source: U.S. Department of Justice, Federal Bureau of Investigation. *Appropriation Request 1979*, p. 43.

FIGURE 8   Types of fingerprints on file.

narrower data base with items of particular interest to state agencies as well as local and county agencies, such as arrest and criminal history records. At the national level, the data base is confined to those files mentioned, but covering the entire nation.[34]

Thus, state and local criminal justice agencies have independent information-processing functions of their own in addition to providing the input for the FBI's NCIC system. For this reason, LEAA has continued to support the development of state and local criminal justice information systems.

Comprehensive Data Systems (CDS) Program

In 1972, LEAA adopted a plan that would encourage each state to set up its own criminal justice data-collection process and comprehensive data system and set aside $20 million in discretionary funds to support the effort.[35] Each comprehensive data system would include:

[34] *Ibid*., pp. 2–9.
[35] Richard Velde. "Law Enforcement Assistance Administration, Programs in Criminal Justice Information and Statistics Systems." In: *Proceedings of the International Symposium on Criminal Justice Information*, p. 17.

TABLE 5   Computerized Criminal History (CCH) Record Content

Identification Segment	Arrest date
Name	Offense(s) charged
FBI identification number	Statute citation
Race	Arrest disposition
Sex	
Date, place of birth	*Judicial Segment*
Height, weight	Court identity
Color of eyes, hair	Offense(s) charged
Skin tone	Disposition date
Scars, marks, tattoos	Disposition
Social Security number	Sentence
Fingerprint classification	
Identification comments	*Supplemental Segment*
State establishing record	Data reflecting changes made by
Date of latest identification	courts or chief executive after
segment update	conviction and sentencing by
State identification number	trial court
Arrest Segment	*Custody/Supervision Segment*
Arresting agency	Status change
Name used	Custody starting date
State identification number	Custody supervision location
Offense date	

Source: Adapted from U.S. Department of Justice, Office of the Attorney General. "The Need for a *Modern* Nationwide Criminal Justice Information Interchange Facility." Slide Presentation, July 1978.

–A criminal justice data center,
–An offender-based transaction statistics system linked to automated criminal histories,
–A management and administrative statistics system,
–A uniform crime reports system,
–A state technical assistance capability.[36]

The most significant aspect of the CDS program has been the development of the offender-based transaction statistics (OBTS) systems based on computerized criminal history records in each state.

Essentially, OBTS represents a new approach to criminal justice statistics. The traditional criminal justice statistical system can be categorized into one of four functional areas: law enforcement statistics, judicial and prosecutory statistics, noninstitutional correctional statistics, and institutional correctional statistics.[37] Each of these approaches

[36] *Ibid*.

[37] See Charles M. Friel, "Offender Based Transactional Statistics: The Concept and Its Utility," in: *Proceedings of the International Symposium on Criminal Justice Information*, pp. 43–46.

to statistics is agency-specific, in that it deals with the activities of a given agency within the criminal justice system as opposed to providing information on the activities of the criminal justice system itself. Also, these systems focus primarily on the workload of the agency.

The offender-based approach to criminal justice statistics differs from the traditional approaches, in that an attempt is made to track the individual offender and his offense through the system regardless of the agencies involved in his processing. In addition, OBTS attempts to document all major decisions involving the offender from the point of arrest to his final exit from the criminal justice system. Whereas traditional systems tend to have agency-specific approaches to statistics, the offender-based concept has a longitudinal, offender-oriented approach.[38] Since OBTS depends on essentially the same information that must be collected for criminal history information systems, both systems can be developed simultaneously.

The LEAA CDS program represents a major effort to develop criminal justice information systems in each of the 50 states. From 1972 to 1978, LEAA spent more than $68 million on direct grants to the states through the CDS program (see Table 6). This figure does not include expenditures that were made using LEAA block grant funds at the state level. While LEAA does not have accurate figures of the total federal monies that have been expended since 1972 on information and statistical systems, the total of block grant funds disseminated to the states for information and statistical systems may be three to five times the amount LEAA has expended in discretionary grants. Such investments, whatever their final total, are testimony to the importance given to the development of information systems in local and state criminal justice agencies.

THE DEVELOPMENT OF CRIMINAL JUSTICE INFORMATION SYSTEMS— STATE AND LOCAL LEVELS

According to LEAA, in 1968, only 10 states had automated, state-level criminal justice information systems. By 1972, 47 states had automated information systems serving at least one component of the system,[39] and an LEAA survey revealed that more than 400 systems were in existence or planned. Forty-six percent of these systems were state-level and 54 percent were local-level operations. In 1976, a

---

[38] *Ibid.*, p. 43.

[39] Velde. "Law Enforcement Assistance Administration, Programs in Criminal Justice," p. 18.

TABLE 6   LEAA CDS Program (Discretionary Funds) Totals

Fiscal Year	Total Grants Awarded
1972	$ 2,074,778
1973	449,868
1974	7,750,552
1975	18,118,033
1976	19,734,420
1977	10,668,856
1978	9,883,452
	$68,679,959

Source: U.S. Department of Justice, Law Enforcement Assistance Administration, Comprehensive Data Systems Program. Special request by author, 1978.

follow-up LEAA survey identified 683 separately defined systems representing 549 jurisdictions.[40]

The types of information, or functions, that an agency chooses to computerize varies widely, as indicated in Table 7. More than 90 different functions are performed by computers in police, court, and corrections areas. The functions that are most frequently computerized are: research/statistics, activity reporting, alphabetic indexes for names, arrests, communications—on-line inquiry, case disposition reports, warrants/wanted persons, crime control, and criminal histories.

In addition, some information systems serve a combination of different agencies for a variety of functions, as Table 8 illustrates. For example, the Criminal Law Uniform Enforcement System of Delaware provides or plans to provide 52 different functions for each category of the criminal justice process.[41] Similarly, the Alabama Law Enforcement System performs or plans to perform 41 tasks.[42] In Hamilton County, Ohio, the Regional Crime Information Center proposes to perform 41 tasks,[43] while regional systems in Lane County, Oregon[44] and Tulsa, Oklahoma[45] will handle 39 functions each. Ac-

[40] U.S. Department of Justice, Law Enforcement Assistance Administration. *1976 Directory of Automated Criminal Justice Information Systems*. Vols. I and II. Washington, D.C., 1976.

[41] U.S. Department of Justice, Law Enforcement Assistance Administration. *1972 Directory of Automated Criminal Justice Information System*. Washington, D.C., 1972, pp. B-168–B-174.

[42] *Ibid.*, pp. B-5–B-10.

[43] *Ibid.*, pp. B-609–B-614.

[44] *Ibid.*, pp. B-666–B-671.

[45] *Ibid.*, pp. B-652–B-656.

TABLE 7 Criminal Justice Information System Functions

	Number of Systems with Function Computerized	
Functions	1972	1976
Activity reporting	93	201
Administration/Finance	80	68
Alimony control	2	9
Alphabetic index	80	166
Arrests	107	168
Assignment–Attorneys	22	49
Assignment–Courtroom	17	45
Assignment–Judges	20	44
Auto registration	57	64
Automated vehicle location		3
Booking	4	
Calendaring/Scheduling	50	84
Case control	58	124
Case disposition reports	73	143
Citation control	51	72
Command and Control	32	26
Communications–Message switching	84	112
Communications–Mobile digital terminals		21
Communications–On-line inquiry	112	165
Communications–Other	61	38
Computer-assisted dispatch	25	54
Computer-assisted instruction	4	8
Corrections personnel		15
Courts personnel		15
Crime laboratory		11
Crime trend analysis	69	94
Criminal associates	34	21
Criminal history	104	122
Criminal statistics	2	
Defendant control	39	44
Docketing	53	76
Driver registration	52	52
Equipment inventory/maintenance	5	
Evidence control	13	14
Field contact reporting	38	43
Fines, collateral bail	37	36
Firearms registration		22
Fire/Civil defense	1	
Geographic location index	1	
Geoprocessing (Geocoding)		62
Grant tracking	19	15
Inmate accounting	56	83
Inmate records	43	63
Institutional programs	1	

TABLE 7   Cont.

Jury list	1	
Jury management	32	32
Juvenile index	43	44
Juvenile records	27	53
Legal information retrieval		13
Licensing registration	35	24
Medical reports	2	
Menu planning	4	4
Micrographics		5
Missing persons	61	68
Mobilization data	1	
Modus operandi	39	44
Narcotics control	16	9
Offender-based transaction statistics		55
Organized crime	20	7
Parole control		39
Parole/Probation records	5	
Pawned articles	2	8
Performance evaluation	40	48
Physical goods inventory	21	20
Planning	51	60
Police personnel	63	68
Police records index		3
Prison industries	8	5
Prisoner behavior models	7	4
Probation control	35	60
Process service control	11	9
Prosecution management		24
Rehabilitation	18	13
Research/Statistics	163	241
Resource allocation	61	71
Simulation/Modeling	21	12
Stolen licenses	75	60
Stolen property–guns	72	67
Stolen property–motor vehicles	90	109
Stolen property–other	73	86
Subjects-in-process	44	46
Summons control	37	36
Test scoring	2	
Traffic accident reporting	16	27
Traffic citations	9	
Training	10	16
Trust fund accounting	5	2
Uniform crime reporting	88	139
Vehicle inspection	12	9
Vehicle maintenance	33	30
Vehicle titles	3	
Warrant control	51	80
Warrants/Wanted persons	101	136
White collar crime	1	4

TABLE 7   Cont.

Witness control	25	31
Workload analysis	59	92
Work release	2	

Source: Adapted from U.S. Department of Justice, Law Enforcement Assistance Administration. *1972 Directory of Automated Criminal Justice Information Systems*, Washington, D.C., 1972; *idem, 1976 Directory of Automated Criminal Justice Information Systems*, Vol. I, Washington, D.C., 1976.

cording to LEAA's sample analysis of criminal justice information systems in operation during 1972, 41 percent served law enforcement agencies, 17 percent served courts, 6 percent served corrections agencies, 8 percent served other criminal justice agencies, and 28 percent served a combination of criminal justice agencies.[46]

TABLE 8   Functional Interrelationships for Criminal Justice Information Systems

Interrelationship	Number of Systems Serving Multiple Functions
Corrections—Courts	15
Corrections—Police	19
Courts—Police	62
Corrections—Courts—Police	75

Source: U.S. Department of Justice, Law Enforcement Assistance Administration. *1976 Directory of Automated Criminal Justice Information Systems*, Vol. I.

On the basis of such aggregate statistics, it is possible to perceive both the nature and extent of computer development in criminal justice agencies since 1968. LEAA has made possible an information explosion in the field of criminal justice. Indeed, without the financial aid of LEAA, as well as its technical and policymaking assistance through Project SEARCH and its CDS program, it is unlikely that such computer systems development could have occurred.

[46] Richard Velde. "Law Enforcement Assistance Administration, Programs in Criminal Justice," p. 18.

TOWARD AN INTEGRATED NATIONAL CRIMINAL JUSTICE INFORMATION SYSTEM

The President's Commission on Law Enforcement and Administration of Justice emphasized that a key problem with the operation of the criminal justice system in the United States was its decentralized, loosely coordinated nature. This line of analysis was supported throughout the 1960s and 1970s by key public officials, who encouraged the idea of a nationwide network of integrated criminal justice information systems as an essential element in a national strategy to fight crime.

The attorney general under President Johnson, Ramsey Clark, wrote, in his well-known work, *Crime in America*, "the criminal justice system has been tragically neglected in America for generations," contending that "it is a system in theory only."[47] In 1971, the Advisory Commission on Intergovernmental Relations stated in its report, *State-Local Relations in the Criminal Justice System*, that the criminal justice process (police, courts, corrections) is not well-integrated, because agencies are fairly autonomous and only loosely coordinate their policies and treatment of offenders. The commission felt that parts of the criminal justice process "function too frequently in isolation, or in ways that are counterproductive to each other."[48] A year before the advisory commission issued its report, the National Commission on the Causes and Prevention of Violence (the Eisenhower Commission) asserted in its report, *Law and Order Reconsidered*, that the system of criminal justice in America was a myth:

> A system implies some unity of purpose and organized interrelationship among component parts. In the typical American city and state, and under federal jurisdiction as well, no such relationship exists. There is, instead, a reasonably well-defined criminal process, a continuum through which each accused offender may pass: from the hands of the police, to the jurisdiction of the courts, behind the walls of a prison, then back onto the street. The inefficiency, fallout, and failure of purpose during this process is notorious.[49]

The National Advisory Commission on Criminal Justice Standards and Goals, an LEAA-supported project, opened its discussion of the

---

[47] Ramsey Clark. *Crime in America.* New York, Pocket Books, 1970, p. 123.

[48] Advisory Commission on Intergovernmental Relations. *State-Local Relations in the Criminal Justice System.* Washington, D.C., U.S. Government Printing Office, 1971, p. 13.

[49] National Commission on the Causes and Prevention of Violence, Task Force on Law and Law Enforcement. *Law and Order Reconsidered.* Washington, D.C., U.S. Government Printing Office, 1969, p. 266.

American criminal justice system by noting the adjectives most commonly used to describe it: "fragmented," "divided," "splintered," and "decentralized." [50] The commission pointed out that words such as fragmented and divided referred not only to demarcations in authority but to differences in philosophy and outlook.

There was general agreement about the fractionated condition of the criminal justice system in America. Both the President's Commission on Law Enforcement and Administration of Justice in 1967 and the national advisory commission in 1973 called for a national strategy to reduce crime and to reform and modernize the criminal justice system. Both bodies suggested that an essential condition for this effort was the need for better and more timely information about crime in America and the performance of criminal justice agencies, as well as about offenders going through the criminal justice process. In turn, the computer was perceived as one of the central tools that could provide for management of such information. Reflecting the sentiments of the president's commission made six years earlier, the national advisory commission noted that what had been talked about for decades was a possibility; that is, due to computers, the nation's criminal justice information could be organized into a useful body of knowledge. The commission observed that "along with many other disciplines, criminal justice has been experiencing an 'information explosion' since the late 1960's." The characteristics of such an explosion were the "steadily increasing capabilities for gathering, processing and transmitting information, and steadily increasing information needs." The commission concluded that "more frequent use of the computer and other automated technology is a national trend." [51]

The computer, therefore, was considered the principal means whereby criminal justice information needs could be fulfilled and an integral step in developing an integrated and coordinated system of criminal justice administration in the United States. [52] The basic design strategy for meeting these information needs was an integrated nationwide network of criminal justice information systems. This strategy was first defined by the president's commission in 1967 and elaborated on and defined in 1973 by the National Advisory Commission

[50] National Advisory Commission on Criminal Justice Standards and Goals. *A National Strategy to Reduce Crime*. Washington, D.C., U.S. Government Printing Office, 1973, p. 31.

[51] *Ibid.*, p. 33.

[52] For a discussion of the development of an integrated network of criminal justice information systems as a prelude to and an integral aspect of the reform of the criminal justice system, see J. M. Silbert, "Criminal Justice Information Systems and the Criminal Justice 'System,'" Doctoral Dissertation, New York, New York University, 1972.

on Criminal Justice Standards and Goals. Essentially, the strategy has focused on a federated approach to the development and integration of criminal justice information systems between local, state, and federal agencies.

The president's commission, in its *Task Force Report: Science and Technology*, observed that the information problem in criminal justice had three principal dimensions. The first was type of information:

Inquiry Information—Facts about wanted persons or property needed on immediate recall ("on-line" in "real-time") by the police.

Personal Information—Containing relevant background facts about people with whom the system must deal.

Management Information—Needed by a criminal justice official on the operation of his agency to help him manage it better.

Statistical Information—On crime, on the nature of criminal careers, and on the operations of criminal justice agencies.[53]

The second dimension referred to the components of the criminal justice system: police, courts, and corrections. The third dimension referred to the government level: federal, state, and local (including county, city, and metropolitan area).

In any integrated information system, all combinations of these dimensions have to be considered. Furthermore, since the administration of criminal justice is primarily a local and state function, any national criminal justice information system must be geared to the requirements of states and localities: "Fundamentally, the information system must be directly accessible to them and they must specify the information they need from other jurisdictions." To the president's commission, such a consideration suggested "a concept of hierarchy of information interchange and information files."[54] This approach gave local and state agencies the bulk of the responsibility for tailoring information systems that would suit their needs. Thus, neither a regional data center approach nor a federally controlled central data bank would be acceptable. Instead, a federated approach was considered to be consistent with the decentralized nature of the American criminal justice system. At the national level, the commission noted there could be a central inquiry system such as the FBI's NCIC. Personal information about adults with criminal records would be included in a directory that would list the formal matters of record with criminal

---

[53] President's Commission on Law Enforcement. *Task Force Report: Science and Technology*, p. 68.
[54] *Ibid.*, p. 70.

justice agencies. Such a directory would include information only about *"serious* crimes." [55]

At the state level, an inquiry file similar to the national file would be retained:

The State file would be more extensive, however, it would include other kinds of files—motor vehicle registrations and gun registrations, for example—and would have a lower threshold of seriousness—persons wanted for nonindictable offenses, less valuable stolen property, etc.

A state would also have a directory recording a person's contacts of record with the State's criminal justice agencies. Here, too, the threshold would be lowered to include offenses not serious enough for the national directory.

In addition, to support court and correctional decision-making some states could establish more detailed records on persons in their directories. This registry could contain such background information as education, employment, military service, and probation reports. [56]

At the county level, court information systems might be established and integrated with local police, county sheriff, or other county correctional functions. In large cities and metropolitan areas, police information systems could be established to provide access to state and national systems for core city police departments and agencies from smaller neighboring cities.

In 1973, the National Advisory Commission on Criminal Justice Standards and Goals followed up the president's commission by endorsing a federated approach to the design of an integrated national criminal justice information system. The national advisory commission also elaborated on the federated approach in areas where the earlier commission had omitted comment or had been incomplete.

Concerning requirements for criminal justice information, the national advisory commission concluded in its *Report on the Criminal Justice System* that, while the police, courts, and correctional agencies each had specific information needs, there were several categories of data that should serve all criminal justice agencies. These categories included "a basic criminal history record, statistics about the activities of the system with respect to offenders, and crime occurrence data." [57]

---

[55] There has been considerable debate over the composition, control, and configuration of the federal link in this network (see Chapters 7 and 8).

[56] President's Commission on Law Enforcement. *Task Force Report: Science and Technology*, p. 71.

[57] National Advisory Commission on Criminal Justice Standards and Goals. *Report on the Criminal Justice System*. Washington, D.C., U.S. Government Printing Office, 1973, p. 38.

It also was noted that each category had been given high priority in the various programs of LEAA and by state and local agencies.

Concerning jurisdictional responsibility, the national advisory commission stated that "choosing the right jurisdictional level at which to apply and use developing criminal justice information systems (was) a most critical decision" and observed that local, state, and federal agencies, proceeding without coordinated plans, had "already spent considerable monies for the hardware and impedimenta of incompatible and duplicative systems....Not only money has been wasted; the human resources, technical talents, and skills available for development of criminal justice information systems have been diffused and dissipated across many redundant development efforts." [58]

Thus, the commission called for the development of an integrated network of criminal justice information systems, as depicted in Figure 9. Four levels corresponded roughly to government jurisdictional levels. The first consisted of the information services and statistical activities conducted by federal agencies such as LEAA and the FBI's NCIC. The second level included the various activities conducted by the states. The third represented the criminal justice information and statistical system maintained for a local jurisdiction, which could be a city, city-county, county, or metropolitan area system serving all components of the criminal justice system. The fourth level represented the information services to be provided for the individual components—police, courts, and corrections.

Communication between the levels was to be maintained through a telecommunication network operating only on vertical interfaces. Horizontal interfaces were not contemplated unless justified by heavy message traffic.

The approach of the national advisory commission in 1973, LEAA since 1968, and the president's commission in 1967 to the development of an integrated national criminal justice information system as a necessary step toward a system of criminal justice was a decentralized or federated approach. Based on the notion that criminal justice is primarily a local and state responsibility, the approach to criminal justice information system development was consistent with this tenet of federalism. Indeed, the national advisory commission in 1973 sought to apply federalism to the problem of criminal justice system design. The result was the intention to develop a decentralized, yet coordinated, network of criminal justice information systems serving the needs of agencies at various levels of government with diverse

[58] *Ibid.*, p. 41.

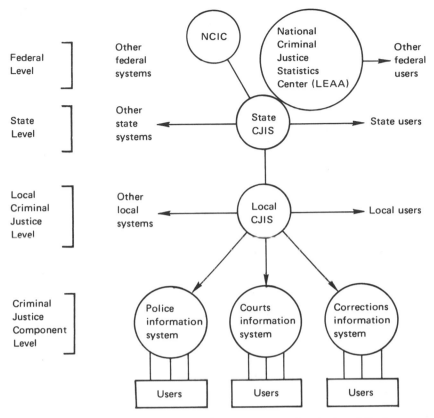

Source: National Advisory Commission on Criminal Justice Standards and Goals. *Report on the Criminal Justice System.* Washington, D.C., U.S. Government Printing Office, 1973, p. 42.

FIGURE 9   Maximum decentralization in an integrated network of criminal justice information systems (CJIS).

responsibilities related to the crime problem and the administration of criminal justice.

LEAA has furthered this intention in recent years with the requirement that funds for the development of state and local criminal justice information systems be dependent on its approval of state-designated master plans for criminal justice information systems, reflecting the standards and goals of the national advisory commission.[59] Generally,

[59] See U.S. Department of Justice, Law Enforcement Assistance Administration, "Comprehensive Data Systems Program" (Revised April 1, 1972), in: *Criminal Justice Data Banks: 1974*, Vol. 1, U.S. Congress, Senate, Committee on the Judiciary, Subcommittee on Constitutional Rights, 93d Congress, 2d Session, 1974, pp. 698–711.

the master plans have aimed at coordinating the development of criminal justice information systems among state and local agencies in efforts to develop integrated and federated criminal justice information systems in each state.

The sum of this national development strategy in the criminal justice information systems area has been an unprecedented drive to apply the new technology in a particular context of public organizations and to apply the technology on a scale never before attempted. Information has been perceived as the key to making the American system of criminal justice more systematic and effective, and the computer has appeared as the essential means to enable the transmission, retrieval, and utilization of the information at each governmental level.

5

The Social Costs of
Criminal Justice Records,
the Affected Public,
and the Problem of
Collective Action

In the preceding chapter, the development of criminal justice information systems in the United States was discussed in its appropriate historical and political context. The aim was to explain the movement for technological innovation from the perspective of the developers of computerized information systems and systems development strategies in the field of criminal justice.

This chapter will focus on the problem of the social costs of criminal justice records. Specific attention will be given to identifying the range of issues and divergent claims that have been advanced in this context and to understanding the response, or lack thereof, by the public affected by criminal justice recordkeeping. This analysis will not provide any answers to the problems of the social costs of criminal justice records, but will clarify the relevant policy concerns and problems as a prelude to the discussion of the politics of public policy formation in the following chapters.

SOCIAL COSTS: THE POLITICS OF
PRINCIPLE AND POLICY

Social costs arising from the activities of public organizations in the United States generally pose problems of principle and of policy. Individuals have certain fundamental moral rights that are guaranteed as legal rights by the Constitution.[1] Individuals, then, are supposed to be legally protected from unreasonable, arbitrary, or capricious governmental action by rights of free speech, free association, due process, equal protection, and privacy. A basic function of such rights is to provide for the internalization of external costs deriving from the activities of public officials.[2]

The existence of fundamental legal rights in the United States does not guarantee that all moral rights of citizens are incorporated in the guarantees of the Constitution, nor that such fundamental rights always will be recognized and respected by public officials. Indeed, an important aspect of political debate and conflict in American politics centers on the problems of interpreting such rights and reconciling competing claims of rights as well as matters of policy.

Political actions in American politics usually are justified in terms of arguments of principle or policy or both. Arguments of policy "justify a political decision by showing that the decision advances or protects some collective goal of the community as a whole."[3] An argument in favor of granting a loan to a large aerospace firm to protect national defense is an argument of policy. An argument of principle, on the other hand, justifies "a decision by showing that the decision respects or secures some individual or group right."[4] An argument in favor of affirmative action to redress past discrimination against a minority is an argument of principle.

In the context of American politics, arguments of principle and policy are the chief grounds of political justification. For example, the justification for a legislative program usually will involve both types of arguments. Many judicial decisions, particularly in cases where no legal precedent or prior history is available, will turn on arguments of both principle and policy. On some occasions, principles may condition policy; on others, policy concerns may condition principles.[5]

Conflicts reflected in arguments of principle or policy involve disputes over rights and goals. "Arguments of principle are arguments intended to establish an individual right; arguments of policy are arguments intended to establish a collective goal."[6] Rights and goals

---

[1] Ronald Dworkin. "Taking Rights Seriously." *New York Review of Books, 17*:23, December 17, 1970.

[2] See, for example, Harold Demsetz, "Toward a Theory of Property Rights," in: *Externalities: Theoretical Dimensions of Political Economy,* edited by Robert J. Staaf and Francis X. Tannian, New York, Dunellen, 1973, pp. 163–175.

[3] Ronald Dworkin. "Hard Cases." *Harvard Law Review, 88*:1059, April 1975.

[4] *Ibid.*

[5] *Ibid.*, pp. 1059, 1060.

[6] *Ibid.*, p. 1067.

possess different distributional characteristics. A political right is "an individuated political aim":

An individual has a right to some opportunity or resource or liberty if it counts in favor of a political decision that the decision is likely to advance or protect the state of affairs in which he enjoys the right, even when no other political aim is served and some political aim is disserved thereby, and counts against that decision that it will retard or endanger that state of affairs, even when some other political aim is thereby served.[7]

A goal, on the other hand, is a nonindividuated political aim; "that is, a state of affairs whose specification does not in this way call for any particular opportunity or resource or liberty for particular individuals."[8]

Collective goals promote trade-offs of benefits and burdens within a community to produce an overall gain for the community as a whole. Both goals and rights may be absolute; however, they are generally compromised to accommodate other goals and rights. The weight of a right or goal is its power to withstand competition from other rights and goals.[9]

In American politics, it is generally believed that fundamental rights should not be outweighed as a matter of course by social goals such as economic prosperity or crime control. The relative weight of rights and goals is not, however, a foregone conclusion. Such weights are products of political debate and conflict and, therefore, are determined by the outcomes of such activity. In some instances, particular rights may bend to social goals in ways that reduce the weight of such rights to minimal levels.[10]

Rights can be both abstract and concrete. An abstract right is "a general political aim the statement of which does not indicate how the general aim is to be weighed or compromised in particular circumstances against other political aims."[11] Abstract rights, such as the right of free speech or due process, serve an important function as political symbols in the context of political action.[12]

Concrete rights, on the other hand, are "political aims that are more precisely defined so as to express more definitely the weight they have

[7] *Ibid.*, p. 1068.
[8] *Ibid.*
[9] *Ibid.*, p. 1069.
[10] *Ibid.*
[11] *Ibid.*, p. 1070.
[12] For a discussion of the symbolic function of rights in American politics, see Stuart A. Scheingold, *The Politics of Rights*, New Haven, Conn., Yale University Press, 1974.

against other political aims on particular occasions."[13] Abstract rights do not account for competing rights, whereas concrete rights reflect the results of such competition.[14]

Social costs arise as problems of competing rights and policies. Contending sides in a political conflict possess different perspectives on the desirable state of the community and the precise weights to be assigned to rights and collective goals, that is, to the distribution of internal and external costs. Such differences are reflected in the substantive and symbolic dimensions of political discourse.

For example, in recent years, the right of privacy has become a useful political symbol. The recognition of this right, in view of increased organizational recordkeeping and computerization and the adverse effects of these activities on individuals, has meant that privacy is not only a concrete right to be reconciled with competing social goals and rights, but, stated abstractly, also is a political resource.[15] The authoritative declaration or affirmation of this right in the context of political debates provides the legitimacy to pursue what is essentially a political course of action "where power relationships loom large and immediate."[16] In this way, the introduction of an abstract right in the context of American politics can work on behalf of change. Furthermore, as Scheingold states, "It is possible to capitalize on the perceptions of entitlement associated with rights to initiate and to nurture political mobilization—a dual process of *activating* a quiescent citizenry and *organizing* groups into effective political units."[17] Because rights carry, by definition, connotations of entitlement, a declaration of a right, such as the right of privacy, may publicize needs by changing the way people think about their individual problems or discontents. On the other hand, this strategy for political change may not be particularly effective. Indeed, Scheingold suggests that "when legal rights run counter to prevailing power relationships, it surely cannot be taken for granted that these rights will be redeemed on demand."[18]

The assertion of abstract rights by individuals and groups may not always lead to such rights being accorded their appropriate weight in the political process. Fundamental rights of citizens often may be given relatively low weight vis-à-vis particular social goals and, there-

---

[13] Dworkin. "Hard Cases," p. 1070.
[14] *Ibid.*, p. 1075.
[15] Scheingold. *Politics of Rights*, pp. 83–96.
[16] *Ibid.*, p. 85.
[17] *Ibid.*, p. 131.
[18] *Ibid.*, p. 86.

fore, they may not be treated as fundamental. Such an outcome effectively contradicts the very reason for having what Dworkin calls an "institution of rights" in the American political system:

> If rights make sense at all, then, the invasion of a relatively important right must be a very serious matter. It means treating a man as less than a man, or as less worthy of concern than other men. The institution of rights rests on the conviction that this is a grave injustice, and that it is worth paying the incremental cost in social policy or efficiency that is necessary to prevent it.[19]

At the heart of the problem of social costs, then, is the conflict over competing rights and social goals. The weight accorded various rights, such as privacy and due process, in relation to competing rights and social goals promoted by public agencies, determines the extent to which reductions of social costs may be accomplished. In this context, promoting the extension or emergence of rights is a costly process. Following the analysis in Chapters 2 and 3, it can be suggested that rights will be developed or extended to internalize external costs when the gains of internalization become greater than the costs of internalization to the involved individuals, groups, and political entrepreneurs.[20] In addition, the marginal cost-return principle of such actors will be directly affected by the costs to public agencies and officials of changing organizational practices, procedures, structures, and goals. The extent to which rights will be taken seriously and external costs will be internalized will depend on the degree to which such changes are costly to agencies and the degree to which agencies are exposed to the problems and demands of individuals affected by external costs or groups and entrepreneurs representing such claims. A clear example of this process occurred in the 1960s when racial minorities were finally extended civil rights which they had laid claim to and fought over for two centuries.

THE ADMINISTRATION OF CRIMINAL JUSTICE: INSTITUTIONALIZING THE CONFLICT OVER SOCIAL GOALS AND INDIVIDUAL RIGHTS

The administration of criminal justice in the United States is political. It engages in the formulation and implementation of public policies that must be reconciled with divergent and often competing rights

[19] Dworkin. "Taking Rights Seriously," p. 28.
[20] Demsetz. "Toward a Theory of Property Rights," p. 164.

and social goals.[21] Roscoe Pound identified this problem some years ago as the "antinomy" of criminal justice:

Criminal Law, as conditioned by its origin and history, has a two-fold nature. On the one hand, it is made up of commands and prohibitions addressed to the individual in order to secure social interests. On the other hand, it is made up of limitations upon the enforcement of those commands and prohibitions in order to secure the individual life.[22]

This internal tension in criminal law is reflected in the conflicts and problems of administering criminal justice. Although there is no easy way to categorize the goals and rights operative in the criminal justice process, it is possible to identify three separate, but interdependent and often conflicting, structures of goals and rights characterizing the administration of criminal justice: the crime control model, the due process model, and the rehabilitative model.[23]

Crime Control Model

The crime control model (CCM) is based on the premise that the repression of criminal conduct is by far the most important function to be performed in the criminal process. The CCM requires that primary attention be paid to the efficiency with which the criminal process operates to screen suspects, determine guilt, and secure appropriate dispositions of persons convicted of crimes. Successful operation of the CCM depends on the maintenance of high rates of apprehension and conviction, and there is a premium on speed and finality. Speed, in turn, depends on uniformity and informality, while finality depends on minimizing the occasions for challenge. The criminal justice process is perceived as a screening process in which

[21] George F. Cole. *Politics and the Administration of Justice.* Beverly Hills, Calif., Sage Publications, 1973, p. 15.

[22] Roscoe Pound. *Criminal Justice in America.* New York, DaCapo Press, 1930, p. 57.

[23] The characterizations of the crime control model and the due process model are drawn from Herbert L. Packer, *The Limits of the Criminal Sanction,* Stanford, Calif., Stanford University Press, 1968, pp. 149–248. A critique of Packer's two models and a partial conceptualization of the rehabilitative model is provided by John Griffiths, "Ideology in Criminal Procedure or a Third 'Model' of the Criminal Process," *Yale Law Journal, 79:*359–417, January 1970. For a more complete presentation of the rehabilitative model, see Francis A. Allen, "Criminal Justice, Legal Values and the Rehabilitative Ideal," in: *Crime, Law, and Society,* edited by Abraham S. Goldstein and J. Goldstein, New York, Free Press, 1971, pp. 271–282; Sol Rubin, *The Law of Criminal Correction,* St. Paul, Minn., West, 1963, pp. 673–694; and Paul W. Tappan, *Crime, Justice and Correction,* New York, McGraw-Hill, 1960.

each successive stage—prearrest investigation, arrest, postarrest investigation, preparation for trial, trial or entry of plea, conviction, disposition—involves a series of routinized operations whose success is gauged primarily by their ability to pass the case along to a successful conclusion. The key to the CCM operation regarding those who are not screened out is the presumption of guilt, which makes it possible for the system to deal efficiently with large numbers of cases. If there is confidence in the reliability of informal administrative fact-finding activities that take place in the early stages of the criminal process, the remaining stages can be relatively perfunctory without any loss of operating efficiency. The presumption of guilt is the operational expression of that confidence.

The opposite of the presumption of guilt, however, is not the presumption of innocence. A presumption of innocence is a direction to officials about how they are to proceed and is not a prediction of outcome. A presumption of guilt is a prediction of outcome; it is descriptive and factual, while the presumption of innocence is normative and legal.

In the CCM, the center of gravity for the criminal justice process lies in the early, administrative fact-finding stages. It is important, then, to place as few restrictions as possible on the character of the administrative fact-finding processes and to limit restrictions to those that enhance reliability. As will be discussed, this view of restrictions on administrative fact finding is reflected consistently in the CCM's view of minimizing regulation on the use of criminal justice records.

Due Process Model

While the CCM may resemble an assembly line, the due process model (DPM) can be regarded as an obstacle course. Each of its successive stages is designed to present impediments to carrying the accused any further in the process. In the DPM, the stress on the finality with which judgments are made is viewed as superior to the efficiency of the process. The key to its operation resides in the presumption of innocence and the reliability of a formal fact-finding and error-minimizing process. The DPM resembles a factory that devotes a substantial part of its input to quality control, necessarily cutting down on quantitative output.

The DPM values the concepts of primacy of the individual and limitations on official power. The combination of stigma and loss of liberty embodied in the result of the criminal process is considered as the heaviest deprivation that government can inflict on an individual. In addition, the processes that culminate in these highly afflictive sanctions are viewed as being coercive, restricting, and demeaning. Because of its potency in subjecting the individual to the coercive power of the state, the criminal justice process must, in this model, be subjected to controls that prevent it from operating with maximum efficiency. According to this ideology, within the context of the DPM, there is acceptance of a substantial diminution in the efficiency with which the criminal justice process operates in the interest of preventing official oppression of the individual.

Rehabilitative Model

In contrast to both the CCM and DPM, the rehabilitative model (RM) begins with an assumption of reconciliatory interests between the state and the individual. Discretion is left in official hands because stress is placed on the individualized treatment of offenders. The aim of the criminal justice process is not merely to be formal and punitive, as in the CCM and DPM, but to be reconciliatory. The intention is to treat the offender as a person, rather than as a member of the special category of criminals. At the point of conviction or admission of guilt, there is no strict demarcation between the individual as a criminal and the rest of society; rather, the individual is seen as "deviant." The task of the criminal justice process is to reintegrate that individual into society after his problem has been properly diagnosed and treated. The RM aims at minimizing the stigma attached to the operation of the criminal justice process, which is placed on the individual, in an effort to downgrade the notion of the individual as a social outcast.

The main consequence of the multiple objectives of the criminal justice process is that the process itself must be governed by a series of delicate balances or adjustments between the competing and conflicting political orientations. While each of the models roughly corresponds to one of the components of the criminal justice system (the police, the courts, and corrections agencies), there still is a great deal of overlap and contradiction. Indeed, within each component of the criminal justice system, one model may be dominant, but the two other models may still be operative. For example, the right of a community to an acceptable measure of lawful and orderly existence is enhanced by prompt and comprehensive investigations of crime and strict application of legal sanctions. At the same time, individuals are entitled to the observance of civil liberties that limit the nature and scope of investigation and to fair treatment that requires, among other things, appropriate procedural safeguards and the presence of adequate and accurate facts as the basis for decisions. The point at which these policies and rights are adjusted or weighed is a problem of public policy formation which has substantial influence on decisions made within the criminal justice process. Indeed, as will be seen in the following chapters, the determination of criminal justice information policy presents itself as just this kind of problem—one whose outcome is determined not only by the nature of the competing claims involved, but also by problems (noted in Chapters 2 and 3) concerning the politics of social costs and public policy formation.

THE SOCIAL COSTS OF CRIMINAL JUSTICE RECORDS: THE CONTEXT OF ISSUES AND JUSTIFICATIONS

The social costs of criminal justice records present a problem of divergent political perspectives about the desirable state of the community and the weight to be accorded various social goals and rights. The debate over the use of criminal justice records has, on the whole, reflected the more fundamental conflicts that characterize the criminal justice process generally. As previously noted, the criminal justice process is governed by a series of adjustments between competing and conflicting social goals and rights that can be represented as divergent models of the criminal justice process. These models form the substantive context in which the problem of criminal justice information arises.

Criminal justice records can include many kinds of records, but this discussion will focus on the arrest record, the conviction record, and the criminal history record or "rap sheet," which are the most widely used records within the criminal justice process. These records are at the center of debate concerning the development of information policy for computerized information systems. Arrest and conviction records are differentiated by the kinds of determination such records ordinarily represent. The arrest record represents a decision by the police to charge an individual with a particular crime, given a reason to take the person into custody in the first place.[24]

A majority of arrests are made without a warrant, and, in most cases, the decision to arrest is made by a patrolman. Similarly, most decisions to detain a suspect after arrest and to conduct an in-custody investiga-

[24] For a comprehensive discussion of the problems and issues regarding the legal and practical difficulties of the decision to arrest, see Wayne LaFave, *Arrest: The Decision to Take a Suspect into Custody*, Boston, Mass., Little, Brown, 1965.

tion are made without review by a high-ranking police officer; if there is a review, it usually is perfunctory. The arrest and the subsequent decision to charge an individual with a crime generally are based on a lesser probability of guilt than is required for arraignment and subsequent judicial proceedings. The arrest record, then, is a record of *suspicion of a crime* and does not represent a record of guilt or conviction in itself. On the other hand, the conviction record represents the outcome of a judicial proceeding wherein an individual is found or pleads guilty to a specific crime. Such a determination is made either on the basis of a trial or a plea-bargaining arrangement between the defendant, the prosecuting attorney, and the presiding judge.[25] In any event, the conviction record represents a formal determination of guilt for a specific offense.

The criminal history record or rap sheet lists an individual's contacts with criminal justice agencies during his lifetime. It may include only records of arrests, only records of arrests followed by convictions, or records of arrests not leading to convictions as well as records of arrests leading to convictions. Thus, the criminal history record is somewhat more complex than either the arrest or conviction record. When a criminal history record consists only of arrests not followed by conviction, it represents a history of suspicion of crimes. When a criminal history record includes only those arrests followed by convictions, it represents a historical record of formal determinations of guilt for specific offenses through appropriate judicial proceedings. And when the criminal history record includes both arrests followed by convictions and arrests not followed by convictions, it becomes a more complex historical record that can be only partly considered a *criminal* record in any strict sense. Records of arrest not followed by conviction usually are not considered criminal records until formal judicial proceedings have determined the fact of guilt; therefore, in this instance, a criminal history record can be regarded partly as a history of criminal offenses and partly as a history of suspicion for criminal offenses.

To understand the nature and extent of social costs that arise from the use of criminal justice records, it is important to remember the distinction between arrest and conviction records, as well as the more complex nature of criminal history records. A number of social costs arising from nonrecognition of the distinction between the essential records of the criminal justice process will be discussed next.

---

[25] See Donald J. Newman, *Conviction: The Determination of Guilt or Innocence Without Trial,* Boston, Mass., Little, Brown, 1966.

Wheeler has observed that, "increasingly in American life, the information upon which we act is drawn neither from direct observation nor informal communication, but from consulting the record about the person in question."[26] Increases in the size and scale of our organizational life, coupled with the increase in the mobility of persons in society, have generated a demand or an expressed need for more and more records upon which decisions about individuals can be based. Such a condition is captured succinctly by Alexander Solzhenitsyn in *Cancer Ward:*

As every man goes through life he fills in a number of forms for the record, each containing a number of questions. . . .There are thus hundreds of little threads radiating from every man, millions of threads in all. If these threads were suddenly to become visible, the whole sky would look like a spider's web, and if they materialized as rubber bands, buses, trams and even people would all lose the ability to move, and the wind would be unable to carry torn-up newspapers or autumn leaves along the streets of the city. They are not visible, they are not material but every man is constantly aware of their existence.[27]

When one considers the generation and use of criminal justice records, benefits that can be derived and costs that may be incurred from having acquired such records can be distinguished. If, however, one considers costs as benefits that are lost, it is possible to perceive more clearly the problems presented by criminal justice records in our society.

The social costs of criminal justice records arise from their widespread availability and dissemination. Indeed, "the United States disseminates arrest and conviction records more widely than any other country in the Western world."[28] The primary reason for the collection and dissemination of arrest records, conviction records, and criminal history records is the belief that such practices are necessary to control and reduce crime. In recent years, however, it has been suggested that the widespread dissemination of these records has not

[26] Stanton Wheeler. "Problems and Issues in Record-Keeping." In: *On Record: Files and Dossiers in American Life.* Edited by Stanton Wheeler. New York, Russell Sage Foundation, 1969, p. 5.

[27] Alexander Solzhenitsyn. *Cancer Ward.* Translated by Nicholas Bethell and David Burg. New York, Bantam Books, 1969, p. 189.

[28] "Prepared Statement of Aryeh Neier, Executive Director, and John H. F. Shattuck, Staff Counsel, American Civil Liberties Union." In: *Criminal Justice Data Banks: 1974.* Vol. I, Hearings. U.S. Congress, Committee on the Judiciary, Subcommittee on Constitutional Rights. 93d Congress, 2d Session, p. 251.

contributed to solving the problem of crime in America as much as it has helped to exacerbate the condition.[29]

At the heart of the problem concerning these social costs has been the controversy over the use of criminal justice records to deny individuals the benefits and services of our society. Many forms of "record discrimination" have been identified. The primary and probably most significant form of record discrimination involves employment in both private industry and public service. Surveys of private employers in various parts of the country have shown that, generally, both individuals with arrest records and individuals with conviction records are refused employment, often without consideration of the distinction between a person who was arrested and released due to insufficient evidence, dismissal, or acquittal and a person who either pleaded guilty or was convicted of a crime. A study of New York area employment agencies revealed that 75 percent of the agencies would not accept for referral an applicant with an arrest record and no conviction.[30] Despite attempts by criminal justice agencies to prevent the dissemination of arrest records, employers often have obtained records from the police, with the result that job applicants are not hired.[31] In a report on the situation in Washington, D.C., the Chief of the Employment and Employee Relations Section of the District of Columbia Personnel Office observed that "many interviewers, receptionists, and employers automatically rule out considering any person where a risk is involved."[32] A representative of the Work Training Opportunities Center of the District of Columbia Department of Public Welfare noted further that employers' attitudes engendered a defeatism among unemployed persons with arrest records: "When an employer asks for a police clearance, the applicant who has been arrested may not return, thinking he will automatically be rejected. He may not even apply for a job for which he is qualified if he thinks he will be asked for a police clearance."[33] The director of the local U.S. Employment Service in Washington, D.C. has stated that many em-

[29] *Ibid.*

[30] E. Sparer. *Employability and the Juvenile Arrest Record.* New York, Center for the Study of Unemployed Youth, New York University, 1966, p. 5.

[31] See "Report of the Committee to Investigate the Effects of Police Arrest Records on Employment Opportunities in the District of Columbia," in: *Criminal Justice Data Banks: 1974,* Vol. II, Appendix, p. 830; and Phillip F. Fishman, "Expungement of Arrest Records: Legislation and Litigation to Prevent Their Abuse," *Clearinghouse Review,* 6:725, April 1973.

[32] "Report of the Committee to Investigate the Effects of Police Arrest Records," p. 830.

[33] *Ibid.*, pp. 830–831.

ployers require a "clean" arrest record as a condition of employment, and that only approximately 15 percent of applicants with records of conviction *or* arrests were placed in jobs.[34] In a study conducted in 1962, 65 out of 75 employers would not consider a person arrested for assault even though he had no conviction.[35] Of 475 private employers interviewed in New York about considering individuals with conviction records, 312 stated unequivocally that they would never hire an exconvict, and 311 stated that they would fire an employee if they discovered that he had a criminal record.[36]

In addition, discriminatory recordkeeping laws and government personnel practices exist at the local, state, and federal levels. An estimated 56 percent of all states, 55 percent of all counties, and 77 percent of all cities ask on their civil service application forms whether an applicant has ever been arrested.[37] In many jurisdictions, an arrest record not followed by conviction is a reason for not hiring job applicants.[38] At the federal level, the Civil Service Commission does not request arrest record information on employment forms, but does on job security forms that are used after the initial consideration of qualifications. On the basis of such forms, both the Civil Service Commission and the Department of Defense conduct investigations concerning the circumstances of an individual's arrest or conviction record.[39]

Another form of record discrimination involves occupational licenses. The standards prescribed by a state legislature for entrance to or continued participation in a licensed occupation may include the individual's age, education, skill, experience, and entrance examination score. Other standards, however, are actually prohibitions, not qualifications. These prohibitions generally take one of three forms:

---

[34] *Ibid.*, p. 832.

[35] Richard D. Schwartz and Jerome H. Skolnick. "Two Studies of Legal Stigma." *Social Problems, 10*:142, 1962.

[36] Barry M. Portnoy. "Employment of Former Criminals." *Cornell Law Review, 55*:306–307, 1970.

[37] Herbert S. Miller. *Guilty But Not Convicted: Effect of an Arrest Record on Employment.* Washington, D.C., Georgetown University Law Center, 1972.

[38] *The Closed Door: The Effect of a Criminal Record on Employment with State and Local Agencies.* Washington, D.C., Manpower Administration, U.S. Department of Labor, 1972, p. 147.

[39] See "Statement of David O. Cooke, Deputy Assistant Secretary of Defense (Administration)," in: *Dissemination of Criminal Justice Information,* Hearings, U.S. Congress, House, Committee on the Judiciary, Subcommittee on Civil Rights and Constitutional Rights, 93d Congress, 1st and 2d Sessions, pp. 382–389; and "Statement of Anthony L. Mondello, General Counsel of the U.S. Civil Service Commission," in: *Dissemination of Criminal Justice Information,* pp. 508–512.

1. Provisions which specifically refer to criminal offenses (e.g., "conviction of a felony") as grounds for denying a license;
2. Provisions which place restrictions or requirements in such a manner as to give licensing agencies wide discretion to refuse a license to an applicant, such as the requirement that the applicant possess "good moral character";
3. Provisions which bar licensing because of offenses involving "moral turpitude".[40]

A total of 1,948 different state statutory provisions affect the licensing of an exoffender because of one or more of these restrictions. Of these, 134 refer to the commission of a criminal offense as grounds for denying a license, and 707 require, as a condition of receiving a license, that the applicant not have committed a criminal offense and that he also possess good moral character.[41] While the terms "good moral character" and "moral turpitude" may be vague, both the courts and licensing agencies interpret them to mean that a person with a criminal record lacks the requisites for a license. In addition, there is evidence that licensing agencies apply the good moral character requirement almost exclusively to persons with an arrest or criminal record. For example, a California legislative study concluded that, as a result of the lack of definitive guidelines, "licensing agencies have been extremely reluctant to deny licenses based on the lack of good moral character *unless the applicant has had an arrest or criminal record.*"[42]

Apart from the direct problem of gaining employment, individuals with arrest or conviction records are denied or have difficulty acquiring a number of significant benefits and services. First, these individuals have difficulty becoming bonded by commercial bonding companies. Although bonding companies may assert that they have no interest in arrest records as such,

it is a stipulation of standard bonding contracts . . . that coverage of the bond shall not apply to any employee from the time that the insured shall have knowledge or information that such employee has committed any fraudulent or dishonest act at any time. The effect of such stipulation upon employers has been to cause them to demand production of arrest records by prospective employees.[43]

---

[40] James W. Hunt, J. E. Bowers, and N. Miller. *Laws, Licenses and the Offender's Right to Work.* Washington, D.C., National Clearinghouse on Offender Employment Restrictions, 1974, p. 5.

[41] *Ibid.*

[42] California Legislature, Senate, Committee on Business and Professions. *Good Moral Character Requirements for Licensure in Business and Professions.* Sacramento, Calif., 1972, p. 3.

[43] "Report of the Committee to Investigate the Effects of Police Arrest Records," p. 831.

Second, individuals with arrest or conviction records are denied common financial services. Life insurance, loans, property insurance, and retail credit are dependent on investigations performed by credit agencies, such as the Retail Credit Company of Atlanta, Georgia, which have access to criminal justice records in almost every city and county in the country. The Retail Credit Company estimates that approximately 73.9 percent of the reports it prepared nationwide "potentially could contain information on arrests or other criminal records."[44]

Third, in certain areas of the country, such as New York City, public housing may be denied due to arrest or conviction records. In many instances, such records serve as "the basis for nondesirability," which the housing authority affirms prior to evictions.[45]

Fourth, arrest or conviction records may bar individuals from participation in various educational programs, either because of the character requirements for individuals participating in such programs or the good moral character requirements of the occupational license that the educational program will enable one to acquire.[46]

In addition to the social benefits and services that may be denied because of record discrimination, individuals may be rejected by or separated from the armed forces due to an arrest or conviction record. According to Department of Defense Directive 5210.9, among the restrictions on appointment, enlistment, or induction into, or retention within, the armed forces are the following:

d. Any criminal, infamous, dishonest, immoral, or notoriously disgraceful conduct, habitual use of intoxicants to excess, drug addiction, or sexual perversion.

e. All other behavior, activities, or associations which tend to show that the member is not reliable or trustworthy.[47]

To acquire relevant information concerning these grounds for rejection by or separation from the armed forces, the Department of Defense checks on the arrest and/or conviction records of each individual at the time of enlistment and on each subsequent occasion when some need arises.[48]

---

[44] Hand-delivered letter to the Honorable Sam J. Ervin from Sutherland, Asbill, and Brennon, Attorneys for Retail Credit Company, by Francis M. Gregory, Jr., March 21, 1974, in: *Criminal Justice Data Banks: 1974*, Vol. I, Hearings, p. 379.

[45] "Testimony of Nancy LeBlanc, Assistant Legal Director, Mobilization for Youth, Inc., New York, N.Y." In: *Dissemination of Criminal Justice Information*, pp. 123–124.

[46] Aryeh Neier. *Dossier*. New York, Stein and Day, 1974, p. 97.

[47] Reprinted in: *Dissemination of Criminal Justice Information*, p. 439.

[48] *Ibid.*, p. 463.

Private investigative agencies also may acquire arrest and conviction records on individuals in the course of conducting specific preemployment or insurance investigations and miscellaneous background reports.[49] Specific investigations also are performed for private individuals or groups who, for various reasons, seek information about other individuals or groups. In 1974, for example, the Standard Oil Company of California engaged a private detective agency to compile extensive personal files, including confidential arrest and criminal records, on the leaders of the People's Lobby, an environmental group, and the leaders' children.[50]

The problems of record discrimination described here have dramatized the price paid by persons with arrest or conviction records. The existence of such problems has led to a fuller articulation of the divergent claims and conflicting social goals that have been at stake in this controversy.

Much of the concern with reducing the social costs of criminal justice records has been justified in terms of the priorities and goals of the due process and the rehabilitative models of the criminal justice process. The priorities given to particular rights and goals in these two models, concerning criminal justice recordkeeping and use both within and outside the criminal justice process, have conflicted with the priorities of the crime control model.

The due process model values the primacy of the individual and limitations on official power. The key to the DPM resides in the presumption of innocence and the reliability of a formal fact-finding and error-minimizing process. Because of this orientation, the DPM tends to place a higher value on the conviction record and a relatively lower value on the arrest record. One implication is that the widespread dissemination of arrest records in the United States amounts to a denial of the presumption of innocence, since the impact of arrest records on individuals is almost as severe as the impact of conviction records. This is especially true in the criminal justice process, where evaluation of arrest records as "prior criminal records" at various stages of the decision process has the effect of treating individuals with prior arrests the same as individuals with prior conviction records.

A second implication of the due process model is the use of inaccurate or incomplete arrest records or criminal history records to make important decisions about individuals.[51] When an incomplete or inaccurate arrest record or criminal history record is used by the

---

[49] James S. Kakalik and Sorrel Wildhorn. *The Law and Private Police.* Vol. 4. Santa Monica, Calif., Rand Corporation, 1971, pp. 53–54.

[50] "People's Lobby Sues Cal Standard." *Los Angeles Times,* January 21, 1975.

[51] There are very few studies on the quality of criminal justice records in the United

police, courts, district attorney, probation or corrections officials, and licensing and other government agencies to adversely affect the interest of the individual, the individual's right to expect that such judgments be made on the basis of information that is as accurate and complete as possible has been ignored. In such a situation, the weight attached by the DPM to the primacy of the individual results in more emphasis on the results of official decision making about the individual than on the operational difficulties of providing accurate and complete information about each individual in the decision-making process. The seriousness of the consequences of official decision making outweighs any claims by public officials that providing accurate and complete information in each case is costly and not very efficient in terms of the total number of cases handled by various government agencies.

Third, equal protection by the law is being denied to persons with arrest records when they are treated as if they are criminals. A person with an arrest record who has not been convicted of a crime should not be treated like a criminal. He is entitled to be treated like other nonconvicts; however, in the course of public and private organizational decision making, usually "his arrest record classifies him with the guilty and he is exposed to all the risks, disabilities and disadvantages that flow from maintenance and dissemination of his record."[52] As a rule, the individual with an arrest record is presumed guilty and, thus, is effectively placed in the ranks of the guilty. In this context, special justification is necessary for such persons to receive the benefits of protection provided by laws that generally are available to those who are not criminals.

Fourth, the DPM implies that it is fundamentally unfair to punish

States; however, those available indicate serious problems. In 1975, the FBI reported that an examination of 835,000 charges revealed that disposition data had not been received on more than 372,000 (45 percent). See U.S. Department of Justice, Federal Bureau of Investigation, *Crime in the United States, 1974,* Washington, D.C., U.S. Government Printing Office, 1975. A national survey of state data centers and repositories completed in 1976 noted that 30 percent of existing criminal records were missing the required data, and 10 percent contained erroneous data. See SEARCH Group, Inc., *The American Criminal History Record,* Sacramento, Calif., 1976. In 1978, a survey of New York City Police Department and New York State Division of Criminal Justice Services rap sheets observed that, when compared with court records, 45 percent of the rap sheets were completely blank for prior arrests and had complete and correct disposition information for only 27 percent in the sample of 2,210 prior arrested listing. See Martin Erdmann, "Affidavit of Richard Faust," in: *Tatum v. Rogers,* 75 Civ. 2782 (CBM), S.D.N.Y. 1977.

[52] "Statement of Aryeh Neier, Executive Director, and John Shattuck, Staff Counsel, American Civil Liberties Union." In: U.S. Congress, House, Committee on the Judiciary, Subcommittee No. 4. *Security and Privacy of Criminal Arrest Records.* Hearings. 92d Congress, 2d Session, 1972, p. 156.

individuals *de facto,* if not *de jure,* for having been suspected of a crime without determination of actual guilt. Since the DPM relies heavily on the formal fact-finding process for determining guilt or innocence and guarding against official abuses of power, there is little or no tolerance for informal decision making that results in forms of punishment as severe as those resulting from the formal process of guilt determination and sentencing.

A fifth implication of the DPM is that the widespread dissemination of an arrest record constitutes a cruel and unusual punishment. Basically, the individual is being punished for his status rather than for an act which has been defined as illegal.[53]

Sixth, the DPM implies that dissemination of an arrest record outside the criminal justice system represents an invasion of privacy. This claim arises not so much because the information will be misconstrued, but because the practice of disseminating arrest records goes beyond the needs of criminal justice and constitutes a break in the interactive process between the individual and the agencies of criminal justice. Such a practice cannot be justified by the reasons for collecting the arrest record (i.e., suspicion or probable cause that an individual committed an offense) and constitutes, especially because of its derogatory nature, an unreasonable usurpation of the individual's claim to control information about himself in contexts where the rights of others are not being harmed or interfered with. Assuming that individual rights such as privacy are subject to qualification only in order to ensure equal protection of the rights of others, it is suggested that, while the claim to privacy does not arise when an arrest record is first generated and used within the criminal justice process, such a claim does become relevant when the arrest record is disseminated for purposes other than those reasonably related to law enforcement and the administration of criminal justice. Otherwise, the individual not only would lose control over information about himself, but would do so in a context where the condition of mutuality that exists between the individual and governmental agencies would no longer hold.[54] In such a situation, unilateral control over information is undertaken—whether directly or indirectly—by agencies or individuals, signifying a substantial loss to the individual's personal identity.[55]

---

[53] See Robinson v. California, 370 U.S. 660 (Superior Ct., LA Co., 1962) and Wheeler v. Goodman, 306 F.Supp.58 (U.S. District Ct., N.C., 1969).

[54] For a discussion of the condition of mutuality as it relates to the concept of privacy, see U.S. Department of Health, Education, and Welfare, Secretary's Advisory Committee on Automated Personal Data Systems, *Records, Computers and the Rights of Citizens,* Washington, D.C., U.S. Government Printing Office, 1973, pp. 38–39.

[55] According to Charles Fried, privacy permits the control of information which

With regard to the conviction record, considerations based on the assumptions and perspective of the rehabilitative model become relevant. A conviction record represents proof that a crime has been committed, but it also is proof that the person convicted has been or is being punished. Although the fact of a conviction should not cause that punishment to continue after a sentence imposed by law has been served, it generally is the case that an individual with a conviction record continues to be subjected to the social and economic liabilities of his record.

Such a situation contravenes the considerations derived from the RM concerning the aim of reintegrating the individual into society on a basis where the strict demarcation between criminals on the one hand and noncriminals on the other hand is minimized. Removing or minimizing the stigma attached to the criminal justice process is possible only if it is assumed that an individual can pay his debt to society for criminal offenses and begin anew without continued reference to his criminal status or history. This is not possible when the person's conviction record is disseminated widely, foreclosing available opportunities to reintegrate himself as a useful member in society.

The policy orientation of the crime control model toward criminal justice information policy is quite different than that of the due process or rehabilitation model. First, since the key to the operation of the CCM is the presumption of guilt, much more emphasis is placed on the reliability of the arrest record than in the DPM. A person whose guilt for a crime is highly probable may escape conviction in a number of circumstances: under the exclusionary rule, certain physical evidence against the individual may not be used; police may violate procedural requirements in obtaining the confession of an individual, thus invalidating the confession; witnesses and victims may refuse to testify; and the individual may be freed on grounds such as insanity and diminished capacity. Thus, while the suspect has not been formally convicted of a crime, the practical realities of the situation (i.e., an arrest record) imply that his guilt is at least as likely as his innocence.

Second, because speed in the handling of cases is important for the efficient operation of the criminal justice process, less emphasis is placed on the accuracy with which the process operates. Seen in the context of the administrative fact-finding process, criminal justice rec-

---

makes the maintenance of various degrees of intimacy in social relationships possible: "even between friends the restraints of privacy apply. . . .The rupture of this balance, by a third party—the state perhaps—thrusting information concerning one friend upon another might well destroy the limited degree of intimacy the two achieved." See Charles Fried, "Privacy," *Yale Law Journal*, 77:485, January 1968.

ords do not have to be completely accurate to be useful, especially with regard to judicial dispositions.

Third, the dissemination of criminal justice records outside the criminal justice system is regarded as a means of preventing crime, because it keeps individuals who have been suspected or convicted of crimes from acquiring jobs or other social or economic benefits or services that they would be likely or be tempted to abuse.

A fourth implication of the crime control model is that no criminal justice records should, under any circumstances, be sealed or purged, since there always is the possibility that an individual who has had contact with the criminal justice system at one time in his life will have contact at another time. Information about individuals must be retained, not only to understand the complete nature of their interactions with criminal justice agencies, but, also, to aid in establishing a possible modus operandi or lead in investigations of specific crimes. Criminal justice records, then, always remain at least potentially useful and should be retained.

Because the CCM is based on the idea that the prevention and control of criminal conduct is by far the most important task of the criminal justice process, criminal justice records are perceived first and foremost as operational tools to aid that process. From this perspective, limitations on the use of such records, which may be suggested as a result of policy choices recognizing the extent of social costs involved with criminal justice records and the claims and goals of the DPM and RM, tend to be regarded as obstructive to the efficient enforcement of laws and to the control of crime.

The weight such divergent claims and goals are to be accorded is by no means clear. Their articulation in the context of the policy formulation process is no guarantee that a reduction in the social costs of criminal justice records will result. In the next section and in subsequent chapters, it will be suggested that the fact that the public affected by criminal justice recordkeeping practices represents a relatively large segment of society does not mean that such a public can or will act to reduce the costs of such record practices to themselves.

THE PUBLIC AFFECTED BY SOCIAL COSTS: THE PROBLEM OF IDENTIFICATION AND COLLECTIVE INACTION

Aside from the debate over conflicting claims and policies, there is the practical problem of the ability of the public, who are affected by criminal justice recordkeeping and use, to effect changes to improve their situation. In this section, the public affected by the social costs of criminal justice records will be identified and the problems members of this public have when engaging in political action will be discussed.

The Relevant Public Affected

The social costs of criminal justice records affect individuals who have been arrested, arrested and tried, and arrested, tried, and sentenced. At the outset, it must be noted that this group does not represent the total body of criminals or suspected offenders in society. The common belief that the general population consists largely of law-abiding people has, in recent years, been refuted by studies indicating that most people, when asked, remember having committed offenses for which, if apprehended, they might have been sentenced. Such studies of "self-reported" crimes have uniformly shown that delinquent or criminal acts are committed by people at all levels of society.[56] And, while most people admit to relatively petty delinquent acts, many report larcenies, automobile thefts, burglaries, and assaults of a more serious nature. In an early study dealing with the criminal behavior of 1,700 adults from New York City, 90 percent admitted that they had committed one or more offenses for which they might have received jail or prison sentences. Thirteen percent of the males admitted to grand larceny, 26 percent to automobile theft, and 17 percent to burglary. Sixty-four percent of the males and 29 percent of the females committed at least one felony for which they had not been apprehended.[57] Since that survey, criminologists have made numerous studies of unreported crime which have strongly confirmed earlier findings. Many people do, in fact, commit one or more crimes during their lifetimes, and such behavior occurs among all social classes, in contrast to what is indicated by criminal justice statistics.[58] In addition, although some of these offenses might have been reported to the police by the victims, the individuals who committed the crimes were not arrested. On

[56] President's Commission on Law Enforcement and Administration of Justice. *Task Force Report: Assessment of Crime*. Washington, D.C., U.S. Government Printing Office, 1967, p. 77.

[57] Jane S. Wallerstein and C. J. Wyler. "Our Law Abiding Law Breakers." *Probation*, 25:107–112, March–April 1947.

[58] For a more comprehensive assessment of the causes of unreported crime in the United States and extensive documentation of previous studies on unreported and undetected crime, see Charles E. Silberman, *Criminal Violence, Criminal Justice*, New York, Random House, 1978, pp. 40–47.

the other hand, a recent study concerned with victimization in the nation's five largest cities found that a significant number of victims of crimes never report them to the police.[59]

Those individuals who bear the social costs of criminal justice records represent only those who have been apprehended by the police and not the total body of criminals or suspected offenders in society. What, then, are the characteristics of this group?

Even though many crimes are not reported and many criminals are never arrested, the number of individuals who are arrested is staggering; however, it has been estimated that fewer than 25 percent of those arrested each year are found guilty of the offense for which they were arrested and only slightly more than another 25 percent are found guilty of any crime at all.[60] Thus, in 1972, of approximately 8.7 million arrests of persons for all criminal acts except traffic offenses,[61] approximately 4 million people were arrested for a crime but were not convicted. A recent study of the number of persons in the United States with arrest or conviction records indicates that this population constitutes approximately 40 million people, representing approximately 25 percent of the total labor force.[62]

National arrest statistics reported by the President's Commission on Law Enforcement and Administration of Justice in 1967 indicated that, when all offenses are considered together, the majority of offenders arrested were white, male, and over 24 years old. For many crimes, however, the peak age of criminality occurred below age 24. For example, the 15-to-17-year-old age group was the highest for burglaries, larcenies, and automobile thefts.[63] In 1972, the FBI, in its Uniform Crime Reports, provided these figures: "nationally, persons under 15 years of age made up 9% of the total police arrests; under

[59] See U.S. Department of Justice, Law Enforcement Assistance Administration, National Criminal Justice Information and Statistics Service, *Crime in the Nation's Five Largest Cities, Advance Report,* Washington, D.C., 1974, pp. 1–5.

[60] "Prepared Statement of Aryeh Neier, Executive Director, and John H. F. Shattuck, Staff Counsel, American Civil Liberties Union." In: *Criminal Justice Data Banks: 1974.* Vol. I, Hearings, p. 253.

[61] U.S. Department of Justice, Federal Bureau of Investigation. *Crime in the United States—1972.* Washington, D.C., U.S. Government Printing Office, 1972, p. 31.

[62] See Neal Miller, *A Study of the Number of Persons with Records of Arrest or Conviction in the Labor Force,* Washington, D.C., U.S. Department of Labor, Office of the Assistant Secretary for Policy, Evaluation, and Research, 1979, p. 23.

[63] Ronald Christensen. "Projected Percentage of U.S. Population with Criminal Arrest and Conviction Records." In: *Task Force Report: Science and Technology.* President's Commission on Law Enforcement and Administration of Justice. Washington, D.C., U.S. Government Printing Office, 1967, p. 78.

18, 26%; under 24, 39%; and under 25, 53%."[64] The FBI attributed these high percentages in youth crime partly to the marked increases in drug-related arrests which had occurred.

The president's commission also found that the probability of a male being arrested at least once during his lifetime was 50 percent, while for a female it was 12 percent; however, for white urban males, the probability was 62 percent, and for black urban males, as high as 90 percent. Nineteen percent of all males and 25 percent of all urban males will be convicted of crimes at some time during their lives, while 5 percent of all females will acquire conviction records.[65] The rate for males was 1,092 per 100,000 population for index offenses plus larceny under $50, while the corresponding rate for females was 164 per 100,000. Since 1960, however, the rate of arrests for females has been increasing more rapidly than the rate for males.[66]

The commission noted that race was almost as important as sex "in determining whether a person is likely to be arrested and imprisoned for an offense. Many more whites than Negroes are arrested every year but Negroes have a significantly higher rate of arrest in every offense category except certain offenses against public order and morals."[67] As indicated, the probability of a black urban male acquiring an arrest record during his lifetime was as high as 90 percent.

Studies of probation records have confirmed that many individuals who come into contact with the criminal justice process come from disorganized families, have had limited access to educational and occupational opportunities, and have been frequently involved in difficulties and conflicts with the criminal justice system.[68]

The relevant public affected by the social costs of criminal justice records reflects a population that is predominantly urban, young, and black and is likely to be unemployed. Indeed, the most significant aspect of crime in the United States is that it is largely a consequence of frustration, collapse of the family, and other social problems caused by poverty and unemployment.

As the president's commission found: "from arrest records, probation reports, and prison statistics a 'portrait' of the offender emerges that progressively highlights the disadvantaged character of his life."[69]

---

[64] U.S. Department of Justice, Federal Bureau of Investigation. *Crime in the United States—1972*, p. 34.
[65] Christensen. "Projected Percentage," p. 224.
[66] *Ibid.*, p. 78.
[67] *Ibid.*
[68] *Ibid.*, p. 79.
[69] *Ibid.*, p. 78.

Incentives to Neither Talk Nor Act

In Chapter 2, it was observed that collective action in large or small groups is dependent on mechanisms for coordinating and pooling of resources. Political action will occur when someone finds it profitable to act. In the absence of mechanisms for coordination and pooling of resources, it is likely that the costs of political transactions will exceed the marginal benefits. The result will be either very limited or minimal contributions by individuals toward the supply of a public good or a reduction of social costs. Political transaction costs will tend to increase with the size of particular groups so that, in large groups, the costs of information, communication, and participation are likely to be higher than in small groups. Coupled with the low levels of resources available for allocation for collective action among certain individuals in society, relatively higher transaction costs in large groups may lead to collective inaction; that is, collective inaction results when members of a public feel inefficacious with respect to their contribution, expect others to feel the same, and do not expect that efforts on their part will change the motivation of others concerning the net benefits of collective action.

At the outset, it is relatively easy to perceive that the relevant public affected by the social costs of criminal justice records is a large group. In 1977, the FBI reported that 10.2 million arrests had been made by law enforcement agencies in the United States, up from 9.6 million in 1976.[70] As noted, the probability that a white urban male will be arrested at least once during his lifetime is 62 percent; for a black urban male, the probability rises to approximately 90 percent. In addition, most arrests in any one year are males under 25 years of age. A large segment of those arrested is unemployed, unemployable, or underemployed and, thus, poor.

The relevant public affected by the social costs of criminal justice records, then, comprises a large group whose composition suggests incentives leading to collective inaction. According to Mancur Olsen, separable and selective incentives are needed to stimulate individuals in a group to act in a group-oriented manner to provide a collective good.[71] The presence or absence of such incentives indicates the like-

---

[70] See U.S. Department of Justice, Federal Bureau of Investigation, *Crime in the United States—1976,* Washington, D.C., U.S. Government Printing Office, 1976, p. 90; and U.S. Department of Justice, Federal Bureau of Investigation, *Crime in the United States—1977,* Washington, D.C., U.S. Government Printing Office, 1977, p. 96.

[71] Mancur Olsen. *The Logic of Collective Action.* Cambridge, Mass., Harvard University Press, 1965, p. 33.

lihood of a collective good being provided to a group. In the case of the relevant public affected by the social costs of criminal justice records, it becomes clear not only that such separable and selective incentives are not present, but that selective *disincentives* exist which lead to collective inaction. Such disincentives tend to raise the costs of political transactions.

The main impact of criminal justice records on individuals focuses on the closing off of employment and other opportunities and benefits that normally are available to persons in society. Individuals with arrest or conviction records have difficulty in obtaining employment in private industry, public service, and licensed occupations, as well as obtaining loans, insurance, credit, public housing, and commercial bonding for selective occupations. In addition to these restrictions, an individual may be rejected by or separated from the armed forces because of his arrest or conviction record, and he also may become the target of private investigations into his background and reputation that are intended to adversely affect his legitimate economic, political, or social pursuits.

The cumulative effect of such forms of record discrimination on individuals is to provide positive incentives to neither talk about nor bear witness to the arrest or conviction record, except under special conditions. To have either an arrest or conviction record constitutes a liability or, as has been suggested, a stigma that the person must respond to by managing such information about himself in a manner that will reduce the personal costs which are likely to be incurred. One manifestation of this strategy is to believe that you are an exception and that other people with similar records are either guilty or not rehabilitated. This theory has been described effectively by Neier.

Writing about Stalin's purges, Nadezhda Mandelstam and Alexander Solzhenitsyn observed that victims who deemed themselves to be innocent nevertheless believed their fellow sufferers to be guilty. Because they thought of others as true criminals, they were unable to join their fellow victims in action to protect themselves.

Few self-help movements have emerged in the United States among people victimized by their records. Those who have been arrested, but not convicted often think their own cases are exceptional but share in the general presumption that other people with similar records are guilty. So many are tarnished by a record of arrest that among them must be a number of those who, in turn, make the decisions to deny jobs to other people who have similar records. Common experience has proven no guarantee of empathy.[72]

[72] Neier. *Dossier,* p. 167.

Thus, individuals stigmatized by such records have not organized, as each individual seeks to escape the consequences of his record by concealing it. Only when they have records that are perhaps most difficult to conceal—of criminal convictions—have individuals joined together to pursue their collective interests. In recent years, exconvicts have formed a number of organizations to concentrate public attention on their plight and to help each other obtain suitable housing and employment.[73] Generally, however, such organizations have not had memberships commensurate to the actual number of individuals eligible and have not had support from individuals with arrests not leading to convictions. As Neier has indicated, "Those with arrest records prefer not to identify themselves or join with others whom they think were probably guilty. Getting by without disclosing the record seems to them the best option."[74]

Minimizing the personal costs of the discrimination caused by an arrest or conviction record entails positive incentives not to act collectively. Management of such information about oneself is perceived as less costly than collective action to reduce the social costs arising from such records.

In addition, prominent segments of the relevant public affected by the social costs of criminal justice records comprise what Olsen has noted are forgotten groups.[75] These are unorganized groups having only limited resources to support political action on their behalf and either no lobby or a very weak lobby to promote their needs and protect their interests. Given that the public affected by the social costs of criminal justice records is composed of large segments of the young, the unemployed, the poor, and the black and other racial minorities, it is not difficult to understand why such a public may be unorganized and not stimulated to act collectively. Traditionally, such groups do not receive the immediate benefits and protections derived from collective action; therefore, they remain the losers in the political allocation of goods. Collective action by individuals comprising such groups

[73] While there are more than 700 groups in the United States that are concerned with prison reform and prisoner civil rights, less than one-third pays any attention to the issue of employment discrimination for exprisoners. Most of these are direct, self-help groups for prisoners that engage in little, if any, organized political lobbying at the local, state, or federal levels. See Mary Lee Bundy and K. R. Harmon, *The National Prison Directory,* Base Vol., Suppl. No. 1, and Suppl. No. 2, College Park, Md., Urban Information Interpreters, 1975–1977.

[74] Neier. *Dossier,* p. 168.

[75] Olsen. *Logic of Collective Action,* p. 165.

is costly and, in the absence of mechanisms for coordination and pooling of resources, unlikely. In the following chapters, the development and efficacy of such mechanisms for political action will be explored in the context of the politics of criminal justice information policy formation.

6

Regulating the Social Costs
of Criminal Justice Records—
the Public Issue Emerges

The patterns of governmental and individual responses to the social costs associated with the use of criminal justice information will be examined here, beginning with the period prior to 1965, when recordkeeping was performed manually, and proceeding to the late sixties and early seventies, when computerized criminal justice information systems were used more and more extensively. This chapter and Chapters 7 and 8 aim to foster an understanding of the efforts to reduce social costs as a problem of public policy. In Chapter 5, it was suggested that, given the size, relevant characteristics, and transaction costs of the public affected by the social costs of criminal justice records, it could be expected that such a public would not engage in collective action. In fact, a number of specific disincentives to collective action by individuals with criminal justice records were noted.

To suggest that a particular public affected by social costs will not engage in collective action does not mean that specific individuals in that public will not seek, through legal or political action, to minimize social costs affecting them, or that particular entrepreneurs or interest groups will not act to provide for the reduction of social costs affecting a larger public. It also does not imply that the public agencies who are largely responsible for such costs will not, under certain conditions, seek to reduce social costs deriving from their productive processes.

Therefore, a public good, such as the reduction of social costs of criminal justice records, can be provided through a number of alternative organizational and decision-making arrangements. Such arrangements may reduce the costs of participation for a large public affected by social costs; however, representation costs may rise as a result of the divergence between the individual preferences and needs of those comprising the affected public and the preferences of public agencies, interest groups, or entrepreneurs in reducing social costs. As noted in Chapter 2, no a priori assumption can be made that the prevailing political or legal processes can guarantee that the social costs of public agencies will be kept at a minimum. The reduction of social costs is equivalent to providing a public good, and such a good generally is costly to provide. The cost depends on the kinds of organizational and decision-making arrangements that govern the formulation of public policy concerning the reduction of social costs as well as the practical effects of such policies.

This chapter focuses on the early patterns in the development of criminal justice information systems and on the policies concerned with the social costs of criminal justice records. Particular attention will be given to those factors affecting what Crenson has called the "issueness"[1] of reducing the social costs of criminal justice records and subsequent results. Chapters 6, 7, and 8 provide a descriptive and historical review of information policy formulation and debate, and Chapter 9 presents an analysis of the politics of reducing social costs, especially in relation to the representation of relevant interests in the policy formation process.

Public issues do not just arise; they have an organizational and entrepreneurial aspect. The latter characteristic is derived from the fact that issues and policies are not simply pieces of abstract political subject matter. As Crenson suggests: "To say that an issue has arisen is to announce the emergence of an informal organization, a body of would-be decision-makers who interact with one another in their efforts to deal with some common concern."[2]

Within the context of the American political system, public policy issues may remain latent until certain individuals or groups find it to their advantage to focus on an administrative, legal, social, or economic problem by suggesting and then demanding that a political response is necessary. The emergence of the public policy issue concerning the social costs of criminal justice records will be detailed in its preliminary stages: first, as an administrative problem and individual concern demanding the sporadic attention of state legislatures and courts, and, second, as an evolving public issue tied to significant technological and political patterns in the middle and late 1960s. How this issue gains community and formal agenda status by being tied to an "ecology"[3] of issues concerned with the impact of information

[1] Matthew A. Crenson. *The Un-Politics of Air Pollution*. Baltimore, Md., Johns Hopkins University Press, 1971, p. 94.
[2] *Ibid.*, p. 157.
[3] *Ibid.*, p. 170.

technology on changing individual values and demands will be described.

THE MANUAL PERIOD PRIOR TO 1965

The social costs associated with the use and dissemination of criminal justice records have not simply arisen *de novo* with the use of computers in criminal justice agencies. Until the incorporation of computers into criminal justice recordkeeping during the 1960s, systems were using manual files of index cards and manila folders, developed during the late 1800s and early 1900s. Traditionally, a positive method for identifying persons with arrest records and histories of prior involvement with criminal justice agencies has been regarded as an indispensable tool of law enforcement.[4] Prior to 1900, the Bertillon system of criminal identification—an effective method of classifying, recording, indexing, and searching photographs, developed by Alphonse M. Bertillon in 1882—was used in the United States. The system was based on measurements of various parts of the body taken with specially designed calipers and recorded with specific photographs and personal appearance data. The measurements provided police with a means of positively identifying individuals and storing and retrieving criminal files that did not rely on names or aliases. Despite certain defects, the Bertillon system served the needs of police for 30–40 years, until criminal identification using fingerprints was introduced.

A system of criminal identification based on fingerprints was put into operation by Scotland Yard in 1900 and later was adopted by American law enforcement agencies and police throughout the world. Several reasons for the adoption of the fingerprint system have been cited:

1. If all the millions of people on earth were fingerprinted, it is safe to say that no two fingerprints would ever be alike.
2. Fingerprints do not change from birth to death, as do the bony structures of the body.
3. It is a very simple operation to take the fingerprints of an individual, and it requires only a few minutes.
4. As indicated before, fingerprints lend themselves to a very simple system of classification by which a fingerprint formula is derived. Since the finger-

[4] V. A. Leonard. *The Police Records System.* Springfield, Ill., Charles C Thomas, 1970, p. 43.

prints of an individual do not change throughout life, the fingerprint formula of each person remains the same from birth to death.

5. Under most conditions, on everything a person touches, he leaves his fingerprints. Many a criminal offender has found his way to the penitentiary through latent fingerprints he left at the scene of the crime.[5]

Although, for a few years, some jurisdictions used both systems of identification, the fingerprint system gradually emerged as the most useful and efficient means of achieving positive identification of individuals arrested and booked for suspected criminal offenses.

During the manual period of recordkeeping, various states established bureaus of criminal identification and statistics to act as depositories for arrest records collected throughout the state and as clearinghouses for information about offenders from other states and jurisdictions. In 1896, New York became the first state to establish a bureau of criminal identification.[6] As part of the prison department, the State Bureau of Criminal Identification was authorized by law to procure and file Bertillon measurements of all prisoners confined or admitted to state prisons, reformatories, and penitentiaries. In 1903, the bureau began filing fingerprints of inmates of the state prisons. Both systems of identification were used until, in 1913, fingerprinting was required by law for all inmates of the state prisons, reformatories, and penitentiaries. A Central Bureau of Criminal Identification was established in 1927 as a division in the Department of Correction, which had replaced the prison department. In 1928, a state law was passed requiring all law enforcement agencies in the state to fingerprint all persons arrested and charged with a felony, misdemeanor, or offense as specified. In addition, it required that a copy of each set of prints be forwarded to the Division of Criminal Identification, Records and Statistics, in the state capitol.

In 1954, the division was separated into the Division of Criminal Identification and the Division of Research. Then, in 1957, to acknowledge the annual receipt of more noncriminal than criminal fingerprints, the word criminal was dropped from the title of the Division of Criminal Identification. The Division of Identification operated a manual information system that collected and disseminated arrest records and criminal history records throughout the state of New York until 1966, when it was transferred to the New York State Identification and Intelligence System (NYSIIS). The criminal files subsequently were computerized.

[5] *Ibid.*, pp. 46–47.
[6] See J. M. Silbert, "Criminal Justice Information Systems and the Criminal Justice 'System,'" Doctoral Dissertation, New York, New York University, 1972, pp. 79–99.

A similar pattern of development occurred in California, where the Bureau of Criminal Identification was established in 1905 in San Quentin Prison.[7] Its primary purpose was to fingerprint inmates and to distribute copies of the prints to major police departments and sheriffs' offices in California for use in identifying subjects who might be arrested again at some future time. In 1917, after much political activity by law enforcement agencies throughout the state, a Bureau of Criminal Identification and Investigation was created under state law. The statute established categories for arrested persons whose fingerprints were to be submitted to the bureau and described what reports on major crimes and stolen, lost, found, or pledged-upon property were to be submitted by local police departments.[8] Local law enforcement departments were not required to report violations of local ordinances or state law misdemeanor violations.

In 1929, a statistical function was added to the bureau, based on recommendations of the California Crime Commission. In 1941, the bureau was integrated into the Department of Justice; when the Department of Justice was reorganized in 1951, the bureau was placed under the Division of Criminal Law and Enforcement. The Bureau of Criminal Statistics, created in 1955 by the legislature, was responsible for processing information relating to police, probation, and court activities. The Departments of Corrections and Youth Authority assumed responsibility for processing their own statistical output. By the late 1960s, the Bureau of Criminal Identification and Investigation had computerized a portion of its records which had been maintained manually since 1918.

By 1965, 42 states had developed central recordkeeping systems for criminal offenders. The systems varied widely, but three basic files generally were maintained: fingerprinting, name index to prints, and criminal history records.[9]

While state bureaus for arrest and criminal history records were being created, the FBI established, in 1924, its Identification Division to serve as a national depository and clearinghouse for fingerprint cards and arrest records collected throughout the United States. The Identification Division collects fingerprint and arrest records submitted by local, state, and federal law enforcement agencies for crimes

---

[7] See John P. Kenney, *The California Police*, Springfield, Ill., Charles C Thomas, 1964, pp. 44–63.

[8] *Ibid.*, p. 54.

[9] Harry Bratt. "Survey of State Criminal Justice Information Systems." In: *Proceedings of the National Symposium on Criminal Justice Information and Statistics Systems*. Edited by Project SEARCH. Sacramento, California Crime Technological Research Foundation, 1970, p. 74.

serious enough to require taking prints. The cumulative record of an individual's arrests, dispositions, and sentences comprises what the FBI calls a criminal history record or rap sheet (see Figure 10).

Prior to 1965, criminal justice agencies throughout the United States maintained extensive files on individuals through the use of fingerprint system and manual files. Fingerprint records and criminal history records were exchanged statewide as well as nationwide via mail and the first teletype systems. Information about individuals could be obtained anywhere in the country.

Given, then, such extensive recordkeeping on the part of criminal justice agencies, what was the focus of information policy during this period?

The main concern relative to criminal justice records was at the level of the state bureaus of criminal identification and statistics. As in New York and California, many of the bureaus were given specific statutory authority to collect and disseminate criminal justice records and statistical information. Much of the legislative activity at the state level during this period centered on authorization statutes for criminal justice recordkeeping and did not deal specifically with the social costs of criminal justice records. Indeed, it was during this period of informality and lack of uniformity at the state and local levels that the widespread dissemination of criminal justice records outside the criminal justice system was initiated. Few criminal justice agencies developed explicit information policies during this period: The information policies that did exist focused on the use and dissemination of criminal justice records rather than on any limitations on their use.

If the problem of the social costs of criminal justice records was apparent during this period, it arose in the context of individual complaints pursued through state courts, that usually were hesitant to interfere with police discretion. In the absence of specific legislative action, the courts indicated that all arrest records could be retained and disseminated freely among criminal justice agencies.[10]

Legislative activity was sporadic.[11] Generally, the problems related

[10] See Donald A. Marchand, *Criminal Justice Records and Civil Liberties: The State of California*, Final Project Report, Sacramento, California Department of Justice, 1973, pp. 113–119.

[11] See, for example, Herbert S. Miller, *The Closed Door: The Effect of a Criminal Record on Employment with State and Local Public Agencies*, Washington, D.C., Manpower Administration, U.S. Department of Labor, 1972, pp. 235–250 (Appendix G, "Expungement Statistics"); also, Congressional Research Service, "Survey of State Statutes on Access to Criminal Records," in: *Criminal Justice Data Banks: 1974*, Vol. II, Appendix, U.S. Congress, Senate, Committee on the Judiciary, Subcommittee on Constitutional Rights, 93d Congress, 2d Session, 1974, pp. 715–717.

UNITED STATES DEPARTMENT OF JUSTICE
Federal Bureau of Investigation
Identification Division
Washington, D.C. 20537
Fictitious Record

The following FBI record, NUMBER 000 000 X, is furnished FOR OFFICIAL USE ONLY. Information shown on this Identification Record represents data furnished FBI by fingerprint contributors. WHERE DISPOSITION IS NOT SHOWN OR FURTHER EXPLANATION OF CHARGE OR DISPOSITION IS DESIRED, COMMUNICATE WITH AGENCY CONTRIBUTING THOSE FINGERPRINTS.

Contributor of Fingerprints	Name and Number	Arrested or Received	Charge	Disposition
SO Clanton AL	John Doe A-000	3-9-65	susp	rel
SO Clanton AL	John J. Doe A-000	6-11-65	vag	rel
SO Clanton AL	John J. Joe A-000	9-18-65	intox	$25 or 25 das; pd
PD Montgomery AL	Joseph Doe CC-000	6-11-66	forg	
St Bd of Corr Montgomery AL	John Joseph Doe C-00000	10-18-66	forg 2nd deg	2 yrs & 1 day par 5-15-67
St Bd of Corr Montgomery AL	Joseph John Doe C-00000	returned 9-5-67	PV (forg 2nd deg)	to serve un- expired term of 2 yrs & 1
PD Montgomery AL	John Doe A-0000	2-20-68	burg & escapee	TOT St Bd of Corr Mont- gomery AL
St Bd of Corr Montgomery AL	John J. Doe C-00000	returned 2-21-68	burg & escapee	2 yrs
USM Jacksonville FL	John J. Doe 00-C	10-14-70	ITSMV	
USP Lewisburg PA	John Joseph Doe 00-NE	11-15-70	ITSMV	18 mos par 8-1-71

FIGURE 10   Manual criminal history record.

to criminal justice records did not become public issues until the 1960s, when concerns with and fears of the use of computers highlighted the costs that had been incurred since the beginning of the manual period.

THE EARLY COMPUTER DEVELOPMENT PERIOD (1965–1970)

Public policy issues are not developed in isolation or at random. As Crenson noted: "One political demand may trigger a series of rationally related demands for things that facilitate the achievement, distribution, or enjoyment of the benefit that was originally requested."[12] Thus, the promotion of one political issue leads to the promotion, or the neglect, of others. To comprehend the ecology of issues occupying the center of public attention during any one period, it becomes necessary to understand why a particular problem has developed into a public policy issue for which particular forms of regulatory action are demanded.

Although from 1965 to 1970 concern about the social costs of criminal justice records developed in the context of the wider problem area of privacy and computers, prior to that time, discussions concerning the social implications of computers had focused on three issues: "the effects of computer-spurred automation on employment levels and work patterns; the extent to which business and government leaders are asking computers to 'decide' questions that call for value judgement rather than fact or trend analysis; and the effects of computerization on the psychological attitudes of citizens toward work."[13] Westin also noted that the concern with privacy during the 1940s and 1950s was "conspicuously absent from these debates over the social implications of computerization."[14] On the other hand, in the early 1960s, popular and scientific concern began to focus on the subject of privacy and computers; however, since computerization had not yet occurred on an extensive level, the concern about the abuses of computerized records remained somewhat hypothetical. It was not until the National Data Center controversy that the computers and privacy issue received national attention as the subject of congressional and political debate.

[12] Crenson. *Un-Politics of Air Pollution*, p. 170.
[13] Alan F. Westin. *Privacy and Freedom*. New York, Atheneum, 1970, p. 298.
[14] *Ibid.*

The Proposed National Data Center

In 1965, the Subcommittee on the Preservation and Use of Economic Data of the Social Science Research Council (SSRC) proposed, in a special report, that the Bureau of the Budget, the precursor to the Office of Management and Budget, establish a National Data Center to coordinate the preservation and use of socioeconomic data. E. S. Dunn, Jr., a consultant to the Office of Statistical Standards of the Bureau of the Budget, was commissioned to respond to the recommendation of the SSRC. He, in turn, recommended the implementation of a National Data Center to facilitate the efficient retrieval of information as the Federal Government branched out into the complex areas of poverty, health, urban renewal, and education, which required new and different uses of data. Although the Dunn Report noted the question of confidentiality of records and information, it simply assumed that no violations of existing rules of confidentiality would take place as a result of the data service, nor would there be any harm in putting data from state and local public agencies into the system or in being able to trace aspects of each person's life through time.

Reaction to the proposal was almost completely negative and alarmed. As Miller notes: "Members of Congress, then newspapers and magazines, and finally several legal periodicals took turns castigating the idea, often in emotive and highly symbolic terms."[15]

In the midst of this controversy, the Committee on the Judiciary, Subcommittee on Administrative Practice and Procedure, headed by Senator Edward V. Long (D.-Mo.), held hearings on the data center idea.[16] Dunn, the principal witness, emphasized that the paramount problem of the data bank would not be the potential invasion of privacy but the greater availability of relevant and traditional types of data for administrative program planning and evaluation. Senator Long cited the need for "proper safeguards."[17] The Long subcommittee noted that, although there was no intention to use such a data center for direct dealings with citizens, it would be relatively easy, technologically, to assign each individual a number and to develop the data into a central dossier bank. The subcommittee also indicated that it felt the potential consequences had not been studied thoroughly,

[15] Arthur R. Miller. *The Assault on Privacy*. Ann Arbor, University of Michigan Press, 1971, p. 57.

[16] U.S. Congress, Senate, Committee on the Judiciary, Subcommittee on Administrative Practice and Procedure. *Invasion of Privacy*. 89th Congress, 1st Session, 1965–1966.

[17] Westin. *Privacy and Freedom*, p. 319.

and that it would continue its investigations while the data center project was being designed.[18]

In 1966, Representative Cornelius Gallagher's (D.-N.J.) Committee held its own hearings on "The Computer and Privacy."[19] As Westin reports, "the committee was hostile to Dunn . . . , the Chairman calling the proposed data center a 'monster', and 'octopus', and a 'great, expensive, electronic garbage pail'."[20] As a result of the hearings, the proponents of the proposal, the Bureau of the Budget and the SSRC, recognized that more careful investigation of safeguards was needed to render a National Data Center acceptable to Congress and the public. Subsequently, the House Committee on Government Operations recommended that "no work be done to establish the national data bank until privacy protection is explored fully and guaranteed to the greatest extent possible to the citizens whose personal records would form its information base."[21] Such a recommendation effectively closed off acceptance of any National Data Center without explicit legislative authorization and safeguards.

In the context of the National Data Center controversy, many other concerns were expressed about evolving technologies and the invasion of privacy. In 1965, Representative Gallagher's Special Subcommittee on the Invasion of Privacy held hearings into personality testing, electronic eavesdropping, lie detectors, mail covers, and loyalty procedures.[22] In addition, a number of books[23] and magazine articles were published during this period detailing the horrors of the technological age; legal and scholarly journals published articles and symposia on privacy;[24] and, in 1967, Professor Alan Westin published his authoritative work, which provided the philosophical and constitutional overview for the notion of privacy in the technological age.[25] In 1968, 1969, and 1970, congressional investigations were directed into the policies and practices of the retail credit industry, particularly with regard to the collection, maintenance, and dissemination of retail

---

[18] *Ibid.*

[19] U.S. Congress, House, Committee on Government Operations, Special Subcommittee on the Invasion of Privacy. *The Computer and Invasion of Privacy.* 89th Congress, 2d Session, 1966.

[20] Westin. *Privacy and Freedom*, p. 319.

[21] Miller. *Assault on Privacy*, p. 58.

[22] U.S. Congress, House. *Computer and Invasion of Privacy.*

[23] See, for example, Vance Packard, *The Naked Society*, New York, Pocket Books, 1964; Myron Brenton, *The Privacy Invaders*, New York, Coward-McCann, 1964; and Jerry M. Rosenberg, *The Death of Privacy*, New York, Random House, 1969.

[24] See, for example, *Law and Contemporary Problems, 31,* Spring 1966.

[25] Westin. *Privacy and Freedom.*

credit reports.[26] This series of investigations and hearings culminated in the passage of the Fair Credit Reporting Act, which, although generally considered a weak bill by privacy advocates, did represent landmark legislation in an area where no regulations had previously existed concerning record collection and dissemination policies and practices.

The fears expressed during this period about the invasion of privacy by modern technology and by large-scale organizations were heightened by the search for new forms of personal expression and life-styles by college-educated youth. The right of privacy became a symbol of the counterculture in an age of bureaucracy and technology.[27] It represented, among other things, an assertion of a radical self, which prescribed that man must achieve a heightened sense of intimacy and self-reflection, even at the expense of institutional stability or political cohesion.[28] In part, then, privacy served as a challenge from one generation to another, of young to old, of the powerless to the powerful, of the unskilled to the technical, of the artist to the technocrat. New life-styles were introduced that reflected concern for a society beginning to resemble the anti-utopias of Orwell, Huxley, and Skinner. New values were being articulated, and new demands were placed on institutions. The counterculture feared oppression and repression of creativity and innovation through powerful technological tools.

The middle and late 1960s represented a period of breakthrough for the issue of privacy and computers on the national community agenda. Technological innovations were being introduced, and individual and social values and demands were changing. The computer was perceived as the essential villain threatening individual liberty and equality and, at the same time, as an indispensable tool for conducting organizational and governmental business. Perhaps one of the most significant and least understood changes during this period was the movement in government and industry to apply advances in technology and science derived from the military and space programs directly toward social problems.[29] An appealing and seemingly obvious logic was reflected in a speech by Senator Gaylord Nelson (D.-Wisc.) in 1965:

[26] See Miller, *Assault on Privacy*, pp. 67–89.
[27] See D. N. Weisstub and C. C. Gotlieb, *The Nature of Privacy*, Ottawa, Canadian Department of Communications/Department of Justice, 1972, p. 28.
[28] See, for example, Theodore Roszak, *The Making of a Counter Culture*, Garden City, N.Y., Doubleday, 1970, p. 49.
[29] See Ida R. Hoos, *Systems Analysis in Public Policy*, Berkeley, University of California Press, 1972.

Mr. President, why can not the same specialist who can figure out a way to put a man in space figure out a way to keep him out of jail?

Why can not the engineers who can move a rocket to Mars figure out a way to move people through our cities and across the country without the horrors of modern traffic and the concrete desert of our highway system?

Why can not the scientists who can cleanse instruments to spend germ-free years in space devise a method to end the present pollution of air and water on earth?

Why can not highly trained manpower, which can calculate a way to transmit pictures for millions of miles in space, also show us a way to transmit enough simple information to keep track of our criminals?

Why can not we use computers to deal with the down-to-earth special problems of modern America?

The answer is we can—if we have the wit to apply our scientific know-how to the analysis and solution of social problems with the same creativity we have applied it to space problems.[30]

Following up on this logic of technological transfer, the President's Commission on Law Enforcement and Administration of Justice looked to science and technology as a significant way of modernizing and increasing the capabilities of criminal justice agencies. As noted in Chapter 4, a new impetus for preventing crime and reforming the criminal justice system in America through the use of computers and scientific methods of management and analysis evolved during this period. This was later reflected in the priorities of the LEAA program: LEAA provided the essential funds to get the technological transfer movement off the ground in the field of criminal justice. As observed in Chapter 4, the widespread development of criminal justice computerized information systems in local and state governments has been due largely to the funds provided through the LEAA program; however, much of this development occurred after 1970. Prior to that time, information systems development had progressed on a more limited basis.

Concern for the social costs of criminal justice records evolved directly from the interaction of the privacy and computers movement with the technological transfer movement in criminal justice. Almost from the very beginning of the privacy and computers debate, the use of criminal records outside of the criminal justice process was singled out as an important example of the problems that computerization would exacerbate. The outcome of the National Data Center controversy pointed out that the problems of privacy presented by any proposed computerized information system had to be acknowledged or

<hr>

[30] Gaylord Nelson. "A Space Age Trajectory to the Great Society." *Congressional Record, III*(Part 20):27242, October 18, 1965.

the system would be the subject of public concern and legislative criticism that might be translated into a cut-off or curtailment of activities.

The President's Commission on Law Enforcement and Administration of Justice

In 1967, the President's Commission on Law Enforcement and Administration of Justice included in its *Task Force Report: Science and Technology* a section entitled "Handling Personal Information,"[31] which assessed the problems of privacy. The commission recognized that whenever records contained derogatory personal information, such records created serious public policy problems despite their usefulness, because:

> The record may contain incomplete or incorrect information.
> The information may fall into the wrong hands and be used to intimidate or embarrass.
> The information may be retained long after it has lost its usefulness and serves only to harass ex-offenders, for its mere existence may diminish an offender's belief in the possibility of redemption.[32]

The commission also observed that, in the past, the inherent inefficiency of manual files provided a built-in protection of privacy. Accessibility to files would be greatly enhanced by the computer; thus, special attention had to be given to protecting privacy.

Acknowledging that such problems had been reviewed in congressional hearings on the National Data Center, the commission noted that the good intentions of men in power could not be relied upon as an adequate privacy safeguard and pointed out that "when dealing with law enforcement data, the rights of society must also be protected."[33] Quoting the executive secretary of the American Civil Liberties Union (ACLU), the report included the following observations regarding the FBI's National Crime Information Center:

> Certain valid law enforcement purposes will be served by the creation of such a data center. Police work and crime detection can be more efficiently

---

[31] President's Commission on Law Enforcement and Administration of Justice. *Task Force Report: Science and Technology.* Washington, D.C., U.S. Government Printing Office, 1967, pp. 74–76.

[32] *Ibid.*, p. 74.

[33] *Ibid.*, p. 75.

pursued if information concerning major crime is readily available to law enforcement officials. In addition, such a center can serve as a source of vital statistical research on crime and police practices in the United States.[34]

Discussing the need for safeguards, the ACLU executive secretary outlined the dangers of incomplete arrest information and information not relevant to crime control purposes, particularly with regard to political expression and beliefs, and proposed "several important safeguards":

> Restricting the information content to matters of record.
> Restricting the dissemination to criminal justice agencies.
> Penalizing improper disclosure.
> Providing individuals access to their records and means for correcting them.[35]

The commission further noted that, a year or so earlier, the New York State Identification and Intelligence System had addressed the problems of handling personal information in a state information system. Basically, their approach placed a limit on the amount of information in the system and protected it through technical means. Physical security and technical means could not guarantee total security. The dangers could be minimized, however, by conscientious administration and by limiting the information recorded to an absolute minimum. Research was needed to determine what should be collected and retained in such systems. The administering organization needed to have a close working relationship with all contributing agencies. The contributing agencies would be responsible for restricting access to information. Also, guidelines would be necessary to evaluate requests for access to the file for reasons not initially anticipated. Furthermore, audit checks would be required of all inquiries to the file, preferably performed by a different agency, as in the military. The commission concluded that the problem needed more study and evaluation.

The Project SEARCH Report on Security and Privacy Considerations

The problems of privacy and criminal justice records were not given specific attention at the federal level again until July 1970, when

[34] Ibid.
[35] Ibid.

Project SEARCH issued a report entitled *Security and Privacy Considerations in Criminal History Information Systems.*[36] The report was the product of the Committee on Security and Privacy of the Project SEARCH Group, which was headed by Dr. Robert R. J. Gallati, the director of NYSIIS, and was written with three objectives in mind:

1. To construct a fundamental working document that enumerates potential security and privacy problems and presents solutions for the guidance of participants in Project SEARCH during the demonstration period.
2. To provide a dynamic framework of essential elements of security and privacy for any future national system which may develop as a result of Project SEARCH.
3. To outline the kinds of security requirements and self-imposed disciplines that the participants have, by their own initiative, levied upon themselves and their colleagues in Project SEARCH.[37]

Acknowledging that a computerized national system for exchanging criminal history data was needed and that Project SEARCH had developed the prototype, the committee explained the security and privacy issues relevant to the system. It concluded that the manual system operated by the FBI's identification division was lacking in two respects:

First, the national system is voluntary, with the national coverage fulfilled only by the FBI, in performing a service to contributors. The lack of mandatory reporting limits file completeness. Second, the elapsed time to obtain the criminal history data through the mail is measured in days and weeks in most places and is, therefore, not useful in police or court actions which must be completed in minutes or hours.[38]

The existing manual system lacked the capability to supply timely and complete information to criminal justice agencies. Project SEARCH proposed development of a prototype computerized national information system to collect and disseminate not only arrest records but information on decisions made about individuals in the courts, probation, and corrections.

Three basic problem areas of such a system related to security and privacy were defined from an operational aspect:

[36] Project SEARCH Committee on Security and Privacy. *Security and Privacy Considerations in Criminal History Information Systems*. Technical Report No. 2. Sacramento, California Crime Technological Research Foundation, 1970.
[37] *Ibid.*, p. 1.
[38] *Ibid.*, p. 2.

Unintentional errors. Ranging from typographic error to mistaken identities, there is always the possibility that the data finally stored in the system will be incorrect, without any intent to make it so. *Misuse of data.* Information can be used out of context or for purposes beyond the legitimate criminal justice functions, both by persons who are actually authorized access and by those who acquire the information even without authorization. *Intentional data change.* The data maintained can be destroyed or modified to accomplish the same objectives as described under misuse, or to restrict the proper and effective performance of criminal justice functions. It has been suggested that organized crime may attempt to penetrate the system for this purpose.[39]

While noting that these problems were not unique to a computerized criminal history system but applied as well to "all partly sensitive public records," the committee did emphasize the particular impact of the computer.

The use of fast-access remote terminals would increase the number of persons and agencies obtaining the data and the actual number of inquiries. Remote terminals would "make it more difficult to control individual access, as the system is generally only able to identify terminals and not operators."[40] Although the computer could reduce the frequency of unintentional error by audits, logs, and edits, the report noted that "the consequences of some types of errors may be substantially amplified simply by the fact that there are many more persons with access and the system response speed may exceed the error detection and correction speed."[41] In addition, the possibilities of misusing data would increase substantially over the manual system, and opportunities for intentional modification or destruction of records would increase proportionately to file centralization of the system. Based on these determinations, the committee realized that "the use of a computer as a basis for the system produces a fundamental, substantive change in both the possibility and consequences of possible problems."[42]

As a first step in its program, the Committee on Security and Privacy drafted a code of ethics that was to be adopted by participants in the information system.[43] Next, it provided a detailed explanation in its report of the implications of security and privacy on the development

---

[39] *Ibid.* (Emphasis added.)
[40] *Ibid.*, p. 6.
[41] *Ibid.*
[42] *Ibid.*
[43] *Ibid.*, pp. 45–46.

of a nationwide computerized criminal history system and recommended system policies related to security and privacy.

The committee suggested that the content of the data to be included in the system be limited to that having characteristics of *public* record, that is:

a. Recorded by officers of public agencies directly and principally concerned with crime prevention, apprehension, adjudication or rehabilitation of offenders.

b. Recording must have been made in satisfaction of public duty.

c. The public duty must have been directly relevant to criminal justice responsibilities of the agency.[44]

Excluded from the files, therefore, would be information concerning juvenile offenders, data on misdemeanor drunk and traffic arrests, and unverified data, such as that from intelligence sources. Participants would adopt permanent programs of data verification, including systematic audits, edits, logs, purging procedures, and limitations on what kinds of data could be included in the system in the future.

Overt access to the system should be limited to criminal justice agencies, and definitional questions should be presented to representatives of all the participating states for resolution. To limit access, certain practical restrictions were recommended:

a. Participating states should limit closely the number of terminals within their jurisdiction to those they can effectively supervise.

b. Each participating state should build its data system around a central computer, through which each inquiry must pass for screening and verification. The configuration and operation of the center should provide for the integrity of the data base.

c. Participating agencies should be instructed that their rights to direct access encompass only requests reasonably connected with their criminal justice responsibilities.[45]

In addition, where a local law, state statute, or valid administrative directive authorizes agencies and boards outside the criminal justice community access to data obtained through the system, efforts should be made to limit the scope of such requirements as much as possible. Furthermore, a study of various state "public record" laws was recommended so that the data in the system could be exempted and considered confidential:

[44] *Ibid.*, p. 11.
[45] *Ibid.*, p. 12.

Problems of access are also raised by the statutes under which interested private citizens may inspect and copy wide categories of public documents, sometimes including criminal justice records. The effect of these rights is to offer access to such records to representatives of the communications media, private investigators, credit bureaus, and all other interested citizens. Whatever the wider justifications for the doctrine of public records, the committee has concluded that no such rights of access should be permitted to data obtained through Project SEARCH, or any future system.[46]

From the beginning, Project SEARCH recognized that the new criminal justice information systems would allow for an increased capability to compile and correlate statistical materials for research, but also acknowledged that certain restrictions had to be placed on the use of data for research if individuals with such records were to be protected. Thus, the committee limited access to research data through screening requirements.[47]

The committee suggested that data disseminated from the system be marked and identifiable as such. Heads of agencies receiving information should sign a nondisclosure agreement, and educational programs should be developed for all who might be expected to use the data from the system.

The citizen's right to have access to and to challenge the contents of his record, consistent with state law, should form an essential part of the system for the following reasons:

First, an important cause of fear and distrust of computerized data systems has been the feeling of powerlessness they provoke in many citizens. The computer has come to symbolize the unresponsiveness and insensitivity of modern life. Whatever may be thought of these reactions, it is at least clear that genuine rights of access and challenge would do much to disarm this hostility.

Second, such rights promise to be the most viable of all the possible methods to guarantee the accuracy of data systems. Unlike more complex internal mechanisms, they are triggered by the most powerful and consistent of motives, self-interest.

Finally, it should now be plain that if any future system is to win public acceptance, it must offer persuasive evidence that it is quite seriously concerned with the rights and interests of those whose lives it will record. The committee can imagine no more effective evidence than authentic rights of access and challenge.[48]

[46] *Ibid.*, p. 27.
[47] *Ibid.*, pp. 12–13.
[48] *Ibid.*, p. 28.

If injuries were to occur from misuse of the system, the committee recommended that civil remedies be adopted where not provided for by state law.

Finally, regarding supervisory authority over the system, the committee suggested that the system participants should elect a board of directors to establish policies and procedures governing the central index operation; that the system should remain fully independent of noncriminal justice data systems; and that a permanent committee of staff members should be established to consider the problems of security and privacy and to conduct studies in that area.[49]

The security and privacy recommendations of Project SEARCH represented the first comprehensive attempt to develop a consistent information policy on the use of criminal justice records, and were merely the prelude for the contemporary development of information policy. The development of guidelines for security and privacy by Project SEARCH, concurrent with the development of the prototype data system, indicated that the problem of the social costs of criminal justice records could not be ignored if comprehensive information systems were to gain public approval. As Dr. Robert Gallati stated at Project SEARCH's National Symposium on Criminal Justice Information Statistics Systems in November 1970:

> The threat to systems like SEARCH lie—not so much in Congressional hearings such as those conducted by Congressman Gallagher and Senator Long and the announced hearings on Federal Data Banks and the Systems and the Bill of Rights (sic) to be conducted by Senator Ervin as Chairman of the Constitutional Rights Subcommittee, but rather in a rising crescendo of public revulsion against potential violations of personal privacy by data banks and systems which have not recognized the problem of privacy and have no plans for safeguards.[50]

The outcome of this debate was a realization that provisions to reduce social costs were necessary in order to implement criminal justice information systems at the local, state, and federal levels. Project SEARCH was not alone in acknowledging this fact. In 1965, NYSIIS had been established with a principle of providing safeguards for privacy and security: It was not a coincidence that the director of NYSIIS at that time, Robert Gallati, also served as the chairman of the SEARCH Committee on Security and Privacy.

Recognition of the social costs of criminal justice records, however, did not extend to the courts and state legislatures during this period;

[49] *Ibid.*, p. 13.

[50] Project SEARCH. *Proceedings of the National Symposium on Criminal Justice Information,* p. 28.

they maintained the pattern developed during the manual period. Both the courts and state legislatures continued to deal with problems of privacy and security in an isolated manner, and any concern with the social costs of criminal justice records remained latent. Policies on criminal justice recordkeeping were legislative responses to crisis situations or specific judicial decisions. Some concerns were voiced about privacy and security considerations in new systems, but such expressions were limited to efforts at developing codes of ethics and self-imposed guidelines. No new regulatory arrangements appeared.

INFORMATION POLICY FORMATION DURING THE EARLY 1970s

Between 1971 and 1974, LEAA provided funds to state and local agencies to commence a major effort to computerize the various information functions necessary for law enforcement and the administration of criminal justice. In addition, the development of a national criminal history information system advanced from the prototype stage with Project SEARCH to the design and implementation stages within the FBI's National Crime Information Center.

With the probability that an integrated national criminal justice information system would be realized by the middle or late 1970s, more public attention was focused on both the potential efforts of computerization and on the extent of social costs derived from manual recordkeeping systems. The principal concern was no longer simply the possible adverse effects of computers but, rather, the need for more effective and systematic policies on the collection, maintenance, and dissemination of criminal justice records. This interest extended to the organizational policies and practices of local, state, and federal agencies. Formulation of information policy moved from informal and abstract stages to determined policy debate about the control and regulation of information and information systems.

The Computerized Criminal History Program of the FBI's National Crime Information Center

Project SEARCH proved that use of a computerized system for the interstate exchange of criminal histories was technically feasible. The next questions concerned who should operate the system and what computerized criminal history information should be maintained at the federal and state levels. During the summer of 1970, the Office of

the Attorney General, the FBI, and LEAA discussed possible alternatives. In a series of memoranda during the course of the summer, the
FBI and LEAA responded to Attorney General John Mitchell's request
for the pros and cons on where the central index should be located.[51]
The five alternatives reviewed are listed in Table 9.

The first alternative, that one state would operate the index, was
rejected by both the FBI and LEAA. Although this alternative would
ensure that the system would be controlled by the states, it had
substantial disadvantages: First, it singled out one state to provide
what essentially is a national service, and there would be a continual
possibility of legislative or policy changes that could affect the program. Second, this alternative would be difficult to fund through
either the federal or state government. Third, the operation of the
computer would be involved with state/federal functions, which would
create administrative problems. Similarly, the second alternative offered the advantage that SEARCH would be controlled by the states in
the same fashion as the Law Enforcement Teletype System (LETS), a
state-operated system which transmitted emergency and administrative messages between law enforcement agencies throughout the
United States. SEARCH was far more complicated than LETS, however,
and required strong management control in the initial phases, which
LETS did not need. Furthermore, a consortium of states would demand congressional approval.

A significant divergence in perspectives arose when alternatives
three, four, and five were considered. The FBI director suggested that
the FBI should maintain a central index for the exchange of criminal
histories with the states. The director noted the prior experience and
expertise of the FBI in three functions. First, the FBI had legal authority and past experience in the area of identification. Title 28, Section
534, of the United States Code specifically established the FBI's authority for its Identification Division, Uniform Crime Reports, and NCIC,
stating that the attorney general shall "acquire, collect, classify, and
preserve identification, criminal identification, crime, and other records; and exchange these records with, and for the official use of,
authorized officials of the Federal Government, the States, cities, and
penal and other institutions."

In addition, since 1924, the Identification Division of the FBI had
served as the national clearinghouse in collecting, storing, and exchanging fingerprint cards with duly authorized local and state agen-

---

[51] Reprinted in: U.S. Congress, Senate, *Criminal Justice Data Banks: 1974*, Vol. II,
Appendix, pp. 369–386.

TABLE 9   Alternatives for the Control of the National Index for the
Exchange of Criminal History Information

Alternative 1

One state could operate a central index.

Alternative 2

A consortium of states could operate the central index.

Alternative 3

The FBI could operate the central index as part of its NCIC.

Alternative 4

LEAA could operate the central index as part of its information services to the states.

Alternative 5

A joint LEAA/FBI computer facility could operate the central index.

---

cies. Furthermore, the director suggested that "any computerized file
of criminal history must continue to be based upon the criminal identification process. This positive means of identification is necessary to
insure the integrity of computerized records. The only Federal agency
with this expertise is the FBI."[52]

Second, the FBI, in operating the only nationwide criminal statistics
service—the Uniform Crime Reports—since 1930, had helped set
standards for local and state law enforcement agencies in connection
with the collection of criminal and other statistics. Also, since 1963, the
FBI had been converting criminal history information on federal offenders in its Careers in Crime Program. The director noted that the
FBI was at the time converting the 1970 federal offender records of
criminal history information for computer storage under the standards adopted by the states. Such records would become a part of a
central index for the exchange of computerized criminal history information with the states.

Third, since 1967, the FBI had operated NCIC, a nationwide computerized law enforcement information system that stores documented
information on crime and criminals and makes it immediately accessible to law enforcement agencies. The director pointed out that this
was "the first use of computers and communication technologies to
link together local, state, and Federal government."[53] While NCIC did
not have criminal records as of 1967, the director noted that

from the beginning, it was planned that NCIC would serve as the central index
for computerized criminal history when it became practical to undertake this

[52] *Ibid.*, p. 377.
[53] *Ibid.*

task. The criminal history, or criminal identification record, has been developed over the years primarily by the law enforcement agencies. In terms of rapid response, it is the police agencies that most urgently need this information. Thus, the computerized criminal history has always been considered a logical extension of NCIC.[54]

NCIC was both a computerized information system and a nationwide communications system. The state computers that would store criminal history information were already linked on-line to the FBI/NCIC computer.

Beyond the FBI's expertise and experience, a consideration was that Project SEARCH had been initiated as a pilot program to demonstrate a computerized exchange of criminal histories among the states: "It did not develop the idea."[55] Moreover, to place the central index in an agency other than the FBI would result in duplication of expenditures at the state and federal levels.

Although LEAA acknowledged that placing the central index in the FBI's NCIC had a number of advantages, it noted some significant disadvantages. One concern was the extent of the criminal history information to be retained in the computerized system: "The Bureau (FBI) has indicated its intention of expanding the central index to include a detailed record of arrests, dispositions, and sentencing information."[56] This constituted a problem both technically and politically. The rap sheet would be considerably longer than the summary information used in the Project SEARCH demonstration and envisioned in an operational system, increasing the information traffic load substantially and necessitating more hardware and communications capabilities. Possible legal and political implications also existed.

If SEARCH were no longer a de-centralized, state-controlled system, the national data bank could loom as an issue. The existence or even hint of such a data bank would arouse certain members of Congress and the public. Although manual records are presently maintained by the FBI and have been for years, detailed arrest information available centrally in computerized form does present questions of privacy.[57]

Such a change in the basic design or concept would greatly reduce the states' ability to control the system:

The current (Project SEARCH) concept provides complete control of the system by the states, while the Bureau's proposal could leave the states with little

[54] *Ibid.*
[55] *Ibid.*
[56] *Ibid.*, p. 375.
[57] *Ibid.*

influence. In the NCIC, even though there is an advisory council, the FBI exercises user policy control.[58]

Finally, the FBI primarily served police needs. SEARCH was intended to serve the entire criminal justice community—police, courts, corrections, probation, parole, and prosecution. It was suggested that "the increased involvement of all parts of the system in SEARCH might be better accomplished under an organization not so closely identified with a particular component."[59]

The SEARCH concept, as developed by LEAA and the states, was a decentralized system operated by the states with the Federal Government providing only the service function of maintaining a limited index and providing message-switching capabilities. LEAA suggested that this task came within its legislative mandate to aid the states in improving and strengthening law enforcement. Since LEAA was about to acquire computer facilities for its Grants Management Information System, Technical Reference Service, and statistical data base, it could incorporate the criminal history exchange system in its plans to provide these automated information services to the states.

The FBI responded by noting that its concept was more efficient and effective than the concept of Project SEARCH and that it did not raise the threat of a national data bank as stated by LEAA. As with NCIC, the states would retain responsibility for record entries to the criminal history system, and the system itself would be voluntary. While the FBI's investigative operations and service functions were related primarily to police needs, they also aided the courts, the prosecution, and corrections agencies.

The FBI rejected any FBI/LEAA joint operation (Alternative 5) as contravening "the principle of fixed responsibility": "The management of an operating system cannot be divided between two agencies. This amounts to management by 'committee' resulting in conflicting interests, delay in decision-making, and other problems."[60]

Having received the views of the two major agencies involved, the attorney general requested that the Office of Management and Budget (OMB) study the alternatives for the future organization and operation of SEARCH. On September 3, 1970, the associate director of OMB, Arnold Weber, provided a management review of Project SEARCH.

The OMB report noted at the outset that Project SEARCH repre-

[58] *Ibid.*
[59] *Ibid.*
[60] *Ibid.*, p. 373.

sented a successful demonstration of the Nixon administration's concept of the "New Federalism." Furthermore, the system developed by the states appeared to be superior to the FBI's manual rap sheet system in a number of ways:

> Much more needed information is made available on each criminal's record. Users can receive the information in a matter of minutes instead of days. It is used and supported by the complete "criminal justice system," which includes the agencies of police, prosecutor, courts, probation, corrections and parole. (The current FBI system is heavily police oriented.)

Thus, the report concluded that

> the States are enthusiastic about the success of Project SEARCH. They created the system and made it work and they are eager to maintain control of future developments. They fear that Federal operation of the central index could lead to the development of a central Federated data bank and complete Federal control.[61]

The problem, as suggested in the OMB report, had two aspects: *what* should be done centrally, and *who* should do it. For the first aspect of the problem, two alternatives were available: either operate a complete central data bank for all criminal histories or operate a central index with limited history data on each offender. Concerning the second aspect of the problem, the report identified the same basic alternatives as those listed in Table 9. After reviewing the relevant findings, the following recommendations were made:

> —That the FBI operate the SEARCH central index on a limited record-length basis, while the States continue to develop and operate their individual, but compatible, automated criminal history systems.
> —That a strong Policy Control Board be established, which would report directly to the Attorney General, to decide the future development and operation of SEARCH. The Policy Control Board should include high-level officials from the FBI, LEAA, and the States, who represent all elements of the criminal justice system. Membership should be structured so that the States have an equal voice with the Federal government in recommending policies for the future direction of SEARCH.
> —That planning be initiated to develop an integrated criminal justice system. This would bring together SEARCH and the related FBI activities. The Policy Control Board should be the center of this planning activity.[62]

On December 10, 1970, Attorney General John Mitchell informed

[61] *Ibid.*, p. 366.
[62] *Ibid.*, p. 368.

LEAA that the FBI would take over management responsibility for the computerized system. The system was called the Computerized Criminal History (CCH) program and was operated as part of the National Crime Information Center, using NCIC computers and communication lines. As noted in Chapter 4, NCIC was developed with the assistance of an advisory group composed of state and local law enforcement personnel from agencies that either had computerized systems or were in the advanced planning stages of such systems. The advisory group was replaced in 1969 by the NCIC Advisory Policy Board. The board was composed primarily of state and local law enforcement personnel and made recommendations on NCIC policy to the FBI director regarding the development of the CCH program. The composition of the NCIC board, however, was not as diverse as that proposed by OMB in its September 1970 recommendations to the attorney general, nor did it report to the attorney general directly.

In March 1971, the NCIC Advisory Policy Board approved the operational concept and record content for the CCH program.[63] The central data bank, as recommended by the board and agreed to by the FBI, would no longer merely direct inquirers to the state where detailed criminal history information could be obtained. Instead, it would contain a detailed criminal history on each offender whose record was entered into the system by the states. Maintaining the complete detailed record of each offender was considered an interim measure, since all users would not have the capability to fully participate at the start of the system.

Ultimately, CCH, as envisioned by the board, was to be a combined single-state/multistate system. For single-state offenders, NCIC would maintain only summary data, and the states would maintain the detailed records. For multistate offenders and for federal offenders, NCIC would maintain the complete record. The summary record would include the reason for arrests, number of arrests and convictions, and specific information on the reason, date, and disposition of the offender's latest arrest and the criminal justice agencies involved. Since FBI studies indicate that approximately 70 percent of rearrests are within the same state, most detailed records would be of single-state offenders and ultimately maintained at the state level.

The NCIC board had, therefore, committed itself to developing an operational system that went beyond the original SEARCH concept in

---

[63] Elmer B. Staats, U.S. Comptroller General. *Development of the Computerized Criminal History Information System*. Report to Senator Sam J. Ervin, Chairman, Subcommittee on Constitutional Rights. Washington, D.C., General Accounting Office, 1974, p. 4.

terms of the Federal Government's involvement. Because the attorney general did not follow all of OMB's recommendations, OMB officials held a meeting on April 26, 1971 with the Department of Justice, LEAA, and FBI representatives to discuss CCH. Two of the major findings, according to a May 11, 1971 OMB memorandum of the meeting, were that:

—Neither the FBI nor LEAA had received copies of the September 1970 OMB report to the Attorney General.

—The FBI was building a central data bank of all criminal records instead of operating a central index as OMB recommended.[64]

On May 13, 1971, OMB's associate director reported to the attorney general that:

—The NCIC Board governing CCH had all police representatives instead of representatives from the total criminal justice system, including the courts, correction, prosecution and parole segments, as OMB recommended.

—The NCIC computer system's policies limited CCH to police use. OMB intended that the system be used by the total criminal justice system.

—The rap sheets used in recording data included data on corrections and courts but those agencies did not have access to that data under the CCH system.[65]

Immediate action in response to these charges was not forthcoming from the attorney general.

A COURT CHALLENGE: MENARD V. MITCHELL

While these developments were taking place, however, lawsuits in the federal and state courts began to challenge several important aspects of the way law enforcement agencies were handling offender records under existing manual procedures. In a series of cases during the 1960s, federal courts ruled in favor of individuals who sued to have their fingerprints returned and their arrest records expunged when charges against them were voluntarily withdrawn or dismissed by the court, or when trial resulted in acquittal.[66] The courts, in these decisions, emphasized that the dissemination of arrest records by law

[64] *Ibid.*, p. 5.
[65] *Ibid.*
[66] See, for example, U.S. v. Kalish, 271 F. Supp. 968 (U.S. Dist. Ct., Puerto Rico 1967); U.S. v. McLeod, 385 F. 2d 734 (5th Cir. 1967); Morrow v. District of Columbia, 417 F. 2d 728 (D.C. Cir. 1969); Wheeler v. Goodman, 306 F. Supp. 58 (U.S. Dist. Ct., N.C. 1969).

enforcement agencies to private and public employers and for license and permit checks operated as a form of punishment for persons who had never been found guilty. This was especially true for black Amer-. icans, who as a group were subject to more arrests than other segments of society. Only the individuals who sued to have their records expunged or to get specific relief were affected; the courts did not issue rulings setting general required practices for police agencies.

In June 1971, the FBI's criminal record procedures received a major blow in the case of *Menard v. Mitchell*.[67] While a student in California, Dale Menard was arrested for burglary, fingerprinted, and detained for two days by the Los Angeles police, but he was released from custody for lack of evidence and was never charged with any crime. The FBI subsequently obtained copies of Menard's fingerprints and other information placed on a criminal identification card. The card showed that Menard had been detained on suspicion of burglary; however, it failed to indicate his release. Menard brought suit to compel the attorney general and the director of the FBI to remove his fingerprints and the accompanying record regarding his detention by the California police from the FBI's criminal identification files. The U.S. District Court for the District of Columbia did not order expungement of the arrest record, but limited disclosure of the record to employees of the FBI, officials of any agency of the U.S. government for possible employment purposes, and officials of any governmental law enforcement agency.

After reviewing the procedures of the FBI's Identification Division and the circumstances of Menard's arrest, Judge Gerhard Gesell drew a clear distinction between a record of arrest and one of conviction. Recognizing that an arrest with or without probable cause was indeed a fact to be considered, Judge Gesell observed that, under our system of criminal justice, "only a conviction carries legal significance as to a person's involvement in criminal behavior."[68] He further noted that an arrest without conviction could not legally be used as the basis for adverse action against an individual.

Menard v. Mitchell raised significant constitutional issues, which required examination of the legality of FBI practices with respect to the dissemination of arrest records. The controversy that the *Menard* case suggested had to be looked at in the broadest context. In fact, the issue centered on the protection of the citizen's right to privacy and the power of the Federal Government to abuse that right. This power had

[67] 430 F.2d 486 (D.C. Cir. 1970), decision upon remand, 328 F. Supp. 718 (D.D.C. 1971).
[68] *Ibid.*, p. 724.

to be kept "in proper check." The FBI would have to show a "compelling public necessity" to disseminate widely a record that clearly invaded the individual's privacy "by revealing episodes in a person's life of doubtful and certainly not determined import."[69] Furthermore, the proper determination of "public necessity" was not within the jurisdiction of the courts or the executive branch, but up to the legislature. Judge Gesell indicated that the nature of the arrest record problem was such that it could not be left to a case-by-case resolution by the courts or to executive discretion. Critical study of this problem was needed, for which the legislature was properly responsible and uniquely capable.[70]

Turning to the main issue, Judge Gesell observed that the FBI's authorization for its Identification Division (28 U.S.C. 534) "must be narrowly interpreted to avoid the serious constitutional issues raised by *Menard*." Congress had "never intended to or in fact did authorize dissemination of arrest records to any state or local agency for purposes of employment or licensing checks."[71] Neither the statute nor the debates mentioned employment, and it could not be assumed that these records could be disseminated for employment or licensing purposes.

In addition, Congress had never intended that arrest records be used for employment or licensing purposes whenever local ordinances or state statutes permitted that such checks be run.[72] Thus, state licensing boards could obtain records from the state justice department's files but not from the FBI.

A significant aspect of Judge Gesell's rationale in this case depended on the fact that not only was there no legal authority for the FBI to disseminate arrest records in this way, but that the present FBI system of collecting, retaining, and disseminating arrest records was unworkable and inefficient, and it further aggravated the social costs of having an arrest record. Looking critically at the FBI system, Judge Gesell recognized the following "principal faults":

1. State and local agencies receive criminal record data for employment purposes whenever authorized by local enactment. These enactments differ state-by-state and even locality-by-locality within a particular state. Thus there is no pattern that finds justification either in terms of overall law enforcement objectives or by category of employment.

---

[69] *Ibid..*, pp. 726–727.
[70] *Ibid.*, p. 727.
[71] *Ibid.*, p. 726.
[72] *Ibid.*

2. The Bureau cannot prevent improper dissemination and use of the material it supplies to hundreds of local agencies. There are no criminal or civil sanctions. Control of the data will be made more difficult and opportunities for improper use will increase with the development of centralized state information centers to be linked by computer to the Bureau.

3. The arrest record material is incomplete and hence often inaccurate, yet no procedure exists to enable individuals to obtain, to correct or to supplant the criminal record information used against them, nor indeed is there any assurance that the individual even knows his employment application is affected by an FBI fingerprint check.

4. The demands made of the Division for employment data have so increased that the Bureau now lacks adequate facilities to service new applicants who fall within its own vague standards of eligibility.

5. In short, with increasing availability of fingerprints, technological developments, and the enormous increase in population, the system is out of effective control. The Bureau needs legislative guidance and there must be a national policy developed in this area which will have built into it adequate sanctions and administrative safeguards. It is not the function of the courts to make these judgments, but the courts must call a halt until the legislature acts.[73]

The only "compelling necessity" that the court was willing to recognize was that of furnishing "arrest data to other law enforcing agencies for strictly law enforcement purposes."[74] When arrest records were used for these purposes, they were subject to due process limitations, and any misuse of the records could be rectified by the courts. The same safeguards could not apply when an arrest record was used for employment purposes; thus, while Menard's arrest record was not expunged, its dissemination outside the Federal Government was limited to law enforcement purposes.

The *Menard* case represented a decisive move by a court to come to grips with the arrest-record problem. The FBI complied with the *Menard* ruling and suspended dissemination of arrest records to state and local agencies for employment and licensing checks. At the same time, the FBI called for legislation to establish guidelines.

PROPOSED FEDERAL LEGISLATION, 1971–1972

In October 1970, Senator Charles McC. Mathias (R.-Md.) sponsored an amendment to the Omnibus Crime Control and Safe Streets Act, requiring LEAA to submit legislation by May 1, 1971 to ensure "the

[73] *Ibid.*, pp. 726–727.
[74] *Ibid.*, p. 727.

integrity and accuracy of criminal justice data collection, processing and dissemination systems funded in whole or in part by the federal government, and protecting the constitutional rights of all persons covered or affected by the act."[75]

In September 1971, the Department of Justice proposed two bills concerning the use and dissemination of criminal justice records. The first bill, S. 2546, was introduced by Senator Roman Hruska on behalf of LEAA on September 20, 1971. The bill, the Criminal Justice Information Systems Security and Privacy Act of 1971, codified the confidentiality and security standards established by the NCIC Advisory Policy Board and authorized the attorney general to alter the scope of the national system as he deemed necessary. The bill met with severe and immediate opposition in Congress for failing to provide adequate protection against misuse of data and was never assigned to a subcommittee for hearings.

The second bill was introduced in Congress during September 1971 by Senator Alan Bible (R.-Nev.) to authorize the exchange of arrest-record information, which had been denied to the FBI by the *Menard* ruling. The senator stressed the importance of criminal record checks to prevent infiltration of organized crime figures into the gambling and liquor industries in Nevada and the need for screening applicants for "sensitive" posts such as "the employment of schoolteachers, the licensing of lawyers, private investigators, real estate agents,"[76] and other positions. The bill was retained in the full Judiciary Committee, but no action was taken in the Ninety-second Congress. Instead, in December 1971, Senator Bible added a rider concerning arrest records to Justice Department supplemental appropriation legislation. The Bible Rider, as it was called, was effective until June 30, 1972, when it was perpetuated by a continuing resolution, under which the Department of Justice had been operating during fiscal year 1973 in lieu of the enactment of its appropriation legislation. It was reiterated in the final House-Senate conference version of the bill for fiscal year 1973 appropriations for the Departments of State, Commerce, Justice, and other agencies, passed by Congress on October 13, and signed by the president on October 27, 1972. Later, as Alan Westin has observed, "there were protests by liberals in Congress that the authorization had been 'sneaked through.'"[77] It came to be regarded

---

[75] Omnibus Crime Control and Safe Streets Act Amendments, P.L. 91-644, Sec. 7(7), 1970.

[76] Alan F. Westin and Michael A. Baker. *Databanks in a Free Society*. New York, Quadrangle Books, 1972, p. 61.

[77] *Ibid*.

as a "stopgap" or "temporary authority" in the 1973 Senate debate on its continuance for fiscal year 1974.[78]

Although the Bible Rider effectively negated the *Menard* ruling and permitted the FBI to disseminate arrest records to state and local agencies for employment and licensing checks, the NCIC Advisory Policy Board was not unmindful that, as a result of the *Menard* case, the CCH program could be jeopardized if confidentiality and security requirements were not strengthened.

NCIC ADVISORY POLICY BOARD

In March 1971, the NCIC Advisory Policy Board had issued a paper delineating its proposed regulations and procedures concerning the accuracy, confidentiality, and security of criminal justice records.[79] To a great degree, the policies and procedures articulated in the NCIC Advisory Policy Board's publication reflected the policies recommended by Project SEARCH's first report on security and privacy, which was reviewed in the previous section. From its inception, the concept of NCIC was to serve as a national index and network for 50 state law enforcement information systems. Local and state governments were responsible for law enforcement and all entry, clearance, modification, and cancellation of criminal justice records. Also, the states were primarily responsible for enforcing discipline, monitoring system use, and assuring compliance with system procedures and policies in their respective jurisdictions. Only state agencies could enter and update records. With its single-state/multistate concept, the NCIC system would maintain complete criminal history records only on interstate and federal offenders and abbreviated criminal history records on all others. The NCIC board noted, however, that until certain states established state-level information systems, full criminal history records would be maintained on intrastate offenders as well as on interstate and federal offenders.

The NCIC board proposed that information in CCH include personal identification data and, for serious violations only, public record data concerning the individual's steps through the criminal justice process. Excluded from the national index would be juvenile offenders; minor

[78] For background on the Bible Rider, see Marchand, *Criminal Justice Records*, pp. 192–193; also, U.S. Congress, Senate, *Criminal Justice Data Banks: 1974*, Vol. II, Appendix, pp. 311–317.

[79] U.S. Department of Justice, Federal Bureau of Investigation, National Crime Information Center, Advisory Policy Board. *National Crime Information Center (NCIC), Computerized Criminal History Program, Background, Concept, and Policy*. Washington, D.C., 1972.

offenses such as drunkenness, vagrancy, and public order offenses; and nonspecific charges of suspicion and investigation. No social history data, such as medical or psychological information, would be included in the system unless such commitments were part of the criminal justice process. All users of the system would be criminal justice agencies or, if using a restricted segment of a multiagency computer center (part of a computer system also containing other government information, especially where a city or county operated a system for all its departments, including the police), the restricted segment using NCIC would have to be under the management control of law enforcement officials. System-derived criminal history data would not be available for licensing or local or state employment checks unless such dissemination was pursuant to state and federal statutes. The NCIC committee stated that the person's right to see and challenge the content of his record should form an integral part of the system.

During the spring of 1972, the policies and procedures of the NCIC Advisory Policy Board were adopted as regulations for the system; however, difficulties with the NCIC/CCH program did not end. In January 1973, the comptroller general of the General Accounting Office issued a report to Congress that identified a need to determine the costs of the NCIC/CCH system as well as to improve reporting procedures.[80] Neither the FBI, LEAA, or state officials knew the cost of a fully operational system, although statements by LEAA and state officials indicated that it could be at least $100 million. Cost information was necessary to enable federal, state, and local governments to determine if they were able or willing to meet the financial requirements of developing and operating the system.

Also, there was the crucial matter of the accuracy and completeness of the data to be entered into the system. The comptroller general noted that a criminal history exchange system is valuable, because it provides criminal justice agencies with complete, accurate, and timely information on all offenders. Under the NCIC system, criminal justice agencies were supposed to report arrests and dispositions within each state to the state's central identification unit, which maintains and controls state criminal records and supplies the data for the national files; however, such reporting was required by law in only 24 states. Citing an LEAA survey conducted between August 1969 and July 1970, the comptroller general indicated that many arrests and their disposi-

---

[80] Elmer B. Staats, U.S. Comptroller General. *Development of a Nationwide Criminal Data Exchange System: Need to Determine Cost and Improve Reporting*. Washington, D.C., U.S. General Accounting Office, 1973.

TABLE 10 Arrest and Disposition Reporting to State Unit

Transaction	Number of states by percent of completeness of arrest and disposition reporting to state identification units*		
	More than 90%	65 to 90%	Less than 65%
Arrests	11	20	18
Disposition	7	11	31

*One state did not provide information on arrests; another state did not provide information on dispositions.

Source: U.S. Comptroller General. *Development of a Nationwide Criminal Data Exchange System: Need to Determine Cost and Improve Reporting.* Washington, D.C., General Accounting Office, 1973, p. 10.

tions were not reported by criminal justice agencies to their state identification units (Table 10). Thus, users could not be certain that the system included all arrest and disposition data. Although both LEAA and FBI officials felt confident that such reporting problems could be worked out, the comptroller general disagreed:

To put a system into operation without first insuring that the information it will process is complete will result in a system that maintains and provides incomplete data to system users. . . . When decisions are being made to set bail, impose sentence, or grant parole, the offender's record should present an accurate and complete history of arrests and dispositions. . . . The failure to restrict dissemination of data on an arrest for which a disposition has not been obtained is a serious system deficiency because it permits dissemination of arrest information without showing whether a person was convicted or found innocent.[81]

In response, both LEAA and the FBI promised to take action about reporting requirements:

—LEAA, under its comprehensive data system program, will not fund data systems in States which do not require mandatory reporting when the States' systems become operational.
—The FBI is continuing to encourage prompt and complete reporting of arrest and disposition data by law enforcement agencies.[82]

Acknowledging that "arrest and disposition reporting should improve as a result of LEAA and FBI actions," the comptroller general maintained reservations:

[81] *Ibid.*, p. 11.
[82] *Ibid.*, p. 13.

The comprehensive data systems program requires only that the States insure that mandatory reporting will be accomplished by the time the States' systems become operational. States therefore can avoid or postpone mandatory reporting by not participating in the comprehensive data systems program or by delaying participation.[83]

MASSACHUSETTS FIGHTS HOOKING UP TO NCIC

In June 1973, the problem of regulations and standards concerning the NCIC/CCH program shifted from the forum of federal agencies to that of the states. In a letter to U.S. Attorney General Elliot Richardson, Governor Francis Sargent of Massachusetts advised that his state would not hook up to NCIC unless "special precautionary steps" were taken "to protect individual rights."[84] In addition, the Criminal History Systems Board, which had been established under a 1972 Massachusetts statute to regulate the use of and access to criminal justice records in the state, refused to grant criminal background information to other federal agencies operating in the state, such as the Small Business Administration and the Defense Investigative Service, an agency of the Defense Department.

The U.S. Attorney in Boston sued the state, claiming that a federal agency takes precedence over state law and should have access to the information in state files regardless of the type of information. Furthermore, the Small Business Administration threatened to withhold $30 million in loans and client aid and the Defense Investigative Service announced it would freeze hiring for 2,400 jobs in the state unless the information was provided.[85]

Governor Sargent and other state officials were not opposed to a computerized file of past criminal offenders, but they felt that the NCIC/CCH program violated constitutional rights and was vulnerable to abuse. Although the NCIC regulations maintained that the system would include only records of serious offenses, Massachusetts officials suggested that such categories often include arrest without conviction and offenses concerning homosexuality and failure to pay alimony. Governor Sargent also expressed serious doubts that "the internal controls and self-policing by line operating agencies or administration

---

[83] *Ibid.*, p. 14.

[84] Robert A. Jones. "Computer War: Massachusetts Bucks the Trend." *Los Angeles Times*, August 17, 1973.

[85] "Governor Doubts Privacy for Records Tied to NCIC." *Computerworld*, July 11, 1973.

can guarantee the integrity of something as sensitive and potentially abusive as ... national criminal information computer systems."[86]

In addition to these objections, the central issue that divided Massachusetts and the federal agencies was the availability of such information to persons or organizations outside the category of law enforcement. As Andrew Klein, a special assistant to Governor Sargent, observed: "The system is only as strong as its weakest link, and that's what scares me."[87] Not only did NCIC permit access to the information by federally insured banks and private employers with state contracts, but it also permitted a variety of secondary access. Data could be made available to credit agencies and private employers through a "friendly cop." In addition, much of the data supplied to such private individuals or agencies could be wrong or outdated. An example cited by Massachusetts officials was the case of Alan Winslow of Auburndale, Massachusetts, who wrote of a scary experience he had in the spring of 1972:

A relative of mine got a job as a deputy sheriff. One bored night, on dispatcher duty, he ran his family through the National Crime Information Center.

Ten out of eleven of us were listed.

His mother was listed because when she was 18, neighbors complained of a noisy sorority party. (No arrests.)

His stepfather, a respected businessman, was listed because he complained to the police that he had received a bad check.

Ten out of eleven of us! No criminal conduct. No criminal record. But we are in the files of NCIC.

The Massachusetts state officials noted that this was "guilt by association":

The worst part are the arrests without convictions. A man gets arrested for, say, car theft. The charges are dropped because he didn't do it, but years later the computer churns out the arrest, and people assume guilt.[88]

In August 1973, a petition was submitted to the attorney general by Governor Sargent and Senator Edward Brooke (R.-Mass.) calling the NCIC regulations "wholly unenforceable, relying on the 'good faith' efforts of individual states." In many cases, they noted, states do not follow arrest records with additional information, "thereby leaving the

[86] Jones. "Computer War."
[87] Ibid.
[88] Ibid.

file replete with arrests that did not result in conviction, or even prosecution, but which are not so designated."[89]

Results of the efforts by Governor Sargent and other state officials began to appear in September 1973. The Department of Justice dropped the suit filed against the state. Deputy Attorney General William D. Ruckelshaus, in announcing the dismissal, said:

> After careful consideration and discussion both with the concerned agencies and with Mr. Gabriel (the U.S. Attorney in Boston), we have concluded that it would be more practical, more appropriate and more effective for the affected federal agencies to seek congressional authorization for such access.[90]

In the meantime, Governor Sargent joined the American Civil Liberties Union in seeking an injunction against CCH until regulations to safeguard its operation were passed. When Attorney General Elliott Richardson promised that Massachusetts' wishes would be complied with, the suit was dropped.[91] Governor Sargent, at the same time, wrote letters to the nation's governors urging them to join him in petitioning the Justice Department and Congress to establish safeguards on the system, which contained the names of "thousands of innocent citizens."[92]

By the end of 1973, it was clearly recognized that national legislation was needed to regulate the NCIC/CCH system. In November, Project SEARCH proposed comprehensive legislation that would control the dissemination of criminal justice records by the states as well as through NCIC. In December, Clarence Kelley, the director of the FBI, said that he would welcome legislation placing controls over the operation of the NCIC/CCH system,[93] thus setting the stage for activities in 1974 aimed at evolving comprehensive national legislation in this area.

State and Local Information Policy Formulation and the Role of LEAA

The controversy over the control and regulation of the NCIC/CCH program highlighted the importance of local and state criminal justice information systems and information policy. As mentioned in Chapter 4, throughout the 1970s, LEAA funds made possible an infor-

---

[89] *Ibid.*

[90] "U.S. Drops Suit for Mass. Files." *Computerworld*, October 3, 1973.

[91] "Mass., ACLU Move to Halt FBI CCH System." *Computerworld*, August 15, 1973.

[92] "Mass. Gov. Sargent Writes Governors on NCIC Curb." *Computerworld*, October 10, 1973.

[93] "Kelley Agrees NCIC Needs Legislated Controls." *Computerworld*, December 5, 1973.

mation explosion that focused on the development of a nationally integrated network of criminal justice information systems at local, state, and federal levels of government. As local and state criminal justice agencies planned and developed new information systems, legislative interest and public concern was expressed about the implications of such systems and the social costs of criminal justice records. To a great degree, such attention was sporadic and widely varied; however, a number of new regulatory schemes and arrangements did develop, dramatizing the range of problems presented by criminal justice records and information systems in state and local governments.

Moreover, as the controversy over the NCIC/CCH program progressed, there was growing recognition that local and state initiatives were not sufficient to cope with the widespread development of local and state criminal justice information systems throughout the country. If criminal justice information was going to be available nationwide, then some form of regulation had to apply throughout the country to minimize the social costs of criminal justice records. It was in this context that, first, Project SEARCH and, then, LEAA undertook the task of establishing standards and regulations concerning criminal justice information policy and information systems.

From its inception, Project SEARCH recognized that the development of a nationally integrated network of criminal justice information systems was contingent on the provision of an adequate framework of standards and regulations that would minimize the social costs of criminal justice records. In July 1970, Project SEARCH issued *Security and Privacy Considerations in Criminal History Information Systems.*[94] The report made clear that, due to the federated nature of the developing criminal justice record system and its fundamental dependence on state and local information systems, the development of privacy and security guidelines and regulations would, of necessity, be dependent on state and local criminal justice information policy formulation. Project SEARCH was developing a model state statute and model administrative regulations that would reconcile, for purposes of uniform requirements relating to privacy and security, "the conflict and diversity of legal structures supporting the identification function in the various states." Furthermore, "federal and state administrative regulations need to be standardized so that they uniformly protect civil liberties."[95]

[94] Project SEARCH. *Security and Privacy Considerations*, p. 7.
[95] *Ibid.*, pp. 7–8.

A MODEL STATE ACT FOR CRIMINAL
OFFENDER RECORD INFORMATION

In May 1971, the Project SEARCH Committee on Security and Privacy issued *A Model State Act for Criminal Offender Record Information*.[96] While application of the model act would improve the efficiency of criminal justice information systems, its primary purpose was to provide for security and privacy. The act "is intended as a model and not as a straight-jacket; it is intended to set out general guidelines, and not to prescribe specific organizational commitments. Alterations may be needed in each state to take fully into account local needs and conditions."[97] The committee observed that the fundamental premise of Project SEARCH was to achieve a balance between the necessary dissemination of criminal information and the protection of civil liberties. The basic question that the committee identified as a constant consideration was: "Is the information collected, stored and disseminated reasonably related to advancing the general welfare, health or safety of society?" While a unified information system might have "untold economic, efficiency and spatial advantages," these were not "the primary considerations. The maintenance of a free society is more important than the argument for efficiency." Thus, "if the statute was to err, it was intentionally designed to err on the side of privacy protection." Because "the future success of any SEARCH-type system depended to a great extent upon the security and privacy protection capabilities of the various states," the committee felt that supportive federal legislation was necessary.[98]

Instead of designing a statute that detailed a specific security and privacy program, which would be applicable directly to present and proposed systems, the committee chose to define a statute that "created a broad framework of objectives and goals within which specific regulation would be formulated by a continuing committee of professionals who would audit, supervise and coordinate system operations."[99] The latter alternative was chosen, since the rigidity of the former type of statute would conflict with the "fluid and dynamic" social situation that existed, "particularly in view of the rapidly evolving technology involved."[100]

[96] Project SEARCH. *A Model State Act for Criminal Offender Record Information*. Technical Memorandum No. 3. Sacramento, California Crime Technological Research Foundation, 1971.
[97] *Ibid.*, pp. 2–3.
[98] *Ibid.*, pp. 7–8.
[99] *Ibid.*, p. 11.
[100] *Ibid.*, p. 12.

The model act was directed at all Criminal Offender Record Information (CORI) files or systems within a state. CORI consisted of

records and data compiled by criminal justice agencies for purposes of identifying criminal offenders and of maintaining as to each offender a summary of arrests, pretrial proceedings, the nature and disposition of criminal charges, sentencing, rehabilitation and release.

On the other hand, the definition of CORI included neither

intelligence, analytical and investigative reports and files, nor statistical records and reports in which individuals are not identified and from which their identities are not ascertainable.[101]

The model act proposed an administrative structure concerned with the regulation and control of CORI. First, the establishment of a Criminal Offender Records Control Committee to regulate the collection, storage, dissemination, and usage of CORI was recommended. This committee was intended as a coordinating body that would draw together criminal justice agencies engaged in the collection and usage of CORI. Membership on the committee was to be drawn from various criminal justice agencies at the local and state levels. Some states might choose a single administrator to perform the tasks of the committee, but in most states a committee would effectively accommodate the various needs and interests of criminal justice agencies.

Second, the model act provided for a Security and Privacy Council, to be appointed by the state governor, to "conduct a continuing study and review of questions of individual privacy and system security in connection with the collection, storage, dissemination and usage of criminal offender record information."[102] Intended chiefly as an advisory body, the council would represent the interests of both the criminal justice community and the general public: "Its members should be broadly representative both of the community and of the relevant interests."[103] It was hoped that such a council would create and maintain greater public confidence in criminal justice recordkeeping:

The Council is intended to be sensitive to problems that the public, or some portions of the public, may think exist in the record keeping system, to identify and examine the system's deficiencies, and to offer prompt and appropriate recommendations for the correction of those deficiencies.[104]

---

[101] *Ibid.*
[102] *Ibid.*, p. 18.
[103] *Ibid.*, p. 31.
[104] *Ibid.*

In addition to the creation of these regulatory arrangements, the act defined specific areas where action was needed. First, the Criminal Offender Records Committee would have to adopt specific regulations and ongoing supervisory programs relating to data verification, purging of CORI, system security, and research uses of CORI. Second, the act required that CORI could be disseminated, whether directly or indirectly, only to criminal justice agencies and such individuals and agencies that are or would be authorized access to such records by statute. The Criminal Offender Records Committee would issue regulations to assure that CORI be disseminated "only in situations in which it is demonstrably required by the individual or agency for purpose of its statutory responsibilities." The committee also would be responsible for determining whether each agency requesting access is authorized such access and for preparing "a finding in writing of its eligibility or noneligibility for such access."[105] Provisions for civil liability and criminal penalties were included to assure that access to CORI would be controlled. Finally, the model act provided that each individual would have the right to inspect and challenge, in case of error, the CORI located in the state that referred to him. Moreover, procedures for appeals through the criminal justice agencies, the committee, and the courts were provided to assure that the individual would be dealt with fairly. Such provisions were included to "guarantee the accuracy of criminal offender records, to prevent unnecessary injuries to individual citizens, and moreover (to) help create wider public confidence in the fairness and accuracy of the record keeping system."[106]

MODEL ADMINISTRATIVE REGULATIONS FOR CORI

The Project SEARCH model state act represented a pioneering effort to regulate and control the collection and use of criminal justice records in state and local agencies. In March 1972, the Project SEARCH Committee on Security and Privacy published *Model Administrative Regulations for Criminal Offender Record Information*,[107] which supplemented the model state act. The SEARCH committee again emphasized the limited purposes for which the regulations were prepared, observing that the regulations simply represented its members' views "as to the rules which are generally appropriate in most of the operating situa-

[105] *Ibid.*, p. 21.
[106] *Ibid.*, p. 36.
[107] Project SEARCH. *Model Administrative Regulations for Criminal Offender Record Information*. Technical Memorandum No. 4. Sacramento, California Crime Technological Research Foundation, 1972.

tions with which we are familiar. They are designed to stimulate thought with regard to a great number of difficult and important problems, and not to discourage other answers, perhaps more responsive to local problems and conditions."[108]

The general intent of the model administrative regulations was to elaborate and specify the provisions of the model state act. In doing so, the model administrative regulations refined the duties and responsibilities of the Criminal Offender Records Committee, as well as state and local criminal justice agencies regarding the regulation of CORI and related systems.

The model administrative regulations required that the Criminal Offender Records Committee conduct a program of public education concerning the purposes, proper use, and control of CORI and supervise training programs and materials for personnel handling CORI or operating criminal justice information systems. The regulations also required that all CORI be stored in a computer dedicated solely to criminal justice or, if this was not possible, in a portion of a computer under the management control of a criminal justice agency. Moreover, CORI could not include information that indicated an intelligence file on an individual existed. Specific requirements were set down for the research of CORI, aimed at minimizing or preventing any injury or embarrassment to individuals.

In addition, the model administrative regulations provided for circumstances under which CORI files could be purged or closed. The Committee on Security and Privacy acknowledged that this was "one of the most difficult and controversial problems facing criminal justice agencies today," and, in several situations, it was "convinced that careful purging programs would contribute significantly to effective programs of rehabilitation."[109] The CORI of an individual whose arrest terminated in a decision in his favor, providing he had no prior conviction record, would be expunged after 60 days and returned to him; the CORI of a person convicted of a serious offense, provided he was not rearrested, in prison, or on probation, would be closed after 10 years; and the CORI of a person convicted of a less serious crime would be closed after 5 years. In addition, a criminal justice agency would be required to notify all agencies to whom CORI was sent that the individual's file be marked closed and not reopened, barring subsequent arrest or statutes in each state requiring inquiry into CORI beyond the 5- and 10-year limitations.

[108] *Ibid.*, pp. 47–48.
[109] *Ibid.*, p. 53.

The model administrative regulations also required that criminal justice agencies maintain a listing of the agencies or individuals, both in and outside the state, to which CORI was released for at least one year. Administrative penalties, in addition to the civil and criminal penalties provided by the model state act, would be applicable to those employees and officers of public agencies who violated provisions of the act or the regulations.

To resolve the difficult problem of access, the SEARCH Security and Privacy Committee provided categories and methods of access to CORI, as well as methods of disseminating CORI by criminal justice agencies. Generally, these provisions aimed at making limited amounts of CORI available "on a carefully circumscribed right-to-know, need-to-know basis for a very limited number of persons and agencies who can establish a creditable claim that their access will serve a criminal justice purpose."[110] Generally, the provisions aimed at excluding "'interested' persons, the media, private investigations, credit bureaus, etc."[111] Tight restrictions were to be placed on dissemination at every level. In addition to restrictions on access, a sensitivity classification and clearance system for CORI and related systems was suggested.

In combination, the Project SEARCH reports on security and privacy considerations formed a remarkably comprehensive approach to the problems of reducing the social costs of criminal justice records. Because Project SEARCH defined its role in terms of research and development, however, the presentation of the model state act and model administrative regulations did not ensure that such recommendations would be adopted by state and local criminal justice agencies. Indeed, the range of local and state activity on behalf of privacy and security varied widely and reflected only partially the information policy orientation of Project SEARCH.

ACTIONS BY THE STATES

During this period, only four states—Alaska, California, Iowa, and Massachusetts—adopted, in whole or in part, the provisions of the model state act and/or model administrative regulations. Only Massachusetts adopted the regulatory and advisory committee outlined in the model state act. Generally, the other states adopted aspects of the model administrative regulations, omitting the Security and Privacy Council and/or the Criminal Offender Records Committee.

[110] *Ibid.*, p. 57.
[111] *Ibid.*

In California, for example, a state assembly bill was drafted in 1971 to create a Security and Privacy Council, appointed by the Governor, in order "to conduct a continuing study and review of questions of individual privacy and security in connection with the collection, storage, dissemination and usage of criminal offender record information."[112] The bill proposed adoption of Project SEARCH's model state act to fill the apparent gap in the handling of privacy and confidentiality concerns by the California Department of Justice. The bill was opposed by the state Department of Finance on the grounds that it was premature and was too liberal an application of the model act to the California situation. It died in committee.[113]

In 1972 and 1973, legislation was passed that specifically rejected the creation of a Criminal Offender Records Committee, choosing instead to delegate authority in these areas to the state attorney general and the state Department of Justice. The attorney general was given explicit responsibility for the security of CORI in local and county criminal justice agencies as well as within the Department of Justice. In addition to securing CORI from unauthorized disclosure, the attorney general was authorized to ensure that CORI be disseminated "only in situations in which it is demonstrably required for the performance of an agency's or officials's functions," to coordinate such activities with those of "interstate systems for the exchange of criminal offender record information," and to initiate for employees of all agencies that handle CORI "a continuing educational program" on its proper use and control. Each agency holding or receiving such records was obligated to "maintain, for such period as is found by the attorney general to be appropriate, a listing of the agencies to which it has released or communicated such information."[114]

A second bill enacted in California defined the minimal data elements that constituted a criminal offender record, stipulated that intelligence and investigative reports not be included, limited access to such records to criminal justice personnel on a need-to-know basis, and required that reporting of such information be made more uniform and efficient throughout the state.[115]

In 1973, Iowa enacted legislation that established a state-level Secu-

---

[112] Donald A. Marchand. "The Issue of Security and Privacy." In: *Proceedings of the International Symposium on Criminal Justice Information and Statistics Systems.* Edited by Project SEARCH. Sacramento, California Crime Technological Research Foundation, 1972, p. 567.

[113] *Ibid.*

[114] Marchand. *Criminal Justice Records*, pp. 146–147.

[115] *Ibid.*, pp. 140–144.

rity and Privacy Council but not a Criminal Offender Records Committee. The law gave the state department of public safety the authority and responsibility concerning the use and control of criminal offender record information in the state; limited information in computer systems to factual data, such as arrest records; required that dispositions be kept of all cases; barred police from putting any type of intelligence data into the computer; prevented police from maintaining any surveillance data; permitted an individual, or his attorney, to examine information about him retained by the state police; provided both civil damages and criminal penalties where public officials maintain illegal information about a citizen; required that the state police review the status of every new arrest every year in order to update it; and provided that computerized arrest records must be destroyed after an individual has been acquitted or the charges against him have been dismissed.[116]

Only Massachusetts voluntarily adopted and implemented most of the provisions of the SEARCH model state act and model administrative regulations. In 1972, the Massachusetts legislature approved an act creating three new regulatory or advisory groups concerned with the use and control of criminal justice information. First, it established a Criminal History Systems Board. Composed primarily of representatives from local and state criminal justice agencies, the board was responsible for providing and exercising control over the installation, operation, and maintenance of a criminal offender record information system in the state. Its mandate included creating a continuing program of data auditing and verification to assure the accuracy and completeness of CORI; assuring the prompt and complete purging of CORI required by any statute or administrative regulation or by order of a court; assuring the security of CORI from all unauthorized disclosures at all levels of operation; maintaining a continuing educational program in the proper use of CORI for all agencies handling such information; limiting dissemination of CORI only to criminal justice agencies and such other individuals and agencies as are authorized access through the board's certification program; promulgating regulations governing the use of CORI for research purposes; supervising the participation by all state and local agencies in any interstate system for the exchange of CORI; and assuring that each individual shall have a right to inspect and challenge his CORI.

Second, the act created a Criminal History System Advisory Committee. Composed largely of the same members that comprised the

---

[116] See U.S. Congress, Senate, *Criminal Justice Data Banks: 1974*, Vol. II, Appendix, pp. 858–863.

Criminal History Systems Board, the advisory committee was responsible for recommending to the board regulations concerning the use and control of CORI; ensuring maintenance of communications between the prime users; coordinating its activities with those of any interstate system for the exchange of CORI; and conducting such inquiries and investigations as deemed necessary.

Third, a Security and Privacy Council was created to oversee the security and privacy of CORI.[117] The council was composed of eight members, specifically including representatives of the general public, state and local government, and one representative of the criminal justice community. The council's specific purpose was to "conduct a continuing study and review and to make recommendations concerning the questions of individual privacy and system security in connection with the collection, storage, dissemination, and usage of criminal offender record information."[118]

Massachusetts had the most extensive regulatory arrangements to control the use of CORI in criminal justice information systems; other states, such as Connecticut, took a different approach. In May 1973, the Connecticut legislature passed a law barring employment discrimination against persons with criminal records. Observing that "the public is best protected when criminal offenders are rehabilitated and returned to society prepared to take their places as productive citizens and that the ability of returned offenders to find meaningful employment is directly related to their normal functioning in the community," the policy of the state assembly was "to encourage all employers to give favorable consideration to providing jobs to qualified individuals, including those who have criminal conviction records."[119]

To realize this intent, the statute provided that a person would not be disqualified from employment in any state agency or occupation, trade, vocation, profession, or business requiring a license, permit, certificate, or registration solely because of a prior conviction of a crime. A denial of suitability for employment or a license or permit was possible only "after considering (1) the nature of the crime and its relationship to the job for which the person has applied; (2) information pertaining to the degree of rehabilitation of the convicted person; and (3) the time elapsed since the conviction or release."[120] If a convic-

---

[117] Massachusetts Security and Privacy Council. *Annual Reports 1973–1974*. Boston, Mass., 1974, p. 1.

[118] Massachusetts General Laws, Chapter 6, Section 170. Reprinted in: U.S. Congress, Senate, *Criminal Justice Data Banks: 1974*, Vol. II, Appendix, pp. 863–869.

[119] *Ibid.*, p. 825.

[120] *Ibid.*, p. 826.

tion for a crime was used as a basis for rejection of an applicant, such a rejection had to be in writing and had to state specifically the evidence presented and the reasons for rejection. In such a case, the individual could appeal the determination through the courts. Under no circumstances were records of arrest which were not followed by a conviction or records of convictions which had been erased to be used, distributed, or disseminated by the state or any of its agencies in connection with an application for employment or for a permit, license, certificate, or registration.

In addition to legislative activity, some state-level criminal justice agencies adopted guidelines and administrative regulations concerning the use and control of information in their systems. For example, in 1970, NYSIIS adopted a code of ethics regarding the proper use and control of CORI. In 1972, NYSIIS issued regulations on privacy and security considerations for all users of the criminal justice information system in response to a "growing concern over the alleged lack of adequate provisions to protect the security of data in its custody and the privacy of the individuals to whom it relates." The regulations were adopted as part of the NYSIIS use and dissemination agreement for all users of its statewide system.[121]

In May 1974, the California attorney general began a $5.2-million program to purge certain criminal files of the California Department of Justice.[122] The purge included records of offenses not of statewide importance and minor and nonspecific offenses, such as disorderly conduct and driving without a license. The program was directed at the manual files and was expected to delete approximately 50 percent of the records retained at the state level.

ACTIONS BY LOCAL GOVERNMENTS

In addition to efforts for regulation at the state level, a number of local governments sought to control the use of criminal justice records. Their efforts ranged from the adoption of administrative regulations by police to the city of Berkeley, California's Committee on the Berkeley Police Department's Records, Access, Privacy, and Retention, and to efforts of regional information systems such as Santa Clara County's Criminal Justice Information Control and Kansas City, Missouri's ALERT II to impose various forms of self-regulation.

[121] *Ibid.*, pp. 654–661.
[122] *Ibid.*, Vol. I, Hearings, pp. 114–115; also, "State Will Destroy 2.5 Million Minor Arrest Records," *Los Angeles Times*, February 23, 1974.

During this period, a few police departments reconsidered their criminal justice record policies. Usually, such activities followed external pressure or public action. Probably one of the earliest efforts in this area was adoption by the Metropolitan Police Department of the District of Columbia of regulations for access to and dissemination of criminal records recommended by a specially appointed board, the Committee to Investigate the Effect of Police Records on Employment Opportunities in the District of Columbia.[123]

The committee was appointed in December 1966 by the president of the Board of Commissioners of the District of Columbia, who characterized the problems that persons with police records faced when seeking employment; he instructed the committee to hear all interested parties, both public and private, either orally or through written statements. Committee members represented various segments of government and private interests. The committee held nine public sessions concerning the effect of the police clearance system. In its report, conscious of

the employers' interest in obtaining full information concerning past acts of misconduct by employees or prospective employees, and responding to the competing interest of employees in the non-disclosure of data that might be unfairly prejudicial or misleading by virtue of incompleteness or incorrections or lack of relevancy,

the committee concluded that "substantial restrictions should be placed upon the availability of raw record data from police files."[124] Its recommendations, which were adopted by the Metropolitan Police Department on October 31, 1967, restrict access to juvenile records to criminal justice purposes; restrict dissemination of raw adult arrest records for law enforcement purposes only; release adult arrest records in a form that reveals only entries relating to offenses which have resulted in conviction or forfeitures of collateral; release arrest records only under a 10-year period; and permit individuals whose records are retained the right to see their records and assure their accuracy and completeness.[125]

A similar effort to safeguard individual rights relating to criminal justice records followed an action by the Berkeley, California City

[123] See "Regulations and Forms Used by the Metropolitan Police Department," in: *Criminal Justice Data Banks: 1974*, Vol. II, Appendix, pp. 836–849.

[124] "Report of the Committee to Investigate the Effect of Police Arrest Records on Employment Opportunities in the District of Columbia." In: *Criminal Justice Data Banks: 1974*. Vol. II, Appendix, p. 834.

[125] *Ibid.*, pp. 834–836.

Council. In December 1971, the council voted unanimously to impose a set of guidelines on the content and use of a new police microfilm record system.[126] The automated Miracode system, financed in part by a grant from the California Council on Criminal Justice, was intended to provide quickly an individual's criminal record to the police.

In its guidelines, the city council stipulated that only conviction records could be automated and that arrest and intelligence records would continue to be processed manually. In addition, any person with a record in the file would be permitted to examine it. The guidelines also ruled out integrating the system into other information exchange systems without prior council approval. The city council then formed the Committee on the Berkeley Police Department's Records, Access, Privacy, and Retention to oversee the policy and procedural difficulties of implementing the system. Since that time, the committee has developed policies and procedures concerning the individual's access to and right to challenge his arrest record, as well as procedures concerning data content, data verification, and the periodic auditing of records by the committee. While the functions of the committee were transferred to the Police Review Commission, the basic information policy established by the committee remained in effect.[127]

A somewhat different approach to restrictions on the use of criminal justice records was adopted by county and regional managers of criminal justice information systems. Generally, managers of such systems sought to adopt codes of ethics and other administrative regulations and guidelines to tighten control over the use of CORI by users during the process of implementing the new automated information systems. Examples of such systems that early on in their existence adopted such voluntary guidelines and self-imposed regulations for users are Santa Clara County's Criminal Justice Information Control (CJIC)[128] and Kansas City's ALERT II regional criminal justice information system.[129]

Although the voluntary approach to the regulation of criminal jus-

---

[126] "Tough Rules on Berkeley Police Files," *San Francisco Chronicle*, December 16, 1971; also, "Miracode System Approved," *Berkeley Gazette*, January 8, 1973.

[127] See "Municipal Ordinance on Privacy and Confidentiality, Berkeley, Calif.," in: *Criminal Justice Data Banks: 1974*, Vol. II, Appendix, pp. 756–760.

[128] See Marchand, *Criminal Justice Records*, pp. 136–138, 358–366.

[129] See Melvin F. Bockelman, "ALERT II: Progress Toward a Computerized Criminal Justice System," in: *Proceedings of the International Symposium on Criminal Justice Information*, pp. 126, 131–132.

tice records that prevailed during this period produced a variety of attempts at introducing new forms of information policy in criminal justice, it resulted in no new forms of regulation in *most* states and localities where criminal justice information systems were developing. Indeed, the development of criminal justice information systems generally has far outpaced the reformulation of criminal justice information policy. Except where there were outside pressures, or the perceived threat of outside pressures, to promote the reformulation of criminal justice information policies to reduce social costs, criminal justice agencies usually did not take action, largely because of the individual agency costs of such activities. As suggested in Chapter 2, providing for reduction of social costs is equivalent to providing a public good. The latter usually is costly to provide due to the incentives of individuals or agencies to act as free riders. In the absence of specific restraints or positive incentives, there is little reason for an agency to bear the costs that such regulation of its information and records entail.

Another related consideration that hindered the reduction of social costs was the problem that arose when local or state agencies attempted to exercise control over the use of their records outside of their jurisdictions. Both the city of Berkeley and the state of Massachusetts attempted to control the use of criminal offender records generated in their jurisdictions in statewide or national criminal information systems, and both, to a great degree, failed.

This was due in large part to their narrow jurisdictional boundaries. The city of Berkeley was not able to persuade the California Department of Justice to adhere to more restrictive information policies, and, similarly, the state of Massachusetts had considerable difficulty and only limited success in persuading the FBI to adopt tighter restrictions on the use of CORI derived from its NCIC/CCH program and its manual identification files. Thus, such jurisdictions depend on the existing laws and policies of other states and localities when participating in statewide or nationwide information systems. The end result is the negation of the effects of information policies aimed at reducing the social costs of criminal justice records by jurisdictions where no reformulation of policies is taking place.

LEAA recognized the limited acceptance of Project SEARCH's policies and regulations regarding CORI and jurisdictional boundaries as a significant problem in need of specific attention. Besides providing support for the Project SEARCH program, LEAA, in January 1971, sent a notice to all directors of state planning agencies to make them aware of the responsibilities regarding privacy and security in relation to funding organized crime programs in the states.[130] Also in 1971, the following special condition was added to the award which funded each state's comprehensive plan: "The grantee agrees to insure that adequate provisions have been made for system security, the protection of individual privacy and the insurance of the integrity and accuracy of data collection."[131] Similar language was subsequently incorporated into LEAA's guidelines as a general condition applicable to all grants from 1971 to date.[132]

LEAA'S COMPREHENSIVE DATA SYSTEM PROGRAM

In May 1972, LEAA took another step toward providing for security and privacy when it established the Comprehensive Data System (CDS) program. The CDS program, as noted in Chapter 4, was designed to encourage the states to establish criminal justice data-collection systems. It made funds available to the states for the establishment of criminal justice data-collection systems and outlined criteria for grant applications. Project SEARCH's recommendations were fully incorporated into the CDS guidelines, which required "the states to develop flexible systems to best address the specific need of each individual state while still having the capability of providing essential uniform data to the National Center for inter-state purposes." Furthermore, LEAA envisioned

a cooperative system for the exchange of criminal histories essentially under the joint control of state governments and the Federal government insofar as it represents federal offenders. The guidelines permit the development of intra-state systems which will be compatible with an eventual interstate system which will include extensive telecommunications and switching capability and an index which will provide only direction information to records held at the state level.[133]

Assuming that a SEARCH-type network for the interstate exchange of criminal history records eventually would be implemented, the CDS program provided for security and privacy by pointing to the Project

[130] U.S. Congress, Senate. *Criminal Justice Data Banks: 1974.* Vol. II, Appendix, pp. 195–196.

[131] *Ibid.*, p. 196.

[132] *Ibid.*, Vol. I, Hearings, p. 300.

[133] "Comprehensive Data System Guidelines for Evaluation of Grant Applications." In: *Criminal Justice Data Banks: 1974.* Vol. II, Appendix, pp. 702–703.

SEARCH reports. The guidelines noted that consideration would be given to the security and confidentiality section of the NCIC Computerized Criminal History Program policy paper as approved by the NCIC Advisory Policy Board. Moreover, the CDS guidelines noted that any application should address at least the following points:

1. Precise rules establishing the types of criminal justice agencies authorized access to the data must be defined.

2. Rules concerning the purposes for which authorized users can gain access to the data bank (e.g. applicants, arrests, investigations, etc.) must be stated, and must be in accordance with state and Federal laws.

3. Policies, procedures, and techniques for the purging, sealing, expunging of records or entries from the system and a plan specified for carrying them out.

4. A physical security plan for the facilities and the terminals on the system must be presented.

5. Adequate audit capability of system operation must be provided, including minimally, a continuous audit trail of all transactions occurring in the system.[134]

The guidelines also required that LEAA not fund the computerization of records when a state permitted the interstate transfer of those records in which the highest offenses were any of 28 stipulated "non-criteria," or minor, offenses.[135]

The CDS program was the primary means at this time through which LEAA tied the future development of local and state criminal justice information systems to a set of minimum development and security and privacy standards. As a result of the program and its requirements, a number of states developed master plans for criminal justice information systems which included manuals concerned with privacy and security. Generally, however, the results of the planning efforts in the states were incomplete. In a survey of 13 master plans reported at the 1974 Project SEARCH International Symposium on Criminal Justice Information and Statistics Systems, only 7 plans included considerations relating to privacy and security.[136]

---

[134] *Ibid.*, pp. 707–708.
[135] *Ibid.*, p. 708.
[136] Donald F. King. "Criminal Justice Information System Master Planning." In: *Proceedings of the Second International Symposium on Criminal Justice Information and Statistics Systems*. Edited by Project SEARCH. Sacramento, California Crime Technological Research Foundation, 1974, p. 106.

LEAA'S NATIONAL ADVISORY COMMITTEE ON
CRIMINAL JUSTICE STANDARDS AND GOALS

In July 1973, the LEAA-supported National Advisory Commission on Criminal Justice Standards and Goals issued a series of reports on the criminal justice system in America. In *Report on the Criminal Justice System*,[137] the commission established a number of standards relating to security and privacy and criminal justice information systems. The commission advised careful supervision of the collection and circulation of criminal justice information, noting that the "problem in establishing a criminal justice information system is to determine who should have access to the files or computer terminals, who should be eligible to receive information from these files, and under what circumstances." It thus recommended that "each State adopt legislation to establish a Security and Privacy Council which is vested with sufficient authority to adopt and administer security and privacy standards for criminal justice information systems."[138] Furthermore, the commission suggested that 50 percent of each council's members should be private citizens.

Although the standards adopted by the commission for data collection, classification, maintenance, and retention, as well as system security, largely reflected and were modeled after the reports of Project SEARCH, the commission's position regarding data dissemination was more definite. It recognized that criminal justice files contained information that was perceived as useful by a "wide range of agencies outside the criminal justice system, for background investigations of potential employees of public agencies and private firms, for determining eligibility for occupational licenses, for credit evaluation, and for general public information supplied by news media," but it also was aware that "potential damage to privacy is increased when the information in criminal justice files is inaccurate, incomplete, misleading and unnecessarily disseminated to persons outside the criminal justice system."[139] Thus, it recommended establishment of strict security and privacy procedures to ensure that information in criminal justice files would be made available only to public agencies that have both a need and a right to know: "The user agency should demon-

---

[137] National Advisory Commission on Criminal Justice Standards and Goals. *Report on the Criminal Justice System*. Washington, D.C., U.S. Government Printing Office, 1973, p. 123.

[138] *Ibid.*

[139] *Ibid.*, pp. 39–40.

strate, in advance, that access to such information will serve a criminal justice purpose."[140]

The standards and goals of the commission regarding privacy and security were reflective of the initial Project SEARCH formulations; however, they stated more definitely the serious concern about reducing the social costs of criminal justice records as an integral element of the criminal justice information system development philosophy: "A strong case is presented that security and privacy cannot be 'tacked on' a system, but must be integrated into the design as a function of the management philosophy."[141]

After their publication, the recommendations of the commission were attached as a basic set of minimum standards of the CDS program together with the Project SEARCH reports. The CDS program represented, then, a major thrust of LEAA in the area of privacy and security during this period. By 1971, LEAA estimated that it had spent more than $300 million on the development of state and local criminal justice information systems.[142] In March 1974, LEAA's Deputy Administrator for Policy Development, Richard Velde, reported that 33 states had indicated a desire to participate in the program by submitting CDS plans, and that 24 plans had been accepted and were being implemented. Velde did not want to "leave the impression that all of these States now have secure information systems which protect the rights of individuals,"[143] since many were merely in the early stages of planning; nevertheless, he did suggest that the CDS program was LEAA's principal means of encouraging the development of state and local criminal justice information policy, which was consistent with its role. This role has been defined in terms of two primary functions: "to serve as a catalyst and to provide financial assistance."[144] More specifically, LEAA sought to provide the coordination necessary to develop a decentralized, but uniform, network of criminal justice information systems and to provide, through research and development as well as a condition of its funding, the minimum standards and policies necessary for reducing the social costs of criminal justice records.

[140] *Ibid.*, p. 123.

[141] *Ibid.*, p. 36.

[142] Richard Velde. "Progress in Criminal Justice Information Systems." In: *Proceedings of the Second International Symposium on Criminal Justice Information*, p. 9.

[143] "Prepared Statement of Richard W. Velde, Deputy Administrator for Policy Development, Law Enforcement Assistance Administration." In: *Criminal Justice Data Banks: 1974.* Vol. I, Hearings, p. 301.

[144] Velde. "Progress in Criminal Justice Information Systems," p. 11.

CONCLUSION

During 1973 and 1974, LEAA efforts to coordinate the development of state and local criminal justice information systems and information policy were overshadowed by the growing controversy over the NCIC/CCH program. Indeed, the two problems were merged into a single concern over the control and regulation of criminal justice information and information systems at the local, state, and federal levels of government, due in large measure to the growing federal presence in the field by the administration of LEAA funds to local and state agencies for information system development and by the control of the interstate exchange system for criminal history records by the FBI. At this time, the focus of policy concern shifted primarily from the states and the Department of Justice to the Congress, as congressional subcommittees proposed comprehensive national legislation to regulate the use of criminal justice information in automated record-keeping systems. The issue concerning the reduction of the social costs of criminal justice records had emerged. What results, if any, that the next steps in the policy process would bring remained to be seen.

7
Regulating the Social Costs
of Criminal Justice Records—
the Politics of Legislative
Initiatives and Nonaction

Bills on thousands of issues are introduced in Congress each session. As suggested in the preceding chapter, each issue is tied to a particular process of emergence which, in turn, will have a good or bad influence on how it will be treated on various community and governmental agendas. The bulk of the legislation that is introduced in Congress each year is not new but carried over from previous sessions for a renewed effort. Any new legislative initiative must compete for the limited attention of congressmen and staff with many other problems and concerns. Not all issues will be "successful." In Chapter 3, it was observed that, although many issues may achieve community agenda status both at the national level and in the states, they fare poorly on various governmental agendas. Why this happens depends in most instances on how the issue emerged and whether it could be developed to counteract containment or opposition efforts as well as to "fit" into the changing priorities and perceptions of public officials at specific points in time.

In this chapter, the legislative history of reducing the social costs of criminal justice records during 1974 and 1975 will be examined, and how this issue achieved congressional agenda status, what key legislative proposals were initiated, and how these proposals were treated and survived will be reviewed.

THE PROMISE OF 1974

The year 1974 promised to be a good year for privacy as a political issue. In January, somewhat ironically amid the almost daily revelations of the Watergate affair, President Nixon listed among the first 10 goals for his administration and Congress that year "an historic beginning in the task of defining and protecting the right of personal privacy for every American."[1] Although he did not specifically mention the growing controversy in the area of criminal justice information systems and the use of criminal justice records, nevertheless, the recognition and specific attention given to the issue of privacy by the president set the tone for upcoming activities in this area.

Many members of Congress believed that the burgeoning technological developments in criminal justice information systems, coupled with the debate over appropriate forms of information policy to minimize the social costs of criminal justice records, demanded more concentrated legislative oversight. Congressional action was especially necessary, since most state and federal legislators were not as yet aware of the relevant issues.[2]

Congressman Don Edwards (D.-Calif.), as chairman of the Subcommittee on Civil and Constitutional Rights of the House Committee on the Judiciary, held exploratory hearings on this subject in 1972 and 1973 and made a number of legislative proposals, which, however, were severely criticized by the Department of Justice.[3] It appeared that little progress would be made without the help and cooperation of the Department of Justice and the criminal justice community. More intensive legislative activity in this area by the Edwards subcommittee, however, was interrupted by its full-time investigation of presidential impeachment.

In early 1974, a task force of Justice Department officials, appointed by then Attorney General Elliot Richardson, released a draft bill that was the first significant comprehensive legislation prepared by the Department of Justice. The bill, S. 2964, was subsequently introduced in the Senate by Senators Roman Hruska (R.-Nebr.) and Sam J. Ervin (D.-N.C.), the ranking Republican member and chairman, respectively, of the Subcommittee on Constitutional Rights. At

---

[1] President Richard M. Nixon. "State of the Union Address." January 30, 1974. *Weekly Compilation of Presidential Documents, 10*(5):115, February 4, 1974.

[2] Mark H. Gitenstein and Clarence D. Kelley. "The Right to Privacy Is American . . . But So Is the Right to Law and Order." *Trial Magazine, 11*:26, January–February 1975.

[3] See U.S. Congress, House, Committee on the Judiciary, Subcommittee No. 4, *Security and Privacy of Criminal Arrest Records*, Hearings, 92d Congress, 2d Session, 1972; also, U.S. Congress, Committee on the Judiciary, Subcommittee on Civil and Constitutional Rights, *Dissemination of Criminal Justice Information*, Hearings, 93d Congress, 1st and 2d Sessions, 1973–1974.

the same time, Senator Ervin introduced a bill on his own, S. 2963, and scheduled hearings for both bills for early March 1974.

Introducing, on behalf of the Department of Justice, S. 2964, the Criminal Justice Information Systems Act of 1974,[4] Senator Hruska observed that, although Senator Ervin's bill took a "somewhat different approach to several aspects of the subject than the Justice Department bill, their fundamental objectives, thrust, and other provisions parallel each other."[5] Moreover, both bills reflected much of the work of Project SEARCH, the National Advisory Commission on Criminal Justice Standards and Goals, and the confidentiality and security policies of the NCIC/CCH program.

Senator Ervin indicated that S. 2963, the Criminal Justice Information Control and Protection of Privacy Act of 1974,[6] was "intended to provide a basis for discussion and hearings. It does not pretend to be a final statement on the subject."[7] Senator Ervin outlined the legislation's most significant features:

The bill is quite detailed and attempts a resolution of all the major privacy and security issues which have arisen in the development of law enforcement data banks. It endeavors to balance the legitimate needs of law enforcement with the requirements of individual liberty and privacy. It would for the first time give firm statutory authority for criminal justice data banks, a major obstacle in the development of such systems. It would impose upon the data banks strict but manageable privacy limitations. Not the least important, the bill also attempts to solve fundamentally important questions of Federal-State relationships in these comprehensive national information systems.[8]

Both proposals were aimed at regulating the use and exchange of criminal justice information and the development of criminal justice information systems; nevertheless, they incorporated fundamentally different approaches to the relevant problem areas.

Criminal Justice Information Systems Act of 1974 (S. 2964, February 5, 1974)

Legislation proposed by the Criminal Justice Information Systems Act of 1974 (Department of Justice [DOJ]) defined three different types of

[4] U.S. Congress, Senate, Committee on the Judiciary, Subcommittee on Constitutional Rights. *Criminal Justice Data Banks: 1974.* Vol. I, Hearings. 93d Congress, 2d Session, 1974, pp. 632–652.

[5] *Ibid.,* p. 629.

[6] *Ibid.,* pp. 590–626.

[7] *Ibid.,* p. 587.

[8] *Ibid.*

criminal justice information: criminal offender record information (CORI), criminal intelligence information, and criminal offender processing information (see Table 11). Defining a criminal justice information system broadly, the DOJ act applied to any criminal justice information system operated by either the Federal Government or a state or local government where funding was provided in whole or in part by the Federal Government. The act also applied to any interstate system and any system operated by a state or local government that was engaged in the exchange of criminal justice information with any federally funded system. Although the DOJ act did not affect lists or systems used by criminal justice agencies for the sole purpose of identifying or apprehending fugitives or wanted persons, it did apply to any criminal justice information obtained from a foreign government or an international agency.

The provisions of the act applied to any criminal justice information system subject to the act and to any agency or person who, directly or indirectly, obtained criminal justice information from such a system. Direct access was limited to authorized officers or employees of a criminal justice agency. As a rule, criminal intelligence information, criminal offender processing information, and CORI could be used

TABLE 11   Criminal Justice Information Systems Act of 1974 (S. 2964, the DOJ Act): Definitions of Criminal Justice Information

---

1. *Criminal Offender Record Information*

Means information contained in a criminal justice information system, compiled by a criminal justice agency for the purpose of identifying individual criminal offenders and alleged offenders and consisting only of identifying data and notations of arrests, the nature and disposition of criminal charges, sentencing, confinement, release, and parole and probation status.

2. *Criminal Intelligence Information*

Means information compiled by a criminal justice agency for the purpose of criminal investigation, including reports of informants and investigators, contained in a criminal justice information system and associated with an identifiable individual. The term does not include criminal offender record information.

3. *Criminal Offender Processing Information*

Includes all reports identifiable to an individual compiled at any stage of the criminal justice process from arrest or indictment through release from supervision. This term does not include criminal intelligence information.

Source: U.S. Congress, Senate, Committee on the Judiciary, Subcommittee on Constitutional Rights. *Criminal Justice Data Banks: 1974.* Vol. I, Hearings. 93d Congress, 2d Session, 1974, pp. 634–635.

only for criminal justice purposes and in accordance with regulations issued by the U.S. attorney general; however, certain exceptions were listed that could be permitted under the supervision of the attorney general. In a particular case or class of cases, criminal intelligence information could be used for reasons of national defense or foreign policy or could be made available to a noncriminal justice component of a federal, state, or local government agency if the information was necessary for the performance of the statutory function of the noncriminal justice component. Under limited conditions, CORI could be made available to the affected individual, to qualified persons for research, or for a purpose not related to criminal justice, if such use was expressly authorized by a court order, a federal statute, executive order, or state statute. In any case where access was permitted to criminal justice information, the agency operating the system had to maintain a log of requests from any other agency or person for that information and the source of the CORI. Such logs had to include information

(1) regarding any request for use for a criminal justice purpose, the identity of the requester, the nature of the information provided and pertinent dates, and

(2) regarding any request for use for a non-criminal-justice purpose, the identity of the requester, the nature, purpose, and disposition of the request, and pertinent dates.[9]

The DOJ act also stipulated that any individual would be entitled to review the CORI about himself contained in any criminal justice information system and to obtain a copy of the information for the purpose of challenge or correction. Each federal or state agency operating a criminal justice information system had to implement regulations to permit such review. Whenever CORI was requested for a noncriminal justice purpose (except in cases of national defense, foreign policy, and with regard to a judge or civil officer whose appointment was subject to confirmation by the Senate), the criminal justice agency had to require that the requester notify the individual that CORI concerning him had been requested and that he had a right to review his record for the purpose of challenge or correction. Moreover, no individual who obtained a copy of his CORI could be required or requested to show or transfer that copy to any person or agency. In any case where an individual disputed the accuracy or completeness of CORI, he could apply for review to the responsible agency, which was required

[9]*Ibid.*, p. 640.

to assess the disputed information and correct and revise the entry accordingly. If the individual was dissatisfied with the decision of the responsible agency, he was to be afforded administrative and judicial review.

Any agency contributing CORI to a criminal justice information system had to ensure that the information it contributed was accurate, complete, and "regularly and accurately revised to include dispositional and other subsequent information."[10] More specifically, no information relating to an arrest could be disseminated without the inclusion of the final disposition of the charges. CORI relating to the arrest of an individual could not be disseminated or used for a noncriminal justice purpose if the individual was acquitted of the charge for which he was arrested, the charge was dismissed, a determination to abandon prosecution of the charge was made by the prosecuting attorney, or an interval of one year had elapsed from the date of arrest with no final disposition and no active prosecution of the charge.

Regarding the retention of CORI, the DOJ act provided that CORI be sealed in accordance with requirements of a court order, a federal or state statute, or regulations issued by the attorney general. At a minimum, such regulations had to provide for the sealing of CORI about an individual who had been free from the jurisdiction or supervision of any criminal justice agency for:

(1) a period of seven years if the individual has previously been convicted of an offense for which imprisonment in excess of one year is permitted under the laws of the jurisdiction where the conviction occurred,

(2) for a period of five years if the individual has previously been convicted of an offense for which the maximum penalty is not greater than imprisonment for one year under the laws of the jurisdiction where the conviction occurred, or

(3) for a period of five years following an arrest if no convictions of the individual occurred during that period, no prosecution is pending at the end of that period, and the individual is not a fugitive.[11]

Moreover, access to sealed records could be permitted only for review by the individual, by court order, or by specific determination of the attorney general.

The security of the contents in each criminal justice information system had to be assured by management control of a criminal justice agency. All criminal justice information systems were subject to the

[10] *Ibid.*, p. 642.
[11] *Ibid.*, p. 645.

security standards promulgated by the attorney general, who also was to provide for "continuous review and periodic audits of the operations of criminal justice information systems" to assure compliance with the standards issued.[12]

Operating procedures of all criminal justice information systems were required to be consistent with the regulations of the attorney general and, at a minimum, to include a program of verification and audit to ensure that CORI is regularly and accurately updated, limit access and dissemination of criminal justice information, provide an administrative review mechanism for challenges by individuals to the accuracy or completeness of their records, undertake an affirmative action program for the training of system personnel, and require a complete and accurate record of access and use made of any information in the systems. Furthermore, each agency operating a criminal justice information system had to publish notice at least once a year of its existence, the nature of the system, record policies, procedures for individual review, and the person immediately responsible for the system.

To enforce such regulations, administrative sanctions could be exercised by the attorney general. Civil and criminal penalties were provided for the unauthorized use, maintenance, or dissemination of criminal justice information included under the act, but good faith reliance on the provisions of the act, applicable law, or regulations and procedures approved by the attorney general constituted a complete defense to a criminal or civil action brought under the act.

Criminal Justice Information Control and Protection of Privacy Act (S. 2963, February 5, 1974)

The Criminal Justice Information Control and Protection of Privacy Act (the Ervin bill) affected a number of different types of criminal justice information. When compared to the DOJ act, the Ervin bill more specifically defined the various types of records used in criminal justice administration, especially in the category of what the DOJ bill had referred to as criminal offender processing information (see Table 12). Also, the Ervin bill was aimed at the regulation of *all* criminal justice data banks operated by federal, state, or local governments.

The Ervin bill reiterated that criminal justice information could only be collected by or disseminated to officers and employees of crim-

---

[12] *Ibid.*, p. 647.

TABLE 12   Criminal Justice Information Control and Protection of Privacy Act of 1974 (S. 2963, the Ervin Bill): Definitions of Criminal Justice Information

1. *Criminal Justice Information*

Means information on individuals collected or disseminated, as a result of arrest, detention, or the initiation of criminal proceeding by criminal justice agencies, including arrest record information, correctional and release information, criminal history record information, conviction record information, identification record information, and wanted persons record information. The term shall not include statistical or analytical records or reports, in which individuals are not identified and from which their identities are not ascertainable. The term shall not include criminal justice intelligence information.

a. *Arrest Record Information*

Means information concerning the arrest, detention, or commencement of criminal proceedings on an individual which does not include the disposition of the charge arising out of that arrest, detention, or proceeding.

b. *Correctional and Release Information*

Means information on an individual compiled by a criminal justice or non-criminal justice agency in connection with bail, pretrial or posttrial release proceedings, reports on the mental condition of an alleged offender, reports on presentence investigations, reports on inmates in correctional institutions or participants in rehabilitation programs, and probation and parole reports.

c. *Criminal History Record Information*

Means information disclosing both that an individual has been arrested or detained or that criminal proceedings have been commenced against an individual and that there has been a disposition of the criminal charge arising from that arrest, detention, or commencement of proceedings. Criminal history record information shall disclose whether such disposition has been disturbed, amended, supplemented, reduced, or appealed by further proceedings, appeal, collateral attack, or otherwise.

d. *Conviction Record Information*

Means information disclosing that a person has pleaded guilty or *nolo contendere* to or was convicted on any criminal offense in a court of justice, sentencing information, and whether such plea or judgement has been modified.

e. *Identification Record Information*

Means fingerprint classifications, voice prints, photographs, and other physical descriptive data concerning an individual which does not include any indication or suggestion that the individual has at any time been suspected of or charged with criminal activity.

f. *Wanted Persons Record Information*

Means identification record information on an individual against whom there is an outstanding arrest warrant including the charge for which the warrant was issued and information relevant to the individual's danger to the community and such other information that would facilitate the regaining of the custody of the individual.

TABLE 12   (Continued)

2. *Criminal Justice Intelligence Information*

Means information on an individual on matters pertaining to the administration of criminal justice, other than criminal justice information, which is indexed under an individual's name or which is retrievable by reference to identifiable individuals by name or otherwise. This term shall not include information on criminal justice agency personnel, or information on lawyers, victims, witnesses, or jurors collected in connection with a case in which they were involved.

Source: U.S. Congress, Senate. *Criminal Justice Data Banks: 1974*. Vol. I, Hearings, pp. 592–596.

inal justice agencies. Conviction record information could be made available for purposes other than the administration of criminal justice only if expressly authorized by state or federal statute. Criminal justice information could be made available to qualified persons for research under regulations to preserve the anonymity of the individuals to whom such information related. Except in specific cases, a criminal justice agency could disseminate to another criminal justice agency only conviction record information. A criminal justice agency could disseminate correctional and release information to another criminal justice agency or to the affected individual or his attorney where federal or state law applied.

The act clearly stated that identification records and information on wanted persons could be disseminated to criminal justice and non-criminal justice agencies only for the purpose of apprehending the subject. The Ervin bill prohibited secondary use of criminal justice information to public agencies and individuals, except by rehabilitation officials and the courts. With the consent of the individual, rehabilitation officials could orally represent the individual's criminal history record to prospective employers if such representation was helpful in obtaining employment for the individual. A court could disclose such information in a published opinion or public criminal proceeding.

An automated criminal justice information system could disseminate criminal justice information only if the inquiry was based on positive identification of the individual by means of identification record information. Only with a class access warrant obtained from a judge could a criminal justice agency make inquiries about individuals on any other basis. Similarly, access to criminal justice information that was sealed would require a class access warrant.

The Ervin bill required that each criminal justice information system adopt procedures reasonably designed to accomplish security, accuracy, updating, and purging. In particular, the bill required minimum standards for sealing or purging criminal justice information. Beyond the seven- and five-year provisions of the DOJ bill, the Ervin bill required "the prompt sealing or purging of criminal history record information in any case in which the police have elected not to refer the case to the prosecutor or in which the prosecutor has elected not to commence criminal proceedings."[13]

For purposes of inspection and challenge, the Ervin bill provided that the individual or his attorney be allowed to receive a copy of the information. Each criminal justice agency and information system was required to adopt and publish specific and detailed regulations for individual record access, review, and challenge. Although, as a rule, an individual who obtains criminal justice information regarding himself could not be required or requested to show or transfer records of that information to any other person or any other public or private agency or organization, conviction record information could be disseminated to noncriminal justice agencies if expressly authorized by state or federal law.

Under the Ervin bill, criminal justice intelligence information could not be maintained in criminal justice information systems or retained in other automated systems.

The most innovative aspect of the Ervin bill was the administrative structure it proposed for the control of criminal justice information systems and information policy formulation. In contrast to the approach of the DOJ bill, which delegated to the attorney general the responsibility for promulgating regulations and standards under the act and for continuous supervision of its implementation, the Ervin bill created a Federal Information Systems Board, which was to be responsible for the administration and enforcement of the act. The board was to be composed of nine members:

One of the members shall be the Attorney General and two of the members shall be designated by the President as representatives of other agencies outside the Department of Justice. The six remaining members shall be appointed by the President with the advice and consent of the Senate. Of the six members appointed by the President, three shall be either directors of statewide criminal justice information systems or members of the Federal Information Systems Advisory Committee at the time of their appointment. The three remaining Presidential appointees shall be private citizens well versed in the law of privacy, constitutional law, and information systems technology.[14]

[13] *Ibid.*, p. 607.
[14] *Ibid.*, p. 612.

The board was given authority to issue regulations as required by the act; review and disapprove regulations issued by a state agency or other criminal justice agency according to the act; exercise its powers, as set out under specific provisions of the act; bring actions for declaratory and injunctive relief according to the act; "operate an information system for the exchange of criminal justice information among the States and the Federal Government"; "supervise the installation and operation of any criminal justice information system or criminal justice intelligence information system operated by the Federal Government"; "conduct an ongoing study of the policies of various agencies of the Federal Government in the operation of information systems"; "require any department or agency of the Federal Government or any criminal justice agency to submit to the Board such information and reports with respect to its policy and operation of information systems or with respect to its collection and dissemination of criminal justice information or criminal justice intelligence information"; and conduct audits as provided by the act. In addition, the board would be required to issue an annual report to Congress and to the president which, at minimum, would contain the results of audits conducted by the board; a summary of public notices filed by criminal justice information systems, criminal justice intelligence information systems, and criminal justice agencies; and "any recommendations the Board might have for new legislation on the operation or control of information systems or the collection and control of criminal justice information or criminal justice intelligence information."[15]

The Ervin bill also required the creation of a Federal Information Systems Advisory Committee which would advise the board on its activities. The committee would be composed of one representative from each state, who would be appointed by the state's governor and serve at the pleasure of the governor.

Finally, the bill required that, beginning two years after its enactment, no criminal justice agency could collect or disseminate criminal justice information to a criminal justice agency which had not adopted all of the operating procedures required by the act and which was located in a state that had failed to create a State Information Systems Board. This board would be an administrative body separate and apart from existing criminal justice agencies and having statewide authority and responsibility for:

1. The enforcement of the provisions of this Act and any State statute which serves the same goals;

[15] *Ibid.*, pp. 613–614.

2. The issuance of regulations, not inconsistent with this Act, regulating the exchange of criminal justice information and criminal justice intelligence systems and the operation of criminal justice information systems; and

3. The supervision of the installation of criminal justice information systems and criminal justice intelligence information systems, the exchange of information by such systems within that State and with similar systems and criminal justice agencies in other States and the Federal Government.[16]

Upon the submission of the two bills in Congress, Senate hearings were scheduled. On March 1, 1974, just prior to the hearings, the U.S. Comptroller General issued a brief report entitled *Development of the Computerized Criminal History Information System.*[17] In an introductory letter to the report, the comptroller general indicated to Senator Ervin that

the principal question which has resulted from our work to date, and which your Subcommittee might wish to pursue in its upcoming hearings, appears to be: What should the national policy be regarding developments in computerized criminal history information systems, and to what extent should the various segments of the criminal justice community and appropriate Federal agencies participate in such policy developments?[18]

Hearings of the Senate Subcommittee on Constitutional Rights

On March 5, 1974, Senator Ervin commenced six days of hearings on the two bills. In his opening remarks, the senator outlined five problem areas that legislation and the hearings should address. The first general issue concerned the quality and accuracy of information that should be allowed to circulate in criminal justice data systems, regardless of whether those systems are computerized. The second problem area concerned what type of information should be made available from police files for agencies and organizations not related to law enforcement, especially commercial establishments. The third problem concerned the types of civil remedies that should be available to a citizen to enforce the dissemination rules set forth in federal legislation and regulations. The fourth problem centered on the collection and dissemination of intelligence or investigative files. The fifth concern was cited by Senator Ervin as probably the most consequen-

[16] *Ibid.*, pp. 617–618.

[17] Elmer B. Staats, U.S. Comptroller General. *Development of the Computerized Criminal History Information System.* Washington, D.C., U.S. General Accounting Office, 1974.

[18] Elmer B. Staats, U.S. Comptroller General. Letter to Sam J. Ervin, Jr., Senator, U.S. Congress, March 1, 1974. In: *Criminal Justice Data Banks: 1974.* Vol. II, Appendix, p. 986.

tial—who should control and operate the manual and automated data systems covered by this legislation?

Shall the law enforcement agencies themselves or an outside independent board make policy? On the Federal level, should policy and regulations issued under this legislation be the exclusive responsibility of the FBI or the Attorney General or should the States have an equal voice?[19]

Although the testimony before the subcommittee indicated general agreement on the need for legislation to regulate the uses of criminal justice records and the development of information systems, from the outset, attention was focused on the debate within the Department of Justice concerning control of the interstate criminal history exchange system. The debate also included any new message-switching and communications system to supplement or replace the National Law Enforcement Telecommunications System, a state-controlled teletype system developed in the mid-1960s to transmit messages between law enforcement agencies nationwide. In his opening remarks to the Senate Subcommittee on Constitutional Rights, Attorney General William Saxbe observed that "in offering this legislation, and in appearing here, I want to state that there is a division of opinion within the Justice Department."[20]

Following Saxbe's testimony, Clarence Kelley, the director of the FBI, confirmed the attorney general's warning about internal division in the Department of Justice. The FBI director reiterated the view that "the overall necessities of law enforcement require that there be one agency with responsibility for management control of the central data bank."[21] Moreover, the CCH concept could not "realize success unless decisions (were) made which provide the FBI with all the management authority necessary to implement the decisions of the NCIC Advisory Policy Board."[22] Kelley also wanted management authority for the FBI with regard to the funding of state efforts and the necessary communication capabilities essential to the reliability and accountability of the CCH program. He characterized the pointer system or index for interstate offenders recommended by SEARCH as uneconomical, stating a preference for the single-state/multistate concept advocated by NCIC.

Concerning the centralizing effect of the DOJ bill, which focused the responsibility over local, state, and federal criminal justice information

[19] U.S. Congress, Senate. *Criminal Justice Data Banks: 1974.* Vol. I, Hearings, p. 7.

[20] *Ibid.,* p. 152.

[21] *Ibid.,* p. 211.

[22] *Ibid.,* p. 212.

systems in the attorney general, Kelley noted that there was nothing particularly ominous about this approach since, in his view, the NCIC Advisory Policy Board was "basically a State organization." The board was composed of 26 members, six of whom were appointed representatives from the fields of prosecution, courts, and corrections. The remaining 20 were law enforcement members elected, according to region, by the users of the NCIC system.

In contrast to the position of the FBI, Deputy Administrator for Policy Development of LEAA Richard Velde recommended that, while the three-tiered board and advisory committee proposed in the Ervin bill could be workable,

> based on five years of experience with Project SEARCH, . . . a group of State representatives designated by the Governors of the several States would be an appropriate and effective vehicle to regulate interstate systems. The group should be created by Federal law and given a federal charter so as to be able to promulgate and enforce meaningful regulations and controls over systems within their jurisdiction. Project SEARCH has fully demonstrated that State representatives can manage complex technical and policy issues and systems of this kind.
>
> With respect to intrastate systems, this should be a matter of State legislative policy, consistent with minimum standards set forth in the federal legislation, as is the case in the regulation and control of electronic surveillance. The SEARCH model bill provision for a State control board, which is contained in S. 2963 and has been adopted in Massachusetts might be an appropriate solution. However, we would not object to the recently passed California law which places regulatory powers in the State Attorney General. But this is a matter best left up to the states.[23]

The position of LEAA was reflective of the overall position of the Project SEARCH group, which generally was against the approach to regulation taken in the DOJ bill and favored providing the states with maximum freedom, consistent with some minimum standards for interstate systems, to determine the scope and nature of their own arrangements for regulating information policy and information systems development. This position was reiterated with regard to the proposed development by the FBI of new message-switching and communications facilities to supplement or replace the National Law Enforcement Telecommunications System (NLETS).[24] In response to this possible action, the executive director of NLETS, C. J. Beddome, noted that NLETS, which was operated by a consortium of states, would resist efforts by the FBI to take over operation of the system.

[23] *Ibid.*, pp. 304–305.
[24] *Ibid.*, p. 318.

The Ervin bill provided yet another approach to the regulation of criminal justice records and information systems. The administrative arrangement that it proposed was perceived by Executive Director Richard C. Wertz and Legislative Committee Chairman Lee M. Thomas of the National Conference of State Criminal Justice Planning Administrators as a compromise between the centralized authority proposed in the DOJ act and the more decentralized authority and voluntary approach promoted by Project SEARCH and LEAA:

Notwithstanding the expenditures of federal money on criminal justice data systems, the majority of actual operation and maintenance will be at the state and local level. Therefore, we feel that the majority of control necessarily placed on those computer systems must likewise remain at the state and local level. Indirect guidance and broad guideline development would, of course, rest with the federal government due in part to the utilization of federal funds for systems development and in part to the interface necessary between federal, state and local information services.

We feel that specific statutory control as well as administrative rules and regulations must be developed by state legislatures and the agencies charged with the operation, maintenance, and control of individual criminal justice information systems. However, we do not feel that states can formulate these rules and regulations governing computer data banks and criminal justice information systems without some guidance from the Federal Government.[25]

Thus, Wertz and Thomas supported the Ervin bill because it attempted to "reach a median ground between federal control and guidance while maintaining the rights of the states to govern themselves," unlike the DOJ bill which removed "too much control from the states and vests not only detailed statutory control but also administrative control in federal government."[26] For these reasons, the Ervin bill was seen as "a step in the right direction," which would be improved by permitting more state and local representatives on the Federal Information Systems Board.

As the Senate hearings came to a close, two key problems needed to be resolved if a bill was going to be passed in 1974. First, although it was conceivable that the approach of the Ervin bill could be reconciled with the differing views of Project SEARCH and LEAA concerning who should control the systems and participate in regulatory decisions, it was clear that progress was limited if the FBI continued to persist in its views. Second, there remained the issue of limiting access to criminal

[25] Ibid., p. 328.
[26] Ibid.

justice records by noncriminal justice government agencies and by private organizations and individuals.

Another Judicial Challenge to the FBI: Menard v. Saxbe

In April 1974, the FBI's position on the handling of criminal justice records was adversely affected by the case of *Menard v. Saxbe.*[27] In *Menard v. Mitchell* in 1971, the plaintiff had been denied expungement of his record from FBI files, but the FBI's ability to distribute his record had been limited. In 1974, the U.S. Court of Appeals for the District of Columbia decided that a cognizable legal injury had occurred and that the courts had the power to expunge arrest and criminal records of local law enforcement agencies. The court found that the *Menard* suit against the FBI was proper insofar as it attacked abuses unique to the FBI's recordkeeping role and that the FBI had no authority to retain the individual's arrest warrant once it was informed by the California police that the police encounter was not deemed an arrest but only a detention. Finally, the court held that the FBI was statutorily precluded from maintaining in its criminal files as an arrest record an encounter with the police that had been established not to constitute an arrest. The FBI was not prohibited, however, from maintaining separate and neutral identification records.

Nine years after his arrest, Dale Menard's records finally had been expunged from the FBI's criminal files. In deciding in Menard's favor, the Court of Appeals noted how the FBI, after numerous appeals by the defendant's mother, had conducted a special review of the case. The review came only after the complaint had been filed in the appeals court and represented merely a change in notation on Menard's record from "Released—Unable to connect with any felony or misdemeanor at this time" to "Released—Unable to connect with any felony or misdemeanor—in accordance with 849b(1)—not deemed an arrest but detention only."

In reviewing the operations of the FBI's Identification Division, the court indicated that the arrestee had been released without being charged. The court noted a firm policy of the FBI that "The FBI does not have authority to decide which fingerprints submitted by law enforcement agencies should be returned. Such a decision rests solely with the original contributor of fingerprints."[28] When the FBI makes the arrest, it removes the arrest cards from its files "on a court order

[27] 498 F.2d 1017 (D.C. Cir. 1974).
[28] *Ibid.*, p. 1022.

only." The FBI had never returned a fingerprint record on its own motion before this case: "Moreover, the Bureau will not amend, alter, or even reveal a record at the instance of a private individual, . . . taking the position not only that the decision to expunge must be made at the local level, but also that disclosure to an individual of the contents of his record will not be permitted." The court concluded that "under its practices, the FBI is not concerned about an inaccuracy, beyond suggesting that the individual contact the local agency."[29]

Turning to the propriety of the action against the FBI, the court decided that while Menard could not point "with mathematical certainty to the exact consequences of his criminal file," he had suffered a "cognizable legal injury." The court suggested that "the disabilities flowing from a record of arrest (had) been well documented: There is an undoubted 'social stigma' involved in an arrest record."[30] Not only would such an individual receive harsher treatment at the hands of criminal justice agencies, he also would be subjected to numerous forms of discrimination outside the criminal justice area due to his record. For these reasons, a court could, through the order of expungement, "vindicate substantial rights" of the individual.

Although the court observed that it could not grant specific relief to Menard for records held by local and state authorities, insofar as Menard's action attacked abuses of the FBI's Identification Division in its unique role in the nationwide information network, the suit against the bureau was proper. Concurring with District Judge Gesell that the recordkeeping practices of the FBI's Identification Division were out of effective control, the appeals court focused on the responsibilities of the FBI in maintaining this information service:

The FBI cannot take the position that it is a mere passive recipient of records received from others, when it in fact energizes those records by maintaining a system of criminal files and disseminating the criminal records widely, acting in effect as a step-up transformer that puts into the system a capacity for both good and harm . . . although the record before us does not contain data concerning the computerization of the FBI's records, it does reveal that a computerization program is proceeding apace, increasing the Division's effectiveness, and enhancing its capacity for both good and harm.

Thus, the court concluded that

having been informed that Menard's encounter with the Los Angeles police authorities was purely fortuitous, the FBI had no authority to retain this record

[29] *Ibid.*
[30] *Ibid.*, p. 1023.

in its criminal files along with the mass of arrest records. This is simply not consistent with the FBI's duty, corollary to its function of keeping identification records, to take appropriate measures to assure this function is discharged responsi(bly) and that the records are reliably informative.[31]

In such cases, when the FBI is apprised that a person has been exonerated after initial arrest, has been released without charge, or has his record changed to "detention only," the court observed that the FBI had the responsibility to expunge the incident from its criminal identification files. Moreover, the FBI could not turn aside its responsibility by claiming that it was powerless to act without a specific and formal request from the local police for withdrawal of the record: "Dependence on other agencies may be sound enough for a practice born of expedience, but it may not be made rigid like a rule of law, in neglect or defiance of basic rights."[32] The FBI, then, was responsible for maintaining an appropriate separation of the various files it was authorized to establish and for preventing the criminal identification files from containing inappropriate material. "Absent clear expression of legislative intent," the court emphasized that it could not conclude that "Congress intended the individual to be threatened by inclusion in the central criminal files, which are kept to facilitate indexing and future reference."[33]

In *Menard v. Saxbe*, it was suggested for the first time that the FBI was civilly liable for information in its files and that state and local agencies were not solely responsible for dispositions. The decision served to undermine the basic premise of the FBI's approach to the management of its Identification Division as well as its CCH program: that the local and state agencies were solely responsible for the accuracy, completeness, and purging of records. In effect, *Menard v. Saxbe* pointed out that the voluntarist approach of the FBI was not merely inefficient but, more importantly, served to increase the social costs of criminal justice records.

The Comptroller General's Assessment of Criminal Record Use

The FBI approach to the management of criminal justice records and the control of the CCH program was questioned further in August 1974 when the U.S. Comptroller General issued a report entitled *How Criminal Justice Agencies Use Criminal History Information*. The comp-

---

[31] *Ibid.*, pp. 1026, 1027–1028.
[32] *Ibid.*, p. 1028.
[33] *Ibid.*, p. 1030.

troller general had been requested by the Senate Subcommittee on Constitutional Rights to determine:

–the extent to which criminal history information was used by Federal, State, and local criminal justice agencies for pre versus postarrest purposes; and
–the extent to which the three components of the criminal justice system, law enforcement, judicial, and corrections agencies, used the information.[34]

The comptroller general's report was based on a survey of requests for criminal history information made to the FBI and to appropriate state agencies in California, Florida, and Massachusetts during a one-week period. These three states were "selected because they were considered by criminal justice officials to be more advanced than many states in the collection and dissemination of criminal history information."[35] The report was divided into two principal sections: The first discussed how state and local criminal justice agencies used criminal history information, the second focused on federal criminal justice agency use of such information.

State and local agencies primarily used criminal history information after a person was arrested. The most frequent recipients of criminal history information, state and local law enforcement agencies, indicated that this information was not used by them when it was received, but that it was placed in the arrested person's file and could be used for prearrest purposes in subsequent investigations.

State and local judicial agencies (prosecutors, courts, probation, and parole) were the major recipients of criminal history information requested by nonfingerprint means. The comptroller general noted that, since requests by this means were less routine than fingerprint card requests, it was "probably more indicative of how criminal justice agencies use the information when they need to know an individual's background."[36] Use of information for judicial purposes was almost three times the use for law enforcement purposes. The information often was requested to secure data upon which to base an opinion regarding the individual's character or risk to society.

Prosecutors wanted complete background data on individuals to help prepare cases. Courts wanted complete background data on which to base decisions regarding bail, probation, or sentencing. Probation officers needed information upon which to base opinions regarding the subjects' character or risk to

[34] Elmer B. Staats, U.S. Comptroller General. *How Criminal Justice Agencies Use Criminal History Information.* Washington, D.C., U.S. General Accounting Office, 1974, p. i.
[35] *Ibid.,* p. 46.
[36] *Ibid.,* p. ii.

society. In some cases these opinions regarded how the probation officer would handle a person placed on probation by the court; in other cases the opinions were transmitted to the courts in the form of preprobation or presentencing reports.[37]

CCH information obtained by computer requests was almost exclusively for law enforcement functions, primarily because most other types of requesting agencies did not have access to CCH terminals. "For example, in California, the 240,000 online criminal history records were directly accessible primarily through terminals located at police departments throughout the State. However, these agencies may have subsequently provided the information to judicial and corrections agencies."[38] Since CCH accounted for only 773, or 1.3 percent, of the 58,465 requests made by state and local agencies in the three states during the one-week period, the comptroller general suggested that it was "too early in CCH's development to be able to draw any definitive conclusions about the uses made of the CCH system."[39]

The comptroller general's survey indicated that law enforcement agencies were the most frequent recipients of criminal history information; however, if the way the information was requested and used was considered, the survey revealed that judicial agencies were the primary users. Accordingly, the report concluded that state and local judicial agencies should play a significant role in determining regulations for the use of CCH information. Although federal criminal justice agencies were more likely to request criminal history information for prearrest purposes, criminal history information previously was used for postarrest purposes by state and local agencies. Often the data was used to help form opinions regarding the individual's character or risk to society:

For example, law enforcement agencies may use the data in postarrest follow-up investigations to prepare more complete cases for the prosecutors. Correctional institutions used the data to help determine the best type of correctional programs and the type of security that is necessary for the person.[40]

Federal postarrest use was significant but it was lower than state and local postarrest use. Federal nonfingerprint requests for judicial purposes, which were less frequent than nonfederal judicial requests, revealed that, of the judicial segment's use of information: 4 percent

[37] *Ibid.*, p. 17.
[38] *Ibid.*
[39] *Ibid.*, p. 18.
[40] *Ibid.*, p. 37.

was used for prosecution of a suspect, 5.6 percent for recommending or setting bail, 21.7 percent for presentencing report preparation, and 5.6 percent for probation and parole supervision decisions.[41]

Generally, however, federal law enforcement agencies proportionally received and used criminal history information more frequently than did state and local law enforcement agencies. There was correspondingly less proportional receipt and use of the data by federal judicial agencies than state and local judicial agencies. With regard to federal representation on any policy board, the comptroller general concluded that, "whereas State and local criminal justice agency representation on any board governing the policy and use of criminal history information should be fairly representative of both law enforcement and judicial agencies, it seems that Federal representation on such a board should be more weighted towards law enforcement agencies."[42]

The report suggested that the historic control by law enforcement agencies over the policies and procedures affecting the use of criminal justice information and information systems needed to be altered substantially to conform to the patterns of use. It proposed that state and local representation be divided between law enforcement and judicial agencies, implying that, since state and local uses of information comprised the bulk of requests to interstate systems, state and local representatives should have substantial control in the determination of information policy and systems control along with federal representatives.

The position of the FBI that the use of criminal records was predominantly for law enforcement purposes and, therefore, that the regulation and control of any CCH program should reflect the priorities of law enforcement was questioned. State and local criminal justice agencies, who made the bulk of requests for information, should have a say in the determination of information policy and control of any interstate information system. The comptroller general's report was practical support for an interstate criminal history exchange system that would serve the criminal justice community as a whole, not simply the law enforcement segment. Regulation of such a system should have substantial state and local representation. In effect, the report supported both the Ervin bill and the contentions of LEAA and Project SEARCH against the DOJ act and the FBI's claim for law enforcement control over the NCIC/CCH program.

---

[41] *Ibid.*
[42] *Ibid.*, p. 41.

Legislative Action in 1974 Ends in Ambiguity

Although criticism increased concerning the use of criminal justice records and the proposed CCH program, the problem of control of the evolving interstate communication system focused in the fall of 1974 on Attorney General Saxbe's approval of an FBI request to add message-switching capability to the NCIC/CCH program.[43] The authorization empowered the FBI to establish a system that would switch any state request for a computerized criminal record from the NCIC/CCH index to the state where the particular record was kept. Every state request would go through the FBI.

Generally, the request for a message-switching capability for the NCIC/CCH program ignored the fact that the states already had the capability of accessing each other's records through the state-run and state-controlled NLETS without FBI involvement. The NCIC Computerized Criminal History program had the participation of only four states; several states had joined and dropped out. Many states never joined because they believed that they neither needed nor wanted the FBI system with its implications of federal control over state and local matters.

In addition, the attorney general's approval of the FBI request met with immediate criticism from the White House and Congress. On October 11, 1974, John Eger, acting director of the White House Office of Telecommunications Policy, submitted a letter to the attorney general criticizing the move. Eger warned that the decision to permit the FBI, rather than the state-operated, state-controlled NLETS system, to control message switching could allow the FBI to "monitor communications between local law enforcement agencies, causing an undesirable shift in the delicate balance between federal and non-federal law enforcement." It could "result in the absorption of state and local criminal data systems into a potentially abusive centralized, federally controlled communications and computer information system."[44]

At the same time, Douglas Metz, acting director of the Domestic Council Committee on the Right of Privacy (a policy group formed by President Nixon), also criticized the move in a letter to the attorney general and urged the Justice Department to "prepare a privacy safeguard plan prior to any decision affecting the data processing or communications component of the NCIC."[45]

[43] "NCIC/CCH Message Switching Approved." *Computerworld*, October 30, 1974.
[44] *Ibid.*
[45] *Ibid.*

On November 13, 1974, Senators Ervin and Hruska, in a joint letter to the attorney general, asked the Justice Department to delay action on the communications plan until privacy legislation that would control the use of criminal information records and systems transmitting such data was enacted by Congress.[46] Project SEARCH endorsed the Ervin bill, calling it "in the best interest of the criminal justice community," and released a resolution affirming that "confusion and inconsistency in the implementation and operation of criminal justice information systems will continue unless the Congress has adopted nationwide standards."[47] The SEARCH endorsement included 11 relatively minor amendments to the bill which subsequently were incorporated by Senator Ervin.

On December 18, 1974, Senator Ervin submitted the final version of his bill to Congress. Noting that the subcommittee had struggled for the past 10 months with balancing the basic interests, Ervin expressed his regret that an agreement had not been reached on a bill prior to his retirement, even though the recent drafts had received favorable responses from "some media and law enforcement groups, Senator Hruska, and the Department of Justice."[48]

The legislation did not pass in 1974; however, the events during the year did focus attention on the key options and problems to be considered in any future deliberations concerning the bills. Furthermore, activities in 1974 clarified the strength and nature of the divergent positions and interests concerned with criminal justice information policy and the development of criminal justice information systems.

THE EVAPORATION OF SUPPORT
FOR LEGISLATION IN 1975

The year 1975 did not begin on an auspicious note. Senator Sam Ervin, the premier advocate in the Congress of the right to privacy and the need for control of personal data in government computer systems, had retired. On February 3, 1975, Senator James O. Eastland (D.-Miss.), the chairman of the Senate Judiciary Committee, appointed Senator John Tunney (D.-Calif.) to be chairman of the Subcommittee on Constitutional Rights. Senator Tunney, who lacked

---

[46] "FBI Message-Switching Draws More Fire." *Computerworld*, November 13, 1974.

[47] "Ervin Criminal Records Privacy Bill Gains Support." *Computerworld*, November 13, 1974.

[48] Sam J. Ervin, Jr., Senator, U.S. Congress. "Statements on Introduced Bills and Joint Resolutions." *Congressional Record, 120*(Part 30): 40735, December 18, 1974.

seniority, was appointed largely because of a 1970 law forbidding members of any major Senate committee to head more than one of its subcommittees and because the five other senators that were eligible declined the position. He pledged to carry on the initiative of the Ervin subcommittee, including the problem of creating an acceptable policy in the area of criminal justice records, and, in the spring of 1975, scheduled hearings on the final Ervin compromise bill as well as the two earlier proposals.

Prior to the hearings, several events occurred both in the Department of Justice and publicly that would ultimately frustrate the progress of legislation in Congress. These events evolved from the FBI's attempt to gain acceptance for a proposal to expand the message-switching capacities of NCIC.

The Controversy Over Message Switching

Prior to 1975, a controversy had been developing between the states, LEAA, and the FBI over the question of upgrading the message-switching capabilities of the National Law Enforcement Telecommunications System (NLETS) and NCIC. The basic concern of the states, including the NLETS organization, was that the FBI, through its development of NCIC, wanted eventually to control all message-switching activities between criminal justice agencies in the United States. Such a move threatened the state-based operations of NLETS and heightened the fears of civil libertarians and others who felt that, with a centralized message-switching capability, the FBI would be able to unduly influence law enforcement activities at the state and local levels. The FBI, on the other hand, perceived such a move as a natural and logical extension of its NCIC recordkeeping and dissemination responsibilities that did not portend the development of a national police force.

SOME BACKGROUND ON NLETS

The National Law Enforcement Telecommunications System was developed in the mid-1960s to transmit emergency and administrative messages between law enforcement agencies in the United States. Since the 1920s and 1930s, police agencies had subscribed to teletype systems so they could communicate quickly with one another. In 1966, the Arizona Highway Patrol was selected to be the home of the automated switching center. LETS, as it was called then, consisted of eight circuits providing interstate communication via telephone lines to all

48 states. Each state had at least one entry point into the network, usually the state's highway patrol, state police, or justice department headquarters.

From its inception, LETS was never conceived as containing its own internal data base. Its sole purpose was to act as a relay station to facilitate communication between the states. Five types of messages were normally transmitted over LETS: names of persons of concern to criminal justice agencies, descriptions of stolen vehicles and property, vehicle and driver's license data, road and weather conditions, and administrative messages.[49]

In December 1973, LETS changed its name to recognize its nationwide coverage and services, becoming NLETS. Since its inception, NLETS has been developed, operated, and governed by the states as a nonprofit organization under the laws of Delaware. Representatives from all 48 member states and the District of Columbia were included in its governing officers, board, and committee structure. All members were charged a monthly user fee to support the organization and to pay for services rendered.

In the early 1970s, NLETS began experiencing severe backlogs in the transmittal of messages between agencies. In busier agencies, backlogs of six and one-half hours to transmit messages were not uncommon. By May 1973, the board of directors decided to upgrade the system by increasing the number of communications lines from the original 8 to 50 and by increasing the speed of the lines. Because the states could not afford to pay for the upgrade, federal LEAA monies were requested. On June 6, 1973, a contract for the upgrade was approved by LEAA for approximately $1.1 million.[50]

MESSAGE SWITCHING AT NCIC

In contrast to NLETS, the NCIC system contains its own data files, which permit inquiry/response exchanges of information in the system through NCIC terminals in FBI field offices and 87 state and local law enforcement agencies. The director of the FBI is responsible for the operation of the NCIC system.

On July 11, 1973, FBI Director Clarence Kelley had requested that

[49] Jet Propulsion Laboratory, California Institute of Technology. "Preliminary National Law Enforcement Telecommunications Requirements." In: *Criminal Justice Data Banks: 1974*. Vol. II, Appendix, p. 730.

[50] See "Application to the Law Enforcement Assistance Administration for Grant Discretionary Funds," in: *Criminal Justice Data Banks: 1974*, Vol. II, Appendix, pp. 676–691.

the attorney general permit the FBI to expand the communications capability of the NCIC system to cover *both* limited message switching for searching/responding to NCIC files and general administrative message switching similar to what NLETS had been performing:

> The communications links to NCIC are dedicated lines between NCIC control terminals at state and metropolitan levels and the NCIC computer at FBI Headquarters. The links now permit access only to NCIC files. The network configuration at this time does not provide the capability of servicing cross traffic needs of the user agencies. However, long range planning by the NCIC Working Groups and the NCIC Advisory Policy Board since early in the development of NCIC included the development of this cross traffic capability (message switching). This capability is a requirement for implementation of the "single-state, multi-state" concept of exchanging criminal history records in the Computerized Criminal Program outlined in the Background, Concept, and Policy document of the NCIC Advisory Policy Board as well as other planning.[51]

The proposal by the FBI to expand NCIC in this way raised immediate questions concerning its authority to do so. The FBI's position on the matter was that its statutory authority for NCIC included "the authority for providing the necessary expanded communications support for NCIC and other official interstate criminal justice communications requirements."[52] Neither LEAA, NLETS, nor the Office of the Attorney General considered the FBI's position acceptable. On August 6, 1973, the Office of Legal Counsel in the Department of Justice had sent a memorandum to the attorney general on whether the FBI had authority to expand its NCIC operation to include general as well as limited message switching. In an ambiguous opinion, the Office of Legal Counsel concluded that, due to the controversy over LEAA and the FBI on this matter, it was preferable for the attorney general to make a policy determination on the matter *before* the legal question of statutory authority was resolved.[53]

Taking note of the advice of the legal counsel, the director of the FBI

[51] Clarence M. Kelley, Director, Federal Bureau of Investigation, U.S. Department of Justice. Memorandum to Elliot L. Richardson, Attorney General. Subject: "Message Switching, National Crime Information Center." July 11, 1973. In: *Criminal Justice Data Banks: 1974.* Vol. II, Appendix, pp. 694–695.

[52] *Ibid.,* p. 695.

[53] Robert G. Dixon, Jr., Assistant Attorney General, Office of Legal Counsel. Memorandum to Elliot L. Richardson, Attorney General. Subject: "Whether the FBI has statutory authority to expand its National Crime Information Center (NCIC) to include message switching." August 6, 1973. In: *Criminal Justice Data Banks: 1974.* Vol. II, Appendix, pp. 695–697.

petitioned the attorney general on September 5, 1973 for approval of his original request, observing that:

> The FBI is prepared to proceed with implementing of plans for providing message switching on the NCIC network. We have the necessary facilities to handle the initial traffic volume and can provide the service ultimately required at a minimal cost when compared with a separate independent message-switching network. In view of the pressing need for the service by the law enforcement community, your early decision on the questions presented in my memorandum of July 11, 1973, would be appreciated.[54]

No response was made by the Office of the Attorney General at that time. Clearly, the FBI request raised significant issues regarding NLETS and LEAA funding that went beyond the technical issue of upgrading NCIC. On January 15, 1974, the FBI director again petitioned for permission to proceed with general and limited message switching at NCIC, arguing that the FBI did have statutory authority and that the NLETS upgrade contract awarded by LEAA was not for a permanent expansion of NLETS but for an interim upgrade pending completion of a comprehensive study of the matter by the Jet Propulsion Laboratory of the California Institute of Technology under contract to LEAA.[55]

Disturbed by the FBI's position, Donald Santarelli, the administrator of LEAA, forwarded to the attorney general on February 1, 1974 a point-by-point refutation of the FBI position, suggesting that federal control of general message switching would be contrary to the principles of the New Federalism, inconsistent at this time, and contrary to the principle of state and local government self-sufficiency and to the evident capabilities of state and local government in the criminal justice telecommunications field. Santarelli concluded that the FBI request should be denied.[56]

---

[54] Clarence M. Kelley, Director, Federal Bureau of Investigation, U.S. Department of Justice. Memorandum to Elliot L. Richardson, Attorney General. Subject: "Message Switching, National Crime Information Center." September 5, 1973. In: *Criminal Justice Data Banks: 1974*. Vol. II, Appendix, p. 697.

[55] Clarence M. Kelley, Director, Federal Bureau of Investigation, U.S. Department of Justice. Memorandum to William B. Saxbe, Attorney General. Subject: "National Crime Information Center (NCIC) Communications—Administrative Message Handling and Switching." January 15, 1974. In: *Criminal Justice Data Banks: 1974*. Vol. II, Appendix, pp. 698–700.

[56] Donald E. Santarelli, Administrator, Law Enforcement Assistance Administration, U.S. Department of Justice. Memorandum to William B. Saxbe, Attorney General. Subject: "FBI Memorandum re NCIC Expansion." February 1, 1974. In: *Criminal Justice Data Banks: 1974*. Vol. II, Appendix, pp. 700–701.

On March 4, 1974, Clay T. Whitehead, director of the White House Office of Telecommunications Policy (OTP), sent a letter to Attorney General Saxbe expressing his doubts about the FBI's role in message switching.[57] On March 7, 1974, John Eger, deputy director of OTP, issued a statement questioning the FBI's position and supporting NLETS:

But now we come to National LETS, clearly a system servicing all the States simultaneously. Should the reasons which guided our earlier policies be replaced? Should we now adopt a new and different policy which justifies a Federally controlled, national network? Should we do it because the Federal Government could operate it more efficiently and economically?

The answer is no and the explanation, stripped of all the rhetoric, is quite simple. The National LETS experiment has worked precisely because, I believe, it has been a volunteer, cooperative State-to-State, user-to-user system based on the mutual respect of members of a non-Federal law enforcement community. The decision to participate is made by each State or locality and should remain that way since the primary purpose of the system is to benefit you. The Federal Government should not flirt with the temptation to control such a service by offering it as an adjunct to its own systems—and here I am talking about a proposal by the FBI to incorporate the functions of NLETS into its National Crime Information Center. On the one hand, we must face the fact that Federal crimes are committed in this country, that crime is not restricted by State or geographical boundaries. Unquestionably, therefore, the FBI has a valid role in law enforcement telecommunications planning. But how is this role to be defined, particularly with regard to national networks and information systems that cut across State and local boundaries? And what of the individual's right to privacy? Such an amalgamation of local, State and interstate communications networks has broad implications in the area of national telecommunications policy.... It seems to me that since the States are responsible and legislatively authorized for collecting and storing sensitive criminal information, they should also have the ultimate control over its dissemination, and therefore, its effect on the citizens who gave them this authority.[58]

Despite these serious uncertainties and criticisms, the FBI, in April 1974, prepared its third request to the attorney general for approval of message switching.[59] In the fall of 1974, Attorney General Saxbe

[57] Clay T. Whitehead, Office of Telecommunications Policy, Executive Office of the President. Letter to William B. Saxbe, Attorney General. March 4, 1974. In: *Criminal Justice Data Banks: 1974.* Vol. II, Appendix, p. 708.

[58] John Eger, Deputy Director, Office of Telecommunications Policy, Executive Office of the President. "Statement." May 7, 1974. In: *Criminal Justice Data Banks: 1974.* Vol. II, Appendix, pp. 710–711.

[59] Clarence M. Kelley, Director, Federal Bureau of Investigation, U.S. Department of

approved the FBI request to add message switching to NCIC; however, by November 1974, public as well as internal government criticism of Saxbe's decision built up to the point that, as mentioned earlier, both Senators Ervin and Hruska requested a delay in this approval of message switching until privacy legislation was enacted. Thus, by the end of 1974, the fate of both the message-switching and the criminal justice records proposals were integrally tied together.

THE MESSAGE-SWITCHING CONTROVERSY IN 1975

The dispute between LEAA and the FBI erupted into an open conflict by January 1975. During 1974, both agencies had generated significant adverse publicity concerning their differences over message switching and the future of the CCH program. On January 27, 1975, at the urging of the Office of the Attorney General, the director of the FBI and the LEAA administrator met at Quantico, Virginia to settle their dispute. In a summary memorandum drafted by Deputy Attorney General Lawrence Silberman for the participants, several decisions or positions were reported to have been reached, aimed at reconciling a whole range of differences between LEAA and the FBI on criminal justice information systems issues:

1. A nationwide computerized criminal history ("CCH") program is highly desirable...The majority of LEAA Comprehensive Data Systems ("CDS") funds have been invested in CCH development. Nevertheless, the FBI questions whether sufficient emphasis has been placed on CCH development by LEAA. Upon receipt of the evaluation of CDS to be completed shortly, the Department will review the LEAA program to promote the development of state and local CCH capabilities.

2. ...LEAA and the FBI should work together to assure that state automated identification projects be compatible with the FBI's automated identification systems, and LEAA should plan its funding of state systems to further such capability.

3. A CCH system should be decentralized to the extent possible, utilizing a "pointer" or "index" system relying on a master index and a decentralized data base rather than a central repository; only federal or federal and multi-state records would be maintained centrally. Such a system is consistent with fundamental principles of federalism...and operational efficiency.

4. A CCH index system should include the capability for limited message switching, which would permit inquiries to the index to be switched to the

---

Justice. Memorandum to William B. Saxbe, Attorney General. Subject: "National Crime Information Center (NCIC) Communications—Administrative Message Handling and Switching." April 30, 1974.

appropriate data base and information transmitted to the inquirer in a single process.

5. The Department agrees that to implement a CCH system . . . it would be appropriate for the FBI to engage in limited message switching to (1) respond fully to NCIC and CCH inquiries and (2) route messages to State and local law enforcement agencies from Federal agencies whenever the message can be routed most effectively using either the NCIC–NLETS access circuit or existing circuits between NCIC–NLETS point of entry facilities at the state level.

6. The Department remains committed to the continued viability of NLETS. The Department will not impinge upon the NLETS state to state telecommunications role.[60]

Despite these compromise positions, the conflict between LEAA and the FBI over message switching continued. As a follow-up to the meeting, however, the FBI director did send a limited message-switching proposal to Attorney General Edward Levi.[61] In April 1975, the Justice Department released the message-switching proposal for public comment.[62]

The responses to the proposal were immediate and overwhelmingly negative. LEAA administrator Richard Velde suggested that the basic question concerning why NCIC should perform message switching was still unanswered and that it was inappropriate to foreclose options currently available to Congress when basic management, telecommunications, and privacy issues were still unresolved.[63]

The Associate Director for Economics and Government of the OMB, Walter Scott, argued that the implementation plan was premature. Like Velde, he observed that many important policy issues were not yet resolved, and, therefore, he could not endorse or otherwise approve of the plan at that time.[64] Similarly, John Eger, acting director of OTP, suggested that fundamental issues must be addressed before

[60] Lawrence H. Silberman, Deputy Attorney General. Memorandum to Clarence M. Kelley, Director, Federal Bureau of Investigation, U.S. Department of Justice; Glen E. Pommerening, Assistant Attorney General for Administration; and Richard W. Velde, Administrator, Law Enforcement Assistance Administration, U.S. Department of Justice. Subject: "NCIC Limited Message Switching Conference—January 27, 1975." n.d.

[61] "NCIC Switching System Bid Put on Levi's Desk." *Computerworld*, February 19, 1975.

[62] U.S. Department of Justice, Federal Bureau of Investigation, National Crime Information Center. *Proposed Limited Message Switching Implementation Plan.* Washington, D.C., 1975.

[63] Richard W. Velde, Administrator, Law Enforcement Assistance Administration, U.S. Department of Justice. Memorandum to Harold R. Tyler, Jr., Deputy Attorney General. Subject: "Proposed NCIC Plan for 'Limited' Message Switching." May 12, 1975.

[64] Walter D. Scott, Associate Director for Economics and Government, Office of Management and Budget, Executive Office of the President. Letter to Harold R. Tyler, Jr., Deputy Attorney General. May 14, 1975.

any plan for a nationwide CCH system could be prepared. Eger feared that the plan could result in the absorption of state and local criminal data systems into a potentially abusive, centralized, federally controlled system. In addition, there were no safeguards prepared for assuring the accuracy of multistate offender records. Eger recommended a comprehensive inquiry involving the attorney general's office, OMB, the Domestic Council on the Right to Privacy, and the White House OTP to evaluate the worth of CCH versus the costs, the available alternatives, the identification and implementation of privacy safeguards, and the proper federal role in criminal justice telecommunications.[65]

Critical responses also were made by Senator Tunney and Congressman Edwards, who sent letters to the Office of the Attorney General attacking the grounds for the issuance of any proposal. Congressman Edwards questioned at the outset "the cavalier assumption that the only obstacle to the proposed operation of this administrative message switching capability is the development of a technically feasible plan."[66] Edwards observed that the controversy was not about technical feasibility but about fundamental policy issues and concerns, such as:

(1) Does the FBI have legislative authority to expand its National Crime Information Center to include message switching?

(2) Would Federal control over message switching be contrary to the principle of state and local government self-sufficiency in the criminal justice telecommunications field?

(3) Would Federal control over message switching be inconsistent with security and privacy considerations at this time?[67]

He also suggested that the Department of Justice had not yet resolved these issues to the satisfaction of Congress and that a dialogue should be initiated between Congress and the executive branch concerning the overall role of the Federal Government in this area.

The arbitrary action of the Department of Justice of avoiding the issues that have been presented over the past two years and going directly to an implementation plan before soliciting Congressional comment is indicative of the potential abuse that we fear from a federally controlled telecommunications system in the area of law enforcement. Centralizing control over the powerful

[65] John Eger, Acting Director, Office of Telecommunications Policy, Executive Office of the President. Letter to Harold R. Tyler, Jr., Deputy Attorney General. May 12, 1975.

[66] Don Edwards, Chairman, Subcommittee on Civil and Constitutional Rights, House, U.S. Congress. Letter to Edward H. Levi, Attorney General. May 12, 1975, p. 1.

[67] *Ibid.*, p. 2.

law enforcement communications system in the hands of the FBI is of questionable propriety.[68]

Senator Tunney questioned the FBI's lead role in this area and suggested that the dissemination of the plan violated the attorney general's agreement with Senator Ervin to refrain from such actions until the subcommittee carefully reviewed the implications.[69] Senator Tunney's letter, however, was received only after the department had sent the plan out for review and therefore could not prevent its dissemination. In a reply to the senator, Deputy Attorney General Harold Tyler, Jr. assured him that "the proposal is not, as you suggest, designed to facilitate the FBI's takeover of the National Law Enforcement Telecommunications System's message-switching capability."[70]

The response of the FBI to the diverse and heated criticism of its message-switching proposal was both defensive and combative. On May 22, 1975, the FBI director forwarded a memorandum to the attorney general complaining that LEAA has challenged the "agreements" at the Quantico, Virginia conference by criticizing the FBI proposal in its memorandum of May 12, 1975 to Deputy Attorney General Tyler.[71] In addition, the FBI prepared point-by-point responses to LEAA and to Edwards' letter of May 12, 1975 on the plan.[72] The FBI obviously considered that most of the policy concerns were resolved at the Quantico conference and that the technical issues were now in the forefront. As for privacy and security concerns, the bureau considered these to have been confronted and resolved "and perhaps all that is needed is an explanation of this to Congress." With regard to the other policy issues, the FBI position was that Mr. Edwards' comments indicated "that he is simply unaware of the great amount of work that has gone on before the issuance of the Plan. Certainly this is not an arbitrary action on the Department's part, but one which is based on a good deal of study and decision making."[73]

[68] *Ibid.*, p. 4.

[69] John V. Tunney, Chairman, Subcommittee on Constitutional Rights, Committee on the Judiciary, Senate, U.S. Congress. Letter to Edward H. Levi, Attorney General. April 14, 1975.

[70] Harold R. Tyler, Jr., Deputy Attorney General. Letter to John V. Tunney, Senator, U.S. Congress. May 14, 1975.

[71] Clarence M. Kelley, Director, Federal Bureau of Investigation, U.S. Department of Justice. Memorandum to Edward H. Levi, Attorney General. Subject: "Proposed NCIC Plan for Limited Message Switching." May 22, 1975.

[72] See U.S. Department of Justice, Federal Bureau of Investigation, "Response to the Letter of Richard W. Velde, Administrator, Law Enforcement Assistance Administration," n.d., and "Response to the Letter of Congressman Don Edwards, Chairman, Subcommittee on Civil and Constitutional Rights, Committee on the Judiciary," n.d.

[73] U.S. Department of Justice. "Response to the Letter of Congressman Don Edwards," pp. 4–5.

By June 1975, it appeared that the Quantico conference consensus between LEAA and the FBI no longer existed. Although on June 12, 1975, the NLETS Board of Directors and the NCIC Advisory Policy Board issued a joint resolution accepting the existence of NLETS and limited message switching for NCIC, and on July 9, 1975, the NLETS board approved limited message switching for NCIC, the public critique of the FBI's plan continued unabated. On June 11, 1975, Congressman John Moss (D.-Calif.) wrote to the president noting that earlier letters to the attorney general concerning the message-switching controversy were answered unsatisfactorily and that he desired the president's concern in resolving the problem of the FBI's message-switching proposal.[74] The White House did not take any immediate action, and it was clear that by June 1975 the controversy over message switching had increased in intensity in the Department of Justice and between the Congress and the executive branch.

Congressional Hearings and "The Final Stages" of Action

In July 1975, both the Tunney and Edwards subcommittees prepared to hold hearings on the compromise Ervin bill, a revision of the DOJ proposal, and a new compromise bill submitted by Senator Tunney.[75] Senator Tunney opened the hearings of the Subcommittee on Constitutional Rights on July 15, 1975 on a hopeful note:

With these hearings we enter the final stages of this subcommittee's exhaustive consideration of the legislative proposals to regulate the flow of criminal justice information and to protect the privacy and other constitutional rights of individuals upon which such information is collected.[76]

Despite the fact that the subcommittee desired to end the four years of legislative and staff debate over an acceptable measure and put the final polish on a workable bill, the witnesses called before the subcommittee were not in agreement on the compromise measures.

Paul Wormeli, vice-president of Public Systems, Inc. and former national director of Project SEARCH, reiterated his and Project SEARCH's support for the compromise measure as the basis for establishing statutory authority in the field and reducing state and local government confusion and uncertainty, as well as judicial decisions

---

[74] John E. Moss, Representative, U.S. Congress. Letter to President Gerald R. Ford. June 11, 1975.

[75] This "new" bill was designated S. 2008 and H.R. 8227.

[76] U.S. Congress, Senate, Committee on the Judiciary, Subcommittee on Constitutional Rights. *Criminal Justice Information and Protection of Privacy Act of 1975.* Hearings. 94th Congress, 1st Session, July 15–16, 1975, p. 1.

that would be overly restrictive and costly. His view was counter-balanced, however, by testimony indicating resistance to any legislation of this kind given by Rocky Pomerance, the police chief of Miami and the president of the International Association of Chiefs of Police.[77] In addition, both the attorney general of Massachusetts and the executive director of the ACLU called for stronger and tighter regulations than were included in the compromise proposals.[78] Deputy Attorney General Tyler expressed serious methodological, technical, and policy differences with significant aspects of the subcommittee bill, continuing to support the original DOJ proposal, reintroduced in 1975, in amended version, against the more restrictive Tunney compromise measure and the Ervin subcommittee proposal of December 1974.

Traditionally, law enforcement in the United States has been a matter of State and local concern, with Federal law enforcement jurisdiction carefully circumscribed. At the same time, Federal, State and local law enforcement agencies continue to cooperate with each other on matters of common concern and routinely exchange information of mutual interest. The advent of the computer has increased the capability for this exchange of information reinforcing the interdependence of law enforcement agencies throughout the country. Recognizing this, both bills extend not only to federal agencies but also to State and local agencies which operate with federal funds, exchange information interstate, or exchange information with federal agencies.

S. 1428 also recognizes the primacy of State and local government in the criminal justice area by avoiding the imposition of strict federal controls on the operations of criminal justice agencies. S. 2008, on the other hand, establishes a federal commission to oversee administration and enforcement of the provisions of the bill with power to issue binding federal regulations, interpretations and procedures. While the bill encourages creation of State agencies to perform these functions within a State, those agencies would be bound by the federally-established guidelines. In our view, this approach intrudes too deeply into the primary responsibilities of the States for the administration of criminal justice.[79]

[77] See "Testimony of Paul K. Wormeli, Vice President of Public Systems, Inc., Sunnyvale, Calif., and Former National Project Director of Project SEARCH," and "Testimony of Rocky Pomerance, Police Chief, Miami Beach, Fla., and President of the International Association of Chiefs of Police," in: *Criminal Justice Information and Protection of Privacy Act of 1975*, pp. 195–205 and 149–156, respectively.

[78] See "Testimony of Honorable Francis X. Bellotti, Attorney General, The State of Massachusetts, Accompanied by Jon Brant, Assistant Attorney General, and Andrew Klein, Special Assistant to the Attorney General," and "Testimony of Aryeh Neier, Executive Director, American Civil Liberties Union," in: *Criminal Justice Information and Protection of Privacy Act of 1975*, pp. 157–195 and 229–248, respectively.

[79] "Testimony of Harold R. Tyler, Jr., Deputy Attorney General, U.S. Department of Justice, Accompanied by Mary Lawton, U.S. Department of Justice." In: *Criminal Justice Information and Protection of Privacy Act of 1975*, p. 220.

Similarly, in the hearings of the House Subcommittee on Civil and Constitutional Rights, although Project SEARCH, state representatives, and the National Conference of State Criminal Justice Planning Administrators supported the Tunney compromise measures, the Justice Department resisted the approaches to regulation included in the compromise measure and the Ervin bill of December 1974.[80] As a result, neither the Edwards nor the Tunney subcommittee hearings reconciled differences in concept and method among contending sides but merely tended to repeat arguments suggested in the 1974 Senate and House hearings over which regulatory approach was best. Given the underlying controversy over message switching, the internal Justice Department conflicts between LEAA and the FBI over the CCH program, and the growing legislative and public criticism of the unresolved policy problems in this area, including the role of the press,[81] the 1975 hearings represented the end of legislative initiatives in the field of criminal justice records and information systems rather than the final step in policy formulation.

During the summer of 1975, the National Association of State Information Systems critiqued the FBI message-switching plan. In November 1975, Attorney General Levi wrote to Senator Tunney and Representative Edwards that the message-switching proposal was tabled pending further legislative consideration of the policy issues involved. The attorney general welcomed legislation in this area, but it was apparent that none would be forthcoming.[82] By the end of 1975, the continued dissension and disagreement between the FBI and LEAA and the growing awareness of and activity by various press associations and lobbyists to prevent restrictions on their First Amendment rights to have access to criminal history records spelled the end of legislative initiatives on the proposals during 1976. In addition, Senator Tunney

[80] See "Testimony of Judge Harold R. Tyler, Deputy Attorney General, Department of Justice, Accompanied by Mary C. Lawton, Deputy Assistant Attorney General, Office of Legal Counsel," in: *Criminal Justice Information Control and Protection of Privacy Act,* U.S. Congress, House, Committee on the Judiciary, Subcommittee on Civil and Constitutional Rights, 94th Congress, 1st Session, 1975, pp. 42–83.

[81] Although in 1974 the press had not been a major reason for holding up action on the criminal justice information policy proposals, the opposite was the case in 1975. For a variety of reasons, which will be explored in Chapter 9, the press played an important role in preventing consensus from being reached on the bills by maintaining its position that First Amendment rights precluded closing off access to criminal history records and arrest records by the media. See, for example, Jerry W. Friedham, Executive Vice President and General Manager, American Newspaper Publishers Association, Letter to John V. Tunney, Chairman, Subcommittee on Constitutional Rights, Committee on the Judiciary, Senate, U.S. Congress, in: *Criminal Justice Information and Protection of Privacy Act of 1975,* pp. 283–286.

[82] "Levi Shelves FBI Message-Switching Plan." *Computerworld,* November 19, 1975.

faced a tough reelection campaign, which effectively hindered any strong initiative he might have begun to move any legislation out of his subcommittee and committee. For a variety of reasons, in the future, Congress would take a less active approach to resolving disputes over criminal information systems and developing information policy to reduce the social costs of criminal justice records.

8

Regulating the Social Costs of Criminal Justice Records— the Issue Returns to the Bureaucracy

When legislative consensus cannot be reached and legislative proposals do not succeed, an issue may return to the status of a nonissue, temporarily or permanently. Also, the focus of the debate on an issue may shift from the legislative to the executive branch, where it may be debated, redefined, and altered with changing problems, concerns, and values. Indeed, organizational policies, procedures, and politics have an influence on whether an issue stays alive and actions are taken to continue the debate or to attempt various types of conflict resolution in the form of administrative bargains or compromises with the key actors involved.

This chapter examines how the issue of reducing the social costs of criminal justice records was treated from 1976 to 1979 in the primary context of organizational rather than legislative politics. It focuses on two major lines of administrative action that had the effect of continuing public and organizational attention on the problem of reducing the social costs of criminal justice records. At the same time, this attention was being subsumed in the basic problem of whether the managerial and political issues involved in NCIC message switching and the CCH program could be resolved. Clearly, these three years were not times of inactivity concerning the problem of criminal information policy; on the contrary, numerous actions were attempted to formulate policies and regulations acceptable to the contending parties involved. The results of this activity and where precisely the issues stand today are perhaps the most challenging questions that this chapter will address.

LEAA'S IMPLEMENTATION OF PRIVACY AND SECURITY REGULATIONS

One of the major lines of administrative activity in the period 1976–1979 has been the effort by LEAA to implement privacy and security regulations nationwide. Towards the latter part of 1973, Congress extended the Omnibus Crime Control and Safe Streets Act of 1968 (the Crime Control Act of 1973). An amendment added to the act by Senator Edward Kennedy (D.-Mass.), a member of the Senate Judiciary Committee, required that LEAA promulgate regulations to provide safeguards for the privacy and security of criminal history record information. Enactment of the Kennedy amendment, as it was called, followed a period of frustrating efforts by both the House and the Senate to pass legislation controlling the nationwide use of arrest records. The Edwards subcommittee had held extensive hearings on arrest records dissemination, which it viewed as the most harmful aspect of criminal justice record use. The subcommittee had been unable to gain consensus on the issue, due to efforts of both the FBI and the Office of the Attorney General, that resisted enactment of such legislation at the time. Thus, in July 1973, Senator Kennedy "tacked on" his amendment to LEAA's primary supporting legislation.[1] Kennedy intended the regulations to be consistent with the recommendations of Project SEARCH, as presented in its report entitled *Security and Privacy Considerations in Criminal History Information Systems*[2] which he read into the *Congressional Record*. The measure was considered temporary by Congress, in view of anticipated efforts to pass more comprehensive legislation; however, it did have a considerable impact on LEAA and its relations with state and local criminal justice agencies.[3]

[1] In 1971, Senator Charles McC. Mathias, Jr. (R.-Md.) had introduced a bill in Congress that incorporated many of the criminal justice information policy recommendations of Project SEARCH and LEAA. The bill was opposed at the time by the FBI and the Department of Defense and, therefore, did not succeed. When the first draft of the Kennedy amendment was circulated to the interested members of the Judiciary Committee, Senators Roman Hruska (R.-Nebr.) and John McClellan (R.-Ark.) felt that the initial treatment was too superficial and requested that Richard Velde, then associate administrator for LEAA and a former legislative staff member for Senator Hruska, review the proposal. Velde suggested changes to broaden justice records, but also to incorporate security, auditing, and record quality features as well, along the lines of the Mathias bill proposed in 1971 and Project SEARCH recommendations.

[2] Project SEARCH. *Security and Privacy Considerations in Criminal History Information Systems.* Technical Report No. 2. Sacramento, California Crime Technological Research Foundation, 1970.

[3] It was thought at the time that the regulations would be replaced within 6–9 months by legislation with more comprehensive policies and requirements. See "'Interim' Privacy Rules Sought Under Justice Plan," *Computerworld*, February 27, 1974.

Section 524(b) of the Crime Control Act of 1973, as amended, provided that:

All criminal history information collected, stored, or disseminated through support under this title shall contain, to the maximum extent feasible, disposition as well as arrest data where arrest data is included therein. The collection, storage, and dissemination of such information shall take place under procedures reasonably designed to insure that all such information is kept current therein; the Administration shall assure that the security and privacy of all information shall only be used for law enforcement and criminal justice and other lawful purposes. In addition, an individual who believes that criminal history information concerning him contained in an automated system is inaccurate, incomplete, or maintained in violation of this title, shall, upon satisfactory verification of his identity, be entitled to review such information and to obtain a copy of it for the purpose of challenge or correction.[4]

In 1974, LEAA issued draft regulations and held hearings in different parts of the country. Then, on May 20, 1975, it published its regulations in the *Federal Register*. The regulations required the states to develop policies and procedures to ensure the privacy and security of criminal history information, especially arrest records. Specifically, these policies and procedures were to be developed in five areas: completeness and accuracy, audit, individual access and review, limitations on dissemination, and security. To assure appropriate compliance, each state accepting or using federal monies to support record-keeping systems was required to prepare a State Privacy and Security Plan describing the policies and procedures to be developed in each of the five areas covered in the regulations. To help the states develop their plans, LEAA provided a grant to Project SEARCH to hold training seminars in five locations around the country. In addition, LEAA made available to each state grants ranging from $12,000 to $20,000 to develop their plans.[5]

In two areas in particular—limits on dissemination and requirement for dedicated systems—the regulations received immediate and intense criticism.

Limits on Dissemination

In its regulations, LEAA, following in part the lead of Project SEARCH, proposed fairly strict standards on the dissemination of criminal his-

---

[4] See U.S. Department of Justice, Law Enforcement Assistance Administration, *Privacy and Security of Criminal History Information, Summary of State Plans*, n.d., p. 1.

[5] See Gary R. Cooper and M. Steven Zehner, "Privacy: The Evolution of an Issue," in: *Proceedings of the Third International Symposium on Criminal Justice Information and Statistics Systems*, edited by SEARCH Group, Inc., Sacramento, Calif., 1976, p. 88.

tory data. Section 20.33 of the regulations issued May 20, 1975, outlined restrictions on the dissemination of all criminal history record information to noncriminal justice groups and agencies for private or public uses not authorized by state or federal statutes. In addition, the use of arrest records that were more than one year old and not included in pending prosecutions were not to be disseminated without proper disposition information. The press was permitted access to criminal justice record information in pending or current criminal justice activities, but its access to past or *historical* records was limited.[6]

These dissemination provisions met with severe criticism from the press and state and local governments. First, the press argued that its traditional First Amendment right to have access to information on criminal justice activities was unreasonably restricted.[7] The press desired to continue its informal practice of gaining access to complete arrest and criminal records of individuals involved in the criminal justice process. Because the press represented a strong voice and lobby concerning the use of criminal records, the provision of the 1975 regulations limiting access to current records was clarified in the 1976 revised regulations to not preclude checks on prior criminal history records if the individual's name was known.[8]

Second, state and local government officials argued that the provision limiting noncriminal justice access to criminal history records to cases only provided by state and federal law was overly restrictive. Many state and local governments provided access to criminal records through executive orders or local ordinances for employment and licensing checks; in some jurisdictions, access was permitted by court rule, decision, or order. Thus, groups with these kinds of access advocated continuation of past practices.

Third, state and local governments, as well as the press, argued against restricting access to arrest records that were more than one year old and did not have dispositions. They suggested that the *complete* record of past involvement with criminal justice agencies was necessary to make legitimate decisions in licensing and employment

---

[6] See "Title 28—Judicial Administration, Chapter 1—Department of Justice, Part 20—Criminal Justice Information Systems," *Federal Register, 40*(98):22114–22119, May 20, 1975.

[7] See, for example, "Privacy Guidelines Limiting," *Washington Post*, December 25, 1975.

[8] See "Title 28—Judicial Administration, Chapter I—Department of Justice, Part 20—Criminal Justice Information Systems," *Federal Register, 41*(55):11715, March 19, 1976, Sec. 20.21, 2(b).

cases, including records that were known to be incomplete in whole or in part but which could have some probative value.

Fourth, criminal justice agencies, university researchers, and others noted that access to criminal justice records for research and statistical purposes had not been included in the 1975 regulations. The 1976 revised regulations limited access to these records for research, evaluative, and statistical activities under a written agreement with a criminal justice agency.[9]

In large measure, the changes made in the 1975 regulations related to limits on the dissemination of criminal justice records were both corrective and conciliatory. LEAA was not in a position to force state and local governments and the press to conform to regulations that these groups found unacceptable, so past practices that were not completely inconsistent with the principles and objectives underlying the regulations were continued.

Shared Versus Dedicated Systems

The second area of controversy concerned whether computer systems containing criminal history records had to be dedicated (e.g., limited to criminal justice users and controlled by criminal justice agencies), or whether these records could be maintained and disseminated, particularly in local and county governments, through computer systems that were managed in a shared environment with other departments in the jurisdiction. The 1975 regulations mandated dedicated computer systems for criminal justice record information. A criminal justice agency was to:

(2) Assure that where computerized data processing is employed, the hardware, including processor, communications control, and storage device, to be utilized for the handling of criminal history record information is dedicated to purposes related to the administration of criminal justice;

(3) Have authority to set and enforce policy concerning computer operations;

(4) Have power to veto for legitimate security purposes which personnel can be permitted to work in a defined area where such information is stored, collected, or disseminated;

(5) Select and supervise all personnel authorized to have direct access to such information;

(6) Assure that an individual or agency authorized direct access is administratively held responsible for (1) the physical security of criminal history

[9] *Ibid.*, Sec. 20.21, 2(b)(4).

information under its control or custody and (2) the protection of such information from unauthorized accesses, disclosures, or disseminations.[10]

These provisions met with intense criticism and acquired national visibility.[11] Most criticisms were made by state and local government officials who had developed or were developing computer systems to serve the needs of multiple agencies, including criminal justice agencies, and who viewed the dedication requirement as unnecessary and not cost-effective.[12] Law enforcement agencies, in particular, supported dedicated systems for three main reasons. First, the security and confidentiality of data could be better protected by a system dedicated to and controlled by criminal justice agencies than by a shared system. Second, dedicated systems would provide better service to law enforcement agencies than shared systems, which, because of service priorities and resource allocations, would not fully satisfy legitimate law enforcement priorities and needs. Third, the trend in computer technology was moving away from the sharing of large systems and toward distributed data-processing facilities involving minicomputers and other telecommunications innovations.[13]

In contrast, state and local government officials argued in favor of the shared computer system concept. First, the confidentiality and security of information could be assured through the establishment and enforcement of appropriate policies and procedures, including hardware security devices and software file lockout or restriction routines. Second, adequate levels of service could be maintained by proper management of service functions and resource allocations in the shared environment. Third, the dedication of computer systems for functional uses would weaken policy and management control of

[10] "Title 28—Judicial Administration, Chapter 1—Department of Justice, Part 20—Criminal Justice Information Systems." *Federal Register*, *40*(98):22115, May 20, 1975, Sec. 20.21 (f).

[11] For reviews of the dedication debate from various perspectives, see Project SEARCH, *Proceedings of the International Symposium on Criminal Justice Information and Statistics Systems*, Sacramento, California Crime Technological Research Foundation, 1972, pp. 573–582; also, O. E. Dial, ed., "Computers: To Dedicate or Not to Dedicate, That is the Question," *Bureaucrat*, *1:*305–378, Winter 1972.

[12] See, for example, "States Blast NCIC Requirement for Dedicated Systems," *Computerworld*, July 30, 1975; "NASIS Opposes Edict Requiring Dedicated Criminal DP Systems," *Computerworld*, August 13, 1975; "NASIS Fights LEAA Regulations," *Computerworld*, August 13, 1975.

[13] See U.S. Department of Justice, Information and Telecommunications Systems Policy Board, "Subject: Dedication to the Criminal Justice Function of Computers Utilized for Handling Criminal Justice Data," Washington, D.C., U.S. Department of Justice, September 12, 1975.

general government officials and managers. In the past, many local and state officials had adopted shared systems to improve management control over computer resources and information management policies in their jurisdictions, in light of state and federal funding and management practices that require dedicated computer systems for more and more program areas.

Throughout 1974 and early 1975, LEAA considered the arguments of both sides. On the one hand, law enforcement groups, such as the International Association of Chiefs of Police, lobbied for dedicated systems; on the other hand, several state and local governments and their associations, such as the National Association of State Information Systems, the Council of State Governments, the National Association of Counties, and the International City and County Management Association, strongly favored permitting individual jurisdictions to decide for themselves the question of a dedicated versus shared environment.

LEAA provided the "local option" by emphasizing in its regulations the need for substantial management involvement by criminal justice agencies in shared systems. At the same time, LEAA clearly indicated that it was up to local and state governments to choose—considering confidentiality, security, finances, and operational characteristics—either a dedicated or shared system or a variation thereof.

Computer operations, whether dedicated or shared, which support criminal justice information systems, operate in accordance with procedures developed or approved by the participating criminal justice agencies that assure that:

(i) Criminal history record information is stored by the computer in such manner that it cannot be modified, destroyed, accessed, changed, purged, or overlaid in any fashion by noncriminal justice terminals.

(ii) Operational programs are used that will prohibit inquiry, record updates, or destruction of records, from any terminal other than criminal justice system terminals which are also designated.

(iii) The destruction of records is limited to designated terminals under the direct control of the criminal justice agency responsible for creating or storing the criminal history record information.

(iv) Operational programs are used to detect and store for the output of designated criminal justice agency employees all unauthorized attempts to penetrate any criminal history record information system, program or line.

(v) The programs specified in (ii) and (iv) of this subsection are known only to criminal justice agency employees responsible for criminal history record information system control or individuals and agencies pursuant to a specific agreement with the criminal justice agency to provide such programs and the programming are kept continuously under maximum security conditions.

(vi) Procedures are instituted to assure that an individual agency authorized direct access is responsible for (A) the physical security of criminal history record information under its control or in its custody and (B) the protection of such information from unauthorized access, disclosure or dissemination.

(vii) Procedures are instituted to protect any central repository of criminal history record information from unauthorized access, theft, sabotage, fire, flood, wind, or other natural or manmade disasters.[14]

Just as in the case of the limits on dissemination, LEAA sought to avoid major confrontations with state and local governments and to arrive at a compromise on the issue of dedicated versus shared computer systems while maintaining standards for protecting the confidentiality and security of criminal history records.

As the states began developing their plans for submittal to LEAA and for implementation of the regulations by December 31, 1977, it became apparent to LEAA that the latter implementation deadline could not be met. Getting the states to comply with this deadline provided a variety of unexpected problems of implementation that LEAA had not adequately anticipated.[15]

State and Local Problems in Implementing the Regulations

Prior to the December 1977 deadline for implementation of the 1976 regulations, LEAA contracted with the Mitre Corporation to conduct a study of the level of state compliance with the regulations and whether the December 1977 deadline could reasonably be met. The study focused on the progress and status of an 18-state survey sample (Arizona, Arkansas, California, Colorado, Florida, Iowa, Kentucky, Maine, Massachusetts, Minnesota, Missouri, New York, Ohio, Oregon, Pennsylvania, Texas, Washington, and Wyoming).

Generally, the Mitre Corporation study found that there were two types of problems hindering the states in complying with the federal privacy and security regulations:

(1) Those that are external to the Regulations and could, perhaps, be better characterized as indicative of the environment in which the Regulations were required to be implemented; and

---

[14] "Title 28—Judicial Administration, Chapter I—Department of Justice, Part 20— Criminal Justice Information Systems." *Federal Register, 41*(55):11715, March 19, 1976. Sect. 20.21 (f)(3)(A).

[15] "Title 28—Judicial Administration, Chapter I—Department of Justice, Part 20— Criminal Justice Information Systems, Extension of Implementation Date," *Federal Register, 42*(98):61595–61596, December 6, 1977.

(2) Those that are internal to the Regulations themselves, that is, problems caused by generalities in language which have caused the states difficulties in interpreting the intent thereof and/or particular stipulations of the Regulations that states have difficulty in implementing.[16]

Volume I of the study reviewed the external problems of implementing the regulations and ranked the 18 states surveyed in three compliance categories: (1) substantial compliance—two states, (2) medium compliance—nine states, and (3) minimal compliance—seven states.[17] The study then presented, in detail, its four major findings about the level of compliance in the states.

The first major finding was that "long-term prior involvement with privacy and security implementation is a reliable indicator of successful compliance. However, commitment to improved privacy and security is also important."[18] The study asserted that such a commitment, even when it has been developed recently, significantly increases likelihood of compliance.

Both states with substantial compliance had comprehensive legislation or a long-term involvement in the area prior to the 1975 regulations and had ongoing implementation activities and well-developed, formal procedures that had been pursued in all areas covered by the regulations. In the nine states with medium compliance, some legislation had been enacted and procedures were being developed to conform to the regulations, but the process of implementation was still incomplete. All the states in this category varied in their approaches; however, commitment on the part of key individuals in lead agencies was a major factor of progress. The states in the minimal compliance category, in contrast, appeared to have little or no enabling legislation and procedures for bringing the information systems into compliance. In five states, attempts were made to draft legislation, but these efforts were either unsuccessful or were not yet completed.[19]

Second, the Mitre study indicated that "comprehensive legislation already in place appears to greatly facilitate compliance progress."[20] Both states with substantial compliance had enacted, several years prior to the regulations, state statutes that addressed all the major

---

[16] Mitre Corporation. *Implementing the Federal Privacy and Security Regulations, Vol. II: Problem Analysis & Practical Responses.* McLean, Va., 1977, p. vii.

[17] Mitre Corporation. *Implementing the Federal Privacy and Security Regulations, Vol. I: Findings & Recommendations of an Eighteen State Assessment.* McLean, Va., 1977, pp. vii–viii.

[18] *Ibid.*, p. viii.

[19] *Ibid.*, pp. 6, 9.

[20] *Ibid.*, p. viii.

requirements that were mandated by LEAA. In the states with medium compliance, only two had enacted a comprehensive legislative package. The other states had either enacted legislation specific to only part of the major categories covered by the regulations or were in the process of enacting legislation. Among the states with minimal compliance, two had no legislation in existence prior to the submission of their plans and had failed to pass any legislation in the interim; however, these states did have aspect-specific legislation pending (e.g., a public disclosure law, a statute limiting dissemination, a mandate for reporting arrests). The other states either had public disclosure laws that were applicable, at least in part, to the information affected by the regulations or had made no attempt to enact legislation.[21]

The third major finding was that "states with highly specific mandates as to what their CSR (central state repositories) file bases should contain and who have actively pursued these mandates have made adequate progress towards compliance. When mandates as to file content lack specificity, or are not stringently pursued, states fared less well in moving towards compliance."[22] All 18 states had organizations designated by statute as central state repositories; the ages of the organizations varied from 4 years to 63 years. Of the two states in substantial compliance, both considered all criminal justice agencies to be covered by the regulations and had mandated and actively pursued the reporting of felony and serious misdemeanor arrest and disposition information.[23]

It would appear that it is the degree to which the mandate to report required information is pursued that reflects most accurately the compliance status of a CSR and, consequently, that of its contributing agencies.... Both states rely essentially on automated systems, but these are augmented by well devised and established manual systems. Hence, it is not merely the presence of an automated capability which explains the successful compliance progress of these states; rather, it is the flow of information through established and rigorously enforced systems which appears to be a prime determinant of their success.[24]

In the states with medium compliance, mandates for reporting arrest and disposition data were only partially applicable or the coverage of the statutes included only LEAA-funded systems. Most states with minimal compliance had statutes that did not specify file content but

[21] *Ibid.*, pp. 13, 14.
[22] *Ibid.*, p. viii.
[23] *Ibid.*, pp. 16, 19.
[24] *Ibid.*, p. 19.

rather were couched in broad language. Thus, the study noted that: "what usually results is a less rigorous pursuit of those stipulations than that characterizing the CSR operations of states with specific legislative mandates."[25]

The fourth significant finding was that four factors (lack of sufficient resources, confusion as to interpretation of the regulations, traditional practices inhibiting change, and tendencies to link compliance with proposed automated data systems) appeared to relate directly, either alone or in some combination, to a state's ability or inability to comply.[26]

In addition to these external problems influencing compliance with LEAA regulations, the Mitre study also identified internal problems that impeded compliance progress and made the December 31, 1977 deadline unrealistic. Of considerable significance was "the lack of specificity in terms both of the meaning and the intent of parts of the Regulations."[27] The general language of the regulations resulted in three problems. The first was uncertainty over the purpose and development of CSRs, which involved:

(a) what its actual role should be—is it a repository only or an overseer/guardian of the activities of its contributing agencies? (b) the content of its CHRI file base—do the Regulations require that all arrest information be retained or may the state be selective? and (c) the extent of the responsibilities of the CSR—should it be the agency responsible for conducting audits of all contributing agencies?[28]

Second, there was confusion over the development of state-local agency relationships:

Since the Federal Government does not consider it appropriate to proscribe the lines of authority for implementation within a state, the Regulations leave open the question of who is to take the initiative in compliance activities. . . . In some states, implementors have perceived their responsibilities as being limited principally to state-level activities. Often, local jurisdictions are doing little to achieve compliance, believing they must wait upon state-level implementors for guidelines and procedures. Frequently, when the state does come out with guidelines and procedures, localities have perceived them as not reflective of local needs and practices. In concert with this problem, many officials at both state and local levels have expressed some degree of uncer-

---

[25] *Ibid.*, p. 20.
[26] *Ibid.*, p. viii.
[27] Mitre Corporation. *Implementing the Federal Privacy and Security Regulations, Vol. II,* pp. 5–6.
[28] *Ibid.*, p. 6.

tainty as to the nature and role that locally maintained repositories of criminal history record information should play versus that of a centralized repository at the state level.[29]

Third, the broad language in the regulations caused many differences in interpretations by both intra- and interstate jurisdictions.

The study also found major impediments to compliance by the states in each of the five areas covered by the LEAA regulations:

—*Completeness and Accuracy:* the lack of a clear and effective mandate, funds and/or technical ability needed for a CSR to introduce or improve an arrest and disposition reporting system, and sufficient time in which to do so.

—*Individual Access and Review:* the lack of standardized, comprehensive policies, applicable to all impacted agencies in a state, which are supported by formalized procedures and the force of state law.

—*Limitations on Dissemination:* the lack of a statewide policy supported by formalized mechanisms and procedures, that is promulgated, pursued and enforced by some responsible agency.

—*Security:* the lack of specific, statewide security standards and the resources required for the full implementation of these standards.

—*Audit:* the lack of both a legislative mandate to conduct audits and of the resources these audits will require.[30]

In summary, the Mitre Corporation study provided a unique overview of the difficulties of implementing the federal regulations. By December 1977, it became clear that the original deadline could not be met. Although the study recommended a five-year, staged approach to implementation, LEAA sought instead to merely extend the deadline for the submittal of implementation schedules and plans by the states to March 1, 1978. The Mitre study noted that aggressive efforts by LEAA would be necessary to achieve compliance by all states in five years;[31] at this time, however, LEAA desired to select a wait-and-see attitude. In large measure, this low-key, incremental strategy was dictated by the continuing concern and debate regarding available resources, message switching, and the CCH program.[32]

---

[29] *Ibid.*, p. 7.

[30] Mitre Corporation. *Implementing the Federal Privacy and Security Regulations, Vol. I*, p. ix.

[31] *Ibid.*, p. xi.

[32] There also was some concern within LEAA over whether the agency should be in a regulatory role vis-à-vis state and local agencies. A regulatory role could put the agency in conflict with these jurisdictions and hinder its ability to deal effectively with state and local agencies in its assistance or funding role, which the agency considered to be of primary importance.

CONFUSION AND TURMOIL WITHIN THE DEPARTMENT OF JUSTICE—THE CASES OF MESSAGE SWITCHING AND CCH CONTINUED

The period from 1976 to 1979 was characterized by a series of events concerning both message switching and the CCH program, which are related by confusion and indecision rather than by decision and action. These events may be better described as episodes in bureaucratic, public interest, and legislative politics that raised doubts about the possibility of developing a nationwide network of integrated criminal justice information systems that would provide acceptable levels of confidentiality and security both in the short and long term. Whether the original concepts of the nationwide network were politically, administratively, and, in some ways, technically premature and overoptimistic also was questioned. These debates are not over; rather, they have taken on an unmistakable air of fatigue and frustration due to the failure to achieve consensus on whom and how the CCH program should be managed and on acceptable policies and procedures for the reduction of the social costs of criminal justice records. In fact, LEAA's attempts to implement the privacy and security regulations have been overshadowed and influenced by the fact that the debate about these questions remains unresolved. Before moving to more definitive conclusions about the problems, it is necessary to assess how this climate of uncertainty, confusion, and indecision developed from 1976 to 1979 and why it occurred.

The Justice Department Attempts to Resolve Internal Conflicts

As observed in Chapter 7, the Office of the Attorney General recognized in 1974 that relations between the FBI and LEAA over message switching and CCH had pretty much broken down. Both agencies had conflicted publicly and privately, which created an image of a department in disarray. The Office of the Attorney General attempted to bring together the FBI director and the LEAA administrator in an effort to formulate acceptable departmental positions by arranging a conference at Quantico, Virginia in January 1975; however, the consensus reached at Quantico was tenuous and broke down as the year progressed.

Despite the apparent failure of the meeting, the Office of the Attorney General pursued the idea that such high-level meetings to deal with an array of information systems and telecommunications policy issues should continue. Establishment of a Department Information and Telecommunications Systems Policy Board, consisting of the deputy attorney general, FBI director, LEAA administrator, and assistant attorney general for administration, originally had been recommended at the Quantico conference. The purpose of this board was "to review all information systems and telecommunications issues with Department-wide implications and make recommendations for decisions by the AG (Attorney General)" as well as "to assure that the Department develops and promotes coordinated compatible telecommunications programs."[33] On July 16, 1975, Attorney General Edward Levi signed the departmental order establishing the board.[34]

The board was established to bring key departmental individuals together to resolve conflicts and problems concerning information and telecommunications systems and to advise the attorney general on departmental positions. Its role did not include decision-making or policy development activities but, rather, study and review. In the three years of its formal existence, the board met sporadically, sometimes with a lapse of more than a year between meetings. Although the board considered a variety of significant issues (see Table 13), it made only a few recommendations, and not all of these were accepted or acted on. For example, during its first two meetings in 1975 (August 27 and September 23), the board deliberated over the proposed limited message-switching implementation plan for the FBI. At the end of the second meeting, the board forwarded to the attorney general its recommendations, which suggested that the plan be promptly implemented after proper consultation with interested legislative members.[35] Shortly thereafter the attorney general tabled the plan, notwithstanding the board's call for prompt action. The lack of incentives within the department for LEAA and the FBI to achieve consensus hampered the effectiveness of the board.[36] In large measure, the

[33] Lawrence H. Silberman, Deputy Attorney General. Memorandum to Clarence M. Kelley, Director, Federal Bureau of Investigation, U.S. Department of Justice; Glen E. Pommerening, Assistant Attorney General for Administration; and Richard W. Velde, Administrator, Law Enforcement Assistance Administration, U.S. Department of Justice. Subject: "NCIC Limited Message Switching Conference—January 27, 1975." April 18, 1975, p. 4.

[34] U.S. Department of Justice. *Order of Edward Levi.* Subject: "Information and Telecommunications Systems Policy Board." Washington, D.C., July 16, 1975.

[35] U.S. Department of Justice, Information and Telecommunications Systems Policy Board. "Recommendation Number 1." September 23, 1975, p. 1.

[36] Both the FBI and LEAA considered the board to be a usurpation of their authority and management prerogatives in their respective fields. In addition, congressional criticism of the Quantico conference and subsequent board efforts focused on the perceived unwillingness of the department and the FBI, particularly, to consult ahead of time with interested congressmen such as Don Edwards and John Moss before

TABLE 13   Topics Formally Considered by the U.S. Department of Justice Information and Telecommunications Systems Policy Board

---

- FBI Automated Fingerprint Identification Systems (AIDS)
- National Crime Information Center/Computerized Criminal History Program (NCIC/CCH)
- Message Switching
- Interstate Organized Crime Index (IOCI)
- Comprehensive Data System (CDS) Program of LEAA
- Nationwide Network of Criminal Laboratories

---

board served as another forum for the conflict rather than as a means for consensus building. Often, it was bypassed entirely for more public assaults on policy positions taken by the FBI and/or LEAA. An example of such bypassing occurred in the spring of 1976 concerning the CCH program.

The FBI's Request to Terminate CCH and the Reaction

At a March 4, 1976 meeting with Attorney General Edward Levi, FBI Director Clarence Kelley expressed his concerns about the future of the FBI criminal history record services, especially the CCH program. On April 16, 1976, Director Kelley forwarded a memorandum to the attorney general providing background information for Levi's discussion with Congressman Don Edwards, including Kelley's "best judgments regarding the future of NCIC/CCH and one very important recommendation for [his] consideration."[37]

Both the background information and the cover memo reviewed the current status and problems with CCH:

SYNOPSIS: The CCH program has not proven successful in terms of state participation occasioned, in chief, by gross underestimates on the costs and efforts required of states to participate. In addition, there are serious governmental relations problems, particularly when cooperation must be secured from all or nearly all of the states to truly insure CCH success. A variety of

---

proceeding with attempts to resolve conflicts between LEAA and the FBI over message switching and the NCIC/CCH program. Although the board has never been formally discontinued, its last reported meeting was on January 11, 1977.

[37] Clarence M. Kelley, Director, Federal Bureau of Investigation, U.S. Department of Justice. Memorandum to Edward H. Levi, Attorney General. Subject: "Future Course of FBI Criminal History Record Services." April 16, 1976, p. 1.

security and privacy concerns continue and increase the complexity of achieving the CCH program's original expectations. Further, at the present time this Bureau is in the untenable position of having to retain duplicates of all criminal history records in Washington rather than decentralizing those records (approximately 70%) wherein all offenses have occurred in a single state, to that state. This inability to return such records to their state of origin, which is a major provision of the CCH program, has resulted from the lack of message-switching authority, which authority would allow the states to obtain from one another all such "single-state offender" records. Thus with the states being restricted to computer communication only with NCIC, as opposed to communicating directly with each other, all criminal histories must be stored and available in the NCIC computer. This lack of interstate CCH message switching has resulted in duplication of records, but even more importantly, it has resulted in a centralized record file which is growing in size every day. On the other hand, and as a separate and distinct operation from the CCH program, the Identification Division continues to provide the primary identification and record services to law enforcement and prosecutive agencies nationally, and these services will not be adversely affected by termination of CCH.[38]

In light of these difficulties with the program, the FBI director recommended that the CCH program be terminated.

The response to Director Kelley's decision was both immediate and critical. On April 28, 1976, the NCIC Advisory Policy Board passed a resolution in support of the CCH program and urged the attorney general "to resolve favorably to continue participation of the FBI as a full partner in improving and expanding the use of CCH within its present concept."[39] On May 14, 1976, LEAA Administrator Richard Velde recommended to Deputy Attorney General Harold R. Tyler, Jr. that any decision by the attorney general on the future of the CCH program be postponed "for a reasonable time" to allow for consideration of all the options for its continuation.[40] LEAA had been critical of the FBI's handling of the CCH program in the past, and Velde obviously felt LEAA's own interests were jeopardized by the decision to terminate:

Our records indicate that by conservative estimate LEAA has awarded more

[38] *Ibid.*

[39] U.S. Department of Justice, Federal Bureau of Investigation, National Crime Information Center, Advisory Policy Board. *Minutes.* Advisory Policy Board Meeting, April 27–28, 1976, New Orleans, La. Appendix C, p. 2.

[40] Richard W. Velde, Administrator, Law Enforcement Assistance Administration. Memorandum to Harold R. Tyler, Jr., Deputy Attorney General. Subject: "Future Course of the Computerized Criminal History (CCH) Program." May 14, 1976, p. 3.

than $27,000,000 since 1972 in direct grants to the states in development of the CCH components of the Comprehensive Data System (CDS) program. The contributions by the states themselves using LEAA block grant funds and their own money and manpower are also a substantial investment which cannot be ignored. A commitment of this magnitude by both the Federal Government and the states should not be summarily written off.[41]

Clearly, LEAA's investments in CDS were threatened by a decision to terminate the CCH program. In a report attached to a memorandum to Tyler dated May 5, 1976, Velde commented that the central issue which had to be resolved was "how will this interstate criminal justice communications network be managed?" Velde recommended that a task force study the options, particularly the establishment of a "Network Agency," possibly by multistate agreement, to manage the network.[42] The decision to terminate CCH, therefore, represented a direct and adverse response to LEAA's efforts with the SEARCH group to decentralize management of the interstate network for message switching and CCH in the states and away from FBI control.[43] In support of the LEAA position, the SEARCH group passed a resolution on May 23, 1976 which suggested that any decision to terminate CCH would be both "premature" and "detrimental to nationally established and recognized goals and objectives for the criminal justice community."[44] In addition, on June 1, 1976, the International Association of Chiefs of Police, normally a strong supporter of FBI policy positions, also criticized the decision to terminate CCH.[45]

By June 1976, it appeared that the predominant opinion of the criminal justice community was to not terminate CCH. In an address before the National Association of Attorneys General, Attorney General Levi noted that the FBI's request was being studied in the depart-

---

[41]*Ibid.*, p. 1.

[42]Richard W. Velde, Administrator, Law Enforcement Assistance Administration, U.S. Department of Justice. Memorandum to Harold R. Tyler, Jr., Deputy Attorney General. Subject: "Establishment of a Task Force on Interstate Criminal Justice Communications Management." Attachment: "Toward Defining a Management Structure for an Interstate Criminal Justice Communications Network." May 5, 1976.

[43]The debate between LEAA and the FBI over the termination of CCH crystallized perhaps more clearly than ever before. In addition, the director's decision to advocate termination of CCH in NCIC also represented somewhat of a victory for the FBI's Identification Division, which was proceeding with plans to automate its identification and arrest record files.

[44]SEARCH Group, Inc. *"Resolution."* Philadelphia, Pa., May 23, 1976.

[45]Glen D. King, Executive Director, International Association of Chiefs of Police, Inc. Letter to Edward H. Levi, Attorney General. June 1, 1976.

ment and that other support services provided by the Identification Division of the FBI to the states would continue.[46] Levi stated that, even if the decision to terminate CCH in the FBI was made, another institution could establish a decentralized computerized criminal history program: "However, the hard questions being asked about the FBI in this area must be addressed to and by any other candidate for the responsibility. This is to say there must be high assurance of accuracy and accountability."[47] The attorney general noted that, although it was possible that he might curtail CCH in the FBI, he had not yet decided the issue. Even if he favored termination, LEAA would not be precluded from pursuing a decentralized system, modeled on the original Project SEARCH concept but with some new management structure.[48]

On June 18, 1976, LEAA presented its comments on the CCH program at a Justice Department Policy Board meeting.[49] LEAA's plan of action recommended options that favored more state input and control and policy positions that placed management of the CCH program outside the FBI (see Table 14). The policy board took no action on LEAA's recommendation, but it did prepare a situation analysis that recommended continuation of the CCH program with further state participation in a decentralized mode.[50]

Sentiment against CCH termination continued to arrive at the Office of the Attorney General throughout the latter part of June and July,[51] and the bureaucratic battle of memos continued. On July 1, 1976, the FBI forwarded two sets of comments to the Office of the Attorney

---

[46] U.S. Department of Justice. "Address by the Honorable Edward H. Levi, Attorney General of the United States, Before the National Association of Attorneys General." Address at the Arneson River Theater, LaVillita, San Antonio, Texas, June 3, 1976, p. 15.

[47] *Ibid.*, pp. 15–16.

[48] *Ibid.*, p. 15.

[49] Richard W. Velde, Administrator, Law Enforcement Assistance Administration, U.S. Department of Justice. "National Computerized Criminal History Program, Comments by the Law Enforcement Assistance Administration." June 18, 1976.

[50] U.S. Department of Justice, Systems Policy Board. "Original Situation Analysis, Topic: National Computerized Criminal History (CCH) Program," June 18, 1976, p. iv.

[51] See, for example, Norman A. Carlson, Director, Bureau of Prisons, U.S. Department of Justice, Memorandum to Harold R. Tyler, Jr., Deputy Attorney General, Subject: "National Crime Information Center/NCIC, Computerized Criminal History/CCH," June 24, 1976; Peter B. Bensinger, Administrator, Drug Enforcement Administration, U.S. Department of Justice, Memorandum to Edward Dolan, Executive Secretary, Systems Policy Board, U.S. Department of Justice, Subject: "Comments on Computerized Criminal History (CCH) Proposals," July 6, 1976; V. L. Hays, Director, Arizona Department of Public Safety, Letter to Edward H. Levi, Attorney General, July 14, 1976.

TABLE 14 LEAA Recommended Plan of Action to Sustain the National Computerized Criminal History Program

1. Immediate denial of the FBI proposal to terminate the CCH program.

2. Immediate authorization for the FBI to conduct message switching limited solely to the interstate exchange of computerized criminal history records identified in the NCIC index. Message content recording to be prohibited under this authorization.

3. Directions to the FBI to return all single-state records to the states within six months and thereafter limit the NCIC file to multistate and federal offenders.

4. Issuance of a department policy supporting the development and use of NLETS for all interstate message traffic other than as defined above for CCH referrals.

5. Creation of an attorney general's policy committee on criminal history records, dominated by state personnel but with federal executive and legislative participation, to conduct a two-year review of CCH system policy and to define long-term objectives, federal-state roles, basic privacy and security policies, and to conduct such other investigations as the attorney general may require.

6. Immediate initiation of a program to establish a Task Force on Interstate Criminal Justice Communications Management and to assist the states in implementing a technologically advanced, nationwide communications network (Interstate Network), which would be designed with sufficient capacity to satisfy all interstate criminal justice communications requirements.

Source: Adapted from Richard W. Velde, Administrator, Law Enforcement Assistance Administration, U.S. Department of Justice. "National Computerized Criminal History Program, Comments by the Law Enforcement Assistance Administration." June 18, 1976. p. 3.

General and the board in response, first, to the board's situation analysis and, second, to the LEAA memorandum of June 18, 1976.[52] Voicing respect for the situation analysis, the FBI reaffirmed the position of the director that had been presented to the attorney general on April 16 and suggested that the FBI's Identification Division was an adequate alternative:

> The FBI's Identification Division can continue to be the primary source at the national level of criminal history record information. The Division's "in-house" operations are being automated and consequently it is expected that these services will be enhanced for the benefit of the entire criminal justice system.[53]

In addition, the bureau noted that state-level efforts did not have to end, nor that the FBI would end support of state efforts:

[52] Clarence M. Kelley, Director, Federal Bureau of Investigation, U.S. Department of Justice. Memorandum to Harold R. Tyler, Jr., Deputy Attorney General. Subject: "Comments on Computerized Criminal History (CCH) Proposals." July 1, 1976.

[53] Ibid., Attachment 1, "Response to Department of Justice Systems Policy Board (Staff) Document Entitled 'Situation Analysis,'" p. 2.

The States' efforts to meet the criminal history record needs in their respective states should not be impeded. State criminal history systems are separate and distinct from the national CCH program and all 50 states should develop their own programs to better serve the needs of their criminal justice communities.[54]

The bureau reiterated these positions in its comments on the LEAA memorandum of April 16 and also rebutted point by point the LEAA recommended plan of action. First, the bureau repeated its position that NCIC should not be constrained to limited message switching for the CCH program, but should be allowed to process administrative messages. Second, the FBI noted that their message-switching plan provided for relocation of single-state records to the states within eight months after approval of the plan. Third, the bureau contended that LEAA's recommendations on the issuance of a departmental policy supporting the development and use of NLETS in all interstate message traffic other than for CCH referrals was unnecessary, since their plan defined these message types.[55] Fourth, the FBI did not agree with the creation of an attorney general's policy committee nor the emphasis on heavier state and public representation to formulate a national policy on the CCH system:

A national policy concerning CCH was created by the NCIC Working Group prior to implementation of an on-line system for CCH on November 29, 1971. This policy, approved by the NCIC Advisory Policy Board (APB), has instituted changes and innovations since that time, being responsive to the needs of NCIC users and society. The APB and its Security and Confidentiality (S&C) Committee and the participants at All Participant Meetings are totally representative of the users of NCIC in general and the CCH File in particular.

There is no reason to believe that the creation of an Attorney General's Policy Committee on criminal history records, dominated by state personnel but with Federal executive and legislative participation, could provide input, over and above that already furnished by the NCICAPB and NCIC users, to make workable a concept we have found, in the absence of certain conditions, to be nonviable.[56]

Fifth, the bureau suggested that the LEAA recommendation to form a Task Force on Interstate Communications Management be tabled

[54] *Ibid*.

[55] *Ibid*., Attachment 2, "Comments on the Document Entitled 'National Computerized Criminal History Program Comments, by the Law Enforcement Assistance Administration, June 18, 1976,'" pp. 4–5, 6, 7.

[56] *Ibid*., p. 8.

until completion of a study by the Law Enforcement Systems Policy Review Group for the Systems Policy Board.[57]

In addition, the bureau noted that, contrary to LEAA's claims, CCH was not a major priority in the CDS program; rather, the primary focus was on statistical systems. Moreover, the bureau suggested that CCH development had been slowed by the primary emphasis of LEAA's guidelines to linking the state Statistical Analysis Center to the CCH program.[58]

On July 28, 1976, LEAA Administrator Velde forwarded a memo to Edward Dolan, a member of the Systems Policy Board, indicating that, despite the FBI's arguments, LEAA's position was unchanged. If the department chose to terminate CCH at NCIC, LEAA still desired to offer assistance to the states by developing their criminal history systems. This also was the FBI's position.[59]

During August and September 1976, the Systems Policy Board met again to consider the controversy between the FBI and LEAA. After its discussions, the board proposed a recommendation to the attorney general that covered five basic points.[60] First, the FBI should decentralize single-state offender records in 12 months and submit to the board a plan to reduce duplication of records in the Identification Division. Second, a study committee of the board should be formed to review all present policies and practices of the NCIC/CCH program and to make recommendations on:

—how the NCIC Advisory Policy Board and the proposed standing committee on the NCIC/CCH program can be structured to include representation of national and state legislative interests in the CCH program.
—those actions which must be taken to make the NCIC/CCH program more attractive to state governments; accelerate program implementation; and rapidly increase the availability, quality, and timeliness of accessing CCH records.[61]

Or, as an alternative, the attorney general should create an advisory committee "composed of state personnel, but with Federal executive and legislative participation" to conduct "a two-year review of CCH

[57] Ibid., p. 9.
[58] Ibid., pp. 10–11.
[59] Richard W. Velde, Administrator, Law Enforcement Assistance Administration, U.S. Department of Justice. Memorandum to Edward Dolan, Systems Policy Board, U.S. Department of Justice. Subject: "National Computerized Criminal History (CCH) Program." July 28, 1976.
[60] U.S. Department of Justice, Systems Policy Board. "Recommendation Number 4." September 1, 1976.
[61] Ibid., p. 2.

system policy and to define long-term objectives, Federal-state roles, basic privacy and security policies, and . . . other related matters."[62] Fourth, NCIC would do limited message switching only, and, fifth, the comptroller general and the chairmen of the appropriate congressional committees should be advised that NCIC limited message switching was approved and that periodic audits of the NCIC/CCH program would be desirable.

The board's recommendations favored LEAA's policy positions rather than the FBI's. In their responses to the deputy attorney general on the proposed board recommendations, the FBI and LEAA confirmed this observation. While LEAA generally supported the board,[63] FBI Director Kelley was critical, noting that the recommendation ignored the April 16 request to terminate and that the continuation of the program under the conditions outlined was unacceptable: "I wish to emphasize that the FBI is not opposed to receiving the views and counsel of outside interested parties, but we are opposed to a further dilution of our management prerogatives over CCH if we are to continue to operate it."[64]

The year 1976 did not end with any firm decision on the board's recommendation by the attorney general. No movement had yet occurred in getting the FBI to modify its position on the NCIC/CCH program. No reply from the attorney general to the FBI director's April 16 termination request would be forthcoming for another 18 months. Meanwhile, the controversy continued in public with a particularly noteworthy example of bureaucratic "strategic retreat."

THE FLAHERTY SWITCH ON MESSAGE SWITCHING

On March 17, 1977, Congressman Don Edwards wrote to the newly appointed attorney general, Griffin Bell, to request the status of the department's consideration of the FBI's request for termination of CCH.[65] In a briefing memorandum dated March 30, 1978, the Assistant

[62]*Ibid.*

[63]Richard W. Velde, Administrator, Law Enforcement Assistance Administration, U.S. Department of Justice. Memorandum to Harold R. Tyler, Jr., Deputy Attorney General. Subject: "Proposed DOJ Systems Policy Board Recommendation Regarding NCIC/CCH Program." September 24, 1976.

[64]Clarence M. Kelley, Director, Federal Bureau of Investigation, U.S. Department of Justice. Memorandum to Harold R. Tyler, Jr., Deputy Attorney General. Subject: "FBI Proposal to Terminate Its Participation in National Crime Information Center (NCIC) Computerized Criminal History (CCH) Program." September 17, 1976, p. 2.

[65]Don Edwards, Chairman, Subcommittee on Civil and Constitutional Rights, Committee on the Judiciary, House, U.S. Congress. Letter to Griffin B. Bell, Attorney General. March 17, 1977.

Attorney General for Administration, Glen E. Pommerening, noted that no action had been taken by Attorney General Levi on the fourth recommendation of the policy board and that Attorney General Bell should "revisit" this issue area and consider the matter on its merits.[66] Shortly thereafter, the FBI director wrote to Attorney General Bell requesting authority to implement message-switching applications "totally unrelated to the Computerized Criminal History (CCH) application."[67] The FBI desired to upgrade NCIC's message-switching capability for want/warrant and all stolen property files (see Chapter 4).

On May 19, 1977, Deputy Attorney General Peter F. Flaherty responded to the FBI request by authorizing that message switching be approved for: "(1) switching messages relating to NCIC files unrelated to CCH and (b) [sic] switching messages at the request of NLETS to and from remote localities, such as Puerto Rico."[68] In addition, Flaherty observed that "the FBI should not terminate its participation in the CCH Program" until it received further advice.[69]

The reaction by Congress to Flaherty's decision on message switching was immediate and intense. Congressional members expressed displeasure at the Flaherty approval. Although the authorization did not involve the CCH program directly, it was felt that the decision was premature and that it violated past agreements between Congress and the Department of Justice over prior consultation in matters of this significance. In addition, fears were expressed in the press and by legislative members that this decision was a prelude to allowing message switching for the CCH program by the FBI. Throughout the rest of May and June, public criticism mounted. Then, on June 27, 1977, Flaherty sent another memorandum to the FBI director suspending his authorization of May 19 and informing the director that:

We are thoroughly reviewing the subject of message switching in the Depart-

[66] Glen E. Pommerening, Assistant Attorney General for Administration. Memorandum to Griffin B. Bell, Attorney General. Subject: "Computerized Criminal History (CCH) Program—Request for Status from Congressman Don Edwards (Action Memorandum)." March 30, 1977, p. 2.

[67] Clarence M. Kelley, Director, Federal Bureau of Investigation, U.S. Department of Justice. Memorandum to Griffin B. Bell, Attorney General. Subject: "Message Switching Over the NCIC Network." April 3, 1977, p. 1.

[68] Peter F. Flaherty, Deputy Attorney General. Memorandum to Clarence M. Kelley, Director, Federal Bureau of Investigation, U.S. Department of Justice. Subject: "Message Switching." May 19, 1977, p. 1.

[69] Peter F. Flaherty, Deputy Attorney General. Memorandum to Clarence M. Kelley, Director, Federal Bureau of Investigation, U.S. Department of Justice. Subject: "FBI Participation in the Computerized Criminal History Program." May 19, 1977, p. 1.

ment of Justice, in cooperation with members of Congress, to determine whether the FBI should be permitted to engage in message switching and, if so, what guidelines should be administered to protect the public. In the course of our review, we will, of course, work closely with FBI personnel.[70]

The affair appeared and disappeared without major impact on the controversy, but the Flaherty "switch" did place further emphasis on the need for congressional consultation and approval before any internal departmental resolution of the message-switching question was possible. This point was given explicit recognition in a letter from Congressman Edwards to Flaherty on July 22, 1977.

Our briefing sessions in June, in addition to subsequent staff contacts with state users, indicate that some deterioration in NCIC responsiveness has occurred over the years. I am most concerned that the principal users, the state criminal justice agencies, have their information needs met in the most timely and reliable fashion available. I understand that certain equipment (front-end) enhancement may serve to meet current state needs while also providing the technical capability to message switch.

While the immediate need for certain functions performed by this equipment may be substantial, I wish to avoid the sort of incremental planning that seems to have characterized the past. Thus while any essential expenditures must be studied as soon as possible, I would like to work with your office in *acquiring* a solid understanding of both *short* and *long* range plans for the future of NCIC, criminal justice telecommunications generally and the entire CCH concept.[71]

In addition, Edwards emphasized that the result of "outside" consultation would be considered by his subcommittee in resolving the message-switching issue and that a definite "timetable" was necessary:

For your additional information, members of my Subcommittee staff along with Library of Congress personnel have been visiting with: (1) state participants in the various systems; (2) private planning and/or evaluation groups; and (3) various technical persons familiar with computer operations and audits. We hope that the information derived from these resources along with that from your office and the FBI will enable us to resolve the problems which are of mutual concern.

---

[70] Peter F. Flaherty, Deputy Attorney General. Memorandum to Clarence B. Kelley, Director, Federal Bureau of Investigation, U.S. Department of Justice. Subject: "Message Switching." June 27, 1977, p. 1. See also "Justice Puts Brakes on FBI Switching, Plans Further Study," *Computerworld,* July 11, 1977.

[71] Don Edwards, Representative, U.S. Congress. Letter to Peter F. Flaherty, Deputy Attorney General. July 22, 1977.

I would recommend that a timetable to deal with all of these issues be developed as soon as possible and I look forward to your views on this suggestion.[72]

Clearly, the Flaherty switch typified the indecision and confusion in the Department of Justice at this time and its sensitivity to legislative and public criticism. The criticisms continued throughout the remainder of 1977 with the appearance of two reports that disapproved of NCIC's message switching and CCH programs.

THE CRITIQUE BY "OUTSIDE EXPERTS"

On July 25, 1977, the Privacy Protection Study Commission delivered its report, *Personal Privacy in an Information Society*,[73] to President Carter and Congress. The president received the report at a public meeting and observed that he would take prompt action on its recommendations. Although the report did not highlight the problems of the social costs of criminal justice records, it did reference the "information policy issues of message switching and CCH at the FBI" and suggested that:

Given the particularly damaging character of the information involved and the potential for misuse, any long-range decision to permit Federal agencies to provide such services should be made only if there is no alternative. Further, the Commission believes that the decision to permit Federal agency operation of such services ought to be made through the legislative process, not unilaterally by the Executive branch of the government.[74]

The Privacy Protection Study Commission had merely set forth a general position on the controversy.[75] The Scientists' Institute for Public Information (SIPI), a public interest group studying the social responsibilities of science and technology, provided a more in-depth

[72] *Ibid.*

[73] Privacy Protection Study Commission. *Personal Privacy in an Information Society*. Washington, D.C., U.S. Government Printing Office, 1977.

[74] *Ibid.*, p. 536.

[75] A few years earlier, the Privacy Protection Study Commission had consciously excluded the consideration of criminal justice records based, in part, on the rationale that this area had been receiving sufficient attention and that the commission had many other areas of recordkeeping to explore. In drafting its report, however, the commission did emphasize the still unresolved character of the criminal information policy debate and the need for further study and action. In addition, it placed particular emphasis on the fact that the Privacy Act of 1974 either "ignored or did not address adequately" this concern and that this was a matter on which Congress and the executive branch needed to take action.

TABLE 15   Thirteen Points of Criticism of NCIC by the Scientists' Institute for Public Information

1. There is no regular auditing of NCIC data and procedures by a relatively independent auditing authority.

2. There has been no in-depth evaluation of the actual benefits of NCIC either performed by the states or by the FBI, despite 10 years of operation.

3. For such a vast system containing over 6½ million records and with 250,000 transactions per day, the hit ratio is not impressive.

4. The downtime of the system is excessive.

5. "Expungement" from the system does not mean true expungement of a record. Back-up tapes and a log are necessarily maintained by NCIC for system reliability purposes. This is a necessary precaution common in computer systems; however, since back-up tapes and a log are maintained, "expungement" ("cancellation," "clear") from NCIC really means that the expunged data is not available on-line but does exist on tapes that are kept at FBI headquarters.

6. There have been at least eight lawsuits resulting from the use of NCIC data, due to false arrest, unlawful search and seizure, or other improper practices. One of the side benefits of not fully expunging data is that law enforcement personnel may defend themselves in lawsuits by pointing to data that had previously been maintained in NCIC at one time and may have given "probable cause" for the law enforcement action that the lawsuit arose over.

7. There has been poor disposition reporting by the courts, which means that arrest records remain in the system without updating of the outcome of that arrest. The arrest records do not drop out of CCH even if no disposition is ever reported.

8. NCIC requires a cumbersome correction and updating procedure. When an entering agency corrects an error or wishes to update a record, it must transmit that data to the central state control terminal, for further transmission to NCIC central headquarters in Washington; however, in addition to the data having to pass through several different steps for correction, this procedure doesn't provide for complete correction or updating of NCIC data.

9. The procedures for the verification and certification of data by the states do not prevent at least some stale and incorrect data from being in NCIC at any given time.

10. People are not informed when a CCH record is maintained on them. They do have the right to check their own file through a cumbersome process and the payment of fees in some cases, but figures were not available on the number of people who actually do check.

11. There are serious security and privacy considerations because between 6,600 and 7,000 terminals can access NCIC nationwide. As the number of terminals increase, with a potential of 45,000 local, state, and federal criminal justice user terminals, the opportunities for abuse also will increase. As long as someone can gain unauthorized access either himself or through an authorized user, the system will be open to abuse.

12. Despite nearly six years of operation, only 11 states are participating in the CCH portion of NCIC by providing some input and, of these, only 2 are fully participating in the sense of providing input of all arrest records.

13. As phrased by Deputy Attorney General Peter F. Flaherty, "... this raises at least *two questions*. One, with direct state-to-state access, through the FBI, would there be a

TABLE 15 (Continued)

tremendous increase in the amount of criminal justice information that would be available on-line? For example, California's CLETS system submits only about 10% of its criminal history data to CCH, determined by the gravity of the offense, residence of the defendant, and other factors. However, with direct access, would the entire CLETS system be available to other states? The Task Force felt that as interconnection increases, problem areas multiply. Two, in this electronic context, due to the design of this central switching system, would this mean that the FBI would control the flow of ever-increasing amounts of criminal justice information throughout the country?"

Source: Adapted from Scientists' Institute for Public Information, Task Force on Science and Technology in the Criminal Justice System, Project on Criminal Justice Information Systems. "Report on Inspection and Briefing at the National Crime Information Center, July 22, 1977, and Follow-up, August 2, 1977." New York, 1977, pp. 1–5.

assessment and critique of NCIC/CCH. SIPI's Task Force on Science and Technology in the Criminal Justice System performed an onsite inspection of NCIC, and was briefed by NCIC staff. The task force then drafted a report which outlined 13 points that were critical of NCIC (see Table 15).[76]

The impact of the SIPI report provided NCIC/CCH critics in Congress and the public an opportunity to raise questions about the value of the program.[77] On September 9, 1977, Congressman Edwards requested comments from the FBI on the report. On September 28, 1977, the FBI presented its rebuttal to the SIPI report at a hearing of the Edwards subcommittee.[78] Basically, the bureau's position was that, despite its flaws and problems (which generally were remedial), NCIC was workable and not as bad as the SIPI report made it appear to be. In addition, the FBI observed that it "welcomed" an on-site independent audit of NCIC to satisfy critics such as the SIPI group.[79]

Although the critiques of the Privacy Protection Study Commission and SIPI caused adverse publicity to the Justice Department and the

[76] See Scientists' Institute for Public Information, Task Force on Science and Technology in the Criminal Justice System, Project on Criminal Justice Information Systems, "Report on Inspection and Briefing at the National Crime Information Center, July 12, 1977, and Follow-up, August 2, 1977." New York, 1977.

[77] See also "Study Questions Worth of NCIC," Computerworld, September 12, 1977. The SIPI Report was in direct response to a request by Representative Don Edwards for outside consultation.

[78] U.S. Department of Justice, Federal Bureau of Investigation. "Comments of the Federal Bureau of Investigation (FBI) on the Report on Inspection and Briefing at the National Crime Information Center (NCIC), Dated August 3, 1977, and Prepared by the Task Force on Science and Technology in the Criminal Justice System of the Scientists' Institute for Public Information." Washington, D.C., September 28, 1977.

[79] See "NCIC Audit, Expansion Pending," Computerworld, October 17, 1977; "FBI Questions Reevaluation of Need for NCIC," Computerworld, October 17, 1977.

FBI, the department's position at this time was that it was trying to create an acceptable position with regard to message switching and CCH. By the end of 1977, despite increasing legislative pressure on the attorney general and the White House, no response to the FBI request to terminate NCIC had been received from the attorney general. The Justice Department did not have a consensus position on either message switching or CCH and continued to exhibit indecision and uncertainty in responding to legislative and public critics.

1978 and 1979—More Questions, More Study, and No Decisions

In November and December 1977, three separate but related series of events occurred that set the stage for developments in 1978 and 1979. The first series represented an attempt by the FBI to procure telecommunications control equipment for NCIC; the second series involved congressional attempts to revitalize the consideration of the major policy, political, and social impact questions concerning NCIC/CCH with the aid of Congress' Office of Technology Assessment; and the third series involved a renewed effort by the Office of the Attorney General and SEARCH Group, Inc. to develop proposals for CCH and message switching that would be acceptable to the states, LEAA, the FBI, and the interested members of Congress, especially Congressman Don Edwards.

THE FBI RUNS INTO PROCUREMENT DIFFICULTIES

On August 10, 1977, the assistant director of the Administrative Service Division of the FBI, Harold Bassett, requested from Frank J. Carr, Commissioner of the Automated Data and Telecommunications Service at the General Services Administration (GSA), that the FBI be provided a delegation of procurement authority (DPA) to obtain telecommunications control equipment for NCIC.[80] The FBI desired to replace its two IBM 2703 communications controllers with faster and more reliable equipment. Essentially, the FBI wanted to upgrade its message-handling capability.[81]

The bureau was provided with a DPA under GSA guidelines for the

[80] Harold N. Bassett, Assistant Director, Administrative Services Division, Federal Bureau of Investigation, U.S. Department of Justice. Letter to Frank J. Carr, Commissioner, Automated Data and Telecommunications Service, General Services Administration. August 10, 1977.

[81] "FBI Message-Switch Plans Never Had GSA Clearance." *Computerworld*, March 20, 1978.

procurement of data-processing equipment and services on November 21, 1977. Recognizing the fact that the FBI was interested in purchasing equipment and software that *could be upgraded* to handle message switching under the CCH program, the GSA commissioner specifically noted that the DPA did not authorize the FBI to acquire the proposed message-switching capability: "Before we can process a request for a DPA to obtain the message switching capability, the FBI must provide us with documentation to confirm that this function is specifically approved by the Deputy Attorney General."[82]

On December 19, 1977, the FBI distributed to potential vendors its request for proposal (RFP) for telecommunications control equipment and software for NCIC. A March 1, 1978 deadline was set. In the cover memorandum, Bassett noted a requirement in the solicitation that "In order to allow for this possible enhancement, offerors are required to include in their proposal the hardware and software components necessary for message switching."[83] Bassett also emphasized that the bureau's current DPA did not include a message-switching option and that another DPA would have to be issued before message-switching equipment could be obtained.[84]

Congressman John Moss (D.-Calif.) publicly protested the RFP as premature and having been initiated without consultation with Congress.[85] On March 8, 1978, Washington Post columnist Jack Anderson criticized, in highly emotive terms, the "insatiable itch" of the FBI to get its hands on a "forbidden" new telecommunications system "that eventually could compile dossiers on virtually every person in the United States." He narrated how the FBI sought the equipment despite the protests of Moss to "sidetrack" its moves. Anderson noted that the RFP included only the option for the message-switching capability, but it was clear that he perceived this move as an ominous sign, going on to say that

Jay Cochran, the FBI's Assistant Director for technical services, argued the solicitation was proper because it advised the bidders that the message switch-

---

[82] Frank J. Carr, Commissioner, Automated Data and Telecommunications Service, General Services Administration. Letter to Harold N. Bassett, Assistant Director Administrative Services Division, Federal Bureau of Investigation, U.S. Department of Justice. November 21, 1977, p. 1.

[83] Harold N. Bassett, Assistant Director, Administrative Services Division, Contracting Officer, Federal Bureau of Investigation, U.S. Department of Justice. Cover Letter for Request for Proposal No. 2014: "Telecommunication Control Equipment for the National Crime Information Center." December 19, 1977, p. 1.

[84] *Ibid.*

[85] See "FBI Message-Switch Plans."

ing system had not actually been authorized. . . . Cochran said he was unaware of the promise that Congress would be consulted. But Congressional sources believe the FBI tried a sneak play, operating on the assumption that if they could get contractors to include specific message switching proposals in the bids, they could confront the Carter Administration and Congress with a fait accompli.[86]

The day after Anderson's column appeared, Congressman Edwards sent a letter to FBI Director William Webster about the "press report," which observed that the FBI had failed to comply with GSA guidelines. Edwards suggested that, although the report was "exaggerated in many respects," nevertheless, it did "bring to light disturbing facts about the Bureau's actions" which had been confirmed by Frank Carr, the commissioner of GSA's Automated Data and Telecommunications Service. Edwards wrote:

> It is my understanding that GSA delegated authority to procure the computer equipment with the express limitation that, since the Bureau lacked approval for message switching, no message switching capability could be required of the equipment. Nonetheless, unbeknownst to GSA and the Congress, the Bureau notified potential vendors that no bids would be considered on equipment which lacked message switching capability...This appears to me to demonstrate either a disturbing incompetence or an intentional defiance of the rules.[87]

The day after receipt of this letter, Carr revoked the FBI's DPA and requested that all vendor proposals be returned unopened.[88] On March 17, 1978, FBI Director Webster responded to Edwards' letter by assuring him that the bureau had "no intention of implementing message switching with the new telecommunication control equipment" without receiving proper permission. Webster disagreed with GSA Commissioner Carr's conclusion that the procurement was faulty; nevertheless, the bureau desired to "be completely open and forthright" and to comply with Carr's decision to revoke the DPA. In a conciliatory note to Congressman Edwards, Webster observed:

> I regret that the actions we have taken with regard to this procurement have

[86] Jack Anderson. "FBI Angles for Computer System." *Washington Post*, March 8, 1978.

[87] Don Edwards, Chairman, Subcommittee on Civil and Constitutional Rights, Committee on the Judiciary, House, U.S. Congress. Letter to William H. Webster, Director, Federal Bureau of Investigation, U.S. Department of Justice. March 9, 1978, pp. 1–2.

[88] Frank J. Carr, Commissioner, Automated Data and Telecommunications Service, General Services Administration. Letter to Jay Cochran, Jr., Assistant Director, Technical Services Division, Federal Bureau of Investigation, U.S. Department of Justice. March 10, 1978.

been misinterpreted; however, I want to assure you that our efforts in this matter have at all times been consistent with the instructions of the Department of Justice and in compliance with what we felt were the expressed wishes of you and your Subcommittee.[89]

Whether the procurement difficulties of the FBI in this case could be called an honest mistake, a misinterpretation, or a "sneaky" move appears somewhat irrelevant. This episode is interesting because it represented an attempt by the bureau to exercise what it considered to be legitimate management prerogatives in an area characterized by conflict, uncertainty, and confrontation. The episode also emphasized the need to address the larger questions prior to dealing with technical and administrative details, so that such details do not become simply an occasion for carrying on the battle over unresolved problems. In the face of unresolved social, political, and legal problems, the seemingly innocuous effort of the FBI to upgrade and procure telecommunications control equipment became another occasion for congressional and public critics to highlight the bureau's and the Justice Department's inability and unwillingness to deal with the fundamental issues involved.[90]

Evaluation of the NCIC/CCH System by the Office of Technology Assessment

During the period when the FBI's procurement efforts were initiated, a series of events occurred that contrasted sharply in both tone and

---

[89] William H. Webster, Director, Federal Bureau of Investigation, U.S. Department of Justice. Letter to Don Edwards, Representative, U.S. Congress. March 17, 1978, p. 2.

[90] As a congressional aide suggested, the basic issue was, and is, trust: To what extent can the FBI be trusted to do what it says it will do in the face of Watergate and domestic intelligence abuses of the last 20 years. A second underlying issue was voiced by a congressional committee staff member: Any procurement of telecommunications equipment for internal or external purposes was suspect, since it would be difficult to ensure that the equipment would be used for the reasons intended and not for some covert or presumably unjustifiable purpose. The FBI has vehemently criticized this position as an obstructive tactic designed to interfere with legitimate operational needs. See "FBI Chief Criticizes Congress," *Washington Post*, September 2, 1978. The more recent attempts of Senator Howard Metzenbaum (D.-Ohio) to bar the Justice Department from using federal funds to acquire any *internal* or *external* message-switching equipment without explicit approval by the House and Senate judiciary committees have maintained the controversy over the credibility of the FBI and congressional distrust of its stated intentions. See "Up Amendment 1578," *Congressional Record, 124* (Part 120):S. 12462, August 3, 1978; and U.S. Congress, Senate Report No. 95-911, Calendar No. 847, *Department of Justice Authorization Bill Fiscal Year, 1979*, 95th Congress, 2d Session, pp. 9–10.

substance with the narrow debate over the FBI's request for proposal. In the early fall of 1977, several House and Senate members asked the Congressional Office of Technology Assessment (OTA) to conduct a complete evaluation of NCIC and, in particular, the CCH and message-switching matters.[91] In November 1977, the first meeting of the OTA informal working group of outside experts and inside staff was held,[92] and in March 1978, the working group completed a draft report entitled "A Preliminary Assessment of the NCIC Computerized Criminal History System."[93] This draft constituted perhaps the most comprehensive analysis of issues and problems that had been developed to date. The report noted that "some of the issues and questions are old," but it emphasized two new characteristics that made consideration of the issues necessary:

(1) What is new is this critical moment of decision for the future development of the system which is now faced by Congress, the Justice Department, and state and local agencies who use such information. They are presented with new opportunities for application and rearrangement of the information processing and telecommunications technology in the light of changes in our society, in our economy, in concepts of federalism, and in the public expectations of effective law enforcement work combined with effective government record-keeping and fair use of information wherever it affects the citizen.

(2) What is new, furthermore, is increased awareness of the need for careful fact finding on matters which may determine the successful structuring of the CCH system according to the changing and varied needs of government and society.[94]

[91] See, for example, Peter Rodino, Jr., Chairman, Committee on the Judiciary, House, U.S. Congress, and Don Edwards, Chairman, Subcommittee on Civil and Constitutional Rights, Committee on the Judiciary, House, U.S. Congress, Letter to Edward M. Kennedy, Chairman of the Board, Office of Technology Assessment, U.S. Congress, September 12, 1977.

[92] The working group members were Adam D'Alessandro, Acting Deputy Commissioner, New York State Division of Criminal Justice Services; Jerry J. Berman, Legislative Counsel, American Civil Liberties Union; Donald G. Ingraham, Office of the District Attorney, Oakland, California; Steve Kolodney, SEARCH Group, Inc.; Kenneth Laudon, Professor, John Jay College of Criminal Justice; Charles Lister, Attorney, Covington & Burling; Michael D. Maltz, Professor, University of Illinois at Chicago Circle, Department of Criminal Justice; Jeffrey A. Meldman, Professor, MIT Sloan School of Management; Brian Ruder, Information Science Laboratory, SRI International; James J. Zurawski, Assistant Deputy Superintendent, Research Development and Data Systems Division, Chicago Police Department; and David T. Stanley, Consultant.

[93] U.S. Congress, Office of Technology Assessment. "A Preliminary Assessment of the NCIC Computerized Criminal History System." Draft Report. March 1978.

[94] *Ibid.*, pp. 13–14; see also "Fears of FBI Switch Plan Grow," *Computerworld*, November 28, 1977.

Both the congressional and OTA perception of the situation necessitated a look at the broad issues and problems and not simply at the narrow questions of law and management. The OTA report, therefore, composed an "NCIC Issues List," which articulated the basic areas and questions that had been raised in the past 10 years on the CCH and message-switching controversy (see Table 16). Although the report did not make any specific recommendations on how these questions should be addressed, it set an agenda for discussion that opened a whole array of concerns and options surrounding the NCIC issue. In addition, the report was perhaps the first document expressing concern over the problem of the social costs of criminal justice records and recognizing the difficulty of formulating privacy and security policy in the absence of data on the extent and nature of the harm accruing to individuals with criminal justice records.

The present climate is clouded by the absence of well-established information on the completeness, ambiguities and accuracy of criminal history data, and on the nature of the injuries to individuals that would be caused by improper use of CCH records or inadequate CCH records. The extent of actual incidence of such injuries is also unknown.

It is important for policymakers to understand the origins, frequency, and consequences of erroneous or incomplete records in order to strike a fair balance between potential harm and potential benefits.[95]

The report recognized that inaccurate records or record discrimination in employment, licensing, and other contexts did harm individuals and emphasized that many of the issues concerning data accuracy, dissemination, disposition reporting, and adverse effects were badly clouded by lack of information. In addition, it noted that the resolution of the division of authority question was "a severe obstacle to the successful development of CCH."[96]

The diversity of political-organizational structures and powers imposed significant obstacles to achieving the CCH concept. Since the system's management problems called for cooperation "among states, between state and local governments, between state and federal governments, among federal agencies, and among components of the criminal justice system at all three levels," a "representative intergovernmental consortium" was called for to manage the system. The question remained, however, "whether sufficient consensus on these matters exists to permit resolution at this time."[97]

[95] U.S. Congress, Office of Technology Assessment. "A Preliminary Assessment of the NCIC Computerized Criminal History System," pp. 13–14.
[96] *Ibid.*, pp. 25, 32.
[97] *Ibid.*, pp. 38, 40.

TABLE 16   NCIC Issues List

1. Information Needs
   a. *Criminal Justice Requirements:* The requirements of the Criminal Justice System for CCH information are not identified sufficiently to support planning and evaluation of an interstate system.
   b. *Constitutional Rights:* The threats to constitutional rights potentially posed by a CCH system are not sufficiently identified for planning and evaluation of an interstate system.

2. Federalism
   a. *Division of Authority:* What authority should be allocated among the units of government to control the contemplated CCH system in terms of efficacy, legality and accountability?
   b. *Cost Apportionment:* How shall the costs of developing and operating the contemplated system be apportioned among federal, state and local governments?

3. Organization, Management and Oversight
   a. *Management Responsibilities:* Considering the decentralized nature of the Criminal Justice System what sort of management structure is required for CCH?
   b. *Oversight:* What oversight mechanisms are needed to ensure that the CCH system will operate in the overall public interest?
   c. *Role of FBI:* Is the FBI the appropriate agency to manage the CCH system?

4. The Planning Process
   a. *Participation in Planning:* How can the needs and interests of the various levels of government, the criminal justice community and other stakeholder groups best be accommodated in the planning and design of the contemplated system?
   b. *Technical Alternatives:* What technical alternatives to the proposed message switching system might offer advantages when the full range of system requirements and social concerns are considered?
   c. *Transition Planning:* Considering the significant change in criminal justice recordkeeping that CCH implies and the long transition period before it can be implemented fully, what aspects of this transitional period require planning now?

5. Long-Term Impacts
   a. *Effects on the Criminal Justice System:* In what ways, desirable, or undesirable, might CCH cause, or contribute to changes in the operation or organization of the criminal justice system?
   b. *The Dossier Society:* To what extent, if any, might CCH contribute to the growth of federal social control, or become an instrument for subversion of the democratic process?
   c. *Privacy and Civil Liberties Trends:* Is there a conflict between maintaining national privacy and civil liberties trends and decentralizing responsibility for the CCH system?

Source: U.S. Congress, Office of Technology Assessment. "A Preliminary Assessment of the NCIC Computerized Criminal History System." Draft Report. March 1978, pp. 18–19.

The report also reviewed and discussed the matters of management, financial oversight, and planning responsibilities concerning CCH and argued for more open and representative management and against the FBI's exclusive management control over the system. Two sets of concerns that challenged the traditional dominance of NCIC and the CCH program by the FBI and law enforcement agencies in particular were cited. The first set of concerns involved questions of political trust:

> The changing political environment has caused many to wonder if there can be sufficient public acceptance of the FBI's role as developer and manager of a national message switching capability for criminal histories. If, as the FBI proposed, the CCH message switching capability is added onto the current FBI NCIC operation, what will prevent future misuse of the system? How will Congress exercise control and oversight, and how can such a system be made accountable to both Congress and the public?

The second set of concerns revolved around the FBI's many "contradictory or at least conflicting" responsibilities:

> The FBI is an investigating agency which also bears a heavy responsibility for the maintenance of criminal records, stolen property records, and the prediction of criminal statistics. It is also involved in a number of programs involving training of state police officials, maintenance of an extensive forensic laboratory, and, significant local aid programs.
> A widely respected principle of the organization suggests that unique functions (like investigation as opposed to criminal statistics) be embedded in specialized and relatively autonomous social units.[98]

Thus, the report suggested that, although separation of functions would have serious impacts on the FBI, the alternative of outside management should be considered.

In addition, the report made it clear that the process of the Justice Department in developing a blueprint for CCH was considered too narrow in terms of the participation of interested groups:

> The essence of the CCH system is that the primary sources and users of the data are the state and local criminal justice agencies.... It is questionable that a blueprint for a workable system can be created without their playing a direct, perhaps even principal role in the planning.
> The nature of the information in the CCH system has raised public concern and debate about privacy and due process. Special interest groups and others have had the opportunity to express their views at several congressional hearings. But there has not been any mechanism for involving these groups in the

[98] *Ibid.*, p. 62.

planning process. Such involvement may be necessary to the development of a workable system.

Also to be considered in the planning process should be the public at large.[99]

Finally, three long-term impacts that the fully developed CCH network might have were examined. The first impact concerned how CCH could either improve the quality of criminal justice decision making or introduce further inequities:

1. Will the proposed CCH system strengthen trends towards administrative justice as opposed to traditional conceptions of legal due process, presumption of innocence, and full, fair, and open hearings?

2. What is the likely effect of the proposed CCH system on the administrative process and relationships between criminal justice agencies?

3. Will the proposed CCH system make it more difficult for former offenders to re-integrate into society and thus impede their rehabilitation?

4. What is the likely impact of use of CCH in criminal justice decision-making on case loads, detention and prison populations, and requirements for judges and attorneys?[100]

The second impact to which the OTA report directed attention was the extent to which CCH might contribute to the growth of social control or subvert the democratic process:

1. To what extent, if any, does the proposed CCH System in combination with other Federal Systems in the Internal Revenue Service, Social Security, and DHEW expand the potential surveillance capacity of the federal government beyond reasonable limits?

2. To what extent, if any, will the development of a national Inter-State CCH capability expand criminal justice demand for and use of CCH records?

3. Given the potential for linkage between the proposed CCH system and the many other, new, massive Federal data banks, to what extent is it advisable for Congress to establish an agency specifically charged with monitoring or controlling these systems?

4. Are the available oversight and auditing mechanisms strong enough to alert Society to adverse consequences in time to avoid or reverse them?[101]

The third long-term impact emphasized in the report was the possible conflict between maintaining national privacy and civil liberties trends and decentralizing responsibility for the CCH system:

---

[99] *Ibid.*, p. 65.
[100] *Ibid.*, p. 87.
[101] *Ibid.*, p. 91.

1. What would be the impact of decentralization of CCH on the opportunity for oversight of constitutional rights protection throughout the country?

2. Would it be more or less possible for interested groups to focus attention on violations or patterns of governmental abuses?

3. Would a decentralized system be more or less responsive to the privacy concerns of individuals?[102]

OTA recognized that the automation of CCH records had precipitated a "long-needed dialog" on record use and abuse issues, which was helping to develop a national criminal information policy as well as "energized reforms" in other areas of recordkeeping. Nevertheless, several serious consequences to the movement were noted:

> Returning CCH files to the states or to another entity, under different umbrellas, might reduce the opportunity for oversight of the way important constitutional rights interests are being protected throughout the country. It is not clear whether interested groups would find it easier or more difficult to turn a spotlight on a violation or pattern of governmental abuses with the intensity sufficient to effect changes. Restructuring of NCIC might result in throwing such political interest groups into an arena dominated by influential police chiefs and political executives in the law enforcement and criminal justice agencies of each state. On the other hand, such a scenario might make it easier to advocate changes and promote oversight in areas of concern not only to constitutional rights groups but those concerned with maintenance of effective criminal justice systems.[103]

The OTA report presented a comprehensive case for reviewing the significant political, social, legal, moral, and organizational issues involved in CCH and initiating an effort to base policy in this area on more accurate assessment of the social costs of criminal justice records and the use and dissemination of these records. The report was intended to expand the agenda for consideration of the CCH controversy; its immediate effect was to justify OTA's interest in a more comprehensive follow-up study.[104] Although the OTA report masterfully reviewed the whole range of long- and short-term issues and questions involved, it had the unintended effect of moving congressional and administrative concerns away, at least in the short-term, from addressing the larger and more fundamental matters and con-

---

[102] *Ibid.*, p. 95.

[103] *Ibid.*, pp. 96–97.

[104] OTA was subsequently granted $425,000 to do a comprehensive study during 1979 of the social impacts of several large-scale information systems including NCIC/CCH, as well as electronic funds transfer (EFT) and electronic mail systems.

centrating instead on a workable reconciliation of the diverse positions within the Department of Justice with congressional concerns over the rights of individuals and the authorization issues involved.[105]

The Department of Justice Presses Ahead

In a letter dated September 29, 1977, Deputy Attorney General Flaherty proposed to Congressman Don Edwards some interim measures that would improve NCIC operations, which included "continuing FBI participation in CCH while taking steps to decentralize the files and adopt a 'blueprint' developed in concert with Congress" and other interested parties, adding message-switching capability to NCIC's computer system but not employing it until the development was approved, negotiating with the General Accounting Office to provide an independent NCIC audit capability, and reviewing NCIC Advisory Policy Board report procedures to ensure maximum effectiveness.[106] On October 20, 1977, Edwards responded to Flaherty's proposal by emphasizing the need to develop standards assuring that CCH records distributed to the states would be protected against misuse. Edwards also suggested that the Department of Justice consider seriously whether message switching should be performed by another agency, such as NLETS, and whether "persons not directly involved in the NCIC System" should be added to the NCIC Advisory Policy Board.[107]

In the midst of this exchange of letters between Flaherty and Edwards, an informal group of officials from the Office of the Attorney General, the FBI, and LEAA and staff members of Edwards' subcommittee initiated an effort to solicit the opinions of various state criminal justice agency officials as the basis for developing program

[105] The sentiment among some activists in Congress was to wait for completion of the OTA comprehensive assessment and, in the meantime, to keep the Justice Department from going ahead with its blueprint activities and the FBI's telecommunications equipment procurement plans. Other activists in Congress, however, such as Congressman Don Edwards, urged the Justice Department to press ahead with its blueprint activities, with only limited reference to the range of issues suggested in the OTA report. In effect, they adopted a pragmatic strategy of letting the department resolve the CCH and message-switching issues, with congressional consultation, to see if a consensus position could be reached.

[106] Peter F. Flaherty, Deputy Attorney General. Letter to Don Edwards, Chairman, Subcommittee on Civil and Constitutional Rights, Committee on the Judiciary, House, U.S. Congress. September 29, 1977.

[107] Don Edwards, Chairman, Subcommittee on Civil and Constitutional Rights, Committee on the Judiciary, House, U.S. Congress. Letter to Peter F. Flaherty, Deputy Attorney General. October 20, 1977.

blueprints which would then be made available for consideration by the executive and legislative branches of federal and state governments. Ten states—considered to be a representative sample—were visited, and state criminal justice officials were asked a series of questions dealing with the needs of the specific state (see Table 17). A total of 49 officials were interviewed, most of whom represented state law enforcement interests rather than judicial or correctional concerns; no members of local government criminal justice agencies were officially

TABLE 17   Questions Asked of State Criminal Justice Officials

1. In discharging intra-state criminal justice responsibilities, is it necessary to acquire out-of-state criminal justice data for (a) wanted persons, (b) wanted properties, and (c) prior criminal offenses?

2. If it is necessary to obtain out-of-state information for (a) wanted persons, (b) wanted properties, or (c) prior criminal offenses, which data could be obtained satisfactorily by means of bilateral agreement between states? Which of this data could be obtained reasonably by means of regional arrangements? Must any of this data be the subject of a routine nationwide inquiry?

3. If a nationwide information interchange facility is required to exchange criminal justice information for (a) wanted persons, (b) wanted properties, or (c) prior criminal offenses, what is the proper and preferred role of any participating federal agency? That is, should the role and responsibility of a participating federal agency be similar to that of a participating state, or should the participating federal agency have responsibility for the administration of the nationwide criminal justice information interchange facility?

4. If a federal agency is to be responsible for the administration of a nationwide criminal justice information interchange facility, should that agency be one which does not have operational law enforcement responsibilities? More specifically, if a federal agency is a proper and preferred agency to administer such a facility, should that responsibility be vested in the FBI?

5. What changes, improvements, etc., are needed in terms of the existing capabilities, procedures, etc., which govern the interjurisdictional exchange of criminal justice information? What problems, if any, are associated with the present criminal identification process in which local criminal justice agencies submit identification requests directly to the FBI? Are the present methods of processing such requests adequate and responsive to the needs of the state criminal justice community? What alternative methods would be preferable?

6. Do the present methods associated with the collection, storage, and exchange of criminal records afford state officials adequate control over access to, and dissemination of criminal records? What, if anything, must be done to remedy any existing shortcomings?

Source: U.S. Department of Justice, Office of the Attorney General. *Representative Viewpoints of State Criminal Justice Officials Regarding the Need for a Nationwide Criminal Justice Information Interchange Facility.* Washington, D.C., 1978, pp. 3–4.

interviewed in any of the states. On March 6, 1978, the Department of Justice issued the report of the working group, entitled *Representative Viewpoints of State Criminal Justice Officials Regarding the Need for a Nationwide Criminal Justice Information Interchange Facility.*[108] The report noted the lack of progress over the years in resolving the "problems associated with the collection and interjurisdictional exchange of criminal justice information," due not to any single source of opposition or for any simple reason, but because of

an uneven appreciation of the intertwined conceptual, institutional, operational and personal privacy considerations,...pronounced differences of opinion concerning the need for collection and exchange of criminal justice information, what agencies should participate in the collection and exchange of criminal justice information, and finally, what information should be collected and exchanged and by what means.

These conflicting and unresolved viewpoints had resulted in a programmatic impasse:

Criminal justice officials have been unsuccessful in obtaining an acceptable program direction, and as a result, duplicative efforts abound, public funds are wasted, confusion and distrust between levels and branches of government has increased, and little progress has been made in improving either the standards governing the collection and exchange of criminal justice information, or the accuracy and currency of the increasing amount of criminal justice information which continues to be exchanged by a variety of means.[109]

Despite the apparent willingness to initiate change and the claim of objectivity in their approach, it was apparent that, by virtue of the state officials selected for the survey, the report confirmed the position of the FBI and Office of the Attorney General on a number of key matters.

On the crucial question of who should manage the network, the report noted that state officials repeatedly and without exception expressed a preference for a federally administered facility.

The state officials frequently pointed out that a federally administered facility is "neutral" in terms of its dealings with state agencies and tends to be uniformly responsive to all states. Further, recognizing the sensitivity of the

---

[108] U.S. Department of Justice, Office of the Attorney General. *Representative Viewpoints of State Criminal Justice Officials Regarding the Need for a Nationwide Criminal Justice Information Interchange Facility.* Washington, D.C., 1978. For a listing of those interviewed, see pp. 5–6.

[109] *Ibid.,* p. 1.

subject matter . . . , many state officials expressed the view that a federally administered facility would be subject to greater scrutiny and, hence, would more likely be in compliance with existing laws, regulations, and policies than a facility administered by a non-federal entity, such as a consortium of states, etc.

While many state officials expressly or implicitly recognized that in the longer term a federal agency other than the FBI could provide the services expected of a nationwide criminal justice information exchange facility, there was a clear consensus that the FBI should continue to provide such services in the foreseeable future.[110]

The credibility problem that the FBI had experienced in recent years was, according to the report, "not a significant issue." As Table 18 suggests, the report did detail criticisms made by state officials about the Justice Department, the FBI, and, to a lesser degree, LEAA; however, its main thrust was to propose a "consensus concept" that would best satisfy the needs of the states. The concept was, on the whole, the pointer index system that had been suggested by LEAA and SEARCH, but it would be under FBI control rather than predominantly state control.[111] The consensus concept offered a compromise between LEAA and the FBI as well as the states in an effort to achieve some progress in resolving problems concerning CCH and the message-switching controversy.

On April 15, Deputy Assistant Attorney General for Administration Edward Dolan forwarded a copy of the report and his recommendation to Attorney General Bell for further action. The consequent events, which caused Bell's consideration of the recommendation to be tabled for the foreseeable future were described by Dolan at the NCIC Advisory Policy Board meeting:

We sent that report and a recommendation to the Attorney General around April 15th. We advised him that the NCIC Advisory Policy Board had set up a special committee and that they had come up with a proposed solution that was essentially consistent with our report. We recommended that a Blue Ribbon Committee of knowledgeable state authorities be constituted as an Attorney General's special task force to make recommendations as to how to upgrade state identification bureaus and decentralize criminal history records, with particular emphasis on involvement of Federal funding.

Shortly after that went to the Attorney General's Office, I received a call from the President's Reorganization Project and I was advised that the President's Reorganization Project on law enforcement would be sending the

---

[110] *Ibid.*, pp. 7–8.
[111] *Ibid.*, pp. 12–15.

TABLE 18   Important Criticisms of State Officials

1. Indecisiveness of the Federal Government's support of NCIC and the CCH program.

2. Fragmented responsibility within the FBI with respect to criminal history records.

3. The direct, routine, and frequently unnecessary submission of fingerprint cards from the arresting agency to the FBI Identification Division.

4. Methods governing the interjurisdictional exchange of criminal records do not meet the needs of state and local criminal justice agencies.

5. Lack of state control over state criminal records presently held in the central repository maintained by the FBI Identification Division.

6. Composition of the NCIC Advisory Policy Board.

7. LEAA funding concepts, particularly the "bundling" of numerous functions within the LEAA Comprehensive Data Systems (CDS) program.

Source: Adapted from U.S. Department of Justice, Office of the Attorney General. *Representative Viewpoints of State Criminal Justice Officials,* pp. 8–11.

President their recommendation as to the reorganization of Federal law enforcement agencies in the near future. I was requested to hold in abeyance our consideration of the CCH matter until their report was cleared through the Office of Management and Budget and the White House. We did hold it in abeyance simply because the Attorney General should not be deciding things that might be inconsistent with what the Reorganization Project was recommending to the President.[112]

On June 1, 1978, a presidential decision memorandum (PDM) had been forwarded by the President's Reorganization Project on Federal Law Enforcement to President Carter, detailing a recommendation to create a Bureau of Information and Statistics in the Department of Justice, which would have included the FBI Identification Division and NCIC. On June 12, 1978, President Carter approved the PDM; however, shortly thereafter, a hold was placed on the approved PDM and the reorganization plan was never enacted.

Subsequently, the Office of the Deputy Assistant General for Administration developed a slide presentation for its "consensus concept," which it began screening for administration representatives and congressional members and staff in mid-July. The purpose of the presentation was to provide an overview of the current CCH and message-switching situation and to recommend "the consensus concept" reflected in the March Report. Neither the attorney general nor

[112] National Crime Information Center Advisory Policy Board. "Minutes" (June 21–22, 1978), pp. 48–49. Mimeographed.

the White House were ready to move on these issues, and no significant changes would have occurred in the short term.

During the developments surrounding the "consensus concept," SEARCH Group, Inc. (SGI), in the spring of 1978, proposed its own "consensus concept" for resolving the CCH and message-switching controversies.

On March 9, 1979, the SGI board of directors adopted a position paper, entitled *A Framework for Constructing an Improved National Criminal History System*.[113] The purpose of the paper was not to develop a "blueprint" but to articulate criteria against which alternative approaches could be evaluated. The paper detailed the key policy positions that SGI supported and the characteristics of a national system consistent with these views. To a great extent, the paper reiterated the basic position of SGI on state versus federal control and emphasized the importance of a national pointer approach to CCH. On April 27, 1978, shortly after the Justice Department issued its own "consensus concept" report, the members of SEARCH Group, Inc. approved and adopted the SGI position paper. Clearly, the consensus concept of the Department of Justice had been countered by the "consensus framework" from SGI. During the remainder of 1978 and 1979, each group advocated its approach to resolving the national policy debate over the CCH program.

CONCLUSION: THE DEVELOPMENT OF CRIMINAL JUSTICE INFORMATION POLICY AS AN ISSUE

Chapter 5 suggested that, given the size and characteristics of the public affected by the social costs of criminal justice records, it could be expected that such a public would not engage in collective action. Chapters 2, 3, and 5 indicated that the development of information policy to reduce the social costs of criminal justice records as an issue was not the result of collective action by the relevant public. During the period from 1965 until the early 1970s, the concern for the social costs of criminal justice records developed in the context of the wider problem area of privacy and computers. Beginning to a large extent with the controversy over the National Data Center, the possible adverse effects of widespread computerization in government and private industry on the privacy and lives of individuals received na-

---

[113] SEARCH Group, Inc. *A Framework for Constructing an Improved National Criminal History System*. Sacramento, Calif., 1978.

tional attention as the subject of congressional and public debate. This period was the breakthrough stage for the issue of privacy and computers on the community and governmental agendas. Fears generated by the potential effects of computers resulted in widespread calls for safeguards. In turn, the outcome of the National Data Center controversy pointed out to the developers of information systems a poignant lesson: Either there was some recognition of the problems of privacy presented by a proposed information system or public concern and legislative interest might cause a cutoff or curtailment of proposed activities.

Almost from the start of the privacy and computers debate, the use of criminal justice records for other than criminal justice purposes was singled out as an important example of the problems that computerization would exacerbate; therefore, proposals to design an integrated network of criminal justice information systems and an interstate criminal history exchange system included various safeguards to minimize the social costs of criminal justice records. Thus, the outcome of this early stage in the formation of the privacy and computers issue was a realization on the part of developers of criminal justice information systems that the uses of criminal justice records, which were mostly unexamined in the manual period, had to be regulated if advanced criminal justice information systems were to be established at local, state, and federal levels.

With the further development, beginning in 1971, of criminal justice information systems at the local and state levels with LEAA funds and the design and implementation of the FBI's NCIC/CCH program, more public attention was focused on the effects of computerization in government and private industry generally and on law enforcement and the administration of criminal justice. In addition, the principal concern was no longer simply the potential adverse effects of computers but rather the need for more effective and systematic information policies concerning the collection, maintenance, and dissemination of criminal justice records. In the next stage, the consideration of criminal justice information policy turned to the organizational policies and practices in local, state, and federal criminal justice agencies. Formulation of information policy moved from the informal and abstract stages to the center of policy debate about the control and regulation of criminal justice information and information systems. At this time, two principal areas of controversy emerged: The first concerned the management and control of the criminal history exchange system and the formulation of appropriate information policy related to the records in that system; the second concerned the role and responsibilities of LEAA for regulating the nature and extent of information policy and information systems in local and state criminal justice agencies.

After initial periods of formulation, the two problem areas merged into a single concern in 1974 and 1975, with the development of a comprehensive national policy to control the use of criminal justice records and a nationwide network of criminal history information systems.

During 1974 and 1975, a number of attempts were made to pass legislation that was acceptable to all the actors involved. Legislative proposals were drafted by the Department of Justice and the Senate and House Subcommittees on Constitutional Rights in an attempt to develop criminal information policies that would protect individual rights and reduce the social costs of criminal justice records, as well as serve the interests of the criminal justice community. Almost from the beginning, however, these efforts met with frustration and resistance from the criminal justice community, the press, and other outside private and public interest groups not satisfied with various provisions of the complex legislation. During 1975 in particular, the controversy over message switching erupted into a full-scale bureaucratic debate between LEAA and the FBI, which began to absorb the energies not only of the parties directly involved, but also the states, public interest groups, and legislative members intent on assuring that individual rights in these matters were properly protected. At this point, legislative initiatives to achieve consensus on criminal justice information policy lost momentum as the focus of concern shifted back to the Department of Justice. A policy was sought that would satisfy the intense organizational interests involved and, at the same time, that would be responsive to concern about the protection of individual rights and the reduction of the social costs of criminal justice records.

The contemporary period of issue development in the area of criminal information policy has, since 1976, continued to be characterized by intense organizational politics at the federal level, coupled with equally intense, if not always consistent, legislative oversight of the process of administrative decision making over the future of the CCH program and message switching by the FBI. State and local governments have made some progress in developing legislative and administrative policies over the use of criminal history records, but the Federal Government has continued a course characterized by misunderstanding, polarization, and, at times, acute infighting and indecision. Although both the Congress and the Department of Justice have, at various times, shown a desire to work together in developing policies, for a variety of reasons, they remain apart.

Thus, the contemporary period of criminal justice information policy development continues to be characterized by frustration and doubt about the prospects of ever establishing a nationwide network of criminal history information systems and information policy responsive to the social impacts of criminal justice records. Neither the developers and advocates of such a network nor the supporters of individual rights have really succeeded. The former have been frustrated in their attempts to proceed with their plans for systems development and reform and have, in the process, consumed a great deal of time and resources; the latter have halted and frustrated attempts to proceed with innovations they consider dangerous to human rights and have, in part, not perceived the opportunity for policy change built into the visibility accorded the use of computer technology in government. In effect, the goal of preventing premature and ill-considered attempts to develop systems that are harmful to human rights have obscured two constructive opportunites: first, the need to develop a fuller awareness of social impacts inherent in technological innovations in the public sector, and, second, the chance to bring lasting reforms in a policy area of low visibility, low intensity, and low general interest but with enormous implications for the social, economic, and moral viability of society.

9

Representation and the Social Costs of Criminal Justice Records

The preceding three chapters focused primarily on the patterns of development of criminal justice information policy concerned with regulating the social costs of criminal justice records. Particular attention was given to the factors influencing the development of criminal justice information policy to reduce social costs as an issue, with the problem of representation as an implicit theme. This chapter will make that theme explicit by reviewing the findings of the previous chapters in the context of the representation of a particular type of interest by the various actors in the public policymaking process.

THE SOCIAL COSTS OF CRIMINAL JUSTICE RECORDS AS AN INTEREST

The primary characteristic of the interest in reducing the social costs of criminal justice records is its "diffusiveness."[1] Reducing the social costs of criminal justice records is equivalent to providing a public or collective good. In theory, a public or collective good may offer a collective benefit; in actuality, the benefit conferred by providing such a good may be differential. Therefore, although protecting privacy and due process rights of individuals vis-à-vis the uses of criminal justice records may collectively benefit all citizens, the benefit offered to individuals *with* criminal justice records, or to those likely to acquire such records, may be differential. In this situation, the outcome of the policy formulation process is likely to be regressive: "Citizens with the

[1] Mark V. Nadel. *The Politics of Consumer Protection.* New York, Bobbs-Merrill, 1971, p. 235.

greatest needs are granted relief only to the extent that such relief is equally beneficial to all."[2] Not all citizens are likely to be equally affected by the recordkeeping practices of criminal justice agencies. Indeed, as suggested in Chapter 5, the public directly affected by the social costs of criminal justice records is not likely to engage in collective action. Rather, this public is likely to constitute what Olsen has characterized as a "forgotten group": a collectivity that has only limited resources to support political action on its behalf and which has either no lobby or a comparatively weak lobby to promote and protect the interests of its members or constituents.

A second important characteristic of the interest in minimizing the social costs of criminal justice records that leads to problems of representation is the variable intensity of the interest. All citizens have an interest in protecting their civil liberties and minimizing the social costs of government activity, but their awareness of this interest generally is lower than their awareness of more immediate and direct interests and, consequently, their interest in minimizing the social costs of criminal justice records is of a lower intensity than their other interests. Thus, the representative seeking to reflect this interest is dealing with an issue that most people do not care very much about; in fact, the interest of most citizens in effective crime control often supersedes the interest in controlling the social costs derived from the activities of criminal justice agencies.

Representation, then, has several significant implications in this context. First, the intensity of this issue, like other issues, depends on the public's perception of its importance and the action being taken on it. Unlike other issues, however, this perception shifts and is not stable. Given the low intensity of interest in the issue, simply to create any perception of its existence is a primary task of representation. Second, the low intensity of the interest gives added importance to symbolic factors. As a subject becomes more important to an individual, he is less likely to be swayed by extraneous and superficial considerations. If his interest is less intense, the individual is likely to be misled by the "symbolic uses of politics," that is, to assume contentedly that the government must be doing *something* about it. Third, the issue's generally low intensity magnifies the importance of disseminating information about it to as wide a public as possible. Low intensity means low visibility, and so the means at hand to disseminate information about the issue become enormously important. Foremost among the means

[2] *Ibid.*, p. 223.

for information dissemination is the press. In addition, special studies of scholars and journalists highlight and integrate the problems into a context familiar to a wider public, and the published reports of government agencies and the hearings of congressional committees focus public attention on the issue and develop the dimensions of the problems to be addressed. Finally, special reports and publications of public interest groups dramatize the problems on which political demands are based.

Another related aspect of the interest in reducing social costs that also leads to problems of representation is the divergence between objective and perceived needs on the part of the public. The community may be moved to respond to the most dramatic and sudden problems, while professional observers may feel that long-range problems present the most difficulty. Representatives of such an interest act as independent agents. This is especially true if bureaucrats are included as representatives. With low-intensity issues, such as the interest in reducing the social costs of criminal justice records, representatives are not faced by many public demands or needs that are perceived by the public and, therefore, are free, within limits, to exercise their choice in defining relevant and irrelevant issues.

This leads to the final difficulty in representing such an interest: "The definition of the interest is inextricably bound up with the conception of what constitutes protection of that interest."[3] Both the FBI and the American Civil Liberties Union may desire to protect the interests of individuals whose names are included in criminal justice information systems. How this is done will depend on their perceptions of the nature of the problems arising from the use and dissemination of criminal justice records. Thus, one characteristic of this type of interest is that groups with nearly opposite approaches to the problem can claim to be the true and worthiest representatives of that interest. A further implication is that, ultimately, the government defines the issue. Public interest groups may present the problem, but the difficulty of outlining this type of diffuse interest means that, in the final analysis, the government will define how the problems are to be resolved. The authority and visibility of the government give legitimacy to its definitions, increasing the prospect that the benefits to be derived from government action will be regressively differential with regard to the public affected by the social costs of criminal justice records.

[3] *Ibid.*, p. 237.

ON REPRESENTING THE INTEREST
IN REDUCING THE SOCIAL COSTS
OF CRIMINAL JUSTICE RECORDS

In Chapter 5, it was suggested that, given the size and relevant characteristics of the public affected by the social costs of criminal justice records, members of that public would not engage in collective action. A number of disincentives to collective action were noted that characterized those groups with criminal justice records; however, as indicated in Chapters 6, 7, and 8, to claim that a particular public affected by social costs will not engage in collective action does not mean that specific individuals in that public will not seek to reduce social costs concerning them through legal or political action. It also does not mean that particular interest groups or entrepreneurs engaged in providing collective goods will not act to reduce social costs affecting a larger public, or even that public agencies will not, under certain conditions, seek to reduce social costs deriving from their productive processes.

Thus, a collective good, such as the reduction of the social costs of criminal justice records, can be provided through a varied pattern of representation that depends on the structure of incentives prevailing among the actors in the policymaking process to represent a nonintense, diffuse, low-visibility interest.

Public Interest Groups and Entrepreneurs—The Advocates

In Chapters 2 and 3, a number of approaches available in the political system for reducing the costs of political action by individual citizens were suggested. Such techniques not only reduce the costs of transactions in politics by individual citizens but also serve to express social preferences which, due to the size of the relevant public and lack of incentives among members of that public to engage in voluntary collective action, might not otherwise be articulated or attended to in the policymaking process. More specifically, some groups have their collective interests organized and represented by political entrepreneurs and the purposive or public interest groups established by such entrepreneurs.

Although it may be irrational or improbable that the community or the public affected by the social costs of criminal justice records would exert influence on behalf of such an interest and assume the necessary costs, political entrepreneurs and public interest groups do so because they can benefit from such activity, either politically or financially. An individual or group of individuals may become professional at representing particular kinds of diffuse interests.

A number of public interest groups and entrepreneurs have sought to represent the nonintense, diffuse interest in reducing the social costs of criminal justice records. The types of representational roles they have assumed are the key to both the sources of their successes and their weaknesses or limitations.

A public interest group or purposive organization is, as Wilson suggests, "one that works explicitly for the benefit of some larger public or the society as a whole and not one that works chiefly for the benefits of its members, except insofar as members derive a sense of fulfilled commitment or enhanced personal worth from the effort."[4] Foremost among the public interest groups that have sought to represent the public affected by the social costs of criminal justice records has been the American Civil Liberties Union (ACLU). Established in 1920 to combat violations of civil liberties resulting from postwar hysteria directed against political dissenters, the ACLU has sought to protect and defend the rights and interests of individuals and groups that it has considered unconstitutionally infringed upon or curtailed. In this regard, much of the ACLU's activities and preoccupations have reflected the temper of the times: It worked to counteract police lawlessness during the Prohibition era and the Communist hysteria during the 1940s and early 1950s and to protect the rights of free speech, assembly, and religion of such diverse groups as the Jehovah's Witnesses, the National Socialist White People's Party, and the Ku Klux Klan.[5]

In the late 1950s, the ACLU focused on protecting the rights of privacy and due process in relation to law enforcement and the administration of criminal justice, beginning with the inaccuracy and incompleteness of the arrest records used by the FBI's Identification Division. In the early 1960s, the ACLU attacked such problems in a more comprehensive manner:

Any individual ought to be able to get his arrest record from the FBI, either directly or through his local police department. Adequate safeguards must be incorporated into any administrative procedure to protect privacy of arrest records from disclosure to unauthorized persons.

Arrest records should always contain a notation whether a person arrested

[4] James Q. Wilson. *Political Organizations.* New York, Basic Books, 1973, p. 46.

[5] See Charles Lam Markmann, *The Noblest Cry: A History of the American Civil Liberties Union,* New York, St. Martin's Press, 1965.

was convicted, acquitted, or released without prosecution. They ought also to allow some opportunity for explanation by the person arrested as to the circumstances surrounding his arrest and prosecution.[6]

During the middle and late 1960s, the ACLU also promoted protection of individual privacy in an era of technological advances and the increased use of new information and surveillance technology.

Whenever a government amasses files about its citizens an inherent threat to liberties exists. The ACLU should work towards statutes setting forth rigorous tests of compelling need. When personal information is transferred between agencies, special protection must be established. The National Data Bank proposals exemplify such use; the seeming insensitivity of its proponents for safeguards underscores the need for legislative protections. The ACLU should oppose establishment of centralized dossier-type data collection. The ACLU believes that the process of converting manual records to computer processing poses a great risk to privacy and due process.[7]

As a public interest group, the ACLU has used many modes of participation to influence public policy formation. One of the primary ways the ACLU has represented the interest of those affected by criminal justice records has been litigation. Its many chapters and affiliates throughout the United States have achieved relief for individuals and have affected the course of public policy. As noted in Chapter 6, such cases as *Menard v. Mitchell* and *Menard v. Saxbe* have been instrumental in pointing out deficiencies in existing recordkeeping practices and in advocating the need for legislative action. These types of cases have had the effect of pressuring agencies to do something in response to the problems presented.[8]

Public interest groups such as the ACLU, as well as private interest groups, engage in legislative lobbying. Both in the states and in the Congress, the ACLU has urged legislative action to alleviate the social costs of criminal justice records. Generally, the ACLU does not submit

[6] "Minutes of Due Process Committee, March 10, 1960." In: American Civil Liberties Union, *Policy Guide of ACLU*. Policy 202. New York, 1970.

[7] "Minutes of Due Process Committee, October 2–3, 1971." In: American Civil Liberties Union, *Policy Guide of ACLU*. Policy 253. New York, 1971.

[8] The ACLU has not been the only organization using test cases as a means of altering administrative or legislative policies. In the fall of 1977, the Legal Aid Society of New York initiated a class action suit against the commissioner of the New York Division of Criminal Justice Services and the New York City Police Department, questioning the retention and dissemination of inaccurate, incomplete, and misleading data in the city's and state's criminal history recordkeeping systems. About 1.1 million persons are included in the plaintiff class whose arrest records are held by these two agencies. See *Tatum v. Rogers*, 75 Civ. 2782 (CBM), S.D.N.Y. 1977.

proposals for drafts of legislation; rather, it criticizes legislative proposals and suggests amendments to conform with its views of adequate action. Much the same as other lobbying organizations, one of its major functions is to keep track of bills through their legislative history, especially to guard against weakening amendments.

Much of the legislative action of the ACLU is directed through its national office, which coordinates the legislative activities of local chapters and affiliates. In addition, no state or local chapter or affiliate takes action regarding national legislation pending before Congress except in accordance with the position taken by the national organization. Thus, much of the legislative lobbying of the ACLU is performed by the national office whenever a national issue is involved. The main communication channel with legislators for such a public interest group consists of testimony at congressional hearings. There also are a variety of informal contacts between congressmen, congressional staff members, and the lobbyists.

Another major function of the public interest group as a lobbying organization is in the area of public relations. Much of the activity of such groups focuses on newsletters, special reports, and other forms of relatively inexpensive activity.[9] The ACLU generally avoids propaganda campaigns, due to their costly nature, although its chapters or affiliates may occasionally engage in local campaigns on significant issues. The ACLU does not make organized attempts to use the press to its own advantages; its publicity network, which is directed toward people who already agree with its views, is largely informational rather than persuasive. In contrast, administrative agencies, such as the FBI and LEAA, regularly provide news releases to focus public and press attention on specific accomplishments.

A fourth function of the public interest group is its ability to expand the affected interest that it represents. This is accomplished by the

---

[9] In 1974, two significant publications were generated as a result of ACLU interest in privacy and computers. The first publication, *Privacy Report*, was published monthly by the Project on Privacy and Data Collection of the ACLU Foundation. The project was established on a nonprofit, tax-exempt basis to monitor increased data collection by state, local, and federal governments, as well as private institutions, and its impact on the individual's right to privacy. The second publication, *Privacy Journal*, was launched by Robert Ellis Smith, the former associate director of the privacy project and the former assistant director of the U.S. Department of Health, Education, and Welfare Office for Civil Rights. Like the *Privacy Report*, the *Privacy Journal* is a subscription publication that reviews current developments in the area of personal data collection by government and private industry, as well as reports on legislation in Congress and the states, including special features on topics of interest and references to publications and reprints available in the field.

formation of informal ad hoc alliances with groups such as the American Bar Association, who share a common interest. These efforts help the organization to expand the range of legitimacy for its policies.[10]

A fifth function of the public interest group as a representative of particular collective interests is its information generating role. Defining the relevant problem appropriately is a key to choosing effective types of corrective measures and also is a source of mobilization for the members of the organization. Communications by organizational leaders are directed not only at public officials and representatives, but also at their own members, to generate support for issues and to expand the organization's areas of concern. New problem areas, such as criminal justice records and privacy and computers, become avenues for mobilizing old members and for developing new forms of involvement in issues and controversies with some potential for organizational development. In this instance, crises in civil liberties help to expand the membership in the organization as well as the range of activities the organization undertakes.

Thus, information generation and problem identification are key activities of the public interest group. Indeed, some public interest groups define the information function as their primary activity. In June 1969, and again in 1970, 1972, and 1976, the Lawyer's Committee for Civil Rights Under Law, with the assistance of the Urban Coalition and later the Center for National Security Studies, published four reports on state and federal performance under the Omnibus Crime Control and Safe Streets Act of 1968. These reports focused on the use of LEAA funds at the federal, state, and local levels. In particular, the reports were critical of the development of criminal justice information systems and the problems of privacy and security arising from such data banks.[11]

---

[10] There are instances where activity is mutually supporting. One example is the National Clearinghouse on Offender Employment Restrictions sponsored by the American Bar Association's Commission on Correctional Facilities and Services, and Criminal Law Section, and funded by the Manpower Administration of the U.S. Department of Labor. The clearinghouse has issued a number of reports, handbooks, and special publications on the problems of offender rights, including the dissemination of criminal history records outside the agencies of criminal justice. In effect, the work of the clearinghouse has been directly complementary and supportive of ACLU efforts.

[11] Lawyer's Committee for Civil Rights Under Law, and Urban Coalition. *Law and Disorder I: State and Federal Performance Under Title I of the Omnibus Crime Control and Safe Streets Act of 1968.* Washington, D.C., Special Projects Office, Lawyer's Committee for Civil Rights Under Law, 1969; Idem. *Law and Disorder II: State and Federal Performance Under Title I of the Omnibus Crime Control and Safe Streets Act of 1968.* Washington, D.C.,

Similarly, the activities of the Scientist's Institute for Public Information (SIPI) in 1977 reemphasized the problems of the National Crime Information Center at a time when legislative interest in this area was stirring once again. The five-page report of the SIPI Task Force was designed not so much to discover new problems but to highlight old problems and difficulties at NCIC, in an effort to influence legislative members, such as Congressman Don Edwards, to act more vigorously and to prod the FBI into a public defense of what the SIPI Task Force considered to be harmful and ineffective administrative practices.[12]

In addition, the work of particular entrepreneurs has augmented and complemented the efforts of public interest groups. Generally, entrepreneurs have supplied information and expertise in pointing out the social costs of criminal justice records and the problems involved in the development of information systems and their possible resolution. They also have urged possible reforms through the medium of books and authoritative reports. In contrast to television and newspaper reporting, books and reports as means of communication document the evidence of the problems more fully and acquaint the public with the range of issues involved. Support is generated through constituency expansion by identifying problem areas and issues while providing a context to which a larger public can relate.

Among the leading entrepreneurs have been "the affirmative minded intellectuals."[13] Such individuals, including lawyers, political scientists, sociologists, and computer scientists, have directed their attention to the interest in reducing the social costs of criminal justice

---

Special Projects Office, Lawyer's Committee for Civil Rights Under Law, 1970; Idem. *Law and Disorder III: State and Federal Performance Under Title I of the Omnibus Crime Control and Safe Streets Act of 1968.* Washington, D.C., Special Projects Office, Lawyer's Committee for Civil Rights Under Law, 1972; Lawyer's Committee for Civil Rights Under Law, Urban Coalition, and Center for National Security Studies. *Law and Disorder IV: State and Federal Performance Under Title I of the Omnibus Crime Control and Safe Streets Act of 1968.* Washington, D.C., Center for National Security Studies, 1976.

[12] There also have been various advocacy groups within the Federal Government which have urged change in this area. Both the Office of Telecommunications Policy in the Executive Office of the President and the Domestic Council Committee on the Right of Privacy, at various times from 1974 to 1976, criticized the more restrictive positions of the FBI and Justice Department on the message-switching and CCH program issues. They suggested alternative approaches and options that favored stronger representation of privacy interests in the decision-making process and information policies that would minimize the social costs of criminal justice records.

[13] Alan F. Westin, ed. *Information Technology in a Democracy.* Cambridge, Mass., Harvard University Press, 1971, p. 150.

records by creating a public record of books and reports.[14] In part, their efforts have been a by-product of the larger concern with privacy and computers; however, on the basis of this kind of linkage, the interest in reducing the social costs of criminal records has been defined and dramatized in a manner that would not otherwise have been available.

The Press

The essence of the representational role of the press is transmission of information to the public. By providing feedback to the reading public, the press gives direction to public opinion about an issue and expands the public attentive to that issue. Many members of the press—reporters, editors, and publishers—have a bearing on the news and its transmission. This discussion deals with the very small group of reporters who represent the interest in reducing the social costs of criminal justice records and regulating the use of criminal justice information systems. There really is no "press" that covers this subject area exclusively; however, there is a diffuse group of reporters who find such stories of interest and have access to appropriate sources.[15]

The literature on the press indicates that there is no systematic process by which reporters decide what events to report on and no generally accepted definition of what is "news."[16] Some criteria of what is newsworthy are more salient than others; for example, the events of the day, the judgment of other reporters, the interest of a news organization or what the reporter perceives as the interest of his news organization, and the reporter's relations with his sources. Also, conflict generally is an accepted criterion of newsworthiness. Physical or verbal confrontation between important groups of people is always good copy.

In addition to the criteria for choosing the story, often, the sources of the story direct the ultimate output of the news. Leaks, although

[14] See, for example, Alan F. Westin, *Privacy and Freedom*, New York, Atheneum, 1970; Arthur R. Miller, *The Assault on Privacy*, Ann Arbor, University of Michigan Press, 1971; James B. Rule, *Private Lives and Public Surveillance*, New York, Schocken Books, 1973; Aryeh Neier, *Dossier*, New York, Stein and Day, 1974; Alan F. Westin and Michael A. Baker, *Databanks in a Free Society*, New York, Quadrangle Books, 1972; and Herbert S. Miller, *The Closed Door: The Effect of a Criminal Record on Employment with State and Local Public Agencies*, Washington, D.C., Manpower Administration, U.S. Department of Labor, 1972.

[15] Nadel. *Politics of Consumer Protection*, pp. 192–193.

[16] *Ibid.*, p. 193.

dramatic, are not the common source of news on criminal information policy and information systems. Much of this material derives from the public record of congressional hearings and from the reports, publications, and analyses of public interest groups, entrepreneurs, and public officials. In addition, occasional dramatic individual cases and conflicts of interests among government officials serve to draw a reporter's attention to a good story.

At the national level, news reporting on the social costs of criminal justice records and information systems has centered on the FBI's dissemination of arrest records by its Identification Division and the controversy surrounding the control and regulation of the nationwide CCH exchange program of NCIC and message switching. At the state and local level, there also have been individual cases concerning the questionable use of criminal records by particular criminal justice agencies and the efforts of local and state governments to develop computerized information systems and regulations for the use of criminal justice records.

Through reporting on the development of these issues and problems and illustrating their significance to the reading public,[17] the press has played a role in expanding the constituency for a nonintense, diffuse, low-visibility interest. By screening information and presenting it in condensed form, the press is, in effect, acting as a "wholesaler" of information.[18] It reduces the costs of presenting information by public interest groups and entrepreneurs and, at the same time, reduces the costs of acquiring information by the public affected by social costs as well as by the larger citizenry. The representational role of the press focuses on increasing public awareness of issues,[19] which helps to generate intensity and visibility for issues that normally are of low intensity and low visibility. In effect, the press forms the key link between the identification of problems and issues and their regulation by reducing information costs and by directing attention to the social costs and the controversies over proposals for their control.[20]

[17] With respect to the social costs of criminal justice records, the reading public is not primarily the general public but a composite of the specific influential individuals directly involved in the controversy, attention groups who monitor developments in the issue area, such as the ACLU, and the attentive public, which is made up of readers who are generally informed on and interested in questions of civil liberties and social impacts of technology. See Roger W. Cobb and Charles D. Elder, *Participation in American Politics: The Dynamics of Agenda-Building,* Boston, Mass., Allyn and Bacon, 1972, pp. 104–108.

[18] Nadel. *Politics of Consumer Protection,* p. 213.

[19] *Ibid.,* p. 192.

[20] The most active segment of the press in reporting on the issues related to criminal

Criminal Justice Agencies

Chapter 2 suggested that, because a public agency equates its internal costs with the total costs of providing a public good or service, it ordinarily will have little or no incentive to reduce social costs arising from its maintenance or productive functions. Such costs are treated as external costs and do not enter into either the total costs calculus of providing a particular level of a public good or service or the internal cost calculus of the agency. In short, it would appear that public agencies responsible for social costs would have no representational role whatever; however, this is not always the case. When the existence of social costs is serious enough to threaten the maintenance of the organization, when social costs affect a group of individuals capable of collective action of some kind against an agency through the political or legal process, or when the reduction or internalization of social costs will benefit the agency in some way, then public agencies can be expected to have some representational role in reducing social costs arising from their productive or maintenance processes. In the context of the social costs of criminal justice records, criminal justice agencies have had selective incentives to develop information policies that would reduce the social costs of criminal records.

As noted in Chapter 6, concern for the social costs of criminal justice records as a public issue developed as part of the wider problem area of privacy and computers, beginning, to a large extent, with the controversy over the National Data Center. The possible adverse effects of widespread computerization in government and industry on the privacy and lives of individuals received national attention as the subject of legislative and public debate, resulting in widespread calls for safeguards. The National Data Center controversy was an important lesson to the developers of criminal justice information systems: If the problems of privacy and other social costs presented by any proposed information system were not recognized, public criticism and legislative inquiry could cause a cutoff or curtailment of proposed activities. Criminal justice agencies, including Project SEARCH, realized the need to review the uses of criminal justice records if they desired to pursue their operational goals of developing advanced criminal justice infor-

---

justice information policy has not been the major papers, such as the *Washington Post,* the *New York Times,* or the *Los Angeles Times,* but a weekly publication in the data-processing industry called *Computerworld,* which has provided the most extensive and in-depth coverage of this area for several years. *Computerworld* reports on economic and technical as well as political and social developments and issues connected with the use and management of computer technology.

mation systems at the local, state, and federal levels. Therefore, since the early computer period, efforts to develop or plan criminal justice information systems were accompanied by either the provision of security and privacy safeguards or the assurance that they would be provided. As early as 1965, the NYSIIS concept included the principle of safeguarding security and privacy. In 1967, the President's Commission on Law Enforcement and Administration of Justice included in the discussion of criminal justice information systems in its *Task Force Report: Science and Technology*, a section entitled "Handling Personal Information." In July 1970, the Project SEARCH Committee on Security and Privacy issued its report on *Security and Privacy Considerations in Criminal History Information Systems*.

Much of the representational role of criminal justice agencies has been linked with their desires to develop computerized information systems and the need to ward off potential threats or severe curtailments of such plans by providing security and privacy safeguards. Indeed, as public interest groups, entrepreneurs, and the press have highlighted the problems of privacy and computers, as well as the specific issues arising from the use and dissemination of criminal justice records, criminal justice agencies have become increasingly aware of and have acted to ensure that *some* safeguards do exist and that manual information policies are revised.

With the widespread development of criminal justice information systems at the local and state levels with LEAA funds since 1971, and the design and implementation of the FBI's NCIC/CCH program and its message-switching component, more public attention has been centered on deficiencies in information policies, which had been largely ignored during the manual recordkeeping period, and on the need for more effective and systematic information policy for the collection, maintenance, and dissemination of criminal justice records. As consideration of criminal justice information policy has focused attention on the information policies and practices of local, state, and federal criminal justice agencies, and as the formulation of information policy has moved from informal and abstract stages to the center of policy debate about the control and regulation of criminal justice information and information systems, criminal justice agencies more often have taken the initiative in developing information policies that suit their needs and plans and have relied less on a reactive posture. Particularly since 1975, for some of the agencies involved in the CCH and message-switching controversy, the promotion of policies responsive to the concern with privacy, confidentiality, and security of criminal records has represented good politics. In the 1970s, both Project

SEARCH and LEAA used their concerns with policy development in this area to highlight and gain support for proposals that have been directly competitive with FBI and Department of Justice positions. In fact, a large measure of LEAA's ability to maintain its own positions related to the CCH program and message switching in the face of intensive FBI lobbying in the Justice Department and Congress has been derived from its active support of privacy and security concerns before sympathetic members of Congress and outside groups. The FBI, on the other hand, has been viewed as less open to such concerns and, therefore, proposals made by the bureau regarding CCH and message switching have been actively resisted by members of Congress who do not trust the FBI to protect individual rights.

For both Project SEARCH and LEAA, taking the offensive on the issue of privacy and security has helped advance systems development proposals and concepts within the Department of Justice, the executive branch, and the Congress. Moreover, by taking an active posture regarding social impact issues, Project SEARCH, in particular, as well as LEAA, have effectively drawn support and cooperation from congressional members and staff, public interest groups, and entrepreneurs who otherwise would be very suspicious, if not completely resistant, to criminal justice agency policy positions and systems development plans in this area.

The Courts

The courts have been important avenues of representation, not so much for the relief that they can grant to individuals affected by the social costs of criminal justice records, but because they are an alternative forum in which public interest groups can pursue their policy preferences through the device of the test case. Cases such as *Menard v. Mitchell* and *Menard v. Saxbe* derive their utility less from the particular relief granted to the individual defendant than from the dramatization and emphasis of deficiencies in existing practices and the need for legislative action. Court proceedings enable alternative representation of nonintense, diffuse interests and permit groups and individuals to extend the meaning and reach of rights such as due process and privacy to new situations. The authoritative declaration or affirmation of the rights of privacy and due process as applied to the social costs of criminal justice records in judicial proceedings provides the legitimacy for public interest groups and entrepreneurs to pursue what is essentially a political course of action. Because, as noted in Chapter 5, the law shapes the context in which American politics is conducted, the invocation of the rights of privacy and due process vis-à-vis the use of information systems works on behalf of political change. Thus, the courts provide an alternative forum for action. In this regard, they offer to public interest groups and entrepreneurs a source of leverage to counteract the claims of criminal justice agencies that criminal justice records are being collected and used responsibly and carefully.[21]

State and Local Governments

Another important avenue of representation for the interest in reducing the social costs of criminal justice. records has been various state and local governments. The criminal justice system in America is a highly decentralized, primarily local and state, function, and the bulk of responsibility for policy formulation rests with state governments and local and county criminal justice agencies. Over the years, this situation has been castigated because of the inefficiency and ineffectiveness of law enforcement and the administration of criminal justice in America. For a number of reasons, decentralization has contributed to the representation of the interest in reducing the social costs of criminal justice records.

First, like the courts, state and local governments have had a significant representational role—not so much for the specific relief afforded citizens with criminal justice records, but because they have constituted alternative forums for political action. As observed in the preceding chapters, although the development of criminal justice information systems generally has far outpaced the reformulation of criminal justice information policy, outside pressures or the threat of outside pressures on criminal justice agencies have promoted the reformulation of criminal justice information policy to reduce social costs. States like Massachusetts and cities like Berkeley, California have attempted to design or adopt new regulatory arrangements aimed at minimizing the social costs of criminal justice records. In such jurisdictions, public interest groups and select entrepreneurs have

[21] The courts have represented one of the key sources of factual information about the connection between social costs of criminal justice records and the practices and policies of criminal justice agencies. Not only have court cases revealed evidence of specific abuses, but they have also led to more extended fact-finding concerning the scope and nature of recordkeeping activities and their negative social and economic effects. See, for example, the survey of the accuracy, completeness, timeliness, and use of criminal history records derived from the New York City Police Department and the New York Division of Criminal Justice Services in *Tatum* v. *Rogers*, 75 Civ. 2782 (CBM), S.D.N.Y. 1977.

found acceptable forums for political action, and the costs of participation for entrepreneurs and public interest groups interested in reformulating criminal justice information policy have been decreased. Policy changes are most easily accomplished where public officials are readily accessible and where the climate of public opinion makes criminal justice agencies less resistant to change.

In addition, the implementation in recent years of LEAA regulations on privacy and security has precipitated a variety of efforts in the states to conform to the regulations. The implementation efforts have varied widely from state to state; nevertheless, the existence of these federal regulations has led to the development of responsive information policies.[22]

A second representational role for localities and states has been to pressure state or federal agencies for changes in policy. As noted in Chapter 6, both the city of Berkeley and the state of Massachusetts have, in the past, attempted to exercise control over the use of their criminal justice records outside their jurisdictions. Both jurisdictions failed in their attempts to do so, but they both brought pressure to bear on the state agency or on the federal agency controlling the larger criminal justice information system to adopt stricter standards and regulations. Massachusetts officials refused to hook up with the FBI's NCIC system until stricter recordkeeping controls were established. The governor and other state officials enlisted the cooperation of other governors in a petition to the Department of Justice requesting stricter standards. Finally, Massachusetts joined the ACLU in seeking a court injunction against the NCIC/CCH program until stricter regulations were adopted.

Although this type of effort did not get immediate results for the state or locality involved, it contributed to the climate of reform which has led at least to the consideration of more comprehensive legislation to control the use of criminal justice records and the development of criminal justice information systems.

A third representational role for localities and states has been in the context of experimenting with various approaches to the design of regulatory arrangements to reduce the social costs of criminal justice records. Some states, like Iowa, Alaska, California, and Massachusetts, adopted, in whole or in part, the provisions of Project SEARCH's model act and/or administrative regulations. Connecticut, on the other hand, dealt with its interest in reducing the social costs of criminal justice

[22] See Chapter 8, "LEAA's Implementation of Privacy and Security Regulations," and Appendix C.

records differently by passing a law barring employment discrimination against persons with criminal records. Similarly, localities like the District of Columbia and Berkeley, California designed regulations to restrict the use of criminal justice records in their jurisdictions. Other jurisdictions controlled the use of criminal justice records through the adoption of guidelines and self-imposed regulations on users of such records. Managers of systems such as Santa Clara County's Criminal Justice Information Control and Kansas City's ALERT II (regional criminal justice information systems) have adopted codes of ethics and other administrative regulations and user guidelines to tighten control over the use of Criminal Offender Record Information (CORI) within their respective systems. Moreover, the implementation of LEAA regulations on privacy and security of criminal history information has precipitated even more concern with developing policies, procedures, and guidelines in the handling of these records. To a large extent, federal regulations have promoted diversity and experimentation in the evolution of appropriate regulations in states and localities where few or no regulations previously existed.

Since comprehensive regulation of a complex area seldom evolves full-blown but is based on prior projects and proposals, the efforts of state and local governments to control the use of either their computerized or manual criminal justice records (or both) serve to cut information costs by directing the attention of public officials, public interest groups, and entrepreneurs to working responses to the problems. Efforts at regulation in one jurisdiction form source materials or precedents for other jurisdictions at the local, state, or federal level.[23]

Thus, not only do state and local governments provide alternative forums for representing nonintense, diffuse, low-visibility interests, reducing the costs of political transactions for public interest groups

[23] In recent years, both LEAA and SEARCH Group, Inc. have provided ways that interested persons from the state as well as the national level can get access to information about what the states are doing in the area of privacy and security policies for criminal records. In January 1978, SEARCH Group, Inc. announced its privacy library and index, which contains more than 1,000 state and local government regulations, laws, and related reports and other materials. SEARCH Group, Inc. published a report entitled *Security and Privacy Rulemaking: Resources, Terms, and References* (SEARCH Technical Memorandum No. 15, Sacramento, Calif., 1978), making available the clearinghouse service to local and state officials and other interested persons. In August 1978, LEAA published its second compendium of state legislation related to privacy and security of criminal history information and, in addition, issued a companion document entitled *Privacy and Security of Criminal History Information: A Guide to Policy Development* (Washington, D.C., 1978), which discussed policy options for criminal justice officials responsible for developing rules for the control of criminal history information.

and entrepreneurs with limited resources, they also provide means whereby other jurisdictions can be pressed to alter or change their policies if further cooperation is to evolve. Opportunities for strategic bargaining then are presented in cases where a state or locality has resources (like its own supply of criminal justice records) that it may hold back if its demands are not accommodated. Finally, the approaches to regulation undertaken by various states and localities serve to cut information costs by serving as source materials or precedents for efforts at regulation in other jurisdictions or at the national level.

Congress

The representational role of Congress in relation to the interest in reducing the social costs of criminal justice records has derived from four sources. First, in the mid-1960s, the issue of privacy and computers became the subject of public attention and congressional debate. As an aspect of the congressional hearings on the National Data Center proposal and as a result of the development of information and surveillance technology, an interest emerged in the social costs of criminal justice records and the use of these records in sophisticated government and private data banks. Civil libertarians were concerned that arrest records of local police agencies would be merged into data banks with welfare, educational, and other types of sensitive personal records. Prior to 1970, much of the congressional activity in this area consisted of expressions of growing concern and interest.

A second facet of congressional interest arose from concern about legislation for criminal amnesty and prisoner rehabilitation, which began to occupy congressional attention in the late 1960s and early 1970s. In the wake of the growing numbers of arrests and convictions of students and other young people for possession and use of marijuana and other stimulant drugs and the context of Draconian penalties for such actions, in October 1970, Congress enacted a federal statute (P.L. 91-513) that decreed the expungement of the arrest and conviction records of all first offenders under 21 years of age charged with simple possession of marijuana or stimulant pills and explicitly restored the individual's status before the arrest or indictment. Following this action, and as a response to the President's Task Force on Prisoner Rehabilitation report on criminal offenders,[24] a proposal

[24] President's Task Force on Prisoner Rehabilitation. *The Criminal Offender: What Shall Be Done?* Washington, D.C., U.S. Government Printing Office, 1970.

was presented in Congress that attempted to nullify the effect of the criminal record in cases of first offenders convicted of federal crimes. Although the proposal did not pass, it indicated the interest of members of Congress in these problems and the need for corrective actions.

A third aspect of congressional interest in this area was a direct result of the Watergate affair and revelations of abuses by the FBI and state and local law enforcement agencies in domestic intelligence operations against politically active groups and individuals.

Like no other event in American history, Watergate has served to point out the problems of unchecked governmental surveillance. One effect in 1974 was to slow down the consideration of legislation concerning criminal justice information systems; however, the more general effect has been to lend support to groups intent on checking the recordkeeping and surveillance activities of government. An interesting effect of Watergate is that privacy has become a popular political issue.

In addition, since 1973, a series of revelations at the national level concerning the FBI's domestic security investigations and intelligence-gathering activities, such as the celebrated COINTELPRO operations, has focused public and congressional attention on the FBI's policies and practices in domestic intelligence and related recordkeeping systems.[25] Moreover, a great deal of congressional interest has, in recent years, concentrated on the capabilities of computer and telecommunications technologies to merge criminal history and intelligence files into more comprehensive and, as viewed by many, dangerous surveillance systems.

A fourth facet of congressional interest was occasioned by the growing federal role in criminal justice recordkeeping. With the use of LEAA funds in the early 1970s to develop local and statewide criminal justice information systems, and with the problems arising from the development of a nationwide criminal history exchange system as part of the FBI's NCIC program and the concerns over message switching, congressional interest has centered on assuring adequate safeguards for the use of criminal justice records and controlling the development of criminal justice information and communication systems.

The focus for much of the activity supporting the interest in reducing the social costs of criminal justice records has come from congres-

---

[25] For the political background concerning the COINTELPRO revelations, as well as a good survey of the content of the FBI documents made public, see Nelson Blackstock, *COINTELPRO, The FBI's Secret War on Political Freedom,* 2nd Edition, New York, Vintage Books, 1976.

sional committees and subcommittees. As key centers of power in Congress, they are important arenas of activity for public interest groups and entrepreneurs, as bases for the promotion of legislative and administrative policies that have been most favorable in this area. They also have an influence on administrative agencies, instigating the agencies to consider approaches and concerns that they otherwise tend to disregard, avoid, or minimize.

Until 1976, the committees and subcommittees that were most active in representing the interest in reducing the social costs of criminal justice records were the Senate Committee on the Judiciary, Subcommittee on Constitutional Rights (later called the Subcommittee on the Constitution) and the House Committee on the Judiciary, Subcommittee on Civil and Constitutional Rights. Since 1976, three other subcommittees in the House and Senate have developed an interest in the area of criminal justice information policy: The Senate Judiciary Committee's Subcommittee on Administrative Practices and Procedures and the House Judiciary Committee's Subcommittee on Crime have focused on the reorganization of LEAA, and the House Committee on Government Operations, Subcommittee on Government Information and Individual Rights, has focused on the general problem of data banks and the rights of privacy and due process. Since legislation in this area, proposed in the 1970s, was never really recommended to full committees, these five subcommittees have been the center of legislative activity in the House and the Senate. In each case, the advocacy or representational roles of the subcommittees have varied with the subcommittee chairmen and the interest of individual members. Three representational roles can be identified which have characterized legislative activity with regard to criminal justice information policy.

First, several of the subcommittees have had the important function of problem identification and information generation. Prior to 1976, both the Senate Subcommittee on Constitutional Rights and the House Subcommittee on Civil and Constitutional Rights held a number of formal hearings on criminal justice records and information systems. In addition, individual chairmen, such as Senator Sam Ervin and Congressman Don Edwards, actively promoted interest in regulating the use of criminal justice records. Each used his position to accrue publicity on the issue area; Senator Ervin, in particular, became synonymous with the advocacy of the right to privacy as related to the use of computers in the Federal Government until his retirement in December 1974. Beginning in 1970 and 1971 with the problem of Army surveillance of civilians using computers, the senator was an active proponent and supporter of privacy legislation, especially criminal justice information policy proposals.

Besides holding hearings, congressional subcommittees have drawn on the research services of the comptroller general of the General Accounting Office, the Congressional Research Service of the Library of Congress, and the Office of Technology Assessment to investigate and present evidence related to the management, use, and relevant options concerning the development of information systems and criminal information policy in the United States. Some subcommittees, such as the House Subcommittee on Civil and Constitutional Rights, have solicited the views of individuals and public interest groups, including the Scientists' Institute for Public Information, to identify problems and suggest alternative ways of dealing with them.

A second representational role of the subcommittees has been to generate alternative legislative proposals to those presented by the executive branch agencies. Staff members in each subcommittee have had specific responsibility for the development of legislative proposals. Generally, these proposals were intended to counteract the more conservative views of criminal justice agencies in reducing the social costs of criminal justice records at the expense of greater information system usage.

A third representational role of the subcommittees has been to monitor the activities of executive branch agencies. The primary instrument of oversight in this area—letter writing—has been used by individual members, including subcommittee chairmen, to request information for clarification, justification, defense, and future deliberation. In recent years, as suggested in the preceding chapter, a major portion of legislative-administrative relations and interactions have been carried on through letters and memoranda. Congressmen John Moss and Don Edwards, in particular, have conducted active correspondence with the executive branch to protest actions taken, to request more detailed information, to prod agencies into action, and to solicit cooperation and input on legislative matters. Legislative oversight of Justice Department actions on the CCH program and message-switching controversy to a great extent has been carried on primarily through informal consultations between legislative and administrative staff members and through letters outlining positions and responses.

The privacy and computers issue and, more specifically, the interest in reducing the social costs of criminal justice records in the face of the widespread development of criminal justice information systems have, for the members of the respective subcommittees involved, represented good politics. Indeed, because the concern for the social costs of criminal justice records generally has been perceived as one aspect of the larger issue, the more limited interest has benefited from inherent features of the privacy and computers issue that have made it popular. In short, it is nearly impossible to argue with a legislator's stand for privacy and against technological autocracy. An important feature of political alignment in these areas has been that Democrats and Republicans alike have asserted that personal privacy and individual rights transcend political partisanship. Both liberals and conservatives have perceived the need for regulation and control of evolving information systems and for the reform of existing information policies in areas such as criminal justice.

The rub in this nonpartisanship comes at the stage when specifics are discussed. In particular, the law and order positions of some conservative legislators have not always coincided with the more civil libertarian bent of liberals or constitutionalists such as Senator Ervin. Thus, nonpartisanship in this context is in part due to the amorphous and abstract nature of the issue. Since definition of the interest is inextricably bound with the conception of what constitutes protection of that interest, Senators Ervin and Hruska were able to submit bills in 1974 that guaranteed the rights of individuals with criminal justice records but that differed considerably as to the extent and nature of acceptable safeguards and controls. For some congressional activists, the interest in reducing the social costs of criminal justice records has simply represented an expression of their more general concern about the right to privacy in society. These activists have focused more on the principles of the issues involved in the CCH and message-switching area than on the managerial and organizational questions involved.

In contrast, others in Congress have been more interested in the practical problems of arriving at a consensus with all the various interests involved for an acceptable information policy in this area. Although they, too, have been interested in the democratic principles such as privacy and due process, they have been more willing to "balance" these concerns against the complex managerial and organizational constraints involved.

Still others in Congress have been interested in this issue area because both the CCH program and message switching involve the FBI. These activists, who have been concerned in recent years in "bringing the FBI under control," have perceived this issue area as one arena where their interests could be pursued.

Finally, some activists in Congress have been introduced to this issue area by focusing on the problems of reorganizing an agency such as LEAA. In this case, they have confronted those aspects of the issue area that the agency is directly responsible for, such as the implementation of privacy and security regulations in the states and the funding of state and local computerized information systems through the Comprehensive Data Systems program.

No conclusion can be made that there is a congressional interest in reducing the social costs of criminal justice records; however, there are several different ways in which this interest "fits" into the concerns and priorities of legislative members and staff and, therefore, into the several different forms of representation it receives.

CONDITIONS OF SUCCESS IN REPRESENTING THE INTEREST IN REDUCING THE SOCIAL COSTS OF CRIMINAL JUSTICE RECORDS

The discussion in the preceding section indicates how a collective good, such as the reduction of the social costs of criminal justice records, can be provided through a particular pattern of representation. The conditions for the successful representation of this interest and some of the difficulties and problems hampering successful representation by the actors in this policymaking process have not been examined.

Much of the effectiveness of public interest groups, entrepreneurs, congressional activists, and the press in representing the interest in reducing the social costs of criminal justice records has been based on widening the scope of conflict, primarily by appealing to and altering public opinion. Information generation and dissemination concerning the social costs of criminal justice records and the development of criminal justice information systems has been only a means toward an end. In this context, the end has been widening the scope of conflict. The significance of doing so has been explored by E. E. Schattschneider and forms the basis for his theory of politics: At the root of all politics is conflict. Such conflict involves both those who are actively engaged and the audience that is attracted to the scene and often influences the outcome. Thus, the basic pattern of politics is based on two propositions:

> The first proposition is that the outcome of every conflict is determined by the extent to which the audience becomes involved in it. That is, the outcome of all conflict is determined by the scope of its contagion. The numbers of people involved determines what happens; every change in the number of participants, every increase or reduction in the number of participants, affects the result. . . . The second proposition is a consequence of the first. The most important strategy of politics is concerned with the scope of conflict.[26]

[26] E. E. Schattschneider. *The Semisovereign People.* New York, Holt, Rinehart and Winston, 1960, pp. 2–3.

The policy stances taken by opposing sides in a conflict depend on the distribution of power and leverage among them. The most powerful interests want to restrict the scope of conflict by involving a limited number of participants and narrowing the definition of problems open to settlement. The weaker interests, on the other hand, seek to widen the scope of conflict by increasing the number of participants and defining the relevant problems open to settlement more broadly. This is done to redress the balance and alleviate the previous lack of power. Thus, the principal representational function of public interest groups, entrepreneurs, congressional activists, and the press, as well as executive branch activists, is to influence public opinion in order to widen the arena in which decisions affecting the public with criminal justice records are made. These actors widen the scope of conflict in the short term by making the public aware of conflicts that potentially may affect them and widen the scope of conflict in the long term by seeking government regulations where none existed before or where existing regulations have been deemed ineffective.

Representation, then, of a nonintense, diffuse, low-visibility interest depends on widening the scope of conflict through dissemination of information to as large a public as possible. As previously mentioned, the low intensity and visibility of the interests make the means of disseminating information very important. In this regard, the press provides a key link in the representation of nonintense, diffuse interests by screening information and providing it in a condensed form. As an information wholesaler, the press cuts the costs of presenting information by public interest groups and entrepreneurs and, at the same time, reduces the costs of acquiring information by those subject to the social costs of criminal justice records and the public at large.

In addition, widening the scope of conflict leads to action by agencies contributing to the problem of social costs. As noted, the representational role of criminal justice agencies is linked with their desires to ward off threats to, or severely curtail, their plans for information system development by providing security and privacy safeguards. Actions taken by public interest groups through the courts, by state and local governments, and by congressional activists are significant in this context because they expand the scope of conflict by pressuring the responsible agencies to reduce social costs through alterations in information policies.

Finally, congressional action concerned with reducing the social costs of criminal justice records and controlling the development of information systems not only expands the scope of conflict but also raises the scale of conflict. Problems of national importance are perceived for which a national policy is demanded.

Conditions for the successful representation of the interest in reducing these social costs hinge on widening the scope of conflict; however, there are limitations and restraints on the ability of public interest groups and entrepreneurs acting through the press, the courts, state and local governments, and Congress to do so. Such problems and difficulties standing in the way of successful representation of this interest have the effect of restricting the scope of conflict as well as reducing the scale of conflict and preventing effective representation of such a collective interest.

The first limitation on the successful representation of the interest in reducing the social costs of criminal justice records arises from the nature of such a nonintense, diffuse, low-visibility interest. Due to its low intensity, representatives, including criminal justice agencies, are not faced by many public demands and thus are free, within limits, to exercise their own choices in defining relevant and irrelevant issues. Since definition of the interest is inextricably bound with the conception of what constitutes its protection, both criminal justice agencies and public interest groups may seek to protect the interests of individuals whose names are included in criminal justice information systems. How this is to be done will depend on their individual perceptions of the nature of the problems arising from use and dissemination of criminal justice records.

Defining the relevant issues, then, influences the scope of conflict. Public interest groups and entrepreneurs will seek to expand the scope of conflict by defining the relevant problems concerning criminal justice records as serious and pervasive, and criminal justice agencies and private interest groups will seek to restrict the scope of conflict by defining the issues and problems as narrowly as possible. Thus, the latter will be attentive to preserving existing patterns of collecting, maintaining, and disseminating criminal justice records with only limited recognition of the need for safeguards on record usage. Private interest groups such as banks, employer associations, savings and loan associations, credit agencies, life insurance companies, and private investigators will aim at restricting the scope of conflict, since they will suffer losses when competing claims are put on the agenda for government decision. Similarly, federal departments now receiving access to criminal justice records, as well as state and local employment officers and licensing authorities, will pursue their claims concerning the legitimacy of their access rights. Finally, within the context of the criminal justice system, law enforcement agencies on the local and state levels and the FBI will seek to guarantee present access to arrest records and controls over criminal justice information systems with only limited concessions to permitting restrictive and costly safeguards on record usage and controls on developing information systems such as the NCIC/CCH program.

A further implication of defining the relevant issues in representing a diffuse, low-intensity, low-visibility interest is the fact that, ultimately, the issues will be defined by the criminal justice agencies that are involved in the formulation of information policy. Public interest groups and entrepreneurs may seek to articulate the problems and possible solutions, but it is the agencies (e.g., the Office of the Attorney General, FBI, LEAA, SEARCH Group, Inc.) that will define the way criminal justice records can be used and criminal justice information systems can be deployed. The authority and visibility of such agencies give legitimacy to their definitions of what is and what is not workable. Although Congress may veto agency proposals and actions, it must rely on the Department of Justice and state and local criminal justice agencies for policy definition and implementation. This dependence puts further emphasis on the representation of existing, known interests at the expense of widening the scope of conflict. For the public affected by the social costs of criminal justice records, this situation increases the prospects that the benefits to be derived from any government action will be regressively differential: Citizens with the greatest needs are granted relief only to the extent that such relief is equally beneficial to all.

A second limitation on representation of the interest in reducing the social costs of criminal justice records derives from the ambivalent role of the press. As suggested, the press plays a key role in the representation of such a diffuse interest by acting as a wholesaler of information. In this role, it helps to cut information and communication costs not only for public interest groups, entrepreneurs, and congressional activists in transmitting information but for those receiving the information. Members of the press involved in such actions, however, represent a relatively small number.

Of equal concern to members of the press—reporters, editors, and publishers—is access to government records. Interest in the press' "right to know" conflicts with interest in restricting the use and dissemination of information about individuals having contact with the criminal justice system. The press played a major role in 1975 and 1976 in resisting any restrictions on its access to criminal justice records. This resistance, coupled with representation of the popular sentiment regarding crime control, has had the effect of negating the role of the press as a wholesaler of information concerning the interest in reducing the social costs of criminal justice records.[27]

---

[27] See, for example, Nussbaum's review of the legislative history of first offender

A third constraint on the successful representation of such a diffuse interest arises from jurisdictional and boundary restraints on the courts as well as local and state governments. The limits of judicial action stem from the fact that courts normally are bound to provide relief only for the case before them. The court can only refer a problem to the legislature for action. Although an individual court's decision may have an effect on administrative agency activity, it can be overridden through legislative action. For example, in 1971, the Bible rider effectively nullified the *Menard v. Mitchell* ruling concerning the FBI's record dissemination procedures. The courts do not offer an avenue for solving public problems as much as they grant relief to individuals and dramatize situations in need of legislative and administrative consideration.

Similarly, local and state governments are limited by their boundaries and jurisdictional restraints from dealing effectively with the questions arising from the interstate transmission of criminal records in a national criminal justice information network. The city of Berkeley and the state of Massachusetts have tried to influence policy formulation at higher levels, but, generally, they have been unsuccessful in achieving any immediate accommodations. Moreover, evaluations of LEAA's efforts to implement privacy and security regulations in the states have highlighted the variations among local agencies in and between individual states that have caused compliance efforts to be more difficult and costly than first expected.

A final constraint on the successful representation of the interest in reducing the social costs of criminal justice records has arisen, somewhat paradoxically, from its link with the general problem area of privacy and computers.

As noted in Chapter 7, 1974 promised to be a good year for the consideration of privacy as a political issue. In the midst of the Watergate crisis, President Nixon had listed privacy among the first 10 goals of his administration. Earlier, in 1973, the Secretary's Advisory Committee on Automated Personal Data Systems of the Department of Health, Education, and Welfare had issued its report on *Records, Computers and the Rights of Citizens.*[28] In February 1974, President Nixon established the Domestic Council Committee on Privacy, chaired by Vice President Gerald Ford, to develop plans to protect the right of privacy of individual citizens.

---

amnesty legislation in New York. Aaron Nussbaum. *A Second Chance, Amnesty for the First Offender.* New York, Hawthorn Books, 1974, pp. 137–235.

[28] U.S. Department of Health, Education, and Welfare, Secretary's Advisory Committee on Automated Personal Data Systems. *Records, Computers and the Rights of Citizens.* Washington, D.C., U.S. Government Printing Office, 1973.

The Ninety-Third Congress was dubbed "the Privacy Congress," as many congressmen and senators began submitting privacy laws in response to the HEW report. The effort was led in the Senate by Senator Sam Ervin and in the House by Congressmen Ed Koch (D.-N.Y.) and Barry Goldwater, Jr. (R.-Calif.). By March 1974, 102 House bills on privacy had been introduced, with 207 sponsors; in the Senate, a number of privacy bills were sponsored by 62 members.[29]

Amidst this flurry of concern and activity, the proposals to develop comprehensive criminal justice data banks were submitted. The efforts to develop such legislation were important, but they were overshadowed by the focus on privacy legislation to control the use of all information systems in the Federal Government. By July 1974, much of the congressional activity focused on the passage of the Privacy Act of 1974, P.L. 93–579. Companion versions of the bill originally had been submitted by Senator Sam Ervin and Congressmen Goldwater and Koch. Due to major differences in each bill and congressional elections in September, the bills were left for consideration until the final month of the year. In December, the House and Senate were reconciled on numerous aspects of the bill, and the Privacy Act of 1974 was passed two days before the close of the session.

In effect, the Ninety-Third Congress had fulfilled its promise of being "the Privacy Congress"; however, in the course of concentrating on the passage of the Privacy Act of 1974, criminal justice databank legislation had been overlooked. Such legislation was reconsidered in 1975; nevertheless, it was clear that amidst the ecology of issues representing the privacy and computers debate, the criminal justice records issue did not have top priority.

CONCLUSION: REPRESENTATION AND CRIMINAL JUSTICE INFORMATION POLICY

In the course of this chapter, it was suggested that prospects for reducing the social costs of criminal justice records are limited and problematic. A number of conditions for successful representation of such an interest were noted, and several significant limitations or constraints on the realization of those conditions in the policy formulation process also were identified. Recognizing the problems of representing a nonintense, diffuse, low-visibility interest such as reducing the social costs of criminal justice records in the existing process of

---

[29] "Privacy: Congress Expected to Vote Controls." *Congressional Quarterly Lobby Report*, September 28, 1974, p. 2614.

policy formulation confirms the hypothesis suggested in Chapter 2: namely, that it cannot be assumed a priori that the prevailing political or legal process can guarantee that the social costs deriving from criminal justice recordkeeping practices can be minimized and adequately entered into the internal cost calculus of public agencies. Indeed, the public affected by such social costs is not likely to engage in collective action because it has positive incentives for collective inaction. Furthermore, existing channels are limited in representing the interest in reducing the social costs of criminal justice records. *Some* level of social cost reduction will be provided, but it will be relatively low, not only in terms of the demands of public interest groups, entrepreneurs, and congressional activists involved in the policy formulation process but the results of changes in information policy on the public affected by criminal justice recordkeeping.

For a number of significant reasons, then, the assumptions of group theory or pluralist politics do not hold in such a context. Prevailing group interactions or legal adjustments of conflicting interests do not offer a guarantee against the occurrence or the reduction of social costs deriving from the use of criminal justice records. Neither does it follow that, because all individuals in a group or public affected by social costs would benefit if they achieved the group objective, such individuals would act to achieve that objective. Thus, it cannot be assumed, as in the perspective of pluralist politics, that all relevant and affected interests are included in specific group or collective forms of action. Significant social costs do not give rise to collective action due to the size of the group affected and the costs of political transactions.

Finally, although alternative mechanisms are available to represent diffuse, low-intensity, low-visibility interests, it cannot be claimed that effective expression of social preferences in reducing social costs will be assured. As noted in Chapters 2 and 3, mechanisms such as direct and indirect delegation, public interest groups, entrepreneurs, and the press may serve to reduce the costs of political action in representing nonintense, diffuse, low-visibility interests, but it cannot be assumed without closer examination whether these forms of representation will effect substantial reductions in the social costs of criminal justice records. Indeed, this chapter has suggested that there are significant limitations on the efficacy of such mechanisms in representing such an interest. To the extent that limitations or constraints persist, the interest in reducing the social costs of criminal justice records is not likely to be represented very effectively.

The fact that the success of activists generally depends on raising the intensity and visibility of the interest they are representing has implications that go beyond simply explaining that success. The importance of the need to intensify and make visible a diffuse interest is that the most dramatic issues come to the fore.[30] Dramatic and immediate problems, such as controlling the use of arrest records, are more rapidly and easily perceived by the public than long-range problems such as the impact of conviction records on rates of recidivism or employment. Since the dramatic issues also are more newsworthy, they are more likely to receive attention from the news media. Thus, successful representation of a diffuse, low-intensity, low-visibility public interest issue will center on the most dramatic problems and leave relatively unattended long-range or more deeply rooted issues.

Furthermore, even if successful representation of such an interest is achieved, it probably will not persist for long, because successful representation of such an interest offers selective benefits to a diffuse public and, simultaneously, offers or imposes concentrated costs on criminal justice agencies. The agencies may have incentives to bear the costs in the short run (due to their interests in developing information systems), but, over the long run, they will feel the burdens of regulation keenly and have a strong incentive to negate the effect of whatever regulation has been imposed.[31] The fact that legislation is adopted does not guarantee that social costs will be reduced. Criminal justice agencies may work hard to "capture" the agency administering the law or to render regulation ineffective when supporters of such legislation have turned their attention to other matters. Thus, without constant vigilance, any legislation passed is likely to be ineffective in reducing social costs.

In summary, obstacles to the successful representation of the interest in reducing the social costs of criminal justice records are, if not overwhelming, at least substantial enough to offer only limited hope of relief to those affected by those costs. It would be premature to forecast the courses of legislation and regulation in this area; however, it is important to understand the conditions for, and the limitations on, the successful representation of these diffuse, low-intensity, low-visibility interests in the context of technology assessment and regulation, for it is within the existing policymaking process that demands for reductions of social costs are made and the control of technological innovations are defined.

---

[30] Nadel. *Politics of Consumer Protection*, p. 245.
[31] See, for example, Matthew Crenson, *The Un-Politics of Air Pollution*, Baltimore, Md., Johns Hopkins University Press, 1971, pp. 139–140.

10
Defining Appropriate Regulatory Arrangements and the Politics and Costs of Regulation

The main emphasis of Chapter 9 concerned representation of the interest in reducing the social costs of criminal justice records in the existing policy formation process. Within the present context of public choice, conditions were suggested for the successful representation of such an interest, as well as some of the existing limitations or constraints.

Politics, however, does not focus exclusively on the existing context of choice. One of the principal aims of engaging in political activity is to alter the context of choice in a favorable direction. The significance of regulation depends not only on the degree to which particular social costs may be reduced but also on changes in regulatory arrangements that affect the prevailing patterns and distribution of political power. Therefore, consideration of proposals for regulation involve inquiry into not only the extent to which the regulations will reduce social costs but also the extent to which they will alter existing patterns of political representation and participation for defining future policy.

The consideration of comprehensive national legislation in 1974 and 1975 suggested that a major shift in regulatory arrangements should occur. Although it is impossible to know precisely whether a shift will occur in the near future, the range of proposed alternatives can be examined to determine how each proposed option addresses the reduction of social costs of criminal justice records and what changes each option implies in the existing pattern of interaction among the actors in the policymaking process.

This chapter will discuss the major approaches to regulation which have been proposed during development of the debate on a national criminal justice information policy (see Table 20). The framework for issue expansion and agenda access presented in Chapter 3 will be used to analyze the comparative political costs and benefits of the approaches to proposed regulations. In doing so, no "best" approach to regulation will be claimed; rather, the focus will be on the comparative advantages and disadvantages of each proposal in reducing social costs, as well as the costs of political transactions, following establishment of new regulatory arrangements for the various actors in the public policymaking process.

ON DEFINING APPROPRIATE REGULATORY ARRANGEMENTS

An important function of regulation is to internalize the externalities for those goods that producers are unable or unwilling to internalize for themselves. It generally is desirable to internalize all the benefits and costs associated with provision of a particular good. Thus, decisions concerning levels of consumption will be more likely to consider the interests of all those whose welfare they influence. If, however, this principle is adhered to without qualification, it may well imply that consumption levels for a good or service of primarily local interest but with some external effects must be determined by the central government. One alternative to regulation of the social costs of criminal justice records might be to let the Federal Government control the use of criminal justice records and criminal justice information systems in local and state governments.[1] A supportive argument might be that, due to the development of a nationwide network of criminal justice information systems, the only way of effectively internalizing the social costs of criminal justice records would be through control by the Federal Government. Traditional state and local control over the information and recordkeeping functions in law enforcement and the administration of criminal justice would be perceived as ineffective in reducing social costs. Nationwide usage and dissemination of criminal justice records through a network of information and communications systems would necessitate federal control over criminal justice information policy.

[1] Wallace E. Oates. *Fiscal Federalism.* New York, Harcourt Brace Jovanovich, 1972, p. 46.

TABLE 20   Proposals for Change in Management of Criminal Justice Information Systems and Formation of Criminal Information Policy

1. Ervin subcommittee bill (1974)
2. Department of Justice bill (1974)
3. Project SEARCH proposal (1974) and SEARCH Group, Inc. consensus framework (1978 and 1979)
4. Compromise Ervin bill with Project SEARCH amendments (1975)
5. DOJ compromise bill (1975)
6. Tunney compromise bill (1975)
7. LEAA proposal for interstate compact (1976)
8. Department of Justice blueprint activities and consensus concept (1978)

The problem with such reasoning is that it disregards an essential feature of the calculus of choice in identifying and reducing social costs: the shift in political transactions costs incurred by such an arrangement.[2] Although permitting a central authority to decide the "right" level of social costs would substantially reduce some transaction costs for the federal agencies involved, the transaction costs for those affected by the regulations, as well as those affected by social costs, might be high. There also would be no guarantee that the central authority would effectively reduce social costs or even that such an authority would know what courses of action to take. Thus, in determining the level of social costs, it is necessary to consider shifts in political transaction costs among relevant actors in the policymaking process. This means that, when assessing proposals for reducing social costs, the anticipated costs or benefits to the various parties must be considered in the context of possible shifts in regulatory approaches.

Chapter 2 noted that social costs were reciprocal; that is, they in-

[2] *Ibid.* See also James M. Buchanan and Gordon Tullock, *The Calculus of Consent: Logical Foundations of Constitutional Democracy,* Ann Arbor, University of Michigan Press, 1965; Vincent Ostrom, "Operational Federalism: Organization for the Provision of Public Services in the American Federal System," *Public Choice,* 6:11–17, Spring 1969; Vincent Ostrom, "Water Resource Development: Some Problems in Economic and Political Analysis of Public Policy," in: *Political Science and Public Policy,* edited by Austin Ranney, Chicago, Markham, 1968, pp. 123–150; Vincent Ostrom, Charles M. Tiebout, and Robert Warren, "The Organization of Government in Metropolitan Areas," *American Political Science Review,* 55:831–842, December 1961; Gordon Tullock, "Federalism: Problems of Scale," *Public Choice,* 6:20–27, Spring 1969; Robert Warren, "A Municipal Services Market Model of Metropolitan Organization," Washington, D.C., Resources for the Future, 1964, pp. 193–204; and Robert Warren, "Federal-Local Development Planning: Scale Effects in Representation and Policy Making," *Public Administration Review,* 30:585–595, November–December, 1970.

volve both internal and external costs. Reducing social costs implies achievement of a more appropriate allocation of internal and external costs. Determining the level of costs is a problem of collective action, which involves strategic interaction between the producer who incurs internal costs and the individuals affected by external costs. The affected individuals are interested in reducing external costs by expanding the scope and scale of conflict, since doing so affects the entrance and treatment of external costs on the community and formal agendas; at the same time, the producer seeks to maintain the status quo by restricting the scope and scale of conflict, thus minimizing the costs of change.

All regulatory proposals are directed at changing the levels of cost allocations between contending parties; each proposal imposes different immediate and long-term costs and benefits on contending sides to a controversy. One cannot assume a priori that the adoption of a new approach will reduce external costs for affected individuals. Public organizations or producers of certain external costs must incur higher internal costs if external costs are to be reduced; therefore, they will either resist or influence regulation to minimize the cost of change. Following the analysis of Chapter 2, such organizations are more likely to use or favor regulatory approaches that alter behavior than approaches that might affect their rules, structures, and goals. In addition, some regulations are likely to be symbolic, providing only an appearance of action to reduce external costs.

All regulatory approaches have a price, which is defined as the trade-off between external and internal costs as well as the costs of political transactions to bring about change in the level of these two types of costs.[3] For purposes of policy analysis, it is important to understand the alternative prices that proposals for regulation imply. In the context of this examination of the social costs of technological innovation in public organizations, three aspects of institutional and political arrangements are significant: the nature and scale of formal organizations and technological development, the size and characteristics of the public affected, and the political community (those who are actually considered when deciding whether and how to provide for reductions in social costs).

In the sections that follow, the various regulatory approaches proposed or used in the debate on formulation of criminal justice information policy will be analyzed on the basis of these three factors. No attempt will be made to give a simple a priori decision rule for the

[3] See Vincent Ostrom, "Water Resource Development," pp. 135–141.

design of regulatory arrangements to reduce social costs. In a world of uncertainty and scarcity of resources, knowing the price of regulatory arrangements in terms of a theoretical optimum standard may not be as significant as assessing the prices of regulatory arrangements and proposals in the context of the give and take of political choice. It is within this context that actual decisions are made and anticipated costs and benefits of change are assessed.

SOME INAPPROPRIATE REGULATORY OPTIONS

Several alternatives examined in this study for the regulation of criminal justice records and recordkeeping have been rejected at one point or another as inappropriate or temporary in nature. This section will consider why these regulatory options have not been perceived as acceptable in the formation of criminal justice information policy.

Basically, six regulatory options have been rejected: prohibition, voluntary action, voluntary standards, compensation, subsidizing collective activity, and administrative rules and procedures directed at state and local government.

Prohibition

At the outset of the controversy concerning privacy and computers, some commentators were convinced that the only way to avoid the social costs of recordkeeping was to ban or prohibit the development of computerized information systems and information networks. It was suggested that barring or severely limiting the use of computers would effectively eliminate social costs. Basically, the advocates of such prohibition were not concerned with any beneficial uses of information technology. In their estimation, the potential for harm clearly outweighed any good that might result from using such machines.

For a number of reasons, outright prohibition can be considered a poor approach. First, as suggested in Chapter 3, social costs are pervasive features of nearly all social processes. To ban the use of computers means that individuals and the community as a whole must forego significant benefits. Outright prohibition misses a fundamental point by focusing exclusively on the computer as the main cause of social costs. No attention is given to the institutional and political contexts in which computer technology is used or the particular uses to which it is put. Significantly, the advocates of outright prohibition overlook the fact that institutional contexts and collective choice arrangements do and can serve to mitigate the negative effects of technological innovations.

A related fact is that the uses of records derived from information systems may be only partly to blame for the social cost problems that arise. As suggested in Chapter 6, introduction of a new technology is not the source of the problem; it is a means for making existing, but seemingly latent, problems worse if current policies and practices are not reconsidered or changed. Many of the problems that arose with the introduction of the computer in the context of law enforcement and the administration of criminal justice were present during the period prior to development of the technology;[4] however, introduction of the new technology occasioned reconsideration of these previously neglected difficulties.[5] The introduction of information technology brings with it new capabilities for good and for bad, but it also, as a positive side effect, highlights aspects of record usage and recordkeeping that otherwise might have been neglected or overlooked. In effect, intentions by public and private agencies to use computers in their organizations made consideration of information policy a significant public concern during the 1960s and 1970s.

Finally, the approach of outright prohibition presumes that the continued suppression of technological innovation is possible. Advocates of such an approach tend to overlook the presence of strong economic and organizational incentives in large public and private organizations to develop and utilize technology wherever possible. As a political strategy, therefore, outright prohibition tends to impose severe costs on those sectors in the society least likely to bear them. Such an approach would impose severe regulatory costs not only by imposing restrictions on sectors of the society in need of such technology but, also, by foregoing the social and economic benefits to be derived from such a powerful innovation.

Voluntary Action

From time to time, it has been suggested that designing regulatory options for reducing social costs is not needed. There is sufficient motivation among individuals affected by social costs for them to take action to relieve or correct their situation. Thus, the approach of voluntary action assumes that there are adequate legal and political

[4] See, for example, Aryeh Neier, *Dossier*, New York, Stein and Day, 1974, Chapter 13, "The Computer Is Not the Villain," pp. 159–166; and Alan F. Westin and Michael A. Baker, *Databanks in a Free Society*, New York, Quadrangle Books, 1972, pp. 341–342.

[5] A similar point is suggested by Westin and Baker, *Databanks in a Free Society*, pp. 342–346.

channels available and that individuals affected by the social costs of criminal justice records will take advantage of them.

As suggested in the preceding chapters, both assumptions are incorrect. There is no a priori basis on which to assume that individuals affected by social costs are willing or able to undertake collective action to deal with this situation. These individuals constitute a group with little or no incentives to engage in collective action, due to the high transaction costs involved and the absence of effective mechanisms for coordination and pooling of resources. Indeed, individuals affected by the social costs of criminal justice records have selective disincentives not to act collectively. Due to the stigma attached to having a criminal record and the cumulative effects of record discrimination in society, it is to the benefit of individuals in this relevant public to neither talk about nor bear witness to the arrest or conviction record. Consequently, the public stigmatized by such records has not organized. Furthermore, when individuals with such records have sought to gain relief from their records, either through the courts or the political process, they have met with only limited success. As noted in Chapter 6, until the late 1960s, most courts were hesitant to interfere with police discretion in handling criminal justice records. When relief was granted, it was essentially limited to specific restrictions on dissemination of arrest and criminal history records. In only a few instances did the courts order that arrest records be expunged or returned to the individual. Legislatures, in turn, were hesitant to provide individuals with criminal records any form of relief. Prior to the 1970s, only a few states had record-sealing provisions or statutes limiting the disclosure of criminal justice records or permitting individuals with such records to review their record and request that any errors or omissions be corrected. In instances where record dissemination restrictions did exist, there seldom were any provisions for holding the agencies or officials criminally or civilly liable for violations.

For these reasons, the voluntary action approach does not stand on its assumptions. Individuals affected by the social costs of criminal justice records have not acted to achieve their common or group interests or to collectively reduce such costs. Furthermore, even in instances where provisions have existed to reduce such costs, they have been seriously deficient.

Voluntary Standards

A third approach to the control of social costs of criminal justice records has been to rely on criminal justice agencies to voluntarily adopt guidelines and standards to control the use of these records. This voluntary approach has taken two forms. Prior to the existence of LEAA, some local and state criminal justice agencies adopted guidelines or standards to control the use of criminal justice records either in response to specific abuses or in the course of developing criminal justice information systems. When LEAA was established, it urged state and local agencies at various times to adopt the Project SEARCH model state act and/or administrative regulations or the standards developed by the National Advisory Commission on Criminal Justice Standards and Goals.

Generally, these two manifestations of the voluntary standards approach have failed. The voluntary approach to regulation of criminal justice records that prevailed during the manual and early computer recordkeeping periods attempted to introduce a variety of new forms of information policy in state and local criminal justice agencies, but failed to introduce any new forms of regulation in states and localities where criminal justice information systems were developing. Except where outside pressures or the perceived threat of outside pressures have existed to promote the reformulation of information policy to reduce social costs, criminal justice agencies have not reduced the social costs of criminal justice records on their own. Even when LEAA-sponsored activities such as Project SEARCH and the National Advisory Commission on Criminal Justice Standards and Goals have designed standards, state and local agencies generally have not voluntarily complied. This is primarily due to the fact that state and local agencies have had little or no incentives to adhere to voluntary standards. Rather, they have had incentives to avoid the costs of such restrictions.

Thus, the voluntary standards approach has been of only limited success. Largely, the incentive structure it sets up simply has been inappropriate for the tasks of reducing the social costs of criminal justice records.

Compensation

A fourth approach to regulation has been compensation. In trying to resolve the incentive problems related to the voluntary standards approach, the compensatory approach aims at providing positive incentives or rewards for desired actions to be taken in reducing social costs. Thus, LEAA has attached specific conditions to its contracts and grants to state and local agencies to assure a reduction in the social costs of criminal justice records. Through its CDS program, LEAA has sought to tie the future development of local and state criminal justice information systems to a set of minimum system development and security and privacy standards. While a number of states have adopted master plans for criminal justice information systems, it is not clear that privacy and security regulations have played an integral part, nor what the effect of such master plans have been on local and state agencies.[6] Compliance on the local level has been on a voluntary basis, suggesting that the compensatory approach, in practice, may be just an offshoot of the voluntary standards approach if the granting agency cannot or will not bear the costs of enforcement of its contract or grant provisions. Generally, LEAA has left enforcement of the conditions of participation in the CDS program to the 50 state planning agencies and has only limited control of efforts for assuring compliance in the implementation of its grant provisions at the local level.

Subsidizing Collective Activity

A fifth approach to regulation has been the subsidizing of collective activity by members of the public affected by the social costs of criminal justice records or by groups representing individuals with criminal justice records. In 1970, LEAA was directed by Congress to allocate a portion of its funds for correctional programs. As part of this emphasis, LEAA funds have supported a variety of projects in the states aimed at expanding offender rights both within and outside of correctional institutions, establishing community employment programs and halfway houses for ex-offenders and providing information on the problems of ex-offenders.[7] By supporting such projects, LEAA has permitted ex-offender self-help groups, as well as religious, legal, and service groups, to promote both directly and indirectly the cause of ex-offenders and the problems they face. Some of these groups have engaged in political activity on behalf of ex-offenders and have supported efforts to reduce the social costs of criminal justice records. In surveys completed in 1975, 1976, and 1977, more than 700 organizations were identified as being involved in correctional change and promoting the cause of ex-offenders.[8] Although not all such

[6] See, for example, Donald F. King, "Criminal Justice Information System Master Planning," in: *Proceedings of the Second International Symposium on Criminal Justice Information and Statistics Systems,* edited by Project SEARCH, Sacramento, California Crime Technological Research Foundation, 1974, p. 206.

[7] U.S. Department of Justice, Law Enforcement Assistance Administration. *6th Annual Report of the LEAA, Fiscal Year 1974.* Washington, D.C., U.S. Government Printing Office, 1974, pp. 31–33.

[8] See Mary Lee Bundy and K. R. Harmon, *The National Prison Directory,* Base Vol., 1975; Mary Lee Bundy and R. G. Whaley, Suppl. No. 1, 1976; Mary Lee Bundy, Suppl. No. 2, 1977; College Park, Md., Urban Information Interpreters.

organizations have received LEAA support, many have received LEAA grants to support some or all of their activities.

Generally, subsidizing collective activity is a byproduct of the LEAA program and not a direct result of LEAA's orientation. The problems with this approach derive from four sources. First, where such groups have supported the promotion of ex-offender rights, they usually have not advanced the cause of individuals with arrest records. Unlike ex-offenders, individuals with arrest records have not organized, nor have they had as many organizations in the states actively promoting their cause.

Second, groups that have received LEAA support have functioned primarily as service groups and secondarily as interest groups promoting the rights of ex-offenders. In most instances, political activity has secured only limited emphasis.

Third, most groups formed by ex-offenders or directed at helping ex-offenders have dealt with the symptoms of record problems and not with the causes; that is, most of the groups have sought to find jobs for ex-offenders and to provide related services but have not dealt directly with the reasons why ex-offenders have difficulties in finding jobs. The fact that conviction records receive wide dissemination in our society usually has been taken as a *given* in outlining group or organizational strategies for ex-offenders.

Fourth, the fact that LEAA has subsidized many projects in recent years to deal with the problems of ex-offenders does not mean that it has had any impact on the policies and practices of using conviction records and criminal history records either within or outside the criminal justice process. As an agency engaged in a wide range of activities, concern with the ex-offender in correctional programs has had little, if any, connection with LEAA's efforts to develop criminal justice information systems.

Administrative Rules and Procedures Directed at State and Local Government

The sixth approach to regulation of the social costs of criminal justice records has been the use of administrative rules and procedures. Both the NCIC Advisory Policy Board and LEAA have adopted administrative rules for privacy and security that are to be followed by agencies participating in the NCIC/CCH program or receiving federal support for criminal justice information systems.

This approach has increased the awareness of privacy and security concerns in many criminal justice agencies and has, as noted in previous chapters, stimulated some innovation and experimentation on the part of state and local governments; nevertheless, this approach suffers from four significant weaknesses. First, the rules are developed by agencies with little incentive to impose significant costs of change on themselves or other agencies that they must deal with on a daily basis. The process of developing and promulgating such rules in administrative agencies typically is characterized by the use of a wide range of discretionary measures by the agency in outlining the methods of regulation and their review and enforcement. Second, such administrative rules generally are weakly enforced. Penalties are seldom invoked, even in the face of information about violations.[9] Third, the development of administrative rules often is used to contain conflict rather than to deal effectively with the problem of reducing the social costs of criminal justice records. Agencies attempt to minimize the costs of change by developing rules and procedures that indicate some action is being taken about problems of public and legislative concern. Such a strategy sometimes has the effect of preempting legislation that might impose more severe costs on the agency: If the agency shows that it is acting to control its problems, then legislation may not be needed. And, fourth, the use of administrative rules and procedures permits significant amounts of discretion to the agencies responding to define what the extent of their compliance will be. In this case, there are strong incentives for state and local governments to meet the minimum acceptable conditions of federal regulations and not to incur additional costs by developing strict compliance policies and practices.

Generally, the approach of administrative rules has been perceived as inadequate and only a stopgap measure. Legislators, public interest groups, and even other public officials have been quick to recognize the limitations of such rules in reducing the social costs of criminal justice records.

REGULATORY ALTERNATIVES FOR A NATIONAL CRIMINAL JUSTICE INFORMATION POLICY

None of the regulatory alternatives in the preceding section have been viewed as appropriate in the development of a national criminal jus-

[9] See, for example, Paul Altmeyer, "ABC News Closeup, The Paper Prison: Your Government Records," Transcript, New York, American Broadcasting Companies, April 25, 1974, pp. 41–46.

tice information policy. Either the regulatory alternatives have posed severe costs in terms of enforcement, or they have assumed incentive structures among the regulators or those affected by social costs that have been inappropriate for the problems being addressed.

The call for a national policy has necessitated the consideration of more comprehensive schemes for regulation by many key participants in the policymaking process. In 1974, efforts to develop comprehensive national legislation centered on two proposals for regulation: the Department of Justice bill and the Ervin bill. Both proposals aimed at regulating the exchange of criminal justice information to protect the constitutional rights and privacy of individuals with criminal records. At the most general level, both bills shared fundamental objectives and a similarity in thrust and provisions, focusing on the regulation of criminal justice records in local, state, and federal systems. Both bills sought to provide rules or minimum standards concerning record dissemination, access, updating, security, and accuracy and included civil and criminal penalties for violation of the provisions and for some enforcement and auditing mechanisms.

Such similarities notwithstanding, however, it was clear that both bills were based on two fundamentally different approaches to regulation and entailed different structures of costs and benefits. These bills were not aimed at merely reducing social costs in the short term but at shifting the context of public choice for future policymaking concerning criminal justice information policy and information systems development.

This section will discuss the significance of these two regulatory proposals as related to the pattern of representation and participation in the policy formation process. Six other positions that have been proposed since 1974 also will be examined: the final Ervin compromise bill with Project SEARCH amendments, the Tunney compromise bill in 1975, the DOJ compromise bill in 1975, the LEAA interstate compact idea, the Project SEARCH state consortium and consensus framework concepts, and the Department of Justice "consensus concept." Each of these proposals represents a variation of the basic regulatory approaches outlined in the original legislative proposals and has important implications for future policymaking and oversight arrangements in this area. As suggested earlier, the political price of regulatory arrangements does not depend only on immediate reductions in social costs but on changes in transaction costs among the contending sides when regulatory arrangements are changed. The assessment of changes in regulatory arrangements is dependent on three important factors: the structure of formal organization and the nature of technological development, the kinds of social costs involved and the size and characteristics of the public affected, and the political community involved in the policy formation process.

The Structure of Formal Organization and Technological Development

In Chapter 4, it was noted that the development of criminal justice information systems at the local, state, and federal levels of government was perceived as an essential step in the reform and modernization of the criminal justice system in America. Both the President's Commission on Law Enforcement and Administration of Justice and the National Advisory Commission on Criminal Justice Standards and Goals called for a national strategy to reduce crime and reform and modernize the criminal justice system, but the principal responsibilities for law enforcement and the administration of criminal justice have remained at local and state levels. The actual development of nationwide criminal justice information systems has occurred largely in the state and local agencies. In addition, the basic approach of LEAA as a catalyst of information system development has been to develop a federated and integrated national criminal justice information system, with the intention of leaving to local and state agencies the major responsibilities for maintaining and disseminating criminal justice information.

Given the decentralized organization in the criminal justice system, as well as decentralized development of criminal justice information systems, what approaches to regulation aimed at setting a criminal justice information policy have been proposed?

The 1974 Ervin bill proposed retention of federated control over the development of criminal justice information policy and information systems and creation of a cooperative federal-state administrative structure for enforcement of this provision. At the federal level, a Criminal Justice Information Systems Board was to be established as an independent agency for administration and enforcement of the act. The board was to have authority to issue general regulations and cease and desist orders, and to impose administrative penalties; it was to supervise the operation of any interstate information system and telecommunications system by authorizing a federal agency, such as the FBI or a federally chartered corporation, to operate the system. Each state, in turn, was required to establish a central administrative agency (or to designate an existing agency) with broad authority to oversee and regulate the operation of criminal justice data banks in the state.

In contrast, the DOJ bill focused administrative and statutory control in the U.S. Attorney General, who was to have almost complete discretion in implementing regulations under the act. No formal role was given to the states for regulating their own data banks. The FBI's NCIC network was to retain control over any interstate information system. The attorney general was to have direct control over the information policies of local and state criminal justice agencies.

In terms of formal organization and information technology development in criminal justice, the DOJ bill would have had a significant centralizing effect on patterns of responsibility. Indeed, in contrast to the Ervin bill, which would have provided a coordinated, federated structure for policy formulation, the DOJ bill would have focused control over local and state information policies in the attorney general.

The six alternatives that have been suggested since 1974 do not represent alterations in the regulatory structures proposed but variations on the basic themes. Prior to 1974, and again in 1978 and 1979, Project SEARCH advocated a "consortium of states" modeled after itself as an appropriate mechanism to regulate the interstate criminal justice information systems network. The consortium was to have been composed of appointed members from each state and would have developed criminal information policy and managed the system on a voluntarist basis, the same as Project SEARCH and NLETS have been managed.

A second decentralized alternative was offered by LEAA in 1976, when it proposed to the Department of Justice Information and Telecommunications System Policy Board an "interstate compact" arrangement as a way of providing control over the interstate communication network to the states. The interstate compact had to be chartered by Congress and, therefore, represented a more formal and permanent arrangement than the consortium concept.

A third decentralized arrangement for regulation in this area was included in the Ervin compromise bill with Project SEARCH's amendments in late 1974 and in the Tunney compromise bill in 1975. The amendments proposed that a Commission on Criminal Justice Information be created with a five-year life cycle. The commission was to have the same responsibilities as the Criminal Justice Information Systems Board in the original Ervin proposal; however, state-level boards were not mandated. Instead, the commission was to encourage each of the states to create or designate an agency to exercise statewide authority and responsibility for enforcement of the act. Although this clause would have provided the states an option with respect to the organization designated to enforce the act, nevertheless, the act would have required minimum policies and standards in each state over the management and use of criminal justice information.

In contrast to the decentralized approach inherent in the first three options, the blueprint activities within the Department of Justice in 1978 advocated a consensus concept, which essentially would retain FBI control over the CCH program and provide the FBI with limited message switching for that purpose. In effect, this option is consistent with the original 1974 DOJ bill and represents a de facto pursuit of that approach to management of the network and the development of criminal justice information policy. The 1978 blueprint activities, therefore, carry on the centralizing effect of the original 1974 department bill, although, in its 1975 compromise bill, the department recommended a Commission on Criminal Justice Information to help advise and study problems in this area. While formal control over state and local criminal justice information policies would not be in the hands of the attorney general and the FBI, the inclination for state and local agencies to depend on the interstate network for direction and federal support in developing their own systems would, at least informally, make them look to the Federal Government for policy development and enactment.

Reducing Social Costs and Granting Relief to the Affected Public

In Chapter 5, it was noted that the social costs of criminal justice records arose mainly from the widespread availability and dissemination of arrest records, conviction records, and criminal history records throughout society. Access to these records on both a formal and informal basis by numerous governmental agencies, private organizations, and individuals resulted in limitations and restrictions on the social, economic, and political opportunities of individuals with such records. Chapter 6 suggested that such social costs were compounded by the inaccuracy and incompleteness of criminal justice records, due to the voluntary nature of reporting dispositions by criminal justice agencies. In both the manual and early computer development periods, the general practice had been to permit individual criminal justice agencies and individual states to establish their own standards and regulations. What resulted was a hodgepodge of statutes, administrative practices, and informal arrangements that were largely responsible for the problems that developed.

In responding to this situation, the Ervin, Tunney, and DOJ bills aimed at requiring minimum standards for local and state agencies to follow in their recordkeeping functions. Generally, the Ervin and Tunney bills provided for more specific requirements concerning record accuracy, access, security, and retention than did the DOJ bills.

The Ervin, Tunney, and DOJ bills would have permitted forms of relief for individuals with criminal justice records, granted rights of access to the individual's record, established correction procedures to be followed if a record was found to be incomplete or incorrrect, and permitted civil courses of action for those individuals who might be harmed by the use or dissemination of their records in violation of provisions of the act. Finally, the bills would have required that individuals be notified when their criminal justice records were being used for noncriminal justice purposes.

State statutes and executive orders permitting noncriminal justice agencies to receive criminal justice records for licensing and employment purposes would have continued under the acts. The Ervin and Tunney bills would have closed off access by the executive order of a governor and required statutory authorizations whenever state or federal noncriminal justice agencies had access to records. The DOJ bills would have permitted grants of access to records by state or federal statute and by executive orders of the governors and the president. Generally, the Ervin and Tunney bills would have prohibited arrest records from being disseminated outside law enforcement agencies; only conviction records were, as a rule, to be disseminated to other than law enforcement or criminal justice agencies. The DOJ bills, on the other hand, would have permitted arrest records to be disseminated to other than law enforcement and criminal justice agencies if the records had dispositions.

Generally, the bills were aimed at establishing minimum standards for criminal justice recordkeeping and record usage. Each proposal sought to cut down on informal and secondary record dissemination and to provide some uniformity in requirements from state to state. In addition, the subcommittee and DOJ bills would have permitted individuals access to their records and forms of relief from injuries caused by improper dissemination or use of their records. Thus, in terms of the responses of both regulatory proposals to the scale of social costs, they undertook similar strategies by providing state and local discretion in formulating regulations within a nationwide context of minimum standards and requirements.

The Ervin and Tunney compromise measures tended to make some concessions for the use and dissemination of criminal justice records, but they also sought to establish minimum standards for the states. Project SEARCH and LEAA also have advocated the development of minimum standards in this area and have pursued the development of standards and goals independent of legislative initiatives. In contrast, the FBI and the Office of the Attorney General largely have left the development of policy up to the FBI and its NCIC Advisory Policy Board, on the premise that the NCIC system in general and the CCH program in particular are voluntary service efforts which should not mandate standards and goals that would influence criminal justice information policy in the states. The Department of Justice, despite public, judicial, and legislative criticism of the voluntarist approach, over the years has consistently maintained that it is up to the states to develop their own policies concerning the records in the interstate system.

The Political Community and Political Representation

Chapter 9 indicated that the successful representation of the interest in reducing the social costs of criminal justice records depends on widening the scope of conflict. It was suggested that the most powerful interests in a conflict want to restrict the scope of the conflict by involving a limited number of participants and narrowing the definition of problems open to settlement. Weaker interests seek to widen the scope of conflict by expanding the number of participants and defining the relevant problems more broadly.

An important aspect of political controversy over the dimensions of the scope of conflict involves not only the generation and dissemination of information to the public to make people aware of relevant conflicts, but also the definition of a regulation scheme that effectively deals with immediate problems and promotes the representational function of advocates in the policy formation process into the stages of administration and implementation. Regulation, therefore, involves not only the definition of standards and guidelines for immediate action but, perhaps more importantly, usually implies a shift, or possible shift, in the patterns of representation and participation for the *future* definition and implementation of policy. In this context, regulatory proposals can be considered from the perspective of how they widen or narrow the scope of conflict. It would be expected that proposals representing the most powerful interests in a controversy would seek to narrow the scope of conflict by restricting participation in future policy formation and by avoiding as much as possible the creation of new forums for information generation and dissemination. On the other hand, proposals for regulation representing the weaker interests would seek to widen the scope of conflict by expanding avenues for participation in future policymaking and by creating new forums for information generation and dissemination.

Even a cursory review of the existing regulatory proposals shows that the expectations concerning the scope of conflict do bear out. The DOJ bills and recent efforts by the department concerning the consensus concept would centralize responsibility for the generation and administration of regulations involving local and state criminal justice agencies in the attorney general. Although the DOJ bill (S. 2964) would have required "appropriate consultation with Federal and State agencies which operate or use criminal justice information systems" before the issuance of regulations implementing the act, and, in 1975, would have established a Commission on Criminal Justice Information to advise and study problems in this area, the attorney general and the Department of Justice would have had the major share of the responsibility for administration and enforcement of the act.

In contrast, the Ervin bills and Tunney compromise measure would have set up a cooperative federal-state administrative structure for enforcement of the act. Membership on the proposed federal Criminal Justice Information Systems Board or the Commission on Criminal Justice Information would have included 13 representatives:

One of the members shall be the Attorney General and two of the members shall be designated by the President as representatives of other Federal agencies outside of the Department of Justice. One of the members shall be designated by the Judicial Conference of the United States. The nine remaining members shall be appointed by the President with the advice and consent of the Senate. Of the nine members appointed by the President, seven shall be officials of criminal justice agencies from seven different states at the time of their nomination, representing to the extent possible all segments of the criminal justice system. The two remaining Presidential appointees shall be private citizens well versed in the law of privacy, constitutional law, and information systems technology. The President shall designate one of the seven criminal justice agency officials as Chairman and such designation shall also be confirmed by the advice and consent of the Senate. Not more than seven members of the Board shall be of the same political party.[10]

[10] U.S. Congress, Senate. S. 2008. *Criminal Justice Information and Protection of Privacy Act of 1975*. Hearings. 94th Congress, 1st Session, 1975.

The acts did not stipulate membership requirements for state agencies, but it was clear that they would have embodied the options for representational structures of the Project SEARCH model act. In addition to representation of the law enforcement community, the option defined by the model act provided for representation of members of the public as well as the judicial and corrections community.

The subcommittee bills in 1974 and 1975 aimed, therefore, at widening participation in the future policy formulation process by dividing responsibilities for criminal justice information policy between state and federal regulatory boards, as well as assuring representation to the judicial and corrections community and the general public. In contrast, the DOJ bill and administrative proposals aimed at restricting the scope of conflict by centralizing responsibility for enforcement of policies in the attorney general. These schemes of regulation would have effectively retained FBI influence in the design of an interstate CCH program and assured that the law enforcement community would continue to have the predominant influence on state and local criminal justice information policies.

Beyond the provision for specific representation in the policy formulation process, both the subcommittee and DOJ approaches would have had an effect on the information generation and dissemination aspects of conflict management. As indicated in Chapter 8, defining the relevant issues and problems does influence the scope of conflict. Information generation and dissemination concerning the social costs of criminal justice records and the development of criminal justice information systems are important in widening or restricting the scope of conflict by affecting the visibility and intensity of the interests involved.

Thus, information generation and dissemination provisions of regulatory proposals do reflect the interests in widening or restricting the scope of conflict. In this regard, the Ervin and Tunney bills would have provided for more specific mechanisms concerning the social costs of criminal justice records and the development of criminal justice information systems than the DOJ approach would have done.

The DOJ bills, for example, would not have required the attorney general to issue detailed reports concerning the administration and enforcement of the act. Once a year, local, state, and federal agencies would have been required to publish notice of their criminal justice information policy and the existence and nature of any criminal justice information system that they operated, and would have had to make periodic reports to the attorney general on request. In the 1975 DOJ proposal, the Advisory Commission would have been required to report annually to the president and to the Congress; however, the range and coverage of reporting was not detailed except in a general manner. In contrast, the subcommittee bills proposed a number of specific problem identification and publication mechanisms. The federal Criminal Justice Information Systems Board (1974) and the Commission on Criminal Justice Information (1975) would have been given authority to conduct an ongoing study of the policies of various agencies of the Federal Government in the operation of information systems. Before implementing any regulations, the board or commission would have had to give notice and hold hearings and to consult with the affected agencies and any other interested parties. They also would have had authority to request periodic reports from federal agencies on criminal justice information policy and information systems and to conduct random annual audits of the practices and procedures of federal agencies handling criminal justice information. In addition, the acts would have required state agencies to conduct annual audits in each state and to make the findings available to the federal regulatory body. Finally, the board or commission would have had to issue an annual report to the Congress and to the president which, at a minimum, would include the results of audits, summaries of orders issued under the act, summaries of any public notices filed by criminal justice agencies on developing systems, and any recommendations for new legislation.

Placement of a public notice on any state or local automated system or any federal manual or automated system also would have been required. Furthermore, any agency proposing a new system or enlarging an existing system would have had to give adequate notice so that affected parties would have enough time to comment. Finally, the acts would have given specific authority to the comptroller general to conduct audits and reviews of the activities of the board and to have access to pertinent data needed for such periodic reviews.

The subcommittee proposals in 1974 and 1975, in contrast to the DOJ proposals, sought to make the policy formation process more visible and specific. Information publication and generation requirements all aimed at assuring that the scope of conflict under which future policy will be made is to be expanded beyond the requirements of the 1974 and 1975 DOJ bills and the DOJ blueprint activities.

CONCLUSION: CRIMINAL JUSTICE INFORMATION POLICY AND THE POLITICS AND COSTS OF REGULATION

At the beginning of this chapter, it was suggested that one of the principal aims of engaging in political activity is to alter the context of choice in a direction that favors one's interests. The significance of regulation depends not only on the degree to which social costs may be reduced in the short term, but also on the changes in prevailing patterns and distributions of political power that are possible through the design of different regulatory arrangements.

This chapter has pointed out that the call for a national criminal justice information policy has necessitated the consideration of a number of alternative schemes for regulation. Several approaches to regulation, which have been previously tried or proposed and which have been viewed as inappropriate, were reviewed. The search for a policy has resulted in the consideration of more comprehensive schemes for regulation.

In the preceding section, proposals were considered from the perspective of the changes each would entail in the contexts of choice. In terms of the analyses in Chapters 2 and 3, it was suggested that, for a number of significant reasons, the subcommittee proposals in 1974 and 1975 represented more appropriate approaches than the DOJ bills in terms of reducing the social costs of criminal justice records.

First, although both approaches would have affected the scale of formal organization and information technology development in criminal justice, the subcommittee proposals would not have resulted in centralizing control over the emerging nationwide network of criminal justice information systems in one federal official. By retaining the federated approach to the regulation of criminal justice information policy under a state-federal administrative structure, it would be possible to tighten control over the interstate transmission of criminal justice information and still permit the states to adjust information policy to information-processing arrangements in each state. The bills would have provided for national minimum standards in this area, but they would not have tied local and state agencies to a federal control structure focused exclusively on the policy formation process of the FBI, LEAA, and the attorney general.

Second, the subcommittee proposals would not have restricted participation in the policy administration process to the priorities of law enforcement alone but would have made the pattern of representation in the administration of the act conform to the patterns of use of criminal justice information within the criminal justice system. Thus, the courts and the corrections community would have had representation corresponding in general with their status as major users of such records as well as major potential contributors to any nationwide system of computerized criminal history records.

Finally, in contrast to the approach of the DOJ bills, the subcommittee bills would have opened more broadly the policy formation process to citizen and public interest group involvement by permitting representation of the latter in policymaking activities and by providing mechanisms whereby policy formulation and administration processes would be more visible.

Thus, in terms of reducing the costs of political transactions, the subcommittee proposals appear to have offered a more satisfactory option to those interested in reducing or minimizing the external costs of criminal justice records. Not only would they have been less costly in terms of regulation, but they also would have offered a higher level of social costs reduction for the use of arrest records as well as conviction and intelligence records.

The fact that the subcommittee proposals would have imposed immediate costs on criminal justice agencies did not portend well for their *political acceptability*.[11] Anticipated costs of such approaches to the FBI and law enforcement agencies and to private and public organizations whose access to records would have been restricted or curtailed suggests that such proposals will continue to generate high levels of resistance. If there are to be compromises on the two approaches, it is likely that they will lean towards the Department of Justice approach and away from the provisions of the subcommittee proposals. As noted in Chapter 2, it is rational for organizations to seek change to reduce external costs and also rational for organizations to minimize the effects of changes on themselves.[12]

Thus, in the end, it cannot be assumed that the passage of national legislation or the development of federal administrative blueprints will have a significant effect on reducing the social costs of criminal justice records for the affected public. The outcome is necessarily problematic, depending on the continued treatment of the issues in the policymaking process and the character of subsequent activities to implement and alter public policy by the actors in the political process.

[11] See Matthew A. Crenson, *The Un-Politics of Air Pollution*, Baltimore, Md., Johns Hopkins Press, 1971, pp. 136–140; also, James Q. Wilson, *Political Organizations*, New York, Basic Books, 1973, pp. 331–337.

[12] James Buchanan has called this phenomenon appropriately the "erosion" of public goods "generated by the individual behavior of persons (or organizations) producing public 'bads.'" James Buchanan. "Public Goods and Public Bads." In: *Financing the Metropolis*. Edited by John P. Crecine. Beverly Hills, Calif., Sage Publications, 1970, p. 52.

PART III

11
Social Costs,
Technological Innovation,
and Public Administration

In treating the problem of interaction of the social costs of technological innovation in public organizations and politics, this study has extended well beyond its admittedly limited empirical base. It would misrepresent the findings of this study to refer to them all as conclusions. Even if the analysis of the social costs of criminal justice records and the politics of information policy formulation were completely certain, it would not account fully for the problems of agenda building and issue development concerning the social costs of technological innovations in public organizations. This study does not account for the problem of social costs in various technological and organizational contexts; it focuses on the social costs of criminal justice records. This issue area is not representative of all the political issues associated with the social costs of technological innovation. The problems of agenda building and issue development in criminal justice records and computers are no doubt different from the problems of agenda building and issue development in other areas of record usage and computer development in public agencies. Granting all these shortcomings, the theoretical approach and findings developed here nevertheless have important implications for the study of the interaction between technology and politics—particularly for the pluralist view of this interaction.

TECHNOLOGICAL INNOVATION AND
THE PROBLEM OF SOCIAL COSTS

The problem of social costs, like the problem of negative externalities in general, presents itself as an ubiquitous aspect of technological innovation. Social interdependence in an increasingly complex, technologically oriented society inevitably leads to the problem of the costs—as well as benefits—of that interdependence. This is especially true when large-scale organizations undertake technological change that affects, directly or indirectly, millions of individuals in society. The development of a nationwide network of criminal justice information systems presents itself as this kind of problem.

As a public policy concern, the phenomenon of social costs presents significant problems of a theoretical and practical nature for the pluralist view of the public policymaking process. As suggested in Chapter 2, the defining characteristics of social costs as uncompensated, reciprocal costs involving jointness of supply and high levels of uncertainty tend to question the basic assumptions of the pluralist perspective concerning the incentives for and the transaction costs involved in political action to reduce such costs. There is no a priori basis for the notion that the prevailing political process can assure that the social costs deriving from technological changes in the production of goods and services, such as law enforcement and the administration of criminal justice, will be kept at a minimum and adequately weighed against the internal cost calculus of public agencies. Will those individuals affected by social costs engage in collective action? Will social costs be internalized through the representation of all affected interests in the policy formation process? To what extent will the political agenda related to the formulation of public policy be directed at reducing social costs deriving from the productive processes of public agencies?

At the heart of the pluralist model of politics is the assumption that organized and effective group pressure will emerge when necessary to counteract suffering, dislocation, and disturbances experienced by individuals in society. Technological change and increasing social complexity leading to the imposition of external costs on many individuals in society will result inevitably in organization for collective action. The existence of external costs will produce disturbances in established relationships and expectations in society and, in turn, will lead to new patterns of interaction aimed at eliminating or restricting the disturbances. These new patterns of interaction often will be generated by the appearance of groups that are organized to counteract existing patterns of group and organizational interaction that are perceived as the causal factors behind the imposition of various external costs. Thus, the political system will move to a new equilibrium position based on the bargains and accommodations made between existing group and organizational interests and the newly emerged pressures for changes in the formulation of public policies in response to perceived disturbances, dislocations, and suffering brought on by technological change.

Such a self-correcting system assumption in the pluralist model of politics reveals, as Mancur Olsen has observed, a serious inconsistency in the theory of politics:

[the analytical pluralists] have assumed that, if a group had some reason or incentive to organize to further its interest, the rational individuals in that group would also have a reason or an incentive to support an organization working in their mutual interest.[1]

This kind of perspective ignores the assessment of the variable transaction costs of political action for individuals in society. Political action will be supplied when someone finds it profitable to do so. In the absence of mechanisms for coordination and pooling of resources, the costs of political transactions probably will exceed the marginal benefits; thus, individuals affected by the social costs of criminal justice records will not necessarily act collectively to reduce such costs. Furthermore, even if these individuals decide to act collectively to provide for reductions in social costs, the reductions are likely to be ineffective. This is true because political transaction costs tend to increase with the size of particular groups or publics. In large groups, the costs of information, communication, and participation are likely to be higher than in smaller groups. The public affected by the social costs of criminal justice records experiences not only high transaction costs and low levels of available resources for political action but also selective individual benefits attached to a strategy of inaction. The cumulative effect of the various forms of record problems on individuals in this relevant public is to provide strong individual incentives to neither talk about nor otherwise bear witness to an arrest or conviction record. The very fact of having either an arrest or conviction record constitutes a liability or stigma that a person usually responds to by managing information about himself in a way that will minimize the personal costs of that record. Thus, political activity by affected individuals constitutes a very costly affair. Reducing the personal costs to oneself of an arrest or conviction record entails positive incentives not to act collectively.

The response to the question concerning the prospects that those affected by social costs will engage in collective action is "It depends."

[1] Mancur Olsen. *The Logic of Collective Action*. Cambridge, Mass., Harvard University Press, 1965, p. 127.

Certainly the self-correcting system assumption of the pluralist model of politics is misdirected, because it does not account for the factors of group size, political transaction costs, and individual incentive structures affecting the possibilities of collective action.

As indicated in Chapters 6, 7, and 8, however, the fact that individuals affected by the social costs of criminal justice records will not engage in collective action does not mean that this public good—the reduction of social costs—will not be provided; it can be and is provided through a varied pattern of representation that depends on the structure of incentives prevailing among the actors in the policy-making process intending to represent a nonintense diffuse interest. Public interest groups, entrepreneurs, the press, and criminal justice agencies, acting through courts, state and local governments, and Congress, do have various incentives to provide for the minimization of social costs of criminal justice records. Those incentives influence the kinds of political actions undertaken, as well as the extent to which social costs reduction is demanded. Successful representation of such an interest depends on widening the scope of conflict. The principal representational function of public interest groups, entrepreneurs, and the press is to affect public opinion so as to widen the arena in which decisions affecting the public with criminal justice records are made.

There are, however, significant limitations or constraints on the representation of a nonintense, diffuse, low-visibility interest, which suggest that social cost reductions are likely to be provided ineffectively. First, criminal justice agencies at local, state, and federal levels often have the signficant advantage of defining what constitutes effective protection of the interest in reducing the social costs of criminal justice records. They may define the relevant issues and problems as narrowly as possible to contain the scope of conflict vis-à-vis the demands of public interest groups and entrepreneurs. Second, the press may not report favorably on the interest in reducing the social costs of criminal justice records because it perceives that its "right to know" is jeopardized by controls on criminal justice information and information systems. Portions of the press may reflect the popular sentiments for crime control and law and order rather than report favorably on the need for regulation and control of the social costs of criminal justice records. Third, local and state governments, as well as the courts, are restricted from effective representation of such an interest due to boundary and jurisdictional restrictions. Also, the interest in reducing the social costs of criminal justice records has, on most occasions, been given relatively low priority by legislators in their efforts to respond to what they perceive as the most significant or politically feasible aspects of the ecology of issues involved in the privacy and computers debate.

The existing patterns of representation are limited in responding to the interest in reducing the social costs of criminal justice records. Some level of social costs reduction will be provided, but it will not be an appropriate level either in terms of the demands of public interest groups, entrepreneurs, state and local government officials, and congressional activists involved in the policy formation process, or in terms of the effects of changes in information policy on the public with criminal justice records.

Clearly, the social costs of criminal justice records will not be internalized through the representation of all affected interests in the policy formation process. Representation of a nonintense, diffuse, low-visibility interest depends on widening the scope of conflict. In this regard, the actors involved in this representational process are not "free and equal."

Robert Dahl has suggested that "a central guiding thread of American constitutional development has been the evolution of a political system in which all the active and legitimate groups in the population can make themselves heard at some crucial stage in the process of decision."[2] Thus, the making of government decisions "is the steady appeasement of relatively small groups."[3]

The fluidity of the representational process as presented by Dahl and other pluralist theorists must be qualified by the biases evident in the existing distribution of political power and initiative. Since successful representation of the interest in reducing the social costs of criminal justice records is based on widening the scope of conflict, the point of departure for the assessment of this process is the relative position taken by each opposing side in the conflict. The most powerful interests want to restrict the scope of conflict by involving a limited number of participants and narrowing the definition of problems open to settlement, while the weaker interests want to widen the scope of conflict by expanding the number of participants and defining the relevant problems more broadly. Consequently, the representational process is shaped by the prevailing "mobilization of bias" and it proceeds, at least in the instance of a nonintense, diffuse interest, on the basis of permitting the most powerful interests to have an edge

[2] Robert A. Dahl. *A Preface to Democratic Theory*. Chicago, University of Chicago Press, 1956, p. 137.
[3] *Ibid.*, p. 146.

concerning how the relevant issues and problems are to be defined. And since, as Schattschneider suggests, the articulation of policy options is an important source of power, the existing mobilization of bias reflected in the representational process tends to assure that the internalization of social costs through effective representation of such an interest is restricted in relation to the cumulative advantages of those actors supporting existing agency and social practices. As Cobb and Elder have observed, "the content of [the] formal agenda will tend to reflect structural and institutional biases found within the [policymaking] system."[4]

Given the restrictions on the prospects for collective action by the public directly affected by the social costs of criminal justice records and the limitations on the successful representation of that interest among the various actors in the policy formulation process, there is little doubt that the political agenda related to the formulation of public policy will be directed only to a limited degree at reducing the social costs of criminal justice records. Indeed, even in those instances where criminal justice agencies have taken the initiative to develop privacy and security safeguards for their information systems, such a strategy has worked to preclude the expansion of conflict. In "facing an important problem before public mobilization on the issue,"[5] criminal justice representatives from Project SEARCH, the NCIC Advisory Policy Board, LEAA, the FBI, and the Office of the Attorney General have been able to control the scope and intensity of conflict concerning the social costs of criminal justice records. By assuming the initiative in defining the issues and relevant concerns, these actors have shaped the development of the political agenda. Also, by influencing the process of definition, they have limited the possible costly impacts of reform proposals on themselves or on their future programs.

Hence, the pluralist model of politics fails to provide insight, on a number of significant grounds, into the dynamics of the policy formulation process in relation to the interest in reducing social costs. It is important to understand the conditions for and the limitations on the successful representation of low-intensity, diffuse, low-visibility interests in the context of technology assessment and regulation, because it is within the existing policymaking process that demands for social cost reductions are made and the control of technological innovations are defined. In this regard, the assumptions of issue generation, self-correction, and fluidity that make up the pluralist model of politics

---

[4] Roger W. Cobb and Charles D. Elder. *Participation in American Politics: The Dynamics of Agenda-Building*. Boston, Mass., Allyn and Bacon, 1972, p. 89.
[5] *Ibid.*, p. 128.

represent, at best, incomplete characterizations of the policymaking "systems" responding to the social costs of technological innovation. A new point of departure is needed, based on the policy process approach to the study of the interaction of politics and technology, if the deficiencies and strengths of the public policymaking process in the assessment of technological innovations and their control are to be comprehended.

POLICY FORMULATION IN PUBLIC AGENCIES AND DEMOCRATIC ADMINISTRATION

This study has attempted to indicate how the policy process approach permits the integration of social costs with collective action and regulation in relation to technological innovations. The previous section noted how the policy approach provides necessary insights into the issue formulation and policy agenda building process that is not otherwise available if reliance is placed on the assumptions and emphasis of the pluralist model of politics.

One salient feature of this process is the fact that criminal justice agencies, as administrative units, have played an integral role in the policymaking process. Even with respect to such apparently internal functions as information generation and use and the subsequent danger of misuse of information technology, administrative agency activities affect various publics in significant ways and, in turn, are substantially involved in the policymaking process which constitutes the response of groups and individuals to adverse effects. It is clear, from historical examples, that politics cannot be viewed as being separate or apart from administration.[6] The actions of administrators in public agencies have both direct and indirect effects on groups and individuals in society, so they are exposed in varying degrees to review and assessment of their decisions and actions by other persons or groups within and outside the governmental system who can exercise some influence over the way decisions are made or actions are pursued. As James D. Thompson has suggested, there is significant interdependence between an organization, its environment, and its technology. In efforts to protect the technical core of its activities,

[6] For a classic statement of the justification behind the distinction between politics and administration, see Woodrow Wilson, "The Study of Administration," *Political Science Quarterly, II:*198–222, June 1887. For a relatively recent critique of the distinction and of the classical school of administration, see Vincent Ostrom, *The Intellectual Crisis in American Public Administration,* University, Ala., University of Alabama Press, 1973.

organizations will seek to "anticipate and adapt to environmental changes which cannot be buffered or leveled."[7] In this regard, they, according to Thompson, will be "most alert to emphasize scoring well on those criteria which are most *visible* to important task-environment elements."[8] It is not difficult to perceive why successful representation of the interest in reducing the social costs of criminal justice records depends on the extent to which the scope of conflict can be expanded, since criminal justice agency responses depend on the visibility of the interest.

In responding to the problem of the social costs arising from the activities of administrative agencies, two important questions arise: What kind and how much influence can outside groups and individuals have on administrative agency decisions and activities, and to what extent can social costs arising from alterations in technology within organizations be reduced as a result of changes in regulatory arrangements?

Chapter 2 suggested that the internal cost calculus of the public agency centers on the maintenance of the organization. Total cost for the provision of a public good is associated with the internal cost calculus of the agency in terms of its maintenance and productive functions. Social costs are treated as external costs and, as such, do not enter into the calculus either of the total cost of providing a public good or of the internal cost calculus of the agency. It would appear that public agencies responsible for social costs would have no direct incentives to reduce social costs, but this is not always the case. Criminal justice agencies have had selective incentives to develop information policies that would reduce to some extent the social costs of criminal records. Primarily, their activity has been tied to the need to protect information system development plans and to respond to increasingly visible concerns about the impacts of information technology on individuals with criminal justice records: But, the effects of such public responses to the problem of social costs are mixed. Although agencies have indeed anticipated public demands and interests in reducing the social costs of criminal justice records and controlling the uses of information technology, they have simultaneously been able to control the scope of conflict and issue definition in the face of demands of public interest groups, entrepreneurs, state and local officials, and congressional activists. Rather than providing an occasion for confrontation, criminal justice agencies have proceeded

---

[7] James D. Thompson. *Organizations in Action*. New York, McGraw-Hill, 1967, p. 21.
[8] *Ibid.*, p. 90. (Emphasis added.)

to adapt to the new demands in the short term and have sought long-term national policies responsive to their needs. The second question, therefore, has become of increasingly central importance: To what extent can social costs arising from alterations in technology within public organizations be minimized as a result of changes in regulatory arrangements?

Exclusive reliance on organizational forms of decision making is costly. Social costs arise from the activities of public agencies not only with respect to the goods produced—that is, public goods—and to limitations on agency boundaries and jurisdictional responsibilities, but also with respect to the character of public organizations themselves. Public agencies as organizations can be seen as alternative decision-making arrangements to that of individual choice. Organizations reduce some of the costs associated with the use of individual choice in providing a public good or service: "The exercise of governmental authority by public officials capable of central direction and control implies that effective sanctions can be mobilized to preclude any holdout strategy and to undertake activities to provide a public good."[9]

Organization, as applied to public agencies providing particular public goods or services, is not without significant institutional weaknesses leading to the generation of social costs. First, the limits on control in public organizations engender "bureaucratic free enterprise" where individuals and groups within an organization proceed with the formulation of their own missions with opportunities for side payoffs, including increases in personal gain and corruption. The most common cases of such enterprise regarding criminal justice records have been where police officers obtain direct payments or favors for providing information on arrested or convicted individuals to employers, political friends, or private investigators. Second, in the absence of an exclusion principle, once a public service is provided, the public agency may be relatively free to induce savings in production costs by shifting some of the burdens and costs of production to particular consumers of the service. Thus, shifts of producer costs to consumers result in increases in social costs. Third, this problem is compounded by instances where new technologies are introduced in organizations and where preferences among groups or the community as a whole are changing.[10] Social costs then will arise as products of changing values and demands vis-à-vis the supply of public services

---

[9] Ostrom. *Intellectual Crisis in American Public Administration*, pp. 58–59.
[10] *Ibid.*, pp. 60–62.

and the structure of public agencies and relations between such agencies at different levels of government. Consequently, changes of information technology have affected the recordkeeping activities within criminal justice agencies as well as the relations between these agencies at different levels of government. This type of situation has, in turn, been affected by changes in public values and demands in response to the privacy and computers debate, as well as the general temper of the times.

Given such problems deriving from public organizations, it is suggested that the interests of those affected by the social costs of agency activities will be considered only to the extent that producers of public services stand exposed to the demands and values of those affected by social costs.

In this regard, Chapter 3 observed that regulation is a costly affair and that social costs must be taken into account in the design or assessment of regulatory arrangements. Although an important function of regulation is to internalize the externalities for those goods that the producers or consumers are either unwilling or unable to internalize for themselves, and since decisions concerning levels of consumption will be more likely to consider the interests of all those whose welfare they influence, it may well be that, if this principle is applied without qualification, consumption levels for a service that is primarily of local or state interest, but has some external effects, must be determined by the Federal Government. No approach to the assessment of regulatory arrangements to reduce social costs should neglect consideration of the costs of regulation. While direction by a central authority may reduce the costs of decision making, there is no guarantee that such a regulatory alternative will not impose significant transaction costs of its own.

Chapter 10 observed that, in responding to the consideration of the design of appropriate regulatory arrangements to reduce social costs, centralized control cannot be considered as the opposite and only adequate alternative to decentralized control. Options may be available that reduce the tendency to centralize control of information technology and information policy formulation at the federal level of government. For this reason, proposals for regulation that offered a federated structure of control offered a more satisfactory arrangement than either the centralized approach, favored by the FBI, or the more decentralized alternatives originally proposed by Project SEARCH and LEAA.

All regulatory arrangements have a price, which is defined in terms of the trade-offs between internal and external costs, as well as the costs of political transactions for contending parties in the policy-making process, but it is hoped that, by examining the nature and scale of organization and technology, the public affected by social costs, and the political community involved in the choice of alternatives—the relevant factors involved in the design of regulatory arrangements—a better understanding of the alternative prices that proposals for regulation imply can be obtained.

All regulatory arrangements, therefore, entail certain costs and benefits. Given this fact, the policy process approach provides a more meaningful perspective by which available regulatory options can be realistically assessed in the context of the dynamics of issue formation, agenda building, and incentives for collective action to reduce the social costs of technological innovations in public organizations.

In doing so, the point of departure taken here is a basic concern of democratic government; that is, continual emphasis on the assessment of decision-making arrangements to meet public needs and demands. In an age when many policy decisions are being made by administrators and when the administrative process is having a greater impact on the lives of individuals, it has become important to reconsider the problems of representation and participation in relation to administrative and technological change. This book has attempted to develop a useful analytical approach that begins with the individual, rather than the organization or group, as the primary unit of analysis and proceeds to articulate a calculus of choice responsive to individual problems and demands in relation to the supply of public goods and services or the reduction of social costs.

In the complex world of government policymaking, no ready-made panacea to plural or administrative decision making, such as "town meeting" democracy or "participatory" democracy, has been found or offered. What has been of central concern is that relevant factors and variables be articulated in the course of public policy formulation, based on the premise that, by understanding the costs and consequences of political choice, significant mistakes might be avoided. In doing so, it has been assumed, as Vincent Ostrom has suggested, that *the structure of public administration cannot be organized apart from the processes of political choice.*[11] It is clear that administration in a democracy cannot be separated from the processes of popular control. So, administration can be democratic only to the extent that limitations on the processes of popular control are recognized and corrected. For it is precisely within the context of political choice and evaluation that

[11] *Ibid.*, p. 66.

technological innovations in public administration and their attendant social costs will be considered and shaped.

ON THE INTERACTION BETWEEN TECHNOLOGY AND POLITICS

The aim of this study has been to move away from the consideration of technology as a general phenomenon and to look at a particular manifestation of technology in a specific context. The intention has been to examine, in relation to the introduction of a specific type of technological innovation, the processes of choice exercised by individual citizens, groups, and organizations in response to the concern about the adverse consequences of such an innovation.

As a result of this study, it can be noted at the outset that technology does not operate autonomously. The relationship between the introduction of information technology in the context of public organizations and the appearance of social costs is not a simple one of cause and effect. As suggested in Chapter 6, the introduction of computerized information systems in criminal justice agencies was not the source of the social costs of criminal justice records as much as the means for making existing, but previously latent, problems worse.

In the early computer development period from 1965 to 1970, the concern for the social costs of criminal justice records developed in the wider problem area of privacy and computers. The National Data Center controversy focused public attention on the possible adverse effects of widespread computerization in government and industry on the privacy and lives of individuals. As a result of this controversy, information policies and practices of public and private organizations that were planning to develop computerized information systems came under specific review both by the organizations themselves and by public interest groups and entrepreneurs intent on highlighting such developments as politically relevant. Because actual implementation of computerized information systems had begun during this period, the real center of controversy did not focus as much on the social costs of computerized records as on the social costs of existing organizational information policies and practices, which computerization, it was thought, could only exacerbate if proper "safeguards" were not developed. The introduction of the computer represented the occasion for reconsideration of information policies and practices that had been operative during the precomputer era. In the early stages of the issue, much attention was given to the *potential* adverse effects of computerization. As further plans for computerization progressed and as actual information systems and networks were implemented, the principal focus shifted from the potential effects of computers to the consideration of deficiencies in information policies and practices left unscrutinized in the manual recordkeeping period. Formulation of information policy moved from the informal and abstract stages to the center of policy debate concerning organizational information policies and practices and the control and regulation of information and information systems.

In the context of organizational recordkeeping, the introduction of computers has had a complex effect. Due to fears about potential misuse and abuse, the introduction of computers has served as the occasion for consideration of regulations involving both manual and automated information and information systems. This technological innovation has made organizational uses of records and recordkeeping systems a public issue where power relationships play a significant role.

At least in terms of the technological innovations reviewed in this study, the uses of the technology for good or bad are linked integrally with the existing policymaking process. Whether technology or particular technologies are used to control or liberate man is not a foregone conclusion but a product of choice involving the processes of issue generation, political agenda formation, and collective action. This point can be illustrated particularly well when examining the manner in which social costs serve as the focus for proposals for regulation.

The existence of social costs is a matter of perception. As Riker and Ordeshook have suggested: "Nearly every social act involves an externality. What one man does limits or expands or varies the options open to another man. Truly, 'no man is an island'. Externalities are therefore inherent in almost every act."[12] Consequently, social costs are related to the interests and political situation of those who are proposing changes in the context of choice. As products of perception, social costs are dependent on the incentives of those affected or others to identify such effects *as costs*, as well as on the context in which a political response is feasible or possible.

The generally low visibility and low intensity of interest in reducing the social costs of criminal justice records magnifies the significance of disseminating information about the issue to as wide an audience as possible. Identifying what can later be cited as serious social costs and

---

[12] William H. Riker and P. C. Ordeshook. *An Introduction to Positive Political Theory.* Englewood Cliffs, N.J., Prentice-Hall, 1973, pp. 289–290.

a sizeable public affected by such costs becomes an essential ingredient in the ability of entrepreneurs, public interest groups, and the press to widen the scope of the conflict.

The effect of political context on social costs is to structure the manner in which political claims representing the interest in reducing social costs are presented. As noted in Chapter 5, social costs arising from the activities of public organizations in the United States pose problems of conflicting individual rights and social goals. Political action is pursued on the basis of seeking recognition for particular individual claims which are justified by reference to constitutional values such as privacy and due process. Public interest groups, entrepreneurs, and public officials invoke constitutional rights in the context of American politics as ways of legitimizing political demands and capitalizing on the perceptions of entitlement connected with rights to initiate and nurture political action. The actual weight accorded various rights and goals is a product of political debate and conflict.

The identification of social costs, then, is intimately connected with the nature of the political context and the incentives of actors in that context to bear the costs of information generation and dissemination. If technological change brings on high social costs, they are costs that will be imposed by men on men and not by machines on men. What appears to be inevitable, in retrospect, may be the consequences of political structures and processes biased in favor of nonrecognition of the social costs of technological changes or in favor of not acting on particular varieties or kinds of social costs due to the mobilization of bias already present in the forums of public choice.

For this reason, this study has aimed at examining the political choices, processes, and efforts involved in controlling the social costs of technological innovation in public organizations before options that are chosen reach the stage where they are considered both inevitable and tyrannous. In particular, the limitations and constraints of the existing policymaking process and the political costs or prices of alternative regulatory arrangements have been analyzed. In doing so, it is hoped that what may have been a premature forecast concerning the tyrannical nature of technological innovation in public organizations may not become a stark reality for those individuals and groups in our society not favored by the mobilization of bias reflected in existing institutions and policymaking processes.

Bibliography

I. BOOKS

Allen, F. A. *The Borderland of Criminal Justice*. Chicago, University of Chicago Press, 1964.

American Friends Service Committee. *Struggle for Justice*. New York, Hill and Wang, 1971.

Anderson, James E. *Public Policy-Making*. New York, Praeger, 1975.

Bachrach, Peter, and Baratz, M. S. *Power and Poverty*. London, Oxford University Press, 1970.

Bauer, Raymond A., and Gergen, Kenneth J., eds. *The Study of Policy Formation*. New York, Free Press, 1968.

Becker, H. A. *Outsiders: Studies in the Sociology of Deviance*. New York, Free Press, 1963.

Bish, Robert L. *The Public Economy of Metropolitan Areas*. Chicago, Markham, 1971.

Black, Duncan. *The Theory of Committees and Elections*. Cambridge, Mass., Cambridge University Press, 1958.

Blackstock, Nelson. *COINTELPRO, The FBI's Secret War on Political Freedom*. 2nd Edition. New York, Vintage Books, 1976.

Blau, Peter. *Dynamics of Bureaucracy*. Chicago, University of Chicago Press, 1963.

Blau, Peter, and Meyer, M. W. *Bureaucracy*. 2nd Edition. New York, Random House, 1971.

Blaug, Mark. *Economic Theory in Retrospect*. Homewood, Ill., Richard D. Irwin, 1968.

Blumberg, Abraham S. *Criminal Justice*. Chicago, Quadrangle Books, 1967.

Boguslaw, Robert. *The New Utopians: A Study of System Design and Social Change*. Englewood Cliffs, N.J., Prentice-Hall, 1968.

Bordua, D. M., ed. *The Police: Six Sociological Essays*. New York, Wiley, 1967.

Breckenridge, Adam C. *The Right to Privacy*. Lincoln, University of Nebraska Press, 1970.

Brenton, Myron. *The Privacy Invaders*. New York, Coward-McCann, 1964.

Buchanan, James M. *The Demand and Supply of Public Goods*. Chicago, Rand McNally, 1968.

Buchanan, James M., and Tullock, Gordon. *The Calculus of Consent: Logical Foundations of Constitutional Democracy*. Ann Arbor, University of Michigan Press, 1965.

Bundy, Mary Lee. *The National Prison Directory*. Supplement No. 2. College Park, Md., Urban Information Interpreters, 1977.

317

Bundy, Mary Lee, and Harmon, K. R. *The National Prison Directory*. Base Volume. Baltimore, Md., Urban Information Interpreters, 1975.

Bundy, Mary Lee, and Whaley, R. G. *The National Prison Directory*. Supplement No. 1. College Park, Md., Urban Information Interpreters, 1976.

Casper, Jonathan D. *American Criminal Justice: The Defendant's Perspective*. Englewood Cliffs, N.J., Prentice-Hall, 1972.

Cicourel, Aaron V. *The Social Organization of Juvenile Justice*. New York, Wiley, 1968.

Clancy, Paul R. *Just a Country Lawyer*. Bloomington, Indiana University Press, 1974.

Clark, Ramsey. *Crime in America*. New York, Pocket Books, 1970.

Cobb, Roger W., and Elder, Charles D. *Participation in American Politics: The Dynamics of Agenda-Building*. Boston, Mass., Allyn and Bacon, 1972.

Cohen, Albert K. *Deviance and Control*. Englewood Cliffs, N.J., Prentice-Hall, 1966.

Cohen, Carl. *Democracy*. New York, Free Press, 1971.

Cole, George F. *Politics and the Administration of Justice*. Beverly Hills, Calif., Sage Publications, 1973.

The Conference Board. *Information Technology: Some Critical Implications for Decision Makers*. New York, The Conference Board, 1972.

Cowan, Paul; Egleson, Nick; and Hentoff, Nat. *State Secrets*. New York, Holt, Rinehart and Winston, 1974.

Crecine, John P., ed. *Financing the Metropolis*. Beverly Hills, Calif., Sage Publications, 1970.

Crenson, Matthew A. *The Un-Politics of Air Pollution*. Baltimore, Md., Johns Hopkins University Press, 1971.

Cross, H. L. *The People's Right to Know*. New York, Columbia University Press, 1953.

Crozier, Michael. *The Bureaucratic Phenomenon*. Chicago, University of Chicago Press, 1963.

Culyer, A. J. *The Economics of Social Policy*. Port Washington, N.Y., Dunellen, 1974.

Dahl, Robert A. *After the Revolution?* New Haven, Conn., Yale University Press, 1970.

————. *A Preface to Democratic Theory*. Chicago, University of Chicago Press, 1956.

Dewey, John. *The Public and Its Problems*. Chicago, Swallow Press, 1927.

Diebold, John. *Man and the Computer: Technology as an Agent of Social Change*. New York, Praeger, 1969.

Diesing, Paul. *Reason in Society*. Urbana, University of Illinois Press, 1962.

Douglas, Jack D., ed. *Freedom and Tyranny: Social Problems in a Technological Society*. New York, Knopf, 1970.

Downie, Leonard, Jr. *Justice Denied*. Baltimore, Md., Penguin Books, 1971.

Downs, Anthony. *An Economic Theory of Democracy*. New York, Harper and Row, 1957.

————. *Inside Bureaucracy*. Boston, Mass., Little, Brown, 1967.

Dvorin, Eugene P., and Simmons, R. H. *From Amoral to Humane Bureaucracy.* San Francisco, Canfield Press, 1972.

Edelman, Murray. *The Symbolic Uses of Politics.* Urbana, University of Illinois Press, 1964.

Elliff, John T. *Crime, Dissent, and the Attorney General.* Beverly Hills, Calif., Sage Publications, 1971.

Ellul, Jacques. *The Technological Society.* New York, Vintage Books, 1964.

Epstein, Edward Jay. *News from Nowhere.* New York, Random House, 1973.

Etzioni, Amitai. *A Sociological Reader on Complex Organizations.* New York, Holt, Rinehart and Winston, 1961.

Ferkiss, Victor C. *Technological Man: The Myth and the Reality.* New York, New American Library, 1969.

Flaherty, David H. *Privacy in Colonial New England.* Charlottesville, University Press of Virginia, 1967.

Francis, Wayne L. *American Politics: Analysis of Choice.* Pacific Palisades, Calif., Goodyear, 1976.

Frankel, Marvin E. *Criminal Sentences.* New York, Hill and Wang, 1972.

Freeman, A. Myrich, III: Haveman, R. H.; and Kneese, Allen V. *The Economics of Environmental Policy.* New York, Wiley, 1973.

Friche, Charles W. *Sentence and Probation.* Los Angeles, Legal Book Store, 1960.

Frohlich, Norman; Oppenheimer, Joe A.; and Young, Oran R. *Political Leadership and Collective Goods.* Princeton, N.J., Princeton University Press, 1971.

Fromm, Erich. *The Revolution of Hope.* New York, Harper and Row, 1968.

Gawthrop, Louis C. *Administrative Politics and Social Change.* New York, St. Martin's Press, 1971.

Germann, A. C.; Day, Frank D.; and Gallati, R. R. J. *Introduction to Law Enforcement and Criminal Justice.* Springfield, Ill., Charles C Thomas, 1973.

Goffman, Erving. *Asylums.* Garden City, N.Y., Doubleday, 1961.

———. *Relations in Public.* New York, Harper and Row, 1971.

———. *Stigma.* Englewood Cliffs, N.J., Prentice-Hall, 1963.

Goldfarb, R. L., and Singer, L. R. *After Conviction.* New York, Simon and Schuster, 1973.

Goldstein, Abraham S., and Goldstein, J., eds. *Crime, Law, and Society.* New York, Free Press, 1971.

Haefele, Edwin T. *Representative Government and Environmental Management.* Baltimore, Md., Resources for the Future, 1973.

Harris, Richard. *Justice.* New York, Avon Books, 1969.

———. *The Fear of Crime.* New York, Praeger, 1968.

Head, John G. *Public Goods and Public Welfare.* Durham, N.C., Duke University Press, 1974.

Hearle, Edward F. R., and Mason, R. J. *A Data Processing System for State and Local Government.* Englewood Cliffs, N.J., Prentice-Hall, 1963.

Hetman, Francois. *Society and the Assessment of Technology.* Paris, Organization for Economic Cooperation and Development, 1973.

Hewitt, W. H. *Police Records Administration.* Rochester, N.Y., Aqueduct Books, 1968.

Hoffman, Lance J. *Security and Privacy in Computer Systems.* Los Angeles, Melville, 1973.

Hood, Christopher. *The Limits of Administration.* London, Wiley, 1976.

Hoos, Ida R. *Systems Analysis in Public Policy.* Berkeley, University of California Press, 1972.

Huxley, Aldous. *Brave New World.* New York, Harper and Row, 1932.

Jacob, Herbert. *Urban Justice.* Englewood Cliffs, N.J., Prentice-Hall, 1973.

Jones, Charles O. *An Introduction to the Study of Public Policy.* Belmont, Calif., Duxbury Press, 1970.

Kapp, K. William. *The Social Costs of Private Enterprise.* New York, Schocken Books, 1950.

Kasper, R. G. *Technology Assessment: Understanding the Social Consequences of Technological Applications.* New York, Praeger, 1972.

Katz, Daniel, and Kahn, Robert L. *The Social Psychology of Organizations.* New York, Wiley, 1966.

Kenney, John P. *The California Police.* Springfield, Ill., Charles C Thomas, 1964.

Kenney, John P., and Pursuit, Dan. *Police Work with Juveniles.* Springfield, Ill., Charles C Thomas, 1965.

Kittrie, Nicholas N. *The Right To Be Different.* Baltimore, Md., Johns Hopkins University Press, 1971.

Kraus, Sidney, and Davis, Dennis. *The Effects of Mass Communication on Political Behavior.* University Park, Pennsylvania State University Press, 1976.

LaFave, Wayne. *Arrest: The Decision to Take a Suspect into Custody.* Boston, Mass., Little, Brown, 1965.

Laudon, Kenneth C. *Computers and Bureaucratic Reform.* New York, Wiley, 1974.

Lemert, Edwin M. *Human Deviance, Social Problems, and Social Control.* Englewood Cliffs, N.J., Prentice-Hall, 1967.

Leonard, V. A. *The Police Records System.* Springfield, Ill., Charles C Thomas, 1970.

Lindblom, Charles E. *The Intelligence of Democracy.* New York, Free Press, 1965.

————. *The Policy-Making Process.* Englewood Cliffs, N.J., Prentice-Hall, 1968.

Lipsky, Michael. *Protest in City Politics: Rent Strikes, Housing, and the Power of the Poor.* Chicago, Rand McNally, 1970.

Loth, David, and Ernst, M. L. *The Taming of Technology.* New York, Simon and Schuster, 1972.

March, James G., and Simon, Herbert A. *Organizations.* New York, Wiley, 1958.

Marcuse, Herbert. *One-Dimensional Man.* Boston, Mass., Beacon Press, 1964.

Margolis, Julius, ed. *The Analysis of Public Output.* New York, National Bureau of Economic Research, 1970.

Markmann, Charles Lam. *The Noblest Cry: A History of the American Civil Liberties Union*. New York, St. Martin's Press, 1965.

Martin, J. P. *Offenders and Employees*. London, Macmillan, 1962.

McCann, Paul D. *American System of Fingerprint Classification*. Albany, New York Department of Correction, 1944.

McCoy, Charles A., and Playford, John, eds. *Apolitical Politics*. New York, Thomas Y. Crowell, 1967.

Medford, Derek. *Environmental Harassment or Technology Assessment?* New York, Elsevier, 1973.

Meek, R. L., and Wade, L. L. *Democracy in America: A Public Choice Approach*. North Scituate, Mass., Duxbury Press, 1976.

Menninger, Karl. *The Crime of Punishment*. New York, Viking Press, 1966.

Mercer, June R. *Labeling the Mentally Retarded*. Los Angeles, University of California Press, 1973.

Merton, Robert K. *On Theoretical Sociology*. New York, Macmillan, 1949.

Mesthene, Emmanuel G. *Program on Technology and Society, 1964–1972, A Final Review*. Cambridge, Mass., Harvard University Press, 1972.

———. *Technological Change*. New York, New American Library, 1970.

———, ed. *Technology and Social Change*. New York, Bobbs-Merrill, 1967.

Michels, Robert. *Political Parties*. New York, Dover, 1915.

Miller, Arthur R. *The Assault on Privacy*. Ann Arbor, University of Michigan Press, 1971.

Mishan, Ezra J. *The Costs of Economic Growth*. New York, Praeger, 1967.

———. *Economics for Social Decisions*, New York, Praeger, 1972.

Mitchell, William, and Mitchell, Joyce. *Political Analysis and Public Policy*. Skokie, Ill., Rand McNally, 1967.

Morris, Norval, and Hawkins, Gordon. *The Honest Politician's Guide to Crime Control*. Chicago, University of Chicago Press, 1970.

Musgrave, Richard A., and Musgrave, Peggy B. *Public Finance in Theory and Practice*. New York, McGraw-Hill, 1973.

Mushkin, Selma J. *Public Prices for Public Products*. Washington, D.C., Urban Institute, 1972.

Nadel, Mark V. *The Politics of Consumer Protection*. New York, Bobbs-Merrill, 1971.

Neier, Aryeh. *Dossier*. New York, Stein and Day, 1974.

Newman, Donald J. *Conviction: The Determination of Guilt or Innocence Without Trial*. Boston, Mass., Little, Brown, 1966.

Niskanen, William A., Jr. *Bureaucracy and Representative Government*. Chicago, Aldine-Atherton, 1971.

———. *Bureaucracy: Servant or Master?* London, Institute of Economic Affairs, 1973.

Nussbaum, Aaron. *A Second Chance, Amnesty for the First Offender*. New York, Hawthorn Books, 1974.

Oates, Wallace E. *Fiscal Federalism*. New York, Harcourt Brace Jovanovich, 1972.

Oettinger, Anthony G. *Run, Computer, Run*. Cambridge, Mass., Harvard University Press, 1964.

Olsen, Mancur. *The Logic of Collective Action*. Cambridge, Mass., Harvard University Press, 1965.

Orwell, George. *1984*. New York, New American Library, 1961.

Ostrom, Vincent. *The Intellectual Crisis in American Public Administration*. University, Ala., University of Alabama Press, 1973.

——. *The Political Theory of a Compound Republic*. Blacksburg, Va., Center for Study of Public Choice, Virginia Polytechnic Institute and State University, 1971.

Packard, Vance. *The Naked Society*. New York, Pocket Books, 1964.

Packer, Herbert L. *The Limits of the Criminal Sanction*. Stanford, Calif., Stanford University Press, 1968.

Parker, T., and Allerton, R. *The Courage of His Convictions*. London, Hutchinson, 1962.

Pennock, J. R., and Chapman, John W. *Nomos XIII: Privacy*. New York, Atherton Press, 1971.

Phillipson, Michael. *Understanding Crime and Delinquency*. Chicago, Aldine, 1971.

Pigou, A. C. *The Economics of Welfare*. London, Macmillan, 1932.

Pitkin, Hanna F. *The Concept of Representation*. Berkeley, University of California Press, 1972.

Pound, Roscoe. *Criminal Justice in America*. New York, DaCapo Press, 1930.

Pressman, Jeffrey L., and Wildavsky, Aaron B. *Implementation*. Berkeley, University of California Press, 1973.

Quinney, Richard. *Critique of Legal Order*. Boston, Mass., Little, Brown, 1973.

Radzinowicz, Leon. *Ideology and Crime*. New York, Columbia University Press, 1966.

Redford, Emmette S. *Democracy in the Administrative State*. New York, Oxford University Press, 1969.

Riker, William H. *The Theory of Political Coalitions*. New Haven, Conn., Yale University Press, 1962.

Riker, William H., and Ordeshook, P. C. *An Introduction to Positive Political Theory*. Englewood Cliffs, N.J., Prentice-Hall, 1973.

Rosenberg, Jerry M. *The Death of Privacy*. New York, Random House, 1969.

Rosengren, William R., and Lefton, Mark. *Organizations and Clients*. Columbus, Ohio, Merrill, 1970.

Roszak, Theodore. *The Making of a Counter Culture*. Garden City, N.Y., Doubleday, 1970.

Rourke, Francis E. *Bureaucracy, Politics, and Public Policy*. Boston, Mass., Little, Brown, 1969.

——. *Bureaucratic Power in National Politics*. Boston, Mass., Little, Brown, 1972.

Rubin, Sol. *The Law of Criminal Correction*. St. Paul, Minn., West, 1963.

Rubington, Earl, and Weinberg, Martin S., eds. *Deviance, The Interactionist Perspective*. New York, Macmillan, 1973.

Rudovsky, David. *The Rights of Prisoners.* New York, Discus Books, 1977.

Rule, James B. *Private Lives and Public Surveillance.* New York, Schocken Books, 1973.

Ruys, P. H. M. *Public Goods and Decentralization.* Tilbury, The Netherlands, Tilbury University Press, 1974.

Schattschneider, E. E. *The Semisovereign People.* New York, Holt, Rinehart and Winston, 1960.

Scheingold, Stuart A. *The Politics of Rights.* New Haven, Conn., Yale University Press, 1974.

Schultz, D. O., and Norton, L. A. *Police Operational Intelligence.* Springfield, Ill., Charles C Thomas, 1968.

Schur, Edwin M. *Crimes Without Victims.* Englewood Cliffs, N.J., Prentice-Hall, 1965.

———. *Our Criminal Society.* Englewood Cliffs, N.J., Prentice-Hall, 1969.

Selznick, Phillip. *TVA and the Grass Roots.* New York, Harper and Row, 1966.

Shklar, Judith N. *Legalism.* Cambridge, Mass., Harvard University Press, 1964.

Simon, Herbert A. *Administrative Behavior.* New York, Free Press, 1945.

Skjie, Stephen S. *Information for Collective Action.* Lexington, Mass., D.C. Heath, 1973.

Skolnick, Jerome H. *Justice Without Trial.* New York, Wiley, 1966.

Staaf, Robert J., and Tannian, Francis X., eds. *Externalities: Theoretical Dimensions of Political Economy.* Port Washington, N.Y., Dunellen, 1973.

Stigler, George J. *The Theory of Price.* New York, Macmillan, 1966.

Taggart, Robert, III. *The Prison of Unemployment.* Baltimore, Md., Johns Hopkins University Press, 1972.

Tannenbaum, Frank. *Crime and the Community.* New York, Ginn, 1938.

Tappan, Paul W. *Crime, Justice and Correction.* New York, McGraw-Hill, 1960.

Teich, Albert H., ed. *Technology and Man's Future.* New York, St. Martin's Press, 1972.

Thompson, James D. *Organizations in Action.* New York, McGraw-Hill, 1967.

Thompson, Victor A. *Bureaucracy and Innovation.* University, Ala., University of Alabama Press, 1969.

Truman, David B. *The Governmental Process.* New York, Knopf, 1951.

Tullock, Gordon. *Private Wants, Public Means.* New York, Basic Books, 1970.

———. *The Politics of Bureaucracy.* Washington, D.C., Public Affairs Press, 1965.

Turner, Roy, ed. *Ethnomethodology.* Baltimore, Md., Penguin Books, 1974.

Ungar, Sanford J. *FBI.* Boston, Mass., Little, Brown, 1976.

Wade, L. L., and Curry, R. L., Jr. *A Logic of Public Policy: Aspects of Political Economy.* Belmont, Calif., Wadsworth, 1970.

Wamsley, Gary L., and Zald, Mayer N. *The Political Economy of Public Organizations.* Lexington, Mass., D. C. Heath, 1973.

Watters, Pat, and Gillers, Stephen, eds. *Investigating the FBI.* Garden City, N.Y., Doubleday, 1973.

Westin, Alan F. *Privacy and Freedom.* New York, Atheneum, 1970.

————, ed. *Information Technology in a Democracy*. Cambridge, Mass., Harvard University Press, 1971.

Westin, Alan F., and Baker, Michael A. *Databanks in a Free Society*. New York, Quadrangle Books, 1972.

Wheeler, Stanton, ed. *On Record: Files and Dossiers in American Life*. New York, Russell Sage Foundation, 1969.

Whisenand, Paul M., and Ferguson, R. Fred. *The Managing of Police Organizations*. Englewood Cliffs, N.J., Prentice-Hall, 1973.

Whisenand, Paul M., and Tamaru, Tug T. *Automated Police Information Systems*. New York, Wiley, 1970.

Whisler, Thomas L. *Information Technology and Organizational Change*. Belmont, Calif., Wadsworth, 1970.

Whitcomb, David K. *Externalities and Welfare*. New York, Columbia University Press, 1972.

Wiener, Norbert. *The Human Use of Human Beings*. New York, Avon Books, 1950.

Wilson, James Q. *Political Organizations*. New York, Basic Books, 1973.

————. *Varieties of Police Behavior*. New York, Atheneum, 1973.

Wilson, O. W. *Police Records*. Chicago, Public Administration Service, 1951.

II. ARTICLES

Albrecht, G. L. "Effects of Computerized Information Systems on Juvenile Courts." *Justice Systems Journal, 2*:102–120, Winter 1976.

"A National Crime Information Center." *FBI Law Enforcement Bulletin, 35*:1–7, May 1966.

"Applicability of the 'New' 4th Amendment to Investigations by Secret Agents: A Proposed Determination of the Emerging 4th Amendment, Right to Privacy." *Washington Law Review, 45*:785, 1970.

"Arrest Record and New York City Public Hiring: An Evaluation." *Columbia Journal of Law and Social Problems, 9*:442–494, Spring 1973.

"Arrest Record Expungement: A Function of the Criminal Court." *Utah Law Review, 1971*:381, Fall 1971.

"Arrest Records—Protecting the Innocent—Misuse of Arrest Records." *Tulane Law Review, 48*:629–648, April 1974.

Askin, Frank. "Police Dossiers and Emerging Principles of First Amendment Adjudication." *Stanford Law Review, 22*:196, 1970.

Ayres, Robert, and Kneese, Allen U. "Production, Consumption and Externalities." *American Economic Review, 59*:282–297, June 1969.

Bachrach, Peter, and Baratz, M. S. "Decisions and Non-decisions: An Analytical Framework." *American Political Science Review, 57*:632, September 1963.

Bain, Harry. "Privacy: What's Happening to a Fundamental Right?" *System Development Corporation Magazine, 10*:1, July–August 1967.

Baker, Michael A. "Record Privacy as a Marginal Problem: The Limits of Consciousness and Concern." *Columbia Human Rights Law Review, 4*:89–100, 1972.

Barrett, David R.; Brown, William; and Cramer, M. "Juvenile Delinquents: The Police, State Courts, and Individualized Justice." *Harvard Law Review,* 79:775–810, 1966.

Bator, Francis. "The Anatomy of Market Failure." *Quarterly Journal of Economics,* 72:351–379, 1958.

Baugher, William Edward. "Interagency Information Sharing: A Legal Vacuum." *Santa Clara Lawyer,* 9:301, 1969.

Baum, Terry. "Wiping Out a Criminal or Juvenile Record." *Journal of the State Bar of California,* 40:816–829, 1965.

Beaney, W. M. "The Right to Privacy and American Law." *Law and Contemporary Problems,* 31:253–271, 1966.

Becker, Louise G. "Congressional Interest in Security and Privacy of Criminal Justice Information Systems." In: *Proceedings, 1975 Carnation Conference on Crime Countermeasures.* Edited by John S. Jackson. Lexington, University of Kentucky, 1975, pp. 1–8.

Beer, Stafford. "Managing Modern Complexity." In: *The Management of Information and Knowledge.* U.S. Congress, House, Committee on Science and Astronautics. Washington, D.C., U.S. Government Printing Office, 1970, p. 60.

Belair, R. R. "Agency Implementation of the Privacy Act and the FOIA." *North Carolina Law Review,* 55:1187–1227, September 1977.

Bish, Robert L. "A Comment on V. P. Duggal's 'Is There An Unseen Hand in Government?' " *Annals of Public and Cooperative Economy,* XXXIX:89–94, January–March 1968.

Black, B. J. "Social Organization of Arrest." *Stanford Law Review,* 23:1087, 1971.

Black, Donald J. "Production of Crime Rates." *American Sociological Review,* 35:733–748, August 1970.

Blau, P. M. "Hierarchy of Authority in Organizations." *American Journal of Sociology,* 73:453, January 1968.

Bloustein, Edward J. "Privacy as an Aspect of Human Dignity: An Answer to Dean Prosser." *New York University Law Review,* 39:962–1007, December 1964.

Bolas, S. M. "Erie County Benefits from Centralized Police Services." *Law and Order,* 22(2):52, 54–55, February 1974.

Booth, Lawrence P. "The Expungement Myth." *Los Angeles Bar Bulletin*:161–166, March 1963.

Boulding, Kenneth E. "The Ethics of Rational Decision." *Management Science,* 12(6):B–165, February 1966.

———. "Towards a Pure Theory of Threat Systems." *American Economic Review,* 53:424–434, May 1963.

Bowen, Howard R. "The Interpretation of Voting the Allocation of Economic Resources." *Quarterly Journal of Economics,* LVIII:27–48, November 1943.

"Branded: Arrest Records of the Unconvicted." *Mississippi Law Journal,* 44:8–46, November 1973.

Brandeis, Louis D., and Warren, Samuel. "The Right to Privacy." *Harvard Law Review,* 4:1890–1891, 1898.

Branscomb, Lewis M. "Why People Fear Technology." *Futurist, 5*:232–233, December 1971.

Breton, Albert. "A Theory of the Demand for Public Goods." *Canadian Journal of Economics and Political Science, XXXII*:455–467, November 1963.

Breton, Albert, and Breton, R. "An Economic Theory of Social Movements." *American Economic Review, 59*:198–205, 1969.

Buchanan, James M. "An Economist's Approach to 'Scientific Politics.'" In: *Perspectives in the Study of Politics.* Edited by M. B. Parsons. Chicago, Rand McNally, 1968, pp. 77–88.

————. "An Individualistic Theory of Political Process." In: *Varieties of Political Theory.* Edited by David Easton. Englewood Cliffs, N.J., Prentice-Hall, 1966, pp. 25–37.

————. "A Public Choice Approach to Public Utility Pricing." *Public Choice, 5*:1–17, Fall 1968.

————. "Public Goods and Public Bads." In: *Financing the Metropolis.* Edited by John P. Crecine. Beverly Hills, Calif., Sage, 1970, pp. 51–71.

————. "Public Goods in Theory and Practice: A Note on the Minasian-Samuelson Discussion." *Journal of Law and Economics, 10*:193–197, 1967.

Bucksbaum, P. "Police Infiltration of Political Groups." *Harvard Civil Rights–Civil Liberties Law Review, 4*:331–344, Spring 1969.

Burgess, Philip M., and Robinson, James A. "Alliances and the Theory of Collective Action." *Midwest Journal of Political Science, 13*:194–218, 1969.

Calabresi, Guido. "Transaction Costs, Resource Allocation, and Liability Rules: A Comment." *Journal of Law and Economics, 11*:67–73, 1968.

Calvani, Terry. "Discrimination on the Basis of Arrest Records." *Cornell Law Review, 56*:470–488, 1971.

Caspari, George. "Developing a Uniform Reporting System on Youthful Offenders." *California Youth Authority Quarterly, 9*:23–27, Spring 1956.

Christie, G. C. "The Right to Privacy and the Freedom to Know: A Comment on Professor Miller's 'Assault on Privacy.'" *University of Pennsylvania Law Review, 19*:970–991, 1971.

Christman, Glen. "Reporting of Offenses in Police Departments." *Journal of Criminal Law and Criminology, 39*:118–124, May–June 1948.

Clynch, E. L. "Spending of LEAA Block Grants by the States." *Justice System Journal, 2*:157–168, Winter 1976.

Coase, R. H. "The Nature of the Firm." *Economica, 4*:386–485, 1937.

Coates, Joseph F. "Technology Assessment: The Benefits . . . the Costs . . . the Consequences." *Futurist, 5*:225–231, December 1971.

Coffee, John C. "Privacy Versus Parens Patriae: The Role of Police Records in the Sentencing and Surveillance of Juveniles." *Cornell Law Review, 57*:571–620, 1972.

Cohen, N. P. "Civil Disabilities: The Forgotten Punishment." *Federal Probation, 35*:19, June 1971.

Cohn, S. A. "Criminal Records: A Comparative Approach." *Georgia Journal of International and Comparative Law, 4*:116, 1974.

Coleman, James S. "Foundations for a Theory of Collective Decisions." *American Journal of Sociology, 71*:615–627, May 1966.

Comber, E. V. "Criminal Justice Study Offers Assistance in Information Management." *Journal of California Law Enforcement, 1*:185–188, January 1967.

Comment: "Access to Governmental Information in California." *California Law Review, 54*:1650, 1966.

Comment: "Discriminatory Hiring Practices Due to Arrest Records—Private Remedies." *Villanova Law Review, 17*:110, 1971.

Comment: "Maintenance and Dissemination of Criminal Records: A Legislative Proposal." *UCLA Law Review, 19*:654, 1972.

Comment: "Preventive Intelligence Systems and the Courts." *California Law Review, 58*:914–939, 1970.

Comment: "The Effect of Expungement on a Criminal Conviction." *Southern California Law Review, 40*:127–147, 1967.

Conover, N. R. "Management Information: Law Enforcement's Forgotten Need." *FBI Law Enforcement Bulletin, 43*(11):3–9, November 1974.

"Constitutional Law—Freedom of Speech—State Police Intelligence System Focusing on Public Protesters Declared Unconstitutional." *Harvard Law Review, 83*:935–942, 1970.

"Constitutional Law: State Reporting System Which Gathered Information on Individuals and Organizations Involved in Civil Disturbances, Protests and Demonstrations Violated the First Amendment." *Vanderbilt Law Review, 23*:180–186, 1969.

Cook, J. G. "Subjective Attitudes of Arrestee and Arrestor as Affecting Occurrence of Arrest." *Kansas Law Review, 19*:173, Winter 1971.

Coon, Thomas F. "Intelligence Files." *Police, 6*:26–27, 79, March–April 1962.

———. "Miscellaneous Files." *Police, 7*:42–44, July–August 1963.

———. "Modern Report Writing." *Police, 6*:34–35, January–February 1962.

Cornelison, R. G. "JURIS (Juvenile Uniform Referral Information System): A Juvenile Court Information System." *Juvenile Justice, 24*(4):35–41, February 1974.

Cressey, Donald R. "Contradictory Directives in Complex Organizations: The Case of the Prison." *Administrative Science Quarterly, 4*:1–19, June 1959.

"Criminal Registration Ordinances: Police Control Over Potential Recidivists." *University of Pennsylvania Law Review, 103*:61–112, 1954.

Crocker, Thomas R. "Externalities, Property Rights, and Transaction Costs: An Empirical Study." *Journal of Law and Economics, 14*:451–464, 1971.

Cunningham, O. K., and Graves, Fred J. "Simplified Report Writing." *Police, 6*:72–73, March–April 1962.

Damaska, M. R. "Adverse Legal Consequences of Conviction and Their Removal: A Comparative Study." *Journal of Criminal Law, Criminology and Police Science, 59*:347–360, September 1968; *59*:542–568, December 1968.

"Davidson v. Dill (Colo.): A Compelling State Interest in Retaining Arrest Records." *University of Pittsburgh Law Review, 35*:205–219, Fall 1973.

Davis, E. M. "Automated Field Interview System." *FBI Law Enforcement Bulletin, 42*(9):24–28, September 1973.

Davis, Otto A., and Winston, A. "On the Distinction Between Public and Private Goods." *American Economic Review, 57*:360–373, May 1967.

Davis, R. M. "Technologists' View of Privacy and Security in Automated Information Systems." *Rutgers Journal of Computers and Law, 4*:264–282, 1975.

Davison, W. T. "Technology and Social Change." *Review of Politics, 34*:172, October 1972.

Deacon, E. R. "Application of Punch Card System to Crimes and Complaints Made Known to the Police." *Pacific Coast International, 5*:11–17, 21, November 1938.

DeBalogh, Frank G. "Public Administrators and the Privacy Thing: A Time to Speak Out." *Public Administration Review, 32*:526–530, September–October 1972.

Demsetz, Harold. "Some Aspects of Property Rights." *Journal of Law and Economics, 9*:61–70, 1966.

———. "The Exchange and Enforcement of Property Rights." *Journal of Law and Economics, 7*:11–26, 1966.

Dial, O. E., ed. "Computers: To Dedicate or Not to Dedicate, That is the Question." *Bureaucrat, 1*:305–378, Winter 1972.

Dill, W. R. "The Impact of Environment on Organizational Development." In: *Concepts and Issues in Administrative Behavior.* Edited by S. Mailick and E. H. VanNess. Englewood Cliffs, N.J., Prentice-Hall, 1962, pp. 94–109.

Dixon, Robert G., Jr. "The Griswold Penumbra: Constitutional Charter for an Expanded Law of Privacy?" *Michigan Law Review, 64*:197, 1965.

Donner, Frank. "The Theory and Practice of American Political Intelligence." *New York Review of Books, 18*:27–39, April 22, 1971.

Dorsen, N., and Rezneck, D. "Gault and the Future of Juvenile Law." *Family Law Quarterly, 1*:1–46, December 1967.

Downs, Anthony. "Theory of Bureaucracy." *American Economic Review, 55*:439, 467, 1965.

———. "Why the Government Budget Is Too Small in a Democracy." *World Politics, XII*:541–564, July 1960.

Draper, H. L. "Privacy and Police Intelligence Data Banks." *Harvard Journal on Legislation, 14*:1–110, December 1976.

Duggal, V. P. "Is There an Unseen Hand in Government?" *Annals of Public and Cooperative Economy, XXXVII*:145–150, April–June 1966.

Dworkin, Ronald. "Hard Cases." *Harvard Law Review, 88*:1057–1109, April 1975.

———. "Taking Rights Seriously." *New York Review of Books, 17*:23–31, December 17, 1970.

Dyba, Jerome E. "Integrating Police Dispatching, Incident Reporting, Records Retrieval, Manpower Reporting." *Police Chief, 36*:30–31, January 1969.

Eckstein, Harry. "Political Science and Public Policy." In: *Contemporary Political Science: Toward Empirical Theory.* Edited by I. deSola Pool. New York, McGraw-Hill, 1967, pp. 121–165.

Eglash, Albert. "Stigma: A Springboard to Mental Health." *Journal of Social Therapy, 6*:44–49, First Quarter 1960.

Ennis, Phillip H. "Crime, Victims and the Police: Crime Commission Shows Dissatisfaction with Police Leads to Incomplete Record of Crime." *Trans-Action,* 4:36–44, June 1967.

"Entrance and Disciplinary Requirements for Occupational Licenses in California." *Stanford Law Review,* 14:533–550, May 1962.

Ericksen, Kai T. "Notes on the Sociology of Deviance." In: *The Other Side, Perspectives on Deviance.* Edited by H. S. Becker. New York, Free Press, 1964, pp. 9–21.

Ervin, Senator Sam J., Jr. "Privacy and Government Investigations." *University of Illinois Law Forum,* 1971:137–153, 1971.

———. "The First Amendment: A Living Thought in the Computer Age." *Columbia Human Rights Law Review.* 4:44–47, Winter 1972

"Expungement of Arrest Records: Police Retention of Data v. Individual Freedom from Governmental Interference." *Rutgers Camden Law Journal,* 4:378, Spring 1973.

"Expungement of Criminal Convictions in Kansas: A Necessary Rehabilitative Tool." *Washburn Law Journal,* 13:93–105, Winter 1974.

"Expungement or Restriction of Arrest Records." *Cleveland State Law Review,* 23:123–134, Winter 1974.

Fanwick, Charles. "Computer Safeguards: How Safe Are They?" *System Development Corporation Magazine,* 10:26, July–August 1967.

Farr, J. A. "Retrospective Technology Assessment." *Technology and Culture,* 18:655–658, October 1977.

"F.B.I. Arrest Records: The Need to Control Dissemination." *Washington University Law Quarterly,* 1970:530, 1970.

"F.B.I. Embarks Upon Development of National Electronic Information System." *Journal of California Law Enforcement,* 1:8–11, July 1966.

"F.B.I. Rap Sheets—An Invasion of Constitutional Rights?" *Catholic University Law Review,* 20:511, 1970.

Ferkiss, Victor C. "Man's Tools and Man's Choices: The Confrontation of Technology and Political Science." *American Political Science Review,* 67:973–980, September 1973.

Ferracuti, Franco, et al. "A Study of Police Errors in Crime Classification." *Journal of Criminal Law, Criminology and Police Science,* 53:113–119, March 1962.

Fishman, Phillip F. "Expungement of Arrest Records: Legislation and Litigation to Prevent Their Abuse." *Clearinghouse Review,* 6:725–733, April 1973.

Flaugher, P. R. "Cincinnati/Hamilton County Regional Crime Information Center: Operations, Security, Ethics." *Police Chief,* 40(10):24, 26–27, October 1973.

Fried, Charles. "Privacy." *Yale Law Journal,* 77:475–493, January 1968.

Friker, E. Kenneth. "The Fingerprinting of Juveniles." *Chicago Kent Law Review,* 43:144–152, 1966.

Frohlich, Norman, and Oppenheimer, Joe A. "I Get By with a Little Help from My Friends." *World Politics,* 23:104–120, October 1970.

Gallati, R. R. J. "Criminal Justice: Computers, Related Technology and the Scientific Method." *Police, 13*:17–26, September–October 1968.

Garfinkel, Harold. "Conditions of Successful Degradation Ceremonies." *American Journal of Sociology, 61*:420–424, March 1956.

Gates, A. L. "Arrest Records: Protecting the Innocent." *Tulane Law Review, 48*(3):629–648, April 1974.

Gerety, T. "Redefining Privacy." *Harvard Civil Rights Law Review, 12*:233–296, Spring 1977.

Gerlack, Gary. "New Cop on the Beat: Nationwide Network Hooked to an FBI Computer Helps Nab Crooks in Seconds, Curb Growing Crime." *National Civic Review, 58*:206–210, May 1969.

Gitenstein, Mark H., and Kelley, Clarence D. "The Right to Privacy Is American. . .But So Is the Right to Law and Order." *Trial Magazine, 11*:26, January–February 1975.

Goldberg, Edward. "Urban Information Systems and Invasions of Privacy." *Urban Affairs, 5*:249–264, March 1970.

Goldberg, Victor P. "Institutional Change and the Quasi Invisible Hand." *Journal of Law and Economics, 17*:461–496, 1974.

Gore, William J. "Decision-Making Research: Some Prospects and Limitations." In: *Concepts and Issues in Administrative Behavior.* Edited by S. Mailick and E. H. VanNess. Englewood Cliffs, N.J., Prentice-Hall, 1962, pp. 49–65.

Gore, William J., and Silander, F. S. "A Bibliographical Essay on Decision Making." *Administrative Science Quarterly, 4*:97–121, June 1959.

Gough, Aidan R. "The Expungement of Adjudication Records of Juvenile and Adult Offenders: A Problem of Status." *Washington University Law Quarterly, 2*:147–190, 1966.

Gouldner, Alvin W. "Red Tape as a Social Problem." In: *Reader in Bureaucracy.* Edited by R. K. Merton, A. P. Gray, B. Hockey, and A. C. Selvin. New York, Free Press, 1952, pp. 410–418.

Greguras, F. J. "Informational Privacy and the Private Sector." *Creighton Law Review, 11*:312–351, October 1977.

Griffin, John I. "The Future of Police Statistics." *Police, 5*:68–71, November–December 1960.

Griffiths, John. "Ideology in Criminal Procedure or a Third 'Model' of the Criminal Process." *Yale Law Journal, 79*:359–417, January 1970.

Grupp, S. E. "Prior Criminal Record and Adult Marihuana Arrest Dispositions." *Journal of Criminal Law, 62*:74, March 1971.

Guetzkow, Harold. "Communications in Organization." In: *Handbook of Organizations.* Edited by J. G. March. Chicago, Rand McNally, 1965, pp. 534–573.

Hathaway, G. O. "Modern Data Processing." *FBI Law Enforcement Bulletin, 35*:6–9, April 1966.

Haney, William V. "Serial Communication of Information in Organizations." In: *Concepts and Issues in Administrative Behavior.* Edited by S. Mailick and E. H. VanNess. Englewood Cliffs, N.J., Prentice-Hall, 1962, pp. 150–165.

Hardin, Garrett. "The Tragedy of the Commons." *Science, 162*:1243–1248, December 1968.

Haskel, Peter B. "The Arrest Record and New York City Public Hiring: An Evaluation." *Columbia Journal of Law and Social Problems, 9*:442–494, 1973.

Head, J. G. "Public Goods and Public Policy." *Public Finance, 17*:197–219, 1962.

Henry, Nicholas. "Bureaucracy, Technology, and Knowledge Management." *Public Administration Review, 35*:572–578, November–December 1975.

Hess, Albert G., and LePoole, Fré. "Abuse of the Record of Arrest Not Leading to Conviction." *Crime and Delinquency, 13*:494–505, 1967.

Hilmen, Dale, and Pettler, Peter D. "Comment: Criminal Records of Arrest and Conviction: Expungement from the General Public Access." *California Western Law Review, 3*:121–134, 1967.

Hirsch, P. "Project SEARCH—Crime Fighters—A Year's Reprieve." *Datamation, 18*(7):95, 97, July 1972.

Hirsch, W. Z. "The Supply of Urban Public Services." In: *Issues in Urban Economics*. Edited by Harvey S. Perloff and Lowden Wingo. Baltimore, Md., Johns Hopkins University Press, 1968, pp. 477–526.

———. "Urban Government Services and Their Financing." In: *Urban Life and Form*. Edited by Werner Z. Hirsch, New York, Holt, Rinehart and Winston, 1963, pp. 129–166.

Hirschman, A. O. "The Principle of the Hiding Hand." *Public Interest, 6*:10, Winter 1967.

Hirsh, Phil. "Privacy: The Basic Questions to Be Found Are Political, not Technical." *Datamation, 6*:161, February 1970.

Hoos, Ida. "Information Systems and Public Planning." *Management Science, 17*:B-658–B-671, June 1971.

———. "When the Computer Takes Over the Office." *Harvard Business Review, 38*:102–111, July–August 1960.

Hoover, J. Edgar. "How Many Crimes? Organized Reporting Is an Essential Weapon in the Offensive Against Organized Crime." *State Government, 7*:55–58, March 1934.

———. "The Confidential Nature of FBI Reports." *Syracuse Law Review, 8*:1, 1956.

Horvitz, J. S. "Expungement of Records: Post Acquittal Recourse for Youthful Offenders." *Justice System Journal, 1*:60–68, September 1975.

Hunter, T. P. "Record Systems in Small Police Departments." *Police, 6*:52, 54, 56, January–February 1962.

"Interchange of Information Battles Organized Crime." *FBI Law Enforcement Bulletin, 31*:3–6, January 1962.

International Commission of Jurists. "The Protection of Privacy." *International Social Science Journal, 24*:3, 1972.

Jacobs, D. H. "Erasure of Criminal Arrest Records: The Connecticut Statute." *Connecticut Bar Journal, 47*:2, 1973.

Jones, R. R. "Complete Advocate: Mitigating Your Client's Record." *California State Bar Journal, 52*:113–116, March–April 1977.

Jourard, Sidney M. "Some Psychological Aspects of Privacy." *Law and Contemporary Problems, 37*:307–318, 1966.

Kafogles, Madelyn L. "Participatory Democracy in the Community Action Program." *Public Choice, 5*:73–85, Fall 1968.

Kalven, Harry, Jr. "Privacy in Tort Law—Were Warren and Brandeis Wrong?" *Law and Contemporary Problems, 31*:326, 1966.

Karabian, Walter J. "Record of Arrest: The Indelible Stain." *Pacific Law Journal, 3*:20–36, 1972.

Karst, Kenneth L. "The Files: Legal Controls Over the Accuracy and Accessibility of Stored Personal Data." *Law and Contemporary Problems, 31*:342–376, Spring 1966.

Katzenbach, Nicholas deB., and Tomc, Richard W. "Crime Data Centers: The Use of Computers in Crime Detection and Prevention." *Columbia Human Rights Law Review, 4*:49–57, Winter 1972.

Kiefer, David M. "Assessing Technology Assessment." *Futurist, 5*:234–239, December 1971.

Kirby, M. D. "Eight Years to 1984: Privacy and Law Reform." *Rutgers Journal of Computers and Law, 5*:487–502, 1976.

Kituse, J., and Cicourel, A. "A Note on the Uses of Official Statistics." *Social Problems, 11*:131–139, 1963.

Kloman, Erasmus H., ed. "A Mini-Symposium on Public Participation in Technology Assessment." *Public Administration Review, 35*:67–82, January–February 1975.

———. "Public Participation in Technology Assessment." *Public Administration Review, 34*:52–61, January–February 1974.

Knight, F. H. "Some Fallacies in the Interpretation of Social Cost." *Quarterly Journal of Economics, 38*:582–606, 1924.

Kogon, Bernard, and Loughbery, Donald L., Jr. "Sealing and Expungement of Criminal Records—The Big Lie." *Journal of Criminal Law, Criminology and Police Science, 61*:378–392, 1970.

Kondos, George. "Criminal Records: Private Rights and Public Needs." *Law and Computer Technology,* 144–149, December 1975.

Kovach, K. A. "Retrospective Look at Privacy and Freedom of Information Acts." *Labor Law Journal, 27*:548–564, September 1976.

Krasnow, E. "Social Investigation Reports in Juvenile Court." *Crime and Delinquency, 12*:150–159, 1965.

Lamberton, Donald M., ed. "The Information Revolution." *Annals of the American Academy of Political and Social Science, 412*:1–151, March 1974.

Lane, R. "Use of Juvenile Court Records in Fixing Subsequent Adult Criminal Proceedings." *Southern California Law Review, 32*:207–211, Winter 1959.

LaPorte, Todd R. "The Context of Technology Assessment: A Changing Perspective for Public Organization." *Public Administration Review, 31*:63–73, January–February 1971.

"LEAA and CCCJ Deny Tot Fingerprinting." *LEAA Newsletter, 3*(2):1, April 1973.

Long, Norton E. "Rigging the Market for Public Goods." In: *Organizations and*

Clients: Essays in the Sociology of Service. Edited by W. R. Rosengren and Mark Lefton. Columbus, Ohio, Charles E. Merrill, 1970.

Longs, E. V. "The Prisoner Rehabilitation Act of 1965." *Federal Probation, 29*:3–7, December 1965.

Lowi, Theodore. "American Business, Public Policy, Case-Studies and Political Theory." *World Politics, 16*:677–715, 1964.

Lundesgaarde, Henry P. "Privacy: An Anthropological Perspective on the Right to be Let Alone." *Houston Law Review, 9*:858–875, 1970–1971.

Lusky, L. "Invasion of Privacy: A Clarification of Concepts." *Political Science Quarterly, 87*:192, June 1972.

MacDonald, M. E. "Computer Support for the Courts—A Case for Cautious Optimism. *Judicature, 57*(2):52–55, August–September 1973.

Majone, G. "Technology Assessment in a Dialectic Key." *Public Administration Review, 38*:52–58, January 1978.

Marks, M. S. "A Commentary (on Retention of Criminal Records)." *Journal of Criminal Law and Criminology, 36*:17–29, May–June 1945.

McCormick, M. J. "Privacy: A New American Dilemma." *Social Casework, 59*:211–220, April 1978.

McDonnell, R. E. "Cooperative Information Sharing Programs for Law Enforcement." *Police Chief, 21*:22–24, 26–31, July 1964.

———. "P.D.'s and Data Processing." *Police Chief, 21*:14, 16, 18, April 1964.

McKean, Roland L. "The Unseen Hand in Government." *American Economic Review, 55*:497–506, June 1965.

Mead, George H. "The Psychology of Primitive Justice." *American Journal of Sociology, 23*:577–602, March 1918.

Michael, D. N. "Speculations on the Relation of the Computer to Individual Freedom and the Right to Privacy." *George Washington Law Review, 33*:270–286, 1965.

Miles, Arthur P. "The Utility of Case Records in Probation and Parole." *Journal of Criminal Law, Criminology and Police Science, 56*:285–293, 1963.

Miller, Arthur B. "Computers, Data Banks and Individual Privacy: An Overview." *Columbia Human Rights Law Review, 4*:1, 1972.

———. "Personal Privacy in the Computer Age: The Challenge of a New Technology in an Information-Oriented Society." *Michigan Law Review, 67*:1089, 1969.

Miller, A. S., and Cox, H. B. "On the Need for a National Commission on Documentary Access." *George Washington Law Review, 44*:213–238, 1976.

Miller, R. I. "Choosing a Consultant—A Guide for the Courts." *Judicature, 57*(2):64–68, August–September 1973.

Minasian, Jara R. "Public Goods in Theory and Practice Revisited." *Journal of Law and Economics, 5*:205–207, 1967.

———. "Television Pricing and the Theory of Public Goods." *Journal of Law and Economics, 7*:71–80, 1964.

Mishan, E. J. "Reflections on Recent Developments in the Concept of External Effects." *Canadian Journal of Economics and Political Science, 31*:3–34, February 1965.

————. "The Relationship Between Joint Products, Collective Goods, and External Effects." *Journal of Political Economy, 77*:329–348, May–June 1969.

Monohan, T. P. "National Data on Police Dispositions of Juvenile Offenders." *Police, 14*:36–45, September–October 1969.

Nader, Ralph; Clark, Ramsey; and Schrag, Peter. "The Invasion of Privacy." *Saturday Review, 54*:18, April 17, 1971.

Nager, George, and Reda, Pietrina J. "The Right of Privacy vs. Victimless Crimes." *Nassau Lawyer, 23*:369–374, May 1974.

National Council on Crime and Delinquency. "Annulment of a Conviction of Crime." *Crime and Delinquency, 8*:97–102, April 1962.

National Crime Information Center. *Newsletter,* January 1974.

"NCIC—A Tribute to Cooperative Spirit." *FBI Law Enforcement Bulletin, 41*:1–7, February 1972. (Reprint)

Neier, Aryeh. "Marked for Life. Have You Ever Been Arrested?" *New York Times Magazine,* April 15, 1973, p. 16.

Neithercutt, M. G. "Consequences of 'Guilty.' " *Crime and Delinquency, 15*:459–462, October 1969.

Note: "Access to Information? Exemptions from Disclosure." *Willamette Law Journal, 13*:135–171, Winter 1976.

Note: "Acquittal Alone Does Not Justify Expungement of Arrest Records." *Utah Law Review, 1975*:535–553, Summer 1975.

Note: "Arrest and Credit Reports: Can the Right of Privacy Survive." *University of Florida Law Review, 24*:681, 1972.

Note: "Arrest Records and the FBI." *Texas Law Review, 53*:1308–1321, August 1975.

Note: "Constitutional Law—Maintenance and Dissemination of Records of Arrest Versus The Right to Privacy." *Wayne Law Review, 17*:995, 1971.

Note: "Constitutional Law—Right to Privacy—Retention of Arrest Records After Acquittal Violates Right of Privacy." *Vanderbilt Law Review, 25*:240, 1972.

Note: "Constitution Does Not Protect an Individual from Being Labeled a Criminal." *Southwestern Law Journal, 30*:781–787, Fall 1976.

Note: "Criminals' Loss of Civil Rights." *University of Florida Law Review, 16*:328, 1963.

Note: "Employment of 'Criminal-Record-Victims' in Missouri." *Missouri Law Review, 41*:349–382, Summer 1976.

Note: "Employment of Former Criminals." *Cornell Law Review, 55*:306, 1970.

Note: "Expungement of Arrest Records." *Minnesota Law Review, 62*:229–249, January 1978.

Note: "Expungement of Arrest Records." *New York Law Forum, 21*:85–95, Summer 1975.

Note: "Expungement of Arrest Records of Exonerated Arrestees." *South Texas Law Journal, 16*:173–197, 1975.

Note: "Expungement of Criminal Convictions in Kansas: A Necessary Rehab. Tool." *Washburn Law Journal, 13*:93–105, Winter 1974.

Note: "Expungement of Records Under the Federal Youth Corrections Act." *Iowa Law Review, 62*:547–567, December 1976.

Note: "Expunging the Arrest Record When There Is No Conviction." *Oklahoma Law Review, 28*:377–389, Spring 1975.

Note: "FBI Has No Statutory Authority to Maintain Files When No Arrest. . . ." *Loyola University Law Review, 8*:238–252, February 1975.

Note: "FBI Retention of Criminal Identification Records." *Rutgers Law Review, 29*:151–171, Fall 1975.

Note: "Federal Privacy Act and Effect on Freedom of Information Act." *New England Law Review, 11*:463–496, Spring 1976.

Note: "FOIA and the Privacy Act Interface: Toward a Resolution of Statutory Conflict." *Loyola University Law Journal, Chicago, 8*:570–593, Spring 1977.

Note: "FOIA's Privacy Exemption and the Privacy Act of 1974." *Harvard Civil Rights Law Review, 11*:596–631, Summer 1976.

Note: "Impact of Expungement Relief on Deportation of Aliens for Narcotics Convictions." *Georgia Law Journal, 65*:1325–1357, June 1977.

Note: "Informational Privacy and Public Records." *Pacific Law Journal, 8*:25–47, January 1977.

Note: "Informational Privacy: the Concept, Its Acceptance and Effect on State Information Practices." *Washburn Law Journal, 15*:273–289, Spring 1976.

Note: "Information Privacy." *Hastings Constitutional Law Quarterly, 3*:229–259, Winter 1976.

Note: "Press and Criminal Record Privacy." *St. Louis University Law Journal, 20*:509–530, 1976.

Note: "Privacy and the Freedom of Information Act." *Administrative Law Review, 27*:275–294, Summer 1975.

Note: "Privacy, Law Enforcement and Public Interest: Computerized Criminal Justice Records." *Montana Law Review, 36*:60–79, Winter 1975.

Note: "Reexamination of LEAA." *Stanford Law Review, 27*:1303–1324, May 1975.

Note: "Restoration of Deprived Rights." *William and Mary Law Review, 10*:924, 1969.

Note: "Retention and Dissemination of Arrest Records." *Santa Clara Law Review, 17*:709–715, Summer 1977.

Note: "Right of Police to Retain Arrest Records." *North Carolina Law Review, 49*:509, 1971.

Note: "Rights of the Innocent Arrestee: Sealing of Records." *Hastings Law Journal, 28*:1463–1507, July 1977.

Note: "Safeguarding the Accuracy of FBI Records." *University of Cincinnati Law Review, 44*:325–332, 1975.

Note: "Texas Open Records Act: Law Enforcement Agencies' Investigatory Records." *Southwestern Law Journal, 29*:431–453, Spring 1975.

Note: "*U.S. v. Miller:* Who Will Watch the Watchers—Informational Privacy." *John Marshall Journal of Practice and Procedure, 10*:629–650, Spring 1977.

Note: "Violation of 4th Amendment and NCIC. . ." *Hofstra Law Review, 4*:881–894, Spring 1976.

Nutter, C. Warren. "The Coase Theorem on Social Cost: A Footnote." *Journal of Law and Economics, 11*:504–505, 507, 1968.

O'Brien, D. M. "Privacy and the Right of Access." *Administrative Law Review, 30*:45–92, Winter 1978.

Olson, Mancur. "The Principle of 'Fiscal Equivalence': The Division of Responsibilities Among Different Levels of Government." *American Economic Review: Papers and Proceedings, LIX*:479–487, May 1969.

Olson, Mancur, and Zeckhauser, Richard. "An Economic Theory of Alliances." *Review of Economics and Statistics, 43*:266–279, August 1966.

Ostrom, Elinor. "Institutional Arrangements and the Measurement of Policy Consequences: Applications to Evaluating Police Performance." *Urban Affairs Quarterly, 6*:447–475, June 1971.

Ostrom, Vincent. "Operational Federalism: Organization for the Provision of Public Services in the American Federal System." *Public Choice, 6*:1–17, Spring 1969.

———. "Water Resource Development: Some Problems in Economic and Political Analysis of Public Policy." In: *Political Science and Public Policy.* Edited by Austin Ranney. Chicago, Markham, 1968, pp. 123–150.

Ostrom, Vincent, and Ostrom, Elinor. "Public Choice: A Different Approach to the Study of Public Administration." *Public Administration Review, 31*:203–216, March–April 1971.

Ostrom, Vincent; Tiebout, C. M.; and Warren, R. "The Organization of Government in Metropolitan Areas: A Theoretical Inquiry." *American Political Science Review, 55*:831–842, December 1961.

Palmer, G. "Privacy and the Law." *New Zealand Law Journal, 1975*:747–756, November 18, 1975.

Pauly, Mark V. "Optimality, 'Public' Goods and Local Governments: A General Theoretical Analysis." *Journal of Political Economy, 78*:572–585, May–June 1970.

Perrow, Charles. "Hospitals, Technology, Structure, and Goals." In: *Handbook of Organizations.* Edited by J. G. March. Chicago, Rand McNally, 1965, pp. 910–967.

Piersante, V. W. "Surveillance Techniques." *Police, 10*:72–78, September–October 1965.

Pipe, G. Russell. "Privacy: Establishing Restrictions on Government Inquiry." *American University Law Review, 18*:516, 1969.

Polansky, L. P. "Contemporary Automation in the Courts." *Law and Computer Technology, 6*(6):122–140, November–December 1973.

"Police Records of Arrest: A Brief for the Right to Remove Them from Police Files." *St. Louis University Law Journal, 17*:263, Winter 1972.

Portnoy, Barry M. "Employment of Former Criminals." *Cornell Law Review, 55*:306–307, 1970.

Project: "The Computerization of Government Files: What Impact on the Individual." *UCLA Law Review, 15*:1371, 1960.

Prosser, William L. "Privacy." *California Law Review, 48*:383, 1960.

Reed, J. P., and Nance, D. "Society Perpetuates the Stigma of a Conviction." *Federal Probation, 36*:27, June 1972.

Regan, Donald H. "The Problem of Social Cost Revisited." *Journal of Law and Economics, 15*:427–437, 1972.

Reiner, G. H., and Igleburer, R. M. "InformationTechnology: Computerized Information Retrieval Systems Have Opened New and Brighter Vistas to Police Chiefs and Others Charged with the Basic Police Function." *Police Chief, 37*:28–31, May 1970.

"Removing the Stigma of Arrest: The Courts, the Legislatures and Unconvicted Arrestees." *Washington Law Review, 47*:659, August 1972.

"Retention and Dissemination of Arrest Records: Judicial Response." *University of Chicago Law Review, 38*:851–874, 1971.

Riesau, V. D. "An Integrated Justice System." *Police Chief, 36*:48–54, February 1969.

Rouzier, V. E. "The Police Administrator and Juvenile Records, Files and Statistics." *Bulletin, 24*:12, 31, Spring 1963.

Rubin, Charles. "Probable Cause in the Police Report." *Journal of California Law Enforcement, 4*:138–142, January 1970.

Rubin, Sol. "The Man with a Record: A Civil Rights Problem." *Federal Probation, 35*:3–7, September 1971.

Ruebhausen, O. M., and Brim, O. G., Jr. "Privacy and Behavioral Research." *Columbia Law Review, 65*:1184–1211, November 1965.

Sagatun, I. J. "Study of Juvenile Record Sealing Practices in California." *Pepperdine Law Review, 4*:543–575, Summer 1977.

Salisbury, Robert H. "An Exchange Theory of Interest Groups." *Midwest Journal of Political Science, 13*:1–32, 1969.

Samuelson, Paul A. "Pitfalls in the Analysis of Public Goods." *Journal of Law and Economics, 10*:199–204, 1967.

———. "Public Goods and Subscription TV: Correction of the Record." *Journal of Law and Economics, 7*:81–83, 1964.

"Saxbe Testifies on Bill Affecting Crime Data." *LEAA Newsletter, 3*(11):1, 12, March 1974.

Schaefer, F. J. "Automatic Data Processing Aids Police Service: A Police Administrator Discusses the Merits of Automatic Data Processing Equipment in Improving Police Services." *FBI Law Enforcement Bulletin, 33*:7–11, April 1964.

Schaefer, J. L. "Federal Youth Corrections Act: The Purposes and Use of Vacating the Conviction." *Federal Probation, 39*:31–38, September 1975.

———. "Use of Expunged Convictions in Federal Courts." *Federal Bar Journal, 35*:107–118, Spring 1976.

Schaffer, Benson. "The Defendant's Right of Access to Presentence Reports." *Criminal Law Bulletin, 3*:674–678, 1967.

Scham, Lawrence. "Police Intimidation Through 'Surveillance' May Be Enjoined as an Unconstitutional Violation of Rights of Assembly and Free Expression." *Clearinghouse Review, 3*[Part I]:130, 137, October 1969; *3*[Part II]:157, 162–164, November 1969.

Schiavo, Pasco L. "Condemned by the Record." *American Bar Association Journal,* 55:540–543, June 1969.

Schwartz, Barry. "The Social Psychology of Privacy." *American Journal of Sociology,* 73:741–752, 1968.

Schwartz, Richard D., and Skolnick, Jerome H. "Two Studies of Legal Stigma." *Social Problems,* 10:133–142, 1962.

"Science and Crime—Engineers Claim a Rosy Outlook But Police Aren't Sure." *Science, 184*(4139):878–881, May 24, 1974.

Selznick, Philip. "Foundations of the Theory of Organizations." *American Sociological Review, 13*:25–35, 1948.

Shapley, D. "Central Crime Computer Project Draws Mixed Reviews." *Science, 197*:138–141, July 8, 1977.

Shappley, W. L., Jr. "Branded Arrest Records of the Unconvicted." *Mississippi Law Journal, 44*:928, 1973.

Shaw, William. "An Introduction to Law Enforcement Electronics and Communications." *Law and Order, 13*(4):44–48, April 1965; *13*(6):30, June 1965.

Shils, E. A. "Privacy: Its Constitution and Vicissitudes." *Law and Contemporary Problems, 31*:281–306, 1966.

Shoup, Carl S. "Standard for Distributing of Free Government Service: Crime Prevention." *Public Finance, 19*:383–392, 1964.

Silvarman, Allen B. I. "Apprehension Report Forms." *Police, 9*:52–54, July–August 1965.

Simon, Herbert. "Theories of Decision-Making in Economics and Behavioral Science." *American Economic Review, 49*:255–257, June 1959.

Smith, David G. "Pragmatism and the Group Theory of Politics." *American Political Science Review, 58*:600–610, September 1964.

Smith, M. E. "Public Dissemination of Arrest Records and the Right to Reputation." *American Journal of Criminal Law, 5*:72–89, January 1977.

Smith, R. C., et al. "Background Information: Does It Affect the Misdemeanor Arrest?" *Journal of Police Science and Administration, 4*:111–113, March 1976.

Stallings, C. Wayne. "Local Information Policy: Confidentiality and Public Access." *Public Administration Review, 34*:197–204, May–June 1974.

Stein, G. "Courts and Computers—Conflicts in Approaches and Goals." *Judicature, 58*(5):222–227, December 1974.

Stein, Melvyn B. "Guilt by Record." *California Western Law Review, 1*:126–135, Spring 1965.

St. John, W. L. "Mechanical Record-Keeping." *Police Chief, 28*:28, 32, June 1961.

Stone, Donald C. "Practical Use of Police Records System." *Journal of Criminal Law and Criminology, 24*:668–678, September–October 1933.

Sussman, A. "Confidentiality of Family Court Records." *Social Service Review, 45*:455, December 1971.

Swan, P. N. "Privacy and Record Keeping: Remedies for the Misuse of Accurate Information." *North Carolina Law Review, 54*:585–640, April 1976.

Sweeney, R. J.; Tollison, R. D.; and Willett, T. D. "Market Failure, The Common Pool Problem and Ocean Resource Exploitation." *Journal of Law and Economics, 17*:179–192, 1974.

Sykes, Gresham M. "The Corruption of Authority and Rehabilitation." *Social Forces, 34*:257–262, March 1956.

Symposium: "Computerized Criminal Justice Information Systems: A Recognition of Competing Interests." *Villanova Law Review, 22*:1171–1213, October 1977.

"Symposium on Privacy and the Law." *University of Illinois Law Forum, 2*:137–178, 1971.

Symposium: "Openness in Government." *Federal Bar Journal, 34*:279–366, Fall 1975.

"The Attorney and the Juvenile Court." *Los Angeles Bar Bulletin, 30*:333, 1955.

"The Collateral Consequences of a Criminal Conviction." *Vanderbilt Law Review, 23*:1, October 1970.

"The National Crime Information Center." *FBI Law Enforcement Bulletin, 43*:8–10, January 1974.

Thompson, F. B. "The Dynamics of Information." *Key Reporter, 38*:2–4, 6, Winter 1972–1973.

Thorsell, B. A., and Klemke, L. W. "Labeling Process: Reinforcement or Deterrent?" *Law and Society Review, 6*:393, Fall 1972.

"Title VIII—Racial Discrimination in Employment—Employer's Use of Record of Arrests Not Leading to Conviction." *Wayne Law Review, 17*:228, January–February 1971.

Toby, Jackson. "An Evaluation of Early Identification and Intensive Treatment Programs for Predelinquents." *Social Problems, 13*:160–175, 1965.

Tresser, T. "After the Bill Is Signed: The Fate of a Juvenile Justice Program." *Human Ecology Forum, 6*:9–12, Summer 1975.

Ullrich, G., and Coon, T. F. "Principles of Surveillance." *Police, 9*:62–65, July–August 1965.

"Use of Prior Crimes to Affect Credibility and Penalty in Pennsylvania." *Pennsylvania Law Review, 113*:382–414, 1964.

Vierra, J. "Computers and the Law." *Police, 13*:95–98, January–February 1969.

Volenick, A. "Juvenile Court and Arrest Records." *Clearinghouse Review, 9*:169–174, July 1975.

Vollmer, August. "The Bureau of Criminal Records." *Journal of Criminal Law and Criminology, 11*:171–180, August 1920.

Wallerstein, Jane S., and Wyler, C. J. "Our Law Abiding Law Breakers." *Probation, 25*:107–112, March–April 1947.

Warren, Robert. "Federal-Local Development Planning: Scale Effects in Representation and Policy Making." *Public Administration Review, 30*:584–595, November–December 1970.

Watson, N. A. "Police Profiles: Interesting Data from Juvenile Delinquency Questionnaires." *Police Chief, 30*:16–18, 40, 42, October 1963.

Webber, L. T. "Keeping Statistics Is Vital to Modern Enforcement of Law." *FBI Law Enforcement Bulletin, 30*:7–9, November 1961.

Weissman, Clark. "Programming Protection: What Do You Want to Pay?" *System Development Corporation Magazine, 10*:30, July–August 1967.

Weizenbaum, Joseph. "On the Impact of the Computer on Society." *Science, 176*:609, May 12, 1972.

Welch, Michael F. "The Effect of a Pardon on License Revocation and Reinstatement." *Hastings Law Journal, 15*:355–359, February 1964.

Whisenand, P. M. "A Data Processing System for Law Enforcement." *Police, 9* [Part I]:35–38, January–February 1965; *10* [Part II]:11–14, November–December 1965.

Wildhorn, Steven Arthur. "Pathological Bureaucracies." In: *Government Lawlessness in America*. Edited by T. L. Becher and V. G. Murray. New York, Oxford University Press, 1971, pp. 224–231.

Wildon, J. C. "Public Goods and Federalism." *Canadian Journal of Economics and Political Science, 32*:230–238, 1966.

Wilkins, Leslie T. "Information and Decisions Regarding Offenders." In: *Police Records Administration*. Edited by W. H. Hewitt. Rochester, N.Y., Aqueduct Books, 1968, pp. 748–755.

Williams, Alan. "The Optional Provision of Public Goods in a System of Local Government." *Journal of Political Economy, 74*:18–33, February 1966.

Wilson, C. J. "Revolution in the Making: Computers in Law Enforcement, A Building Block Method for Installing an Ultimate System a Step at a Time." *Police Chief, 35*:60–61, September 1968.

Wilson, Woodrow. "The Study of Administration." *Political Science Quarterly, II*:198–222, June 1887.

III. HEARINGS, REPORTS, AND SPEECHES

Advisory Commission on Intergovernmental Relations. *Making the Safe Streets Act Work: An Intergovernmental Challenge*. Washington, D.C., U.S. Government Printing Office, 1968.

———. *State-Local Relations in the Criminal Justice System*. Washington, D.C., U.S. Government Printing Office, 1971.

Altmeyer, Paul. "ABC News Closeup. The Paper Prison: Your Government Records." New York, American Broadcasting Companies, 1974. Transcript.

American Civil Liberties Union. *Annual Reports*. Vol. VII. July 1962–December 1969. New York, Arno Press and The New York Times, 1970.

———. *Policy Guide of ACLU*. NewYork, 1974.

American Trial Lawyers Foundation, Annual Chief Justice Earl Warren Conference on Advocacy in the U.S. *Privacy in a Free Society, Final Report*. Cambridge, Mass., 1974.

Arizona State Justice Planning Agency. *A Master Plan for Criminal Justice Information Systems for the State of Arizona*. Phoenix, 1974.

Armer, Paul. *Social Implications of the Computer Utility*. Santa Monica, Calif., Rand Corporation, 1967.

Attorney General's First Annual Report: Federal Law Enforcement and Criminal

Justice Assistance Activities. Washington, D.C., U.S. Government Printing Office, 1972.

Baran, Paul. *Communications, Computers and People*. Santa Monica, Calif., Rand Corporation, 1965.

——. *On Distributed Communications. IX. Security, Secrecy, and Tamper-Free Considerations*. Santa Monica, Calif., Rand Corporation, 1964.

——. *On the Engineer's Responsibility in Protecting Privacy*. Santa Monica, Calif., Rand Corporation, 1968.

——. *Some Caveats on the Contribution of Technology to Law Enforcement*. Santa Monica, Calif., Rand Corporation, 1967.

Bish, R. L., and Ostrom, V. *Understanding Urban Government: Metropolitan Reform Reconsidered*. Washington, D.C., American Enterprise Institute, 1973.

Brictson, R. C. *Computers and Privacy, Implications of a Management Tool*. Santa Monica, Calif., Systems Development Corporation, 1968.

Byrd, R., Senator, U.S. Congress. "Computerized Criminal History Databanks." *Congressional Record, 120*(Part 2):2227–2228, February 5, 1974.

California Crime Technological Research Foundation. *CTRF 1973 Annual Report*. Sacramento, 1974.

California Department of Justice, Division of Law Enforcement, Program Planning Office. *Local California Automated Criminal Justice Systems*. Sacramento, 1973.

California Intergovernmental Board on Electronic Data Processing. *Successful Development of EDP in California Governments, Manual of Guidelines*. Vols. I and II. Sacramento, n.d.

——. *Survey of EDP Activities in State and Local Government*. Sacramento, 1970.

——. *The Intergovernmental Challenge of EDP in California*. Sacramento, 1971.

California Legislature, Assembly Committee on Statewide Information Policy. *A Final Report of the California State Assembly Statewide Information Policy Committee*. Sacramento, 1970.

——. "Hearings." Sacramento, September 2 and 22, 1969. Transcript.

California Legislature, Assembly Interim Committee on Criminal Procedure. A Public Hearing—Records of Arrest, AB2016." Los Angeles, November 12, 1959. Transcript.

——. "Erasure of Arrest Records." Sacramento, June 10, 1964. Transcript.

California Legislature, Assembly Select Committee on the Administration of Justice. *Security and Privacy and Criminal History Information Systems*. Sacramento, 1971.

California Legislature, Joint Legislature Audit Committee. *Report on Pre-Delinquency Programs Funded by California Council on Criminal Justice*. Sacramento, 1973.

California Legislature, Senate, Committee on Business and Professions. *Good Moral Character Requirements for Licensure in Business and Professions*. Sacramento, 1972.

California Office of Criminal Justice Planning. *A Master Plan for Criminal Justice Information Systems for the State of California.* Sacramento, 1974.

California, State Bar of, and the Schools of Law of the University of California and University Extension, University of California, Los Angeles. *Law in a Free Society, A Casebook on Privacy.* Los Angeles, 1972.

Canadian Department of Communications/Department of Justice. *Privacy and Computers.* Ottawa, 1972.

Carroll, J. M.; Baudot, J.; Kirsh, Carol; and Williams, J. I. *Personal Records: Procedures, Practices and Problems.* Ottawa, Canadian Department of Communications/Department of Justice, 1972.

Christensen, R. "Projected Percentage of U.S. Population with Criminal Arrest and Conviction Records." In: *Task Force Report: Science and Technology.* By the President's Commission on Law Enforcement and Administration of Justice. Washington, D.C., U.S. Government Printing Office, 1969, pp. 216–218.

Colorado State Council on Criminal Justice. *A Master Plan for Criminal Justice Information Systems for the State of Colorado.* Denver, 1973.

Committee for Economic Development. *Reducing Crime and Assuring Justice.* New York, June 1972.

Daniels, D., Representative, U.S. Congress. "Jobs and Crime." *Congressional Record, 121* (Part 8):9422, April 8, 1975.

Davis, Otto A., and Kemien, M. I. "Externalities, Information and Alternative Collective Action." Joint Committee Print. In: *The Analysis and Evaluation of Public Expenditures: The PPB System.* Vol. 1. Joint Economic Committee, 91st Congress, 1st Session, 1969, pp. 67–86.

Dennis, Robert L. *Security in the Computer Environment.* Santa Monica, Calif., Systems Development Corporation, 1966.

Dobrovir, William A. "Justice in Time of Crisis." Staff Report. Washington, D.C., District of Columbia Committee on the Administration of Justice Under Emergency Conditions, 1969. Mimeographed.

Domestic Council Committee on the Right of Privacy and the Council of State Governments. *Privacy, A Public Concern.* Washington, D.C., Executive Office of the President, 1975.

Drinan, Robert, Representative, U.S. Congress. "Department of Justice Regulations on Criminal Justice Information Systems." *Congressional Record, 121* (Part 2):16151–16152, May 22, 1975.

Edwards, Don, Representative, U.S. Congress. "Arrest Record Information in Jeopardy." *Congressional Record, 119* (Part 28):37013, November 14, 1973.

———. "Criminal Justice Information Systems." *Congressional Record, 121* (Part 1):92–93, January 14, 1975.

———. "Introduction of Bill to Regulate the Operation of Criminal Data Banks." *Congressional Record, 119* (Part 21):27757–27758, August 2, 1973.

———. "Introduction of Legislation Protecting the Right of Privacy." *Congressional Record, 120* (Part 2):2105, February 5, 1974.

Erdmann, Martin. "Affidavit of Richard Faust." In: *Tatum v. Rogers.* 75 Civ. 2782 (CBM), S.D.N.Y., 1978.

————. "Plaintiff's Pretrial Memorandum of Law." In: *Tatum v. Rogers*. 75 Civ. 2782 (CBM), S.D.N.Y., 1977.

Ervin, Sam J., Jr., Senator, U.S. Congress. "A Letter from Jocelyn." *Congressional Record, 121*(Part 11):14471, May 14, 1974.

————. "Developing Consensus on Criminal Justice Databank Legislation." *Congressional Record, 120*(Part 16):21473–21474, June 26, 1974.

————. "Introduction of S. 2963—The Criminal Justice Information Control and Protection of Privacy Act of 1974." *Congressional Record, 120*(Part 2):2210–2221, February 5, 1974.

————. "Police Data Bank Legislation and the GAO Report." *Congressional Record, 120*(Part 23):30577–30578, September 10, 1974.

————. "Restricting the Use of Computerized Criminal Justice Information." *Congressional Record, 120*(Part 5):5801–5811, March 7, 1974.

————. "Senate Adopts Arrest Records Amendment." *Congressional Record, 119*(Part 17):22255, June 29, 1973.

————. "Statements on Introduced Bills and Joint Resolutions." *Congressional Record, 120*(Part 30):40735–40747, December 18, 1974.

Executive Office of the President, Office of Management and Budget. "Management Review of Project SEARCH for the Department of Justice." Washington, D.C., 1970. Mimeographed.

Executive Office of the President, Office of Telecommunications Policy. *Activities and Programs, 1975–1976*. Washington, D.C., U.S. Government Printing Office, 1977.

Fanwick, Charles. *Maintaining Privacy of Computerized Data*. Santa Monica, Calif., Systems Development Corporation, 1966.

————. "The Role of the Courts in a Statewide Criminal Justice Information System." Speech before Symposium, "Automation in the Courts, Its Impact on Record-Making and Record-Keeping, Implications for the Private Citizen and the Public," sponsored by the Association of the Bar of the City of New York. New York City, November 5, 1971.

Gellman, H. S. *Statistical Data Banks and Their Effects on Privacy*. Ottawa, Canadian Department of Communications/Department of Justice, 1972.

Godfrey, E. D., Jr., and Harris, Don R. *Basic Elements of Intelligence*. Washington, D.C., U.S. Department of Justice, Law Enforcement Assistance Administration, November 1971.

Gotlieb, C. C., and Hume, J. N. P. *Systems Capacity for Data Security*. Ottawa, Canadian Department of Communications/Department of Justice, 1972.

Greenawalt, Kent. *Legal Protections of Privacy*. Washington, D.C., Office of Telecommunications Policy, Executive Office of the President, 1975.

Greenwood, Peter W., et al. *Prosecution of Adult Felony Defendants in Los Angeles County: A Policy Perspective*. Santa Monica, Calif., Rand Corporation, 1973.

Harrington, M., Representative, U.S. Congress. "Massachusetts Takes Firm Stand on Citizen Protection—It's Congress's Turn Now." *Congressional Record, 119*(Part 20): 25788, July 24, 1973.

Harvard University. *Program on Technology and Society, 1964–1972, A Final Review*. Cambridge, Mass., Harvard University Press, 1972.

Hellman, J. J. *Privacy and Information Systems: An Argument and an Implementation*. Santa Monica, Calif., Rand Corporation, 1970.

Hoos, Ida R. *Systems Analysis in Social Policy*. Research Monograph No. 19. Westminster, England, Institute of Economic Affairs, 1969.

Hruska, Roman, Senator, U.S. Congress. "Introduction of S. 2964—Criminal Systems Act of 1974." *Congressional Record, 120*(Part 2):2221–2227, February 5, 1974.

Hunt, James W.; Bowers, J. E.; and Miller, N. *Laws, Licenses and the Offender's Right to Work*. Washington, D.C., National Clearinghouse on Offender Employment Restrictions, 1974.

International Business Machines Corporation. *The Considerations of Data Security in a Computer Environment*. New York, 1970.

Johnson, President Lyndon Baines. "Crime, Its Prevalence and Measures of Prevention." Message to the Congress, March 8, 1965. *Congressional Quarterly Almanac*. Washington, D.C., Congressional Quarterly Service, 1965, pp. 1394–1397.

Jones, Martin V. *Some Basic Propositions*. A Technology Assessment Methodology, Vol. I. McLean, Va., Mitre Corporation, 1971.

Jordan, F. J. E. *Privacy, Computer Data Banks, and the Constitution*. Ottawa, Canadian Department of Communications/Department of Justice, 1972.

Judicial Council of California, Administrative Office of the Courts. *Final Report for an Integrated Court Automation/Information System*. Vols. I and II. Sacramento, Arthur Young and Company, 1972.

———. *Phase II Report, Potential Applications Analysis for a Study to Design an Integrated Court Automation/Information System*. Sacramento, Arthur Young and Company, 1972.

Kakalik, James S., and Wildhorn, Sorrel. *The Law and Private Police*. Vol. 4. Santa Monica, Calif., Rand Corporation, 1971.

Lawyer's Committee for Civil Rights Under Law, and Urban Coalition. *Law and Disorder I: State and Federal Performance Under Title I of the Omnibus Crime Control and Safe Streets Act of 1968*. Washington, D.C., Special Projects Office, Lawyer's Committee for Civil Rights Under Law, 1969.

———. *Law and Disorder II: State and Federal Performance Under Title I of the Omnibus Crime Control and Safe Streets Act of 1968*. Washington, D.C., Special Projects Office, Lawyer's Committee for Civil Rights Under Law, 1970.

———. *Law and Disorder III: State and Federal Performance Under Title I of the Omnibus Crime Control and Safe Streets Act of 1968*. Washington, D.C., Special Projects Office, Lawyer's Committee for Civil Rights Under Law, 1972.

Lawyer's Committee for Civil Rights Under Law, Urban Coalition, and Center for National Security Studies. *Law and Disorder IV: State and Federal Performance Under Title I of the Omnibus Crime Control and Safe Streets Act of 1968*. Washington, D.C., Center for National Security Studies, 1976.

"LEAA Program Is a Crime." *Congressional Record, 121*(Part 2):1299, January 27, 1975.

"LEAA Reports on Agency's Progress." *Congressional Record, 121*(Part 6): 7888–7890, March 20, 1975.

Los Angeles Police Department, Advance Planning Division, Advanced System Development Section. *LAPD and Computers, 1972–73*. Los Angeles, 1973.

Marchand, Donald A. *Criminal Justice Records and Civil Liberties: The State of California*. Final Project Report. Sacramento, California Department of Justice, 1973.

Massachusetts Security and Privacy Council. *Annual Reports 1973–1974*. Boston, Mass., 1974.

Mathias, Charles McC., Senator, U.S. Congress. "The Injustice of Arrest Records." *Congressional Record, 120*(Part 16):20755, June 24, 1974.

Mazzoli, R., Representative, U.S. Congress. "Arrest Records: Permanent Stigma." *Congressional Record, 121*(Part 5):6148, March 11, 1975.

McClory, R., Representative, U.S. Congress. "The Criminal Justice Information Systems Act of 1974." *Congressional Record, 120*(Part 7):8553, March 27, 1974.

Miller, Herbert S. *The Closed Door: The Effect of a Criminal Record on Employment with State and Local Public Agencies*. Washington, D.C., Manpower Administration, U.S. Department of Labor, 1972.

————. *Guilty But Not Convicted: Effect of an Arrest Record on Employment*. Washington, D.C., Georgetown University Law Center, 1972.

Mitre Corporation. *Implementing the Federal Privacy and Security Regulations*. Vols. I and II. McLean, Va., 1977.

Mossman, Frances I., and King, John L. *Municipal Information Systems: Evaluation of Policy Related Research, Disclosure, Privacy and Information Policy*. Vol. V. Irvine, Public Policy Research Organization, University of California, 1974.

National Academy of Sciences. *Technology Assessment: Processes of Assessment and Choice*. Washington, D.C., U.S. Congress, House, Committee on Science and Astronautics, 91st Congress, 2d Session, 1969.

National Advisory Commission on Civil Disorders. *Report*. Washington, D.C., U.S. Government Printing Office, 1968.

National Advisory Commission on Criminal Justice Standards and Goals. *A National Strategy to Reduce Crime*. Washington, D.C., U.S. Government Printing Office, 1973.

————. *Report on Corrections*. Washington, D.C., U.S. Government Printing Office, 1973.

————. *Report on the Courts*. Washington, D.C., U.S. Government Printing Office, 1973.

————. *Report on the Criminal Justice System*. Washington, D.C., U.S. Government Printing Office, 1973.

————. *Report on the Police*. Washington, D.C., U.S. Government Printing Office, 1973.

National Association for State Information Systems. *Information Systems Technology in State Government, 1973 Report*. Lexington, Ky., Council of State Governments, 1973.

————. *Information Systems Technology in State Government, 1974–1975 Report*. Lexington, Ky., Council of State Governments, 1975.

National Commission on the Causes and Prevention of Violence, Task Force on Law and Law Enforcement. *Law and Order Reconsidered*. Washington, D.C., U.S. Government Printing Office, 1969.

National Probation and Parole Association, Advisory Council of Judges. *Guides for Juvenile Court Judges*. New York, 1957.

New York State Assembly and National Conference of State Legislators. *Privacy in the States*. Conference Report. New York, June 1978.

New York State Identification and Intelligence System. *System Development Plan*. New York, Georgian Press, 1967.

New York Supreme Court, First and Second Judicial Departments, Appellate Divisions, The Departmental Committees for Court Administration. *Automation in the Courts: Its Impact on Record-Making and Record-Keeping; Implications for the Private Citizen and the Public*. New York, 1971.

Niblett, B. G. F. *Digital Information and the Privacy Problem*. Informatics Studies, Vol. II. Paris, Organization for Economic Cooperation and Development, 1971.

Nixon, President Richard M. "State of the Union Address." January 30, 1974. *Weekly Compilation of Presidential Documents*, 10(5):113–122, February 4, 1974.

Oakland Police Department. "Most Common Documents on Which a Defendant's Name Will Appear from Perpetration to Disposition." In: California Legislature, Assembly Interim Committee on Criminal Procedure. *Erasure of Arrest Records*. Appendices II–a and III–a. Sacramento, 1964.

Organization for Economic Cooperation and Development. *Automated Management in Public Administration*. Informatics Studies, Vol. IV. Paris, 1973.

———. *Methodological Guidelines for Social Assessment of Technology*. Paris, 1975.

Petersen, H. E., and Turn, R. *System Implications of Information Privacy*. Santa Monica, Calif., Rand Corporation, 1967.

President's Commission on Federal Statistics. *Federal Statistics*. Vols. I and II. Washington, D.C., U.S. Government Printing Office, 1971.

President's Commission on Law Enforcement and Administration of Justice. *Task Force Report: Assessment of Crime*. Washington, D.C., U.S. Government Printing Office, 1967.

———. *Task Force Report: Corrections*. Washington, D.C., U.S. Government Printing Office, 1967.

———. *Task Force Report: Courts*. Washington, D.C., U.S. Government Printing Office, 1967.

———. *Task Force Report: Juvenile Delinquency*. Washington, D.C., U.S. Government Printing Office, 1967.

———. *Task Force Report: Organized Crime*. Washington, D.C., U.S. Government Printing Office, 1967.

———. *Task Force Report: Police*. Washington, D.C., U.S. Government Printing Office, 1967.

———. *Task Force Report: Science and Technology*. Washington, D.C., U.S. Government Printing Office, 1967.

———. *The Challenge of Crime in a Free Society*. Washington, D.C., U.S. Government Printing Office, 1967.

President's Reorganization Project, Federal Data Processing Reorganization Study, General Government Team Report. *Information Technology: Challenges for Top Program Management in the General Government.* Washington, D.C., National Technical Information Service, 1978.

President's Task Force on Prisoner Rehabilitation. *The Criminal Offender: What Shall be Done?* Washington, D.C., U.S. Government Printing Office, 1970.

Privacy Protection Study Commission. *Personal Privacy in an Information Society.* Washington, D.C., U.S. Government Printing Office, 1977.

Project SEARCH. *Designing Statewide Criminal Justice Statistics Systems: The Demonstration of a Prototype.* Technical Report No. 3. Sacramento, California Crime Technological Research Foundation, 1970.

———. *Model Administrative Regulations for Criminal Offender Record Information.* Technical Memorandum No. 4. Sacramento, California Crime Technological Research Foundation, 1972.

———. *A Model State Act for Criminal Offender Record Information.* Technical Memorandum No. 3. Sacramento, California Crime Technological Research Foundation, 1971.

———. *Newsletter.* Vol. I, No. I. Sacramento, California Crime Technological Research Foundation, 1969.

———. *Security and Privacy Considerations in Criminal History Information Systems.* Technical Report No. 2. Sacramento, California Crime Technological Research Foundation, 1970.

———, ed. *Proceedings of the International Symposium on Criminal Justice Information and Statistics Systems.* Sacramento, California Crime Technological Research Foundation, 1972.

———, ed. *Proceedings of the National Symposium on Criminal Justice Information and Statistics Systems.* Sacramento, California Crime Technological Research Foundation, 1970.

———, ed. *Proceedings of the Second International Symposium on Criminal Justice Information and Statistics Systems.* Sacramento, California Crime Technological Research Foundation, 1974.

"Report of the Republican Task Force on Privacy." *Congressional Record, 121*(Part 141):H9234–H9238, September 12, 1978.

Scientists' Institute for Public Information, Task Force on Science and Technology in the Criminal Justice System, Project on Criminal Justice Information Systems. "Report on Inspection and Briefing at the National Crime Information Center, July 12, 1977, and Follow-up, August 2, 1977." New York, 1977.

SEARCH Group, Inc. *Access to Criminal Justice Information.* Technical Memorandum No. 14. Sacramento, 1977.

———. *Criminal Justice Information: Perspective on Liability.* Technical Memorandum No. 12. Sacramento, 1977.

———. *Security and Privacy Rulemaking: Resources, Terms, and References.* Technical Memorandum No. 15. Sacramento, 1978.

———. *Standards for Security and Privacy of Criminal Justice Information.* 2nd Edition. Technical Report No. 13. Sacramento, 1978. (Revised)

————. *The American Criminal History Record.* Technical Report No. 14. Sacramento, 1976.

————, ed. *Proceedings of the Third International Symposium on Criminal Justice Information and Statistics Systems.* Sacramento, 1976.

Seckel, Joachem P. *Employment and Employability Among California Youth Authority Wards: A Survey.* Research Report 30. Sacramento, Youth and Corrections Agency, 1962.

Shapiro, Norman, and Turn, Rein. *Privacy and Security in Databanks Systems: Measures of Effectiveness, Costs and Protector-Intruder Interactions.* Santa Monica, Calif., Rand Corporation, 1972.

Sharp, J. M. *Regulatory Models.* Ottawa, Canadian Department of Communications/Department of Justice, 1972.

Silbert, J. M. "Criminal Justice Information Systems and the Criminal Justice 'System.'" Doctoral Dissertation. New York, New York University, 1972.

Smith, Charles P. "Coordination and Control of Computer Technology in State Government: Constraints and Strategies." Doctoral Dissertation. Los Angeles, School of Public Administration, University of Southern California, 1970.

Sparer, E. *Employability and the Juvenile Arrest Record.* New York, Center for the Study of Unemployed Youth, New York University, 1966.

"The People's Forum: The Privacy Battleground." Report. Jointly Sponsored by AFL-CIO Maritime Trades Department and Transportation Institute. Washington, D.C., 1971.

"Tribute to Professor Alan F. Westin's Work on Privacy." *Congressional Record, 120*(Part 30):40620, December 17, 1974.

Tunney, J., Senator, U.S. Congress. "Message Switching." *Congressional Record, 121*(Part 12):15664–15667, May 21, 1975.

"Up Amendment 1578." *Congressional Record, 124*(Part 120):S.12462, August 3, 1978.

U.S. Comptroller General. *Development of a Nationwide Criminal Data Exchange System: Need to Determine Cost and Improve Reporting.* Washington, D.C., U.S. General Accounting Office, 1973.

————. *Development of the Computerized Criminal History Information System.* Report to Senator Sam J. Ervin, Chairman, Subcommittee on Constitutional Rights. Washington, D.C., U.S. General Accounting Office, March 1, 1974.

————. *How Criminal Justice Agencies Use Criminal History Information.* Washington, D.C., U.S. General Accounting Office, 1974.

U.S. Congress, House, Committee on Government Operations, Subcommittee on the Invasion of Privacy. *The Computer and Invasion of Privacy.* 89th Congress, 2d Session, 1966.

U.S. Congress, House, Committee on Science and Astronautics, Subcommittee on Science, Research, and Development. *Technical Information for Congress.* 92d Congress, 1st Session. April 15, 1971.

U.S. Congress, House, Committee on the Judiciary, Subcommittee No. 4. *Security and Privacy of Criminal Arrest Records.* Hearings. 92d Congress, 2d

Session. March 16, 22, 23, April 13, 26, 1972.

U.S. Congress, House, Committee on the Judiciary, Subcommittee on Civil and Constitutional Rights. *Criminal Justice Information Control and Protection of Privacy Act.* 94th Congress, 1st Session. July 14, 17, and September 5, 1975.

————. *Dissemination of Criminal Justice Information.* Hearings. 93d Congress, 1st and 2d Sessions. July 26, August 2, September 26, October 11, 1973, and February 26, 28, March 5, 28, April 3, 1974.

U.S. Congress, House, Committee on the Judiciary, Subcommittee on Crime. *Restructuring the Law Enforcement Assistance Administration.* 95th Congress, 1st and 2d Sessions. August 15, October 3, 4, 20, 1977, and March 1, 1978.

U.S. Congress, Office of Technology Assessment. "A Preliminary Assessment of the NCIC Computerized Criminal History System." Draft Report. March 1978.

U.S. Congress, Senate, Committee on the Judiciary. *Department of Justice Authorization Bill Fiscal Year 1979.* Senate Report No. 95–911. May 25, 1978, pp. 9–10.

U.S. Congress, Senate, Committee on the Judiciary, Subcommittee on Administrative Practice and Procedure. *Invasion of Privacy.* 89th Congress, 1st and 2d Sessions. 1965–1966.

U.S. Congress, Senate, Committee on the Judiciary, Subcommittee on Constitutional Rights. *Criminal Justice Data Banks: 1974.* Vol. I, Hearings, and Vol. II, Appendix. 93d Congress, 2d Session. March 1974.

————. *Criminal Justice Information and Protection of Privacy Act of 1975.* Hearings. 94th Congress, 1st Session. July 15, 16, 1975.

————. *Drug Abuse Data Banks: Case Studies in the Protection of Privacy.* Staff Study. 93d Congress, 2d Session. November 1974.

————. *Federal Data Banks and Constitutional Rights.* Vol. 4. 92d Congress, 2d Session. 1974.

————. *Federal Data Banks, Computers and The Bill of Rights.* Part I, Hearings, and Part II, Appendix. 92d Congress, 1st Session. February–March 1971.

U.S. Department of Health, Education, and Welfare, Secretary's Advisory Committee on Automated Personal Data Systems. *Records, Computers and the Rights of Citizens.* Washington, D.C., U.S. Government Printing Office, July 1973.

U.S. Department of Justice, Federal Bureau of Investigation. *Appropriation Request 1979. Testimony of William H. Webster, Director, Federal Bureau of Investigation, Before the House Subcommittee on Appropriations, on March 16, 1978.* Washington, D.C., 1978.

————. "Comments of the Federal Bureau of Investigation (FBI) on the Report on Inspection and Briefing at the National Crime Information Center (NCIC), Dated August 3, 1977, and Prepared by the Task Force on Science and Technology in the Criminal Justice System of the Scientists' Institute for Public Information." Washington, D.C., September 28, 1977.

————. *Crime in the United States, Fiscal Year 1971.* Washington, D.C., U.S. Government Printing Office, 1971.

————. *Crime in the United States—1972*. Washington, D.C., U.S. Government Printing Office, 1972.

————. *Fiscal Year 1975 Annual Report*. Washington, D.C., U.S. Government Printing Office, 1975.

————. *Fiscal Year 1976 Annual Report*. Washington, D.C., U.S. Government Printing Office, 1976.

————. *Fiscal Year 1977 Annual Report*. Washington, D.C., U.S. Government Printing Office, 1977.

————. *Fiscal Year 1978 Annual Report*. Washington, D.C., U.S. Government Printing Office, 1978.

————. "Response to the Letter of Richard W. Velde, Administrator, Law Enforcement Assistance Administration." Washington, D.C., n.d.

U.S. Department of Justice, Federal Bureau of Investigation, National Crime Information Center (NCIC). *Proposed Limited Message Switching Implementation Plan*. Washington, D.C., April 14, 1975.

U.S. Department of Justice, Federal Bureau of Investigation, National Crime Information Center, Advisory Policy Board. *National Crime Information Center (NCIC), Computerized Criminal History Program, Background, Concept and Policy*. Washington, D.C., 1972.

————. *National Crime Information Center (NCIC), Computerized Criminal History Program, Background, Concept and Policy*. Washington, D.C. 1974.

————. *National Crime Information Center, Computerized Criminal History Program, Background, Concept and Policy*. Washington, D.C., 1976.

U.S. Department of Justice, Law Enforcement Assistance Administration. *1st Annual Report of the Law Enforcement Assistance Administration, Fiscal Year 1969*. Washington, D.C., U.S. Government Printing Office, 1969.

————. *2nd Annual Report of the LEAA, Fiscal Year 1970*. Washington, D.C., U.S. Government Printing Office, 1970.

————. *3rd Annual Report of the LEAA, Fiscal Year 1971*. Washington, D.C., U.S. Government Printing Office, 1971.

————. *4th Annual Report of the LEAA, Fiscal Year 1972*. Washington, D.C., U.S. Government Printing Office, 1972.

————. *5th Annual Report of the Law Enforcement Assistance Administration, Fiscal Year 1973*. Washington, D.C., U.S. Government Printing Office, 1973.

————. *6th Annual Report of the LEAA, Fiscal Year 1974*. Washington, D.C., U.S. Government Printing Office, 1974.

————. *1972 Directory of Automated Criminal Justice Information Systems*. Washington, D.C., 1972.

————. *1976 Directory of Automated Criminal Justice Information Systems*. Vols. I and II. Washington, D.C., 1976.

————. *Privacy and Security of Criminal History Information: A Guide to Policy Development*. Washington, D.C., 1978.

————. *Privacy and Security of Criminal History Information, Compendium of State Legislation*. Washington, D.C., 1978.

————. *Privacy and Security Planning Instructions*. Revised. Washington, D.C. 1976.

U.S. Department of Justice, Law Enforcement Assistance Administration, National Criminal Justice Information and Statistics Service. *Crime in the Nation's Five Largest Cities, Advance Report.* Washington, D.C., 1974.

———. *Criminal Victimization in the United States, January—June 1973.* Vol. I. Washington, D.C., 1974.

———. *National Survey of Court Organization.* Washington, D.C., 1973.

———. *Sourcebook of Criminal Justice Statistics—1973.* Washington, D.C., 1973.

———. *Sourcebook of Criminal Justice Statistics—1974.* Washington, D.C., 1974.

———. *Survey of Inmates in Local Jails, 1972, Advance Report.* Washington, D.C., 1974.

U.S. Department of Justice, Law Enforcement Assistance Administration, Office of the General Counsel. *Index to the Legislative History of the Omnibus Crime Control and Safe Streets Act of 1968.* Washington, D.C., 1973.

U.S. Department of Justice, Office of the Attorney General. *Representative Viewpoints of State Criminal Justice Officials Regarding the Need for a Nationwide Criminal Justice Information Interchange Facility.* Washington, D.C., 1978.

———. "Summary of Responses to NCIC Proposed Limited Message Switching Implementation Plan." Washington, D.C., May 19, 1975. Mimeographed.

———. "The Need for a *Modern* Nationwide Criminal Justice Information Interchange Facility." Washington, D.C., July 1978. Copy of Slide Presentation.

Usprich, S. J. *The Theory and Practice of Self-Regulation.* Ottawa, Canadian Department of Communications/Department of Justice, 1972.

Velde, Richard W. "Project SEARCH." Speech Before the National Crime Information Center Working Committee. Washington, D.C., January 12, 1971.

Ware, W. H. *Security and Privacy in Computer Systems.* Santa Monica, Calif., Rand Corporation, 1967.

Warren, Robert. *Government in Metropolitan Regions: A Reappraisal of Fractionated Political Organization.* Davis, Institute of Governmental Affairs, University of California, 1966.

Weisstub, D. N., and Gotlieb, C. C. *The Nature of Privacy.* Ottawa, Canadian Department of Communications/Department of Justice, 1972.

Williams, J. S. *Legal Protection of Privacy.* Ottawa, Canadian Department of Communications/Department of Justice, 1972.

Zimmerman, D. H. "Paper Work and People Work: A Study of a Public Assistance Agency." Doctoral Dissertation. Los Angeles, University of California, 1966.

IV. OFFICIAL CORRESPONDENCE (LETTERS, MEMORANDA, AND ORDERS)

Acting Chairman, U.S. Civil Service Commission. Letter to Roy L. Ash, Director, Office of Management and Budget, Executive Office of the President. November 4, 1974.

Bastian, Lloyd A. Draft memorandum to Glen E. Pommerening, Assistant Attorney General for Administration. Subject: "Summary of Responses to NCIC Proposed Limited Message Switching Plan—Responses Provided by DAG's Office on May 16, 1975." May 19, 1975.

Beddome, C. J., Executive Director, National Law Enforcement Telecommunications System, Inc. Memorandum to National Law Enforcement Telecommunications System, Inc. Officers and Board of Directors. Subject: "Discussion Document, Interstate Exchange of Criminal History Information." December 11, 1975.

Buell, Frank B., Chief, National Crime Information Center, Federal Bureau of Investigation, U.S. Department of Justice. Letter to William Hiner, Communications Manager, Telecommunications Service Center, Department of Justice. October 18, 1977.

Buggs, John A., Staff Director, U.S. Commission on Civil Rights. Letter to William Skidmore, Assistant Director for Legislative Reference, Office of Management and Budget, Executive Office of the President. November 7, 1974.

Cannon, James. Letter to Representative John E. Moss, U.S. Congress. July 11, 1975.

Carlstrom, Robert, Legislative Analyst, Office of Management and Budget, Executive Office of the President. Memorandum for File. Subject: "Criminal Justice Information Control and Privacy." August 11, 1975.

Chapman, Dudley, Associate Counsel to the President. Memorandum to William Skidmore, Chief, Business, General Government Branch, Office of Management and Budget, Executive Office of the President. Subject: "Justice Draft Bill: 'Criminal Justice Information System Security and Privacy Act.'" January 9, 1974.

Clark, Jerry N., Office of Criminal Justice, Department of Justice. Memorandum to William Skidmore, Legislative Referral, Office of Management and Budget, Executive Office of the President. Subject: "Comments of Associate Counsel to the President Re 'Criminal Information Systems Security and Privacy Act.'" January 21, 1974.

Clements, G. P., Jr., Deputy Secretary of Defense. Letter to Attorney General William B. Saxbe, with Attachment. "Changes to S. 2964 Requested by the Department of Defense." March 1, 1974.

Colby, W. E., Director, Central Intelligence Agency. Letter to James O. Eastland, Chairman, Committee on the Judiciary, Senate, U.S. Congress, with Attachment: "S. 1428 Criminal Justice Information." n.d.

Cooke, D. O., Deputy Assistant Secretary of Defense. Letter to Lawrence H. Silberman, Deputy Attorney General. October 24, 1974.

Daunt, Jerome J., User Systems, Inc. Letter to Don Edwards, Chairman, Committee on the Judiciary, House, U.S. Congress. September 21, 1977.

Davis, Ruth M., Director, Institute for Computer Sciences and Technology, National Bureau of Standards. Letter to Clarence M. Kelley, Director, Federal Bureau of Investigation, U.S. Department of Justice. July 13, 1976.

Dolan, Edward, Director, Information and Communications Systems Staff, Office of Management and Finance, Department of Justice. Letter to Richard Harris, Director, Division of Justice and Crime Prevention, Department of Justice. October 4, 1977.

Edwards, Don, Chairman, Subcommittee on Civil and Constitutional Rights, Committee on the Judiciary, House, U.S. Congress. Letter to Edward H. Levi, Attorney General. May 12, 1975.

————. Letter to Griffin B. Bell, Attorney General. March 17, 1977.

————. Letter to Peter F. Flaherty, Deputy Attorney General. July 22, 1977.

————. Letter to Peter F. Flaherty, Deputy Attorney General. October 20, 1977.

Eger, John, Acting Director, Office of Telecommunications Policy. Letter to Harold R. Tyler, Jr., Deputy Attorney General. May 12, 1975.

Flaherty, Peter F., Deputy Attorney General. Letter to Burch Bayh, Chairman, Subcommittee on the Constitution, Committee on the Judiciary, Senate, U.S. Congress. September 30, 1977.

————. Letter to John E. Moss, Representative, U.S. Congress. September 30, 1977.

————. Letter to Richardson Preyer, Chairman, Subcommittee on Government Information and Individual Rights, Committee on Government Operations, House, U.S. Congress. September 30, 1977.

————. Memorandum to Clarence M. Kelley, Director, Federal Bureau of Investigation, U.S. Department of Justice. Subject: "FBI Participation in the Computerized Criminal History Program." May 19, 1977.

————. Memorandum to Clarence M. Kelley, Director, Federal Bureau of Investigation, U.S. Department of Justice. Subject: "Message Switching." May 19, 1977.

————. Memorandum to Clarence M. Kelley, Director, Federal Bureau of Investigation, U.S. Department of Justice. Subject: "Message Switching." June 27, 1977.

General Counsel, Department of the Treasury. Letter to the Director, Office of Management and Budget, Executive Office of the President, with Enclosure. May 14, 1974.

General Manager, U.S. Atomic Energy Commission. Letter to Wilfred H. Rommel, Assistant Director for Legislative Reference, Office of Management and Budget, Executive Office of the President, with Enclosure: "Proposed Letter to Honorable Peter W. Rodino, Jr." May 16, 1974.

Hampton, Robert E., Chairman, U.S. Civil Service Commission. Letter to James T. Lynn, Director, Office of Management and Budget, Executive Office of the President. June 11, 1975.

Harris, Richard N., Chairman, Association of State Criminal Justice Planning Administrators. Letter to James T. Lynn, Director, Office of Management and Budget, Executive Office of the President. December 29, 1976.

Hoffman, Martin R., General Counsel of the Department of Defense. Letter to James T. Lynn, Director, Office of Management and Budget, Executive

Office of the President, with Attachment: "Department of Defense Comments on a Draft Bill, 'Criminal Justice Information Control and Protection of Privacy Act of 1974.'"

Holton, Linwood, Assistant Secretary for Congressional Relations, U.S. Department of State. Letter to Roy L. Ash, Director, Office of Management and Budget, Executive Office of the President. May 20, 1974.

Kelley, Clarence M., Director, Federal Bureau of Investigation, U.S. Department of Justice. Letter to Dr. Ruth M. Davis, Director, Institute for Computer Sciences and Technology, National Bureau of Standards. July 9, 1976.

————. Memorandum to Assistant Attorney General for Administration, Office of Management and Finance. Subject: "Law Enforcement Systems Policy Review Group of the Department of Justice Systems Policy Board." June 4, 1976.

————. Memorandum to Edward H. Levi, Attorney General. Subject: "Proposed NCIC Plan for Limited Message Switching." May 22, 1975.

————. Memorandum to Griffin B. Bell, Attorney General. Subject: "Message Switching Over the NCIC Network." April 3, 1977.

————. Memorandum to William B. Saxbe, Attorney General. Subject: "National Crime Information Center (NCIC) Communications—Administrative Message Handling and Switching." April 30, 1974.

Kleppe, Thomas S., Administrator, Small Business Administration. Letter to James M. Frey, Assistant Director for Legislative Reference, Office of Management and Budget, Executive Office of the President. June 13, 1975.

Lawton, Mary C., Deputy Assistant Attorney General, Office of Legal Counsel. Memorandum to the Attorney General. Subject: "Status of Criminal Justice Privacy Legislation (H.R. 61)—Message Switching." December 2, 1975.

McAlvey, Gary D., Chairman, SEARCH Group, Inc. Letter to Harold R. Tyler, Jr., Deputy Attorney General. May 9, 1975.

McCloskey, Robert J., Assistant Secretary for Congressional Relations, Department of Health, Education, and Welfare. Letter to James T. Lynn, Director, Office of Management and Budget, Executive Office of the President. June 11, 1975.

Metz, Douglas W., Acting Executive Director, Domestic Council on the Right of Privacy. Letter to Lawrence Silberman, Deputy Attorney General. September 11, 1974.

————. Letter to Lawrence Silberman, Deputy Attorney General. October 25, 1974.

Mondello, Anthony L., General Counsel, U.S. Civil Service Commission. Letter to William V. Skidmore, Jr., Office of Management and Budget, Executive Office of the President. November 19, 1973.

Moss, John E., Representative, U.S. Congress. Letter to Edward H. Levi, Attorney General. May 27, 1975.

————. Letter to Griffin B. Bell, Attorney General. October 18, 1977.

————. Letter to President Gerald R. Ford. June 11, 1975.

————. Letter to President Gerald R. Ford. June 28, 1975.

Pommerening, Glen E., Assistant Attorney General for Administration. Memorandum to Griffin B. Bell, Attorney General. Subject: "Computerized Criminal History (CCH) Program—Request for Status from Congressman Don Edwards (Action Memorandum)." March 30, 1977.

————. Memorandum to the Deputy Attorney General. Subject: "NCIC Message Switching." May 23, 1974.

————. Memorandum to the Deputy Attorney General. Subject: "Summary of Responses to NCIC Proposed Limited Message Switching Implementation Plan." May 21, 1975.

Proffer, Lanny, Special Assistant, National Governors' Conference. Letter to Harold R. Tyler, Jr., Deputy Attorney General. May 19, 1975.

Saxbe, William B., Attorney General. Letter to James O. Eastland, President Pro Tempore, Senate, U.S. Congress. November 18, 1974

————. Letter to Senator Roman L. Hruska, U.S. Congress. October 26, 1974.

Scott, Walter D., Associate Director for Economics and Government, Office of Management and Budget, Executive Office of the President. Letter to Harold R. Tyler, Jr., Deputy Attorney General. May 14, 1975.

————. Memorandum to Roy L. Ash, Director, Office of Management and Budget, Executive Office of the President. Subject: "Justice's Draft Bill 'Criminal Justice Information System Security and Privacy Act of 1973.'" n.d.

————. Memorandum to William Skidmore, Legislative Referral, Office of Management and Budget, Executive Office of the President. Subject: "Criminal Justice Information Systems Draft Bill (Your Question of January 8 concerning access by private investigations)." January 11, 1974.

Skidmore, William V., Jr., Chief, Business, General Government Branch, Office of Management and Budget, Executive Office of the President. Memorandum to Mr. Bray, Office of Management and Budget, Executive Office of the President. Subject: "Meeting in Mr. Scott's Office on the 'Criminal Justice Information Systems Security and Privacy Act' with Enclosure, 'Suggested Change to Section 11 of the Proposed Criminal Justice Information Systems Security and Privacy Act of 1973.'" November 6, 1973.

————. Memorandum to David Bray, Office of Management and Budget, Executive Office of the President. Subject: "Discussion Paper for Meeting in Mr. Scott's Office, 4:45 p.m., November 7, 1973, re OMB's Position on Justice's Draft Bill Cited as the 'Criminal Justice Information Systems Security and Privacy Act.'" November 6, 1973.

————. Memorandum to James Frey, Office of Management and Budget, Executive Office of the President. Subject: "Justice's Draft Bill on Criminal Justice Information Control and Privacy." n.d.

————. Memorandum to Leonard Garment. Subject: "Justice's Draft Bill Cited as the 'Criminal Justice Information Systems Security and Privacy Act.'" December 5, 1973.

————. Memorandum to Will Rommel, Office of Management and Budget, Executive Office of the President. Subject: "Criminal Justice Information Draft Bill." October 31, 1974.

————. Memorandum to Will Rommel, Office of Management and Budget, Executive Office of the President. Subject: "Criminal Justice Information Legislation (S. 2963) (Follow-up of My Memo of September 25, 1974)." October 8, 1974.

————. Memorandum to Wilfred Rommel, Office of Management and Budget, Executive Office of the President. Subject: "Justice Legislative Proposal—'Criminal Justice Information Systems Security and Privacy Act of 1973.'" Attachments: (A) "Justice and Privacy Act of 1973: 'Summary of Provisions'" and (B) "Summary of Agencies' Positions." October 18, 1973.

————. Memorandum to Walter Scott, Office of Management and Budget, Executive Office of the President. Subject: "Justice Draft Bill Cited as the 'Criminal Justice Information Systems Security and Privacy Act.'" November 1, 1973.

Slack, John, Chairman, Subcommittee on State, Justice, Commerce and Judiciary, Committee on Appropriations, House, U.S. Congress. Letter to Harold R. Tyler, Jr., Deputy Attorney General. May 12, 1975.

Tidd, J. Thomas, Acting General Counsel. Letter to Roy L. Ash, Director, Office of Management and Budget, Executive Office of the President. November 19, 1973.

"Title 28—Judicial Administration, Chapter I—Department of Justice, Part 20—Criminal Justice Information Systems." *Federal Register, 40*(98): 22114–22119, May 20, 1975.

"Title 28—Judicial Administration, Chapter I—Department of Justice, Part 20—Criminal Justice Information Systems." *Federal Register, 41*(55):1175, March 19, 1976 with Amendments of December 6, 1977, Reprint, pp. 1–6.

"Title 28—Judicial Administration, Chapter I—Department of Justice, Part 20—Criminal Justice Information Systems, Extension of Implementation Date." *Federal Register, 42*(98):61595–61596, December 6, 1977.

Tyler, Harold R., Jr., Deputy Attorney General. Letter to John E. Moss, Representative, U.S. Congress. July 16, 1975.

————. Letter to Richard D. Parsons, Associate Director and Counsel, Domestic Council, The White House. October 16, 1975.

————. Memorandum to Heads of Offices, Boards, Divisions and Bureaus. Subject: "Standard Operating Procedures for the Department of Justice Systems Policy Board." April 14, 1976.

Uhlmann, Michael M., Assistant Attorney General, Office of Legislative Affairs, Department of Justice. Letter to James T. Lynn, Director, Office of Management and Budget, Executive Office of the President. August 7, 1975.

U.S. Department of Justice. "Response to the Letter of Congressman Don Edwards, Chairman, Subcommittee on Civil and Constitutional Rights, Committee on the Judiciary." Washington, D.C., n.d

U.S. Department of Justice, Federal Bureau of Investigation, National Crime

Information Center, Advisory Policy Board. "Minutes." June 21–22, 1978. Mimeographed.

U.S. Department of Justice, Federal Bureau of Investigation, National Crime Information Center, Advisory Policy Board, and the National Law Enforcement Telecommunications Systems, Inc. *Joint Resolution* on "The National Crime Information Center Proposed Limited Message Switching Implementation Plan." June 12, 1975.

U.S. Department of Justice, Information and Telecommunications Systems Policy Board. "Automated Fingerprint Identification Systems." Staff Analysis. n.d.

———. "CDS Record Conversion Issue Working Paper." INSLAW, Attachment IV, September 10, 1975.

———. "FBI Position: Interstate Organized Crime Index (IOCI)." n.d.

———. "OBTS/CCH Issue Paper." n.d.

———. "Position Paper, Interstate Organized Crime Index (IOCI)." October 24, 1975.

———. "Recommendation Number 1." September 23, 1975.

———. "Summary Statement of FBI and OMB Viewpoints on the IOCI Project Proposal and Proposal Modifications." n.d.

U.S. Department of Justice, Office of Management and Finance. "Background Paper for Deputy Attorney General and Staff, Interstate Organized Crime Index (IOCI)." December 5, 1975.

———. *Order* of Edward Levi, Attorney General. "Department of Justice Systems Policy Board." February 25, 1976.

———. *Order* of Edward Levi, Attorney General. "Information and Telecommunications Systems Policy Board." July 16, 1975.

———. *Presentation of Project 80 Background Perspectives.* n.d.

Velde, Richard W., Administrator, Law Enforcement Assistance Administration, U.S. Department of Justice. Memorandum to Harold R. Tyler, Jr. Subject: "Proposed NCIC Plan for 'Limited' Message Switching." May 12, 1975.

Weinberger, Caspar W., Secretary, Department of Health, Education, and Welfare. Letter to James T. Lynn, Director, Office of Management and Budget, Executive Office of the President. July 23, 1975.

Wolf, Mark L., Special Assistant to the Attorney General. Letter to Don Edwards, Chairman, Subcommittee on Civil and Constitutional Rights, Committee on the Judiciary, House, U.S. Congress. May 16, 1975.

———. Memorandum to Clarence M. Kelley, Director, Federal Bureau of Investigation, U.S. Department of Justice; Glen E. Pommerening, Assistant Attorney General for Administration; Richard W. Velde, Administrator, Law Enforcement Assistance Administration, U.S. Department of Justice. Subject: "NCIC Limited Message Switching Conference, January 27, 1975." April 18, 1975.

Wormeli, Paul K., Deputy Administrator for Administration, Law Enforcement Assistance Administration, U.S. Department of Justice. Memorandum to Edward Dolan, Executive Secretary, Systems Policy Board, Department of Justice. Subject: "The Need for a Task Force on Interstate Criminal Justice Communications Management." September 10, 1975.

Zelenko, Leo J., Acting President, National Law Enforcement Telecommunications Systems, Inc. Letter to Harold R. Tyler, Jr., Deputy Attorney General. May 12, 1975.

V. NEWSPAPER ARTICLES

Computerworld. "A Look Inside NCIC," by Daniel R. Kashey. December 12, 1977.

———. "Around-the-Clock System Aids Police." November 20, 1974.

———. "Attorney General Delays OK of Message-Switching Plan." July 23, 1975.

———. "Broken Glass Fingers Burglary Suspect." February 13, 1974.

———. "California DOJ Opposes Proposal for Dedicated Justice Systems." May 29, 1974.

———. "Computerized Criminal Histories: A 7-Year Blunder?" July 17, 1974.

———. "Conn. to Draft Privacy Law for Crime Data." February 20, 1974.

———. "Corrections Plan Stresses Program Continuity." December 12, 1973.

———. "Court Disallows NCIC Data as Evidence." January 22, 1975.

———. "'Criminal History File' Keeps Track of Jockey's Violations." July 24, 1974.

———. "Criminal Justice Systems are States' Responsibility." December 12, 1973.

———. "Developing Nations Seen Major Market for Justice Systems." May 29, 1974.

———. "DP to Help Cut Arrests." January 23, 1974.

———. "Ervin Criminal Records Privacy Bill Gains Support." November 13, 1974.

———. "Ervin, Justice Department Privacy Bills Go to Congress; Strong Effort Seen." February 13, 1974.

———. "Ervin, Justice Privacy Bills Split on Enforcement." February 20, 1974.

———. "FBI Message-Switching Draws More Fire." November 13, 1974.

———. "FBI Must Erase Crime Records of Not Guilty." May 1, 1974.

———. "FBI Prohibits CCH Access from Police Car Terminals." July 10, 1974.

———. "FBI Questions Reevaluation of Need for NCIC." October 17, 1977.

———. "FBI's NCIC Has Problems." July 25, 1973.

———. "FBI Wants More Control Over Crime Systems: GAO." March 13, 1974.

———. "Fears of FBI Switch Plan Grow." November 28, 1977.

———. "Frightening Statistics." November 6, 1974.

———. "House Pushing Privacy Board to Watch Data Bank Operations." October 17, 1973.

———. "Inaccurate Records Jeopardize Criminal Histories System." November 18, 1974.

———. "Instant Access Crime File Use Growing in Arrest Decisions." November 6, 1974.

———. "'Interim' Privacy Rules Sought Under Justice Plan." February 27, 1974.

———. "Iowa Police Still Have 'Suspected' File." March 6, 1974.

———. "Justice Limits Arrest Data Dissemination." June 11, 1975.

———. "Kelley Agrees NCIC Needs Legislated Controls." December 5, 1973.

———. "L.A. Justice Systems Safeguards Called Adequate." February 27, 1974.

———. "Law Enforcement Conferences Spice April Offerings." March 20, 1974.

———. "Law Enforcers Defend Need for Maintaining 'Historical' Records." May 15, 1974.

———. "Maintenance of Crime Data Needs Proper 'Checks and Balances.'" May 29, 1974.

———. "Menard Case 'Impacts' Pending Bills." May 29, 1974.

———. "NASIS Fights LEAA Regulations." August 13, 1975.

———. "NCIC Audit, Expansion Pending." October 17, 1977.

———. "NCIC/CCH Message Switching Approved." October 30, 1974.

———. "NCIC Safeguards Publicized, Give Right to Challenge." January 16, 1974.

———. "NCIC Switching System Bid Put on Levi's Desk." February 19, 1975.

———. "New York Forced Out of CCH System for Failure to Update 'Rap Sheet' Files." July 3, 1974.

———. "Nixon's Privacy Message May Receive Extra Care." February 6, 1974.

———. "Nixon to 'Propose' National Criminal Justice System." January 23, 1974.

———. "Nixon Wants Privacy Shield for All." March 6, 1974.

———. "'NLETS' Official Calls for National Policy." November 27, 1974.

———. "One Little Crime Leads to Another." August 22, 1973.

———. "Police Came Calling on Command from California City Citizens." July 10, 1974.

———. "Police Systems Differ in Approach, Sophistication." October 9, 1974.

———. "Police Voice Opposition." February 1974.

———. "Privacy Bills Too 'Restrictive.'" August 28, 1974.

———. "Privacy Board Essential." November 6, 1974.

———. "Privacy Brings Problems." February 20, 1974.

———. "Privacy 'Cause' May Beget Unusable Law." May 28, 1974.

———. "Privacy Report Warns Against Federal EFT, FBI Switch." July 25, 1977.

———. "Privacy Threat Seen Inherent in Data Bank Existence." November 21, 1973.

———. "Records Challenger Has Right to Trial." November 13, 1974.

———. "Reinforcing the Syndrome." December 27, 1974.

———. "Richardson Plans Laws on NCIC CCH Safeguards." October 10, 1973.

———. "SEARCH Group Defines Standards Concepts for Crime Reporting." October 9, 1974.

———. "States Blast NCIC Requirement for Dedicated Systems." July 30, 1975.

————. "State Users Approve FBI Message-Switching System." July 9, 1975.

————. "Study Questions Worth of NCIC." September 12, 1977.

————. "Suing for Privacy." March 20, 1974.

————. "Tampering Charge Leads to Guilty Plea by Former Policeman." October 29, 1975.

————. "The Long Arm of NCIC." February 6, 1974.

————. "Time Ripe to Act on Privacy Issue, NBS Panel Agrees." November 28, 1973.

————. "Time to Bury CCH." July 24, 1974.

————. "Tough Guides Pushed to Ensure 'Highest Protection.'" November 21, 1973.

Law Enforcement News. "Task Force Report Raps Crime Data Center, Questioning Its Values as a Crime Fighting Tool." October 4, 1977.

Los Angeles Daily Journal. "Computers, Law and Ethics," by Reid C. Lawlor. Report Section. October 21, 1972, p. 28.

Los Angeles Times. "ACLU Sues to Kill Police List of Allegedly Dangerous Blacks." December 13, 1974.

————. "Court Curbs Use of Crime Records at Trial." August 17, 1974.

————. "Criminal Rehabilitation 'A Myth,' Saxbe Says." October 1, 1974.

————. "Data Bank Plans Seen as Endangering Privacy." June 5, 1975.

————. "Dear Abby: An Officer Ticketed for Oblivion." August 11, 1974.

————. "FBI Explains Computer System for Crime Data." January 3, 1974.

————. "FBI Seeks to Control Crime Data." March 1, 1974.

————. "Forged Fingerprint Leads to Nightmare for Innocent Man." September 11, 1974.

————. "Levi Defers Action in Criminal Data." November 11, 1975.

————. "1984 Closing in on California, Report Warns." February 23, 1974.

————. "Nixon Acts to Halt Data Banks Misuse." February 24, 1974.

————. "No Substantial Drop in Crime for 5–10 Years, Official Warns." November 24, 1974.

————. "People's Lobby Sues Cal Standard." January 21, 1975.

————. "Privacy: An Important Victory." February 19, 1974.

————. "Privacy vs. The Computer." February 5, 1974.

————. "Protesters Win $12 Million Suit." January 17, 1975.

————. "Records of 600 Arrested in Isla Vista Riots Being Erased." December 10, 1974.

————. "Reduction in FBI Force, Anticrime Funds Proposed." February 4, 1975.

————. "Rules Should Limit Computers' Prying." March 10, 1974.

————. "Soaring Crime Rate Is Severe Setback, Saxbe Warns U.S." August 28, 1974.

————. "State Will Destroy 2.5 Million Minor Arrest Records." February 23, 1974.

————. "Suit Attacks 'Big Brother' Spying on Texans by State Police Agents." September 23, 1974.

————. "Technology Requires a New Balance of Rights." March 10, 1974.

————. "TV Director Sued for $1 Million by Ex-Wife." September 7, 1978.

————. "U.S. Facing Demands to Curb Computer Data on Individuals." February 3, 1974.

————. "U.S. Urges Rules on Use of Criminal Files." February 14, 1974.

New York Times. "Big Brother's Data Bank." January 20, 1974.

————. "Computer Experts Question Value of F.B.I. Crime Information Center." September 5, 1977.

————. "Controversy Over FBI Plan to Set Up NCIC System." November 16, 1975.

————. "FBI Agrees to Expunge Arrest Records." July 15, 1975.

————. "FBI Data: How Much Is Too Much?" October 27, 1974.

————. "Hart Says Administration Undermines Privacy Right." March 3, 1974.

————. "Kelley Says FBI Never Plans to Monitor Communications of State and Local Government." July 15, 1975.

————. "LEAA's Velde Tells Editors About Changes in Policy on Releasing Criminal Information." March 18, 1976.

————. "Levi Postpones FBI's Plan to Extend Its Criminal Justice Communications Network." November 16, 1975.

————. " 'Privacy' Wanted but Vague." February 3, 1974.

————. "Rehnquist Says 'Benefit Programs' Threaten Privacy More Than Crime Data Do." September 29, 1974.

————. "Report on FBI Plan to Establish NCIC." October 29, 1975.

Open Forum. "Jury Duty as Ex-Felon's Right, ACLU Suit Claims." July–August 1975.

————. "Juveniles: Citizens Without Justice." November 1974.

Santa Barbara News Press. "Expunging the Record." May 10, 1970.

————. "No Redress for the Innocent." April 19, 1970.

————. "The Price of Innocence." April 26, 1970.

U.S. Department of Justice *New Release.* "Message Switching." November 10, 1975.

Washington Post, "Computer Banks on Individuals Hit." June 5, 1975.

————. "Computer Storage of Criminal Records." (Editorial) July 26, 1975.

————. "Concern Over New LEAA Criminal Record Guidelines Viewed." December 25, 1975.

————. "FBI Chief Criticizes Congress." September 2, 1978.

————. "FBI Computer Bank Safeguards Detailed." January 3, 1974.

————. "Justice Department Proposes New Rules on Crime Data Bank." April 21, 1975.

————. "Privacy and Criminal Justice Data Banks." September 12, 1976.

————. "Privacy Guidelines Limiting." December 25, 1975.

————. "Proposals to Suppress and Expunge Criminal Records Reviewed." March 29, 1975.

————. "Supreme Ct. Decisions on Privacy." (Editorial) July 11, 1976.

————. "U.S. Supreme Court Rules on Police Use of Criminal Data." March 24, 1976.

VI. OTHER BIBLIOGRAPHIES

Harrison, Annette. *The Problem of Privacy in the Computer Age: An Annotated Bibliography*. 2 Volumes. Santa Monica, Calif., Rand Corporation, 1967–1970.

Matthews, Joseph R., and Smith, Stephanie O. *Municipal Information Systems: Evaluation of Policy Related Research, Project Bibliography and Research Abstracts*. Vol. X. Irvine, Public Policy Research Organization, University of California, 1974.

The Computer in the Public Service: An Annotated Bibliography 1966–1969. Chicago, Public Administration Service, 1970.

Appendix A

94TH CONGRESS
1ST SESSION

S. 2008

IN THE SENATE OF THE UNITED STATES

JUNE 25 (legislative day, JUNE 6), 1975

Mr. TUNNEY introduced the following bill; which was read twice and referred to the Committee on the Judiciary

A BILL

To protect the constitutional rights and privacy of individuals upon whom criminal justice information has been collected and to control the collection and dissemination of criminal justice information, and for other purposes.

1   *Be it enacted by the Senate and House of Representa-*

2   *tives of the United States of America in Congress assembled,*

3   That this Act may be cited as the "Criminal Justice Infor-

4   mation Control and Protection of Privacy Act of 1975".

5   TITLE I—PURPOSE AND SCOPE

6   FINDINGS

7   SEC. 101. The Congress hereby finds and declares that—

8   (a) The responsible maintenance, use, and dissemina-

9   tion of complete and accurate criminal justice information

II—O

★(Star Print)

365

1   among criminal justice agencies is recognized as necessary

2   and indispensable to effective law enforcement and criminal

3   justice and is encouraged.

4   (b) The irresponsible use or dissemination of inaccurate

5   or incomplete information, however, may infringe on individ-

6   ual rights.

7   (c) While the enforcement of criminal laws and the reg-

8   ulation of criminal justice information is primarily the re-

9   sponsibility of State and local government, the Federal

10 Government has a substantial and interconnected role.

11   (d) This Act is based on the powers of the Congress—

12   (1) to place reasonable restrictions on Federal

13   activities and upon State and local governments which

14   receive Federal grants or other Federal services or

15   benefits, and

16   (2) to facilitate and regulate interstate commerce.

17   DEFINITIONS

18 SEC. 102. As used in this Act—

19   (1) "Automated" means utilizing electronic computers

20 or other automatic data processing equipment, as distin-

21 guished from performing operations manually.

22   (2) "Dissemination" means any transfer of information,

23 whether orally, in writing, or by electronic means.

24   (3) "The administration of criminal justice" means any

25 activity by a criminal justice agency directly involving the

1 apprehension, detention, pretrial release, posttrial release,

2 prosecution, defense, adjudication, or rehabilitation of ac-

3 cused persons or criminal offenders or the collection, storage,

4 dissemination, or usage of criminal justice information.

5 (4) "Criminal justice agency" means a court or any

6 other governmental agency or subunit thereof which as its

7 principal function performs the administration of criminal

8 justice and any other agency or subunit thereof which per-

9 forms criminal justice activities but only to the extent that

10 it does so.

11 (5) "Criminal justice information" means arrest record

12 information, nonconviction record information, conviction

13 record information, criminal history record information, and

14 correctional and release information. The term does not in-

15 clude criminal justice investigative information or criminal

16 justice intelligence information.

17 (6) "Arrest record information" means notations of

18 arrest, detention, indictment, filing of information, or other

19 formal criminal charge on an individual which does not in-

20 clude the disposition arising out of that arrest, detention,

21 indictment, information, or charge.

22 (7) "Criminal history record information" means ar-

23 rest record information and any disposition arising therefrom.

24 (8) "Conviction record information" means criminal

25 history record information disclosing that a person has

1   pleaded guilty or nolo contendere to or was convicted of
2   any criminal offense in a court of justice, sentencing informa-
3   tion, and whether such plea or judgment has been modified
4   or reversed.

5   (9) "Nonconviction record information" means crimi-
6   nal history record information which is not conviction record
7   information.

8   (10) "Disposition" means information disclosing that
9   a decision has been made not to bring criminal charges or
10   that criminal proceedings have been concluded, abandoned,
11   or indefinitely postponed.

12   (11) "Correctional and release information" means in-
13   formation on an individual compiled in connection with bail
14   or pretrial or posttrial release proceedings, reports on the
15   physical or mental condition of an alleged offender, reports
16   on presentence investigations, reports on inmates in correc-
17   tional institutions or participants in rehabilitation programs,
18   and probation and parole reports.

19   (12) "Criminal justice investigative information" means
20   information associated with an identifiable individual com-
21   piled by a criminal justice agency in the course of conduct-
22   ing a criminal investigation of a specific criminal act including
23   information pertaining to that criminal act derived from re-
24   ports of informants and investigators, or from any type of
25   surveillance. The term does not include criminal justice in-

1 formation nor does it include initial reports filed by a crim-

2 inal justice agency describing a specific incident, not indexed

3 or accessible by name and expressly required by State or

4 Federal statute to be made public.

5 (13) "Criminal justice intelligence information" means

6 information associated with an identifiable individual com-

7 piled by a criminal justice agency in the course of conducting

8 an investigation of an individual relating to possible future

9 criminal activity of an individual, or relating to the reliability

10 of such information, including information derived from re-

11 ports of informants, investigators, or from any type of sur-

12 veillance. The term does not include criminal justice in-

13 formation nor does it include initial reports filed by a

14 criminal justice agency describing a specific incident, not

15 indexed or accessible by name and expressly required by

16 State or Federal statute to be made public.

17 (14) "Judge of competent jurisdiction" means (a) a

18 judge of a United States district court or a United States

19 court of appeals; (b) a Justice of the Supreme Court of the

20 United States; (c) a judge of any court of general criminal

21 jurisdiction in a State; or (d) for purposes of section 208

22 (b) (5), any other official in a State who is authorized by a

23 statute of that State to enter orders authorizing access to

24 sealed criminal justice information.

1   (15) "Attorney General" means the Attorney Gen-
2   eral of the United States.

3   (16) "State" means any State of the United States,
4   the District of Columbia, the Commonwealth of Puerto Rico,
5   and any territory or possession of the United States.

6   APPLICABILITY

7   SEC. 103. (a) This Act applies to criminal justice in-
8   formation, criminal justice investigative information, or
9   criminal justice intelligence information maintained by
10   criminal justice agencies—

11   (1) of the Federal Government,

12   (2) of a State or local government and funded in
13   whole or in part by the Federal Government,

14   (3) which exchange information interstate, and

15   (4) which exchange information with an agency
16   covered by paragraph (1), (2), or (3) but only to the
17   extent of that exchange.

18   (b) This Act applies to criminal justice information,
19   criminal justice intelligence information and criminal justice
20   investigative information obtained from a foreign govern-
21   ment or an international agency to the extent such informa-
22   tion is commingled with information obtained from domestic
23   sources. Steps shall be taken to assure that, to the maximum
24   extent feasible, whenever any information subject to this Act
25   is provided to a foreign government or an international

1 agency, such information is used in a manner consistent

2 with the provisions of this Act.

3   (c) The provisions of this Act do not apply to—

4   (1) original books of entry or police blotters,

5   whether automated or manual, maintained by a criminal

6   justice agency at the place of original arrest or place of

7   detention, not indexed or accessible by name and re-

8   quired to be made public;

9   (2) court records of public criminal proceedings or

10   official records of pardons or paroles or any index there-

11   to organized and accessible by date or by docket or file

12   number, or organized and accessible by name so long as

13   such index contains no other information than a cross

14   reference to the original pardon or parole records by

15   docket or file number;

16   (3) Public criminal proceedings and court opinions,

17   including published compilations thereof;

18   (4) records of traffic offenses maintained by depart-

19   ments of transportation, motor vehicles, or the equivalent,

20   for the purpose of regulating the issuance, suspension,

21   revocation, or renewal of drivers' licenses;

22   (5) records relating to violations of the Uniform

23   Code of Military Justice but only so long as those records

24   are maintained solely within the Department of

25   Defense; or

1   (6) statistical or analytical records or reports in

2   which individuals are not identified and from which their

3   identities are not ascertainable.

4   TITLE II—COLLECTION AND DISSEMINATION OF

5   CRIMINAL JUSTICE INFORMATION, CRIMI-

6   NAL JUSTICE INVESTIGATIVE INFORMA-

7   TION, AND CRIMINAL JUSTICE INTELLI-

8   GENCE INFORMATION

9   DISSEMINATION, ACCESS, AND USE OF CRIMINAL JUSTICE

10   INFORMATION—CRIMINAL JUSTICE AGENCIES

11   SEC. 201. (a) With limited exceptions hereafter de-

12   scribed, access to criminal justice information, criminal justice

13   investigative information, and criminal justice intelligence in-

14   formation shall be limited to authorized officers or employees

15   of criminal justice agencies, and the use or further dissemina-

16   tion of such information shall be limited to purposes of the

17   administration of criminal justice.

18   (b) The use and dissemination of criminal justice in-

19   formation shall be in accordance with criminal justice agency

20   procedures reasonably designed to insure—

21   (1) that the use or dissemination of arrest record

22   information or nonconviction record information is re-

23   stricted to the following purposes—

24   (A) The screening of an employment applica-

25   tion or review of employment by a criminal justice

1   agency with respect to its own employees or appli-

2   cants,

3   (B) The commencement of prosecution, deter-

4   mination of pretrial or posttrial release or detention,

5   the adjudication of criminal proceedings, or the

6   preparation of a presentence report,

7   (C) The supervision by a criminal justice

8   agency of an individual who had been committed

9   to the custody of that agency prior to the time the

10   arrest occurred or the charge was filed,

11   (D) The investigation of an individual when

12   that individual has already been arrested or detained,

13   (E) The development of investigative leads

14   concerning an individual who has not been arrested,

15   when there are specific and articulable facts which,

16   taken together with rational inferences from those

17   facts, warrant the conclusion that the individual has

18   committed or is about to commit a criminal act and

19   the information requested may be relevant to that

20   act,

21   (F) The alerting of an official or employee of

22   a criminal justice agency that a particular individual

23   may present a danger to his safety, or

24   (G) Similar essential purposes to which the in-

S. 2008--2

1   formation is relevant as defined in the procedures

2   prescribed pursuant to the section; and

3   (2) that correctional and release information is dis-

4   seminated only to criminal justice agencies; or to the

5   individual to whom the information pertains, or his attor-

6   ney, where authorized by Federal or State statute, court

7   rule, or court order.

8   IDENTIFICATION AND WANTED PERSON INFORMATION

9   SEC. 202. Personal identification information, including

10 fingerprints, voice prints, photographs, and other physical

11 descriptive data, may be used or disseminated for any offi-

12 cial purpose, but personal identification information which

13 includes arrest record information or criminal history record

14 information may be disseminated only as permitted by this

15 Act. Information that a person is wanted for a criminal

16 offense and that judicial process has been issued against him,

17 together with an appropriate description and other informa-

18 tion which may be of assistance in locating the person or

19 demonstrating a potential for violence, may be disseminated

20 for any authorized purpose related to the administration of

21 criminal justice. Nothing in this Act prohibits direct access by

22 a criminal justice agency to automated wanted person infor-

23 mation.

1 DISSEMINATION, ACCESS AND USE OF CRIMINAL JUSTICE

2   INFORMATION—NONCRIMINAL JUSTICE AGENCIES

3   SEC. 203. (a) Except as otherwise provided by this Act,

4 conviction record information may be made available for

5 purposes other than the administration of criminal justice

6 only if expressly authorized by Federal or State statute.

7   (b) Arrest record information indicating that an indict-

8 ment, information, or formal charge was made against an

9 individual within twelve months of the date of the request

10 for the information, and is still pending, may be made avail-

11 able for a purpose other than the administration of criminal

12 justice if expressly authorized by Federal or State statute.

13 Arrest record information made available pursuant to this

14 subsection may be used only for the purpose for which it

15 was made available and may not be copied or retained by the

16 requesting agency beyond the time necessary to accomplish

17 that purpose.

18   (c) When conviction record information or arrest rec-

19 ord information is requested pursuant to subsections (a) or

20 (b), the requesting agency or individual shall notify the

21 individual to whom the information relates that such in-

22 formation about him will be requested and that he has the

1 right to seek review of the information prior to its dissemi-
2 nation.

3   (d) Criminal justice information may be made available
4 to qualified persons for research related to the administration
5 of criminal justice.

6   (e) A criminal justice agency may disseminate criminal
7 justice information, upon request, to officers and employees
8 of the Immigration and Naturalization Service, consular
9 officers, and officers and employees of the Visa Office of the
10 Department of State, who require such information for the
11 purpose of administering the immigration and nationality
12 laws. The Attorney General and the Secretary of State shall
13 adopt internal operating procedures reasonably designed to
14 insure that arrest record information received pursuant to
15 this subsection is used solely for the purpose of developing
16 further investigative leads and that no decision adverse to
17 an individual is based on arrest record information unless
18 there has been a review of the decision at a supervisory
19 level.

20   (f) A criminal justice agency may disseminate criminal
21 justice information, upon request, to officers and employees
22 of the Bureau of Alcohol, Tobacco, and Firearms, the United
23 States Customs Service, the Internal Revenue Service and
24 the Office of Foreign Assets Control of the Department of
25 the Treasury, who require such information for the purpose

1   of administering those laws under their respective jurisdic-

2   tions. The Attorney General and the Secretary of the Treas-

3   ury shall adopt internal operating procedures reasonably

4   designed to insure that arrest record information received

5   pursuant to this subsection is used solely for the purpose of

6   developing further investigative leads and that no decision

7   adverse to an individual is based on arrest record informa-

8   tion unless there has been a review of the decision at a

9   supervisory level.

10   (g) The Drug Enforcement Administration of the

11   United States Department of Justice may disseminate crimi-

12   nal record information to federally registered manufacturers

13   and distributors of controlled substances for use in connec-

14   tion with the enforcement of the Controlled Substances Ad-

15   ministration Act.

16   (h) Nothing in this Act prevents a criminal justice

17   agency from disclosing to the public factual information con-

18   cerning the status of an investigation, the apprehension, ar-

19   rest, release, or prosecution of an individual, the adjudication

20   of charges, or the correctional status of an individual, if such

21   disclosure is reasonably contemporaneous with the event to

22   which the information relates. Nor is a criminal justice

23   agency prohibited from confirming prior arrest record infor-

24   mation or criminal record information to members of the

25   news media or any other person, upon specific inquiry as

1 to whether a named individual was arrested, detained, in-

2 dicted, or whether an information or other formal charge was

3 filed, on a specified date, if the arrest record information or

4 criminal record information disclosed is based on data ex-

5 cluded by section 103 (b) from the application of this Act.

6 DISSEMINATION, ACCESS, AND USE OF CRIMINAL JUSTICE

7   INFORMATION—APPOINTMENTS   AND   EMPLOYMENT

8   INVESTIGATIONS

9   SEC. 204. (a) A criminal justice agency may disseminate

10 criminal justice information, whether or not sealed pursuant

11 to section 208, criminal justice intelligence information, and

12 criminal justice investigative information to a Federal, State,

13 or local government official who is authorized by law to ap-

14 point or nominate judges, executive officers of law enforce-

15 ment agencies or members of the Commission on Criminal

16 Justice Information created under section 301 or any State

17 board or agency created or designated pursuant to section

18 307, and to any legislative body authorized to approve such

19 appointments or nominations. The criminal justice agency

20 shall disseminate such information concerning an individual

21 only upon notification from the appointing or nominating

22 official that he is considering that individual for such an

23 office, or from the legislative body that the individual has

24 been nominated for the office, and that the individual has

1 that such an investigation will be conducted and that access

2 to this type of information will be sought.

3 (c) Any information made available pursuant to this

4 section may be used only for the purpose for which it is

5 made available and may not be redisseminated, copied, or

6 retained by the requester beyond the time necessary to ac-

7 complish the purpose for which it was made available.

8 SECONDARY DISSEMINATION OF CRIMINAL JUSTICE

9 INFORMATION

10 SEC. 205. Any agency or individual having access to,

11 or receiving criminal justice information is prohibited, di-

12 rectly or through any intermediary, from disseminating such

13 information to any individual or agency not authorized to

14 have such information; except that correctional officials

15 of criminal justice agencies, with the consent of an individual

16 under their supervision to whom the information refers, may

17 orally represent the substance of the individual's criminal

18 history record information to prospective employers or other

19 individuals if they believe that such representation may be

20 helpful in obtaining employment or rehabilitation for the

21 individual.

22 METHOD OF ACCESS TO CRIMINAL JUSTICE INFORMATION

23 SEC. 206. (a) Except as provided in section 203 (d) or

24 in subsection (b) of this section, a criminal justice agency

25 may disseminate arrest record information or criminal his-

1   been notified of the request for such information and has

2   given his written consent to the release of the information.

3   (b) A criminal justice agency may disseminate arrest

4   record information and criminal history record information

5   to an agency of the Federal Government for the purpose

6   of an employment application investigation, an employment

7   retention investigation, or the approval of a security clear-

8   ance for access to classified information, when the Federal

9   agency requests such information as a part of a comprehen-

10   sive investigation of the history and background of an in-

11   dividual, pursuant to an obligation to conduct such an

12   investigation imposed by a Federal statute or Federal execu-

13   tive order, and pursuant to agency regulations setting forth

14   the nature and scope of such an investigation. Arrest record

15   information or criminal history record information that has

16   been sealed may be made available only for the purpose of

17   the approval of a security clearance. For investigations con-

18   cerning security clearances for access to information classi-

19   fied as top secret, criminal justice intelligence information

20   and criminal justice investigative information may be made

21   available pursuant to this subsection. At the time he files

22   his application, seeks a change of employment status, ap-

23   plies for a security clearance, or otherwise causes the initia-

24   tion of the investigation, the individual shall be put on notice

1   tory record information only if the inquiry is based upon

2   identification of the individual to whom the information re-

3   lates by means of name and other personal identification

4   information. After the arrest of an individual, such informa-

5   tion concerning him shall be available only on the basis of

6   positive identification of him by means of fingerprints or other

7   equally reliable identification record information.

8   (b) Notwithstanding the provisions of subsection (a),

9   a criminal justice agency may disseminate arrest record in-

10 formation and criminal history record information for criminal

11 justice purposes where inquiries are based upon categories

12 of offense or data elements other than personal identification

13 information if the criminal justice agency has adopted pro-

14 cedures reasonably designed to insure that such information

15 is used only for the purpose of developing investigative leads

16 for a particular criminal offense and that the individuals

17 to whom such information is disseminated have a need to

18 know and a right to know such information.

19   SECURITY, ACCURACY, AND UPDATING OF CRIMINAL

20   JUSTICE INFORMATION

21   SEC. 207. (a) Each criminal justice agency shall adopt

22 procedures reasonably designed at a minimum—

23   (1) to insure the physical security of criminal justice

24   information, to prevent the unauthorized disclosure of the

25   information, and to insure that the criminal justice in-

S. 2008--3

1   formation is currently and accurately revised to include

2   subsequently received information and that all agencies

3   to which such information is disseminated or from which

4   it is collected are currently and accurately informed of

5   any correction, deletion, or revision of the information;

6   (2) to insure that criminal justice agency personnel

7   responsible for making or recording decisions relating to

8   dispositions shall as soon as feasible report such disposi-

9   tions to an appropriate agency or individual for inclusion

10   with arrest record information to which such disposi-

11   tions relate;

12   (3) to insure that records are maintained and kept

13   current for at least three years with regard to—

14   (A) requests from any other agency or person

15   for criminal justice information, the identity and

16   authority of the requester, the nature of the informa-

17   tion provided, the nature, purpose, and disposition

18   of the request, and pertinent dates; and

19   (B) the source of arrest record information and

20   criminal history information; and

21   (4) to insure that criminal justice information may

22   not be submitted, modified, updated, or removed from

23   any criminal justice agency record or file without verifi-

24   cation of the identity of the individual to whom the

25   information refers and an indication of the person or

1   agency submitting, modifying, updating, or removing

2   the information.

3   (b) If the Commission on Criminal Justice Informa-

4 tion finds that full implementation of this section is infeasible

5 because of cost or other factors it may exempt the provisions

6 of this section from application to information maintained

7 prior to the effective date of this Act.

8   SEALING AND PURGING OF CRIMINAL JUSTICE

9   INFORMATION

10   SEC. 208. (a) Each criminal justice agency shall adopt

11 procedures providing at a minimum—

12   (1) for the prompt sealing or purging of criminal

13   justice information when required by State or Federal

14   statute, regulation, or court order;

15   (2) for the prompt sealing or purging of criminal

16   justice information relating to an offense by an individual

17   who has been free from the jurisdiction or supervision of

18   any criminal justice agency for a period of seven years,

19   if the individual has previously been convicted and such

20   offense is not specifically exempted from sealing by a

21   Federal or State statute;

22   (3) for the sealing or purging of arrest record in-

23   formation after a period of two years following an arrest,

24   detention, or formal charge, whichever comes first, if no

25   conviction of the individual occurred during that period,

1 no prosecution is pending at the end of the period, and

2 the individual is not a fugitive; and

3 (4) for the prompt purging of criminal history rec-

4 ord information in any case in which a law enforcement

5 agency has elected not to refer the case to the prosecutor

6 or in which the prosecutor has elected not to file an

7 information, seek an indictment or other formal criminal

8 charge.

9 (b) Criminal justice information sealed pursuant to this

10 section may be made available—

11 (1) in connection with research pursuant to sub-

12 section 203 (d) ;

13 (2) in connection with a review by the individual

14 or his attorney pursuant to section 209;

15 (3) in connection with an audit conducted pur-

16 suant to section 304 or 310;

17 (4) where a conviction record has been sealed and

18 an indictment, information, or other formal criminal

19 charge is subsequently filed against the individual; or

20 (5) where a criminal justice agency has obtained

21 an access warrant from a State judge of competent

22 jurisdiction if the information sought is in the posses-

23 sion of a State or local agency, or from a Federal judge

24 of competent jurisdiction if the information sought is in

25 the possession of a Federal agency. Such warrants may

1 be issued as a matter of discretion by the judge in cases

2 in which probable cause has been shown that (A)

3 such access is imperative for purposes of the criminal

4 justice agency's responsibilities in the administration of

5 criminal justice, and (B) the information sought is not

6 reasonably available from any other source or through

7 any other method.

8 (c) Access to any index of sealed criminal justice in-

9 formation shall be permitted only to the extent necessary to

10 implement subsection (b). Any index of sealed criminal

11 justice information shall consist only of personal identifica-

12 tion information and the location of the sealed information.

13 ACCESS BY INDIVIDUALS TO CRIMINAL JUSTICE INFORMA-

14 TION FOR PURPOSES OF CHALLENGE

15 SEC. 209. (a) Any individual shall, upon satisfactory

16 verification of his identity and compliance with applicable

17 rules or regulations, be entitled to review any arrest record

18 information or criminal history record information concern-

19 ing him maintained by any criminal justice agency and to

20 obtain a copy of it if needed for the purpose of challenging

21 its accuracy or completeness or the legality of its mainte-

22 nance.

23 (b) Each criminal justice agency shall adopt and pub-

24 lish rules or regulations to implement this section.

25 (c) The final action of a criminal justice agency on a

1   request to review and challenge criminal justice information
2   in its possession as provided by this section, or a failure to
3   act expeditiously on such a request, shall be reviewable pur-
4   suant to a civil action under section 308.

5   (d) No individual who, in accord with this section,
6   obtains information regarding himself may be required or
7   requested to show or transfer records of that information to
8   any other person or any other public or private agency or
9   organization.

10   CRIMINAL JUSTICE INTELLIGENCE INFORMATION

11   SEC. 210. (a) Criminal justice intelligence information
12   may be maintained by a criminal justice agency only for
13   official criminal justice purposes. It shall be maintained in
14   a physically secure environment and shall be kept separate
15   from criminal justice information.

16   (b) Criminal justice intelligence information regarding
17   an individual may be maintained only if grounds exist con-
18   necting such individual with known or suspected criminal
19   activity and if the information is pertinent to such criminal
20   activity. Criminal justice intelligence information shall be
21   reviewed at regular intervals, but at a minimum whenever
22   dissemination of such information is requested, to determine
23   whether such grounds continue to exist, and if grounds do
24   not exist such information shall be purged.

25   (c) Within the criminal justice agency maintaining the

1 information, access to criminal justice intelligence informa-

2 tion shall be limited to those officers or employees who have

3 both a need to know and a right to know such information.

4   (d) Criminal justice intelligence information may be

5 disseminated from the criminal justice agency which collected

6 such information only to a Federal agency authorized to re-

7 ceive the information pursuant to section 204 or to a crimi-

8 nal justice agency which needs the information to confirm

9 the reliability of information already in its possession or for

10 investigative purposes if the agency is able to point to specific

11 and articulable facts which taken together with rational in-

12 ferences from those facts warrant the conclusion that the indi-

13 vidual has committed or is about to commit a criminal act

14 and that the information may be relevant to the act.

15   (e) When access to criminal justice intelligence infor-

16 mation is permitted under subsection (c) or when such

17 information is disseminated pursuant to subsection (d) a

18 record shall be kept of the identity of the person having ac-

19 cess or the agency to which information was disseminated,

20 the date of access or dissemination, and the purpose for which

21 access was sought or information disseminated. Such records

22 shall be retained for at least three years.

23   (f) Direct remote terminal access to criminal justice

24 intelligence information shall not be permitted. Remote termi-

25 nal access shall be permitted to personal identification infor-

1   mation sufficient to provide an index of subjects of criminal

2   justice intelligence information and the names and locations

3   of criminal justice agencies possessing criminal justice intelli-

4   gence information concerning such subjects and automatically

5   referring the requesting agency to the agency maintaining

6   more complete information.

7   (g) An assessment of criminal justice intelligence in-

8   formation may be provided to any individual when necessary

9   to avoid imminent danger to life or property.

10   CRIMINAL JUSTICE INVESTIGATIVE INFORMATION

11   SEC. 211. (a) Criminal justice investigative informa-

12   tion may be maintained by a criminal justice agency only

13   for official law enforcement purposes. It shall be maintained

14   in a physically secure environment and shall be kept sep-

15   arate from criminal justice information. It shall not be main-

16   tained beyond the expiration of the statute of limitations for

17   the offense concerning which it was collected or the sealing

18   or purging of the criminal justice information related to such

19   offense, whichever occurs later.

20   (b) Criminal justice investigative information may be

21   disclosed pursuant to subsection 552 (b) (7) of title 5 of

22   the United States Code or any similar State statute, or pur-

23   suant to any Federal or State statute, court rule, or court

24   order permitting access to such information in the course of

25   court proceedings to which such information relates.

1   (c) Except when such information is available pursu-

2 ant to subsection (b), direct access to it shall be limited to

3 those officers or employees of the criminal justice agency

4 which maintains the information who have a need to know

5 and a right to know such information and it shall be dissem-

6 inated only to other governmental officers or employees who

7 have a need to know and a right to know such information

8 in connection with their civil or criminal law enforcement

9 responsibilities. Records shall be kept of the identity of per-

10 sons having access to criminal justice investigative informa-

11 tion or to whom such information is disseminated, the date of

12 access or dissemination, and the purpose for which access is

13 sought or files disseminated. Such records shall be retained

14 for at least three years.

15   (d) Criminal justice investigative information may be

16 made available to officers and employees of government

17 agencies for the purposes set forth in section 204.

18 TITLE III—ADMINISTRATIVE PROVISIONS; REG-

19   ULATIONS,   CIVIL   REMEDIES;   CRIMINAL

20   PENALTIES

21   COMMISSION ON CRIMINAL JUSTICE INFORMATION

22   SEC. 301. CREATION AND MEMBERSHIP.—(a) There

23 is hereby created a Commission on Criminal Justice Infor-

24 mation (hereinafter the "Commission") which shall have

25 overall responsibility for the administration and enforcement

1 of this Act. The Commission shall be composed of thirteen

2 members. One of the members shall be the Attorney General

3 and two of the members shall be designated by the President

4 as representatives of other Federal agencies outside of the

5 Department of Justice. One of the members shall be desig-

6 nated by the President on the recommendation of the Judicial

7 Conference of the United States. The nine remaining mem-

8 bers shall be appointed by the President with the advice and

9 consent of the Senate. Of the nine members appointed by the

10 President, seven shall be officials of criminal justice agencies

11 from seven different States at the time of their nomination,

12 representing to the extent possible all segments of the crim-

13 inal justice system. The two remaining Presidential appoint-

14 ees shall be private citizens well versed in the law of privacy,

15 constitutional law, and information systems technology, and

16 shall not have been employed by any criminal justice agency

17 within the five years preceding their appointments. Not

18 more than seven members of the Commission shall be of

19 the same political party.

20 (b) The President shall designate one of the seven

21 criminal justice agency officials as Chairman and such desig-

22 nation shall also be confirmed by the advice and consent of

23 the Senate. The Commission shall elect a Vice Chairman

24 who shall act as Chairman in the absence or disability of the

25 Chairman or in the event of a vacancy in that office.

1   (c) The designated members of the Commission shall

2 serve at the will of the President. The Attorney General

3 and the appointed members shall serve for terms of five

4 years. Any vacancy shall not affect the powers of the Com-

5 mission and shall be filled in the same manner in which the

6 original appointment or designation was made.

7   (d) Seven members of the Commission shall constitute

8 a quorum for the transaction of business.

9   SEC. 302. COMPENSATION OF MEMBERS.— (a) Each

10 member of the Commission who is not otherwise in the serv-

11 ice of the Government of the United States shall receive a

12 sum equivalent to the compensation paid at level IV of the

13 Federal Executive Salary Schedule, pursuant to section 5315

14 of title 5, prorated on a daily basis for each day spent in the

15 work of the Commission, and shall be paid actual travel ex-

16 penses, and per diem in lieu of subsistence expenses when

17 away from his usual place of residence, in accordance with

18 section 5 of the Administrative Expenses Act of 1946, as

19 amended.

20   (b) Each member of the Commission who is otherwise

21 in the service of the Government of the United States shall

22 serve without compensation in addition to that received for

23 such other service, but while engaged in the work of the

24 Commission shall be paid actual travel expenses, and per

25 diem in lieu of subsistence expenses when away from his

1   usual place of residence, in accordance with the provisions

2   of the Travel Expenses Act of 1949, as amended.

3   (c) Members of the Commission shall be considered

4   "special Government employees" within the meaning of

5   section 202 (a) of title 18.

6   SEC. 303. DURATION OF COMMISSION.—The Commis-

7   sion shall exercise its powers and duties for a period of five

8   years following the first appropriation of funds for its activi-

9   ties and the appointment and qualification of a majority of

10 the members. It shall make a final report to the President

11 and to the Congress on its activities as soon as possible after

12 the expiration of the five-year period and shall cease to exist

13 thirty days after the date on which its final report is sub-

14 mitted.

15 SEC. 304. POWERS AND DUTIES.— (a) For the purpose

16 of carrying out its responsibilities under the Act, the Com-

17 mission shall have authority—

18   (1) after consultation with representatives of crimi-

19   nal justice agencies subject to the Act, and after notice

20   and hearings in accordance with the Administrative

21   Procedures Act, to issue such regulations, interpretations,

22   and procedures as it may deem necessary to effectuate

23   the provisions of this Act, including regulations limit-

24   ing the extent to which a Federal criminal justice

25   agency may perform telecommunications or criminal

1   identification functions for State or local criminal justice

2   agencies or include in its information storage facilities,

3   criminal justice information, or personal identification in-

4   formation relative to violations of the laws of any State;

5   (2) to conduct hearings in accordance with sec-

6   tion 305;

7   (3) to bring civil actions for declaratory judgments,

8   cease-and-desist orders, and such other injunctive relief

9   as may be appropriate against any agency or individual

10   for violations of the Act or of its rules, regulations, in-

11   terpretations or procedures;

12   (4) to make studies and gather data concerning the

13   collection, maintenance, use, and dissemination of any

14   information subject to the Act and compliance of crimi-

15   nal justice agencies and other agencies and individuals

16   with the provisions of the Act;

17   (5) to require from each criminal justice agency

18   information necessary to compile a directory of criminal

19   justice information systems subject to the Act and pub-

20   lish annually a directory identifying all such systems and

21   the nature, purpose, and scope of each;

22   (6) to conduct such audits and investigations as it

23   may deem necessary to insure enforcement of the Act;

24   and

25   (7) to delay the effective date of any provision of

1   this Act for up to one year, provided that such delay

2   is necessary to prevent serious adverse effects on the

3   administration of justice.

4   (b) The Commission shall report annually to the Presi-

5   dent and to the Congress with respect to compliance with

6   the Act and concerning such recommendations as it may have

7   for further legislation. It may submit to the President and

8   Congress and to the chief executive of any State such interim

9   reports and recommendations as it deems necessary.

10   SEC. 305. HEARINGS AND WITNESSES.—(a) The Com-

11   mission, or, on authorization of the Commission, any three

12   or more members, may hold such hearings and act at such

13   times and places as necessary to carry out the provisions of

14   this Act. Hearings shall be public except to the extent that

15   the hearings or portions thereof are closed by the Commis-

16   sion in order to protect the privacy of individuals or the

17   security of information protected by this Act.

18   (b) Each member of the Commission shall have the

19   power and authority to administer oaths or take statements

20   from witnesses under affirmation.

21   (c) A witness attending any session of the Commission

22   shall be paid the same fees and mileage paid witnesses in

23   the courts of the United States. Mileage payments shall be

24   tendered to the witness upon service of a subpena issued on

25   behalf of the Commission or any subcommittee thereof.

1   (d) Subpenas for the attendance and testimony of wit-

2 nesses or the production of written or other matter, required

3 by the Commission for the performance of its duties under

4 this Act, may be issued in accordance with rules or pro-

5 cedures established by the Commission and may be served

6 by any person designated by the Commission.

7   (e) In case of contumacy or refusal to obey a subpena

8 any district court of the United States or the United States

9 court of any territory or possession, within the jurisdiction

10 of which the person subpenaed resides or is domiciled or

11 transacts business, or has appointed an agent for the receipt

12 of service or process, upon application of the Commission,

13 shall have jurisdiction to issue to such person an order re-

14 quiring such person to appear before the Commission or a

15 subcommittee thereof, there to produce pertinent, relevant,

16 and nonprivileged evidence if so ordered, or there to give

17 testimony touching the matter under investigation; and any

18 failure to obey such order of the court may be punished as

19 contempt.

20   (f) Nothing in this Act prohibits a criminal justice

21 agency from furnishing the Commission information re-

22 quired by it in the performance of its duties under this Act.

23   SEC. 306. DIRECTOR AND STAFF.—There shall be a

24 full-time staff director for the Commission who shall be ap-

25 pointed by the President by and with the advice and consent

1   of the Senate and who shall receive compensation at the

2   rate provided for level V of the Federal Executive Salary

3   Schedule, pursuant to section 5316 of title 5. The President

4   shall consult with the Commission before submitting the

5   nomination of any person for appointment as staff director.

6   Within the limitation of appropriations and in accordance

7   with the civil service and classification laws, the Commission

8   may appoint such other personnel as it deems advisable:

9   *Provided, however,* That the number of professional per-

10 sonnel shall at no time exceed fifty. The Commission may

11 procure services as authorized by section 3109 of title 5,

12 but at rates for individuals not in excess of the daily equiv-

13 alent paid for positions at the maximum rate for GS–18 of

14 the General Schedule under section 5332 of title 5.

15   STATE INFORMATION SYSTEMS REGULATIONS

16   SEC. 307. (a) The Commission shall encourage each

17 of the States to create or designate an agency to exercise

18 statewide authority and responsibility for the enforcement

19 within the State of the provisions of the Act and any related

20 State statutes, and to issue rules, regulations, and procedures,

21 not inconsistent with this Act or regulations issued pursuant

22 to it, regulating the maintenance, use, and dissemination of

23 criminal justice information within the State.

24   (b) Where such agencies are created or designated, the

25 Commission shall rely upon such agencies to the maximum

1 extent possible for the enforcement of the Act within their

2 respective States.

3   (c) Where any provision of this Act requires any crim-

4 inal justice agency to establish procedures or issue rules or

5 regulations, it shall be sufficient for such agencies to adopt

6 or certify compliance with appropriate rules, regulations,

7 or procedures issued by any agency created or designated

8 pursuant to subsection (a) of this section or by any other

9 agency within the State authorized to issue rules, regulations,

10 or procedures of general application, provided such rules,

11 regulations or procedures are in compliance with the Act.

12   CIVIL REMEDIES

13   SEC. 308. (a) Any person aggrieved by a violation of

14 this Act or regulations promulgated thereunder shall have

15 a civil action for damages or any other appropriate remedy

16 against any person or agency responsible for such violation.

17 An action alleging a violation of section 209 shall be avail-

18 able only after any administrative remedies established pur-

19 suant to that section have been exhausted.

20   (b) The Commission on Criminal Justice Information

21 System shall have a civil action for declaratory judgments,

22 cease-and-desist orders, and such other injunctive relief as

23 may be appropriate against any criminal justice agency in

24 order to enforce the provisions of the Act.

25   (c) If a defendant in an action brought under this sec-

1   tion is an officer or employee or agency of the United States

2   the action shall be brought in an appropriate United States

3   district court. If the defendant or defendants in an action

4   brought under this section are private persons or officers or

5   employees or agencies of a State or local government, the

6   action may be brought in an appropriate United States dis-

7   trict court or in any other court of competent jurisdiction.

8   The district courts of the United States shall have jurisdiction

9   over actions described in this section without regard to the

10   amount in controversy.

11   (d) In any action brought pursuant to this Act, the

12   court may in its discretion issue an order enjoining main-

13   tenance or dissemination of information in violation of this

14   Act or correcting records of such information or may order

15   any other appropriate remedy, except that in an action

16   brought pursuant to subsection (b) the court may order

17   only declaratory or injunctive relief.

18   (e) In an action brought pursuant to subsection (a),

19   any person aggrieved by a violation of this Act shall be

20   entitled to actual and general damages but not less than

21   liquidated damages of $100 for each violation and reasonable

22   attorneys' fees and other litigation costs reasonably incurred.

23   Exemplary and punitive damages may be granted by the

24   court in appropriate cases brought pursuant to subsection

1   (a). Any person or agency responsible for violations of

2   this Act shall be jointly and severally liable to the person

3   aggrieved for damages granted pursuant to this subsection:

4   *Provided, however,* That good faith reliance by an agency

5   or an official or employee of such agency upon the assurance

6   of another agency or employee that information provided

7   the former agency or employee is maintained or dissemi-

8   nated in compliance with the provisions of this Act or any

9   regulations issued thereunder shall constitute a complete

10   defense for the former agency or employee to a civil damage

11   action brought under this section but shall not constitute

12   a defense with respect to equitable relief.

13   (f) For the purposes of this Act the United States

14   shall be deemed to have consented to suit and any agency

15   of the United States found responsible for a violation shall

16   be liable for damages, reasonable attorneys' fees, and litiga-

17   tion costs as provided in subsection (e) notwithstanding

18   any provisions of the Federal Tort Claims Act.

19   (g) A determination by a court of a violation of inter-

20   nal operating procedures adopted pursuant to this Act should

21   not be a basis for excluding evidence in a criminal case

22   unless the violation is of constitutional dimension or is other-

23   wise so serious as to call for the exercise of the supervisory

24   authority of the court.

1   CRIMINAL PENALTIES

2   SEC. 309. Any Government employee who willfully

3   disseminates, maintains, or uses information knowing such

4   dissemination, maintenance, or use to be in violation of this

5   Act shall be fined not more than $10,000.

6   AUDIT AND ACCESS TO RECORDS BY THE GENERAL

7   ACCOUNTING OFFICE

8   SEC. 310. (a) The Comptroller General of the United

9   States shall from time to time, at his own initiative or at the

10 request of either House or any committee of the House of

11 Representatives or the Senate or any joint committee of the

12 two Houses, conduct audits and reviews of the activities of

13 the Commission on Criminal Justice Information under this

14 Act. For such purpose, the Comptroller General, or any of

15 his duly authorized representatives, shall have access to and

16 the right to examine all books, accounts, records, reports,

17 files, and all other papers, things, and property of the Com-

18 mission or any Federal or State agencies audited by the

19 Commission pursuant to section 304 (a) (6) of this Act,

20 which, in the opinion of the Comptroller General, may be

21 related or pertinent to his audits and reviews of the activities

22 of the Commission. In the case of agencies audited by the

23 Commission, the Comptroller General's right of access shall

24 apply during the period of audit by the Commission and for

25 three years thereafter.

1   (b) Notwithstanding any other provision of this Act,

2   the Comptroller General's right of access to books, accounts,

3   records, reports, and files pursuant to and for the purposes

4   specified in subsection (a) shall include any information

5   covered by this Act. However, no official or employee of

6   the General Accounting Office shall disclose to any person

7   or source outside of the General Accounting Office any such

8   information in a manner or form which identifies directly or

9   indirectly any individual who is the subject of such

10   information.

11   PRECEDENCE OF STATE LAWS

12   SEC. 311. Any State law or regulation which places

13   greater restrictions upon the maintenance, use, or dissemina-

14   tion of criminal justice information, criminal justice intelli-

15   gence information, or criminal justice investigative informa-

16   tion or which affords to any individuals, whether juveniles or

17   adults, rights of privacy or other protections greater than

18   those set forth in this Act shall take precedence over this Act

19   or regulations issued pursuant to this Act with respect to any

20   maintenance, use, or dissemination of information within

21   that State.

22   APPROPRIATIONS AUTHORIZED

23   SEC. 312. For the purpose of carrying out the provi-

24   sions of this Act, there are authorized to be appropriated

25   such sums as the Congress deems necessary.

1   SEVERABILITY

2   SEC. 313. If any provision of this Act or the application

3 thereof to any person or circumstance is held invalid, the

4 remainder of the Act and the application of the provision to

5 other persons not similarly situated or to other circumstances

6 shall not be affected thereby.

7   REPEALERS

8   SEC. 314. The following provisions of law are hereby

9 repealed:

10   (a) the second paragraph under the headings en-

11   titled "Federal Bureau of Investigation; Salaries and

12   Expenses" contained in the Department of Justice Ap-

13   propriations Act, 1973; and

14   (b) any of the provisions of the Privacy Act of

15   1974 (Public Law 93–579, 88 Stat. 1896), applicable

16   to information covered by this Act.

17   EFFECTIVE DATE

18   SEC. 315. The provisions of sections 301 through 307

19 and of sections 310 and 312 of this Act shall take effect upon

20 the date of enactment and members, officers, and employees

21 of the Commission on Criminal Justice Information may

22 be appointed and take office at any time after that date.

23 Provisions of the remainder of the Act shall take effect one

1   year after the date of enactment: *Provided, however,* That

2   the Commission may, in accordance with section 304 (b),

3   delay the effective date of any provision for up to one addi-

4   tional year.

Appendix B

Federal Privacy and Security Regulations for Criminal History Information

Title 28—Judicial Administration

CHAPTER I—DEPARTMENT OF JUSTICE

PART 20—CRIMINAL JUSTICE INFORMATION SYSTEMS

On May 20, 1975, regulations were published in the FEDERAL REGISTER (40 FR 22114) relating to the collection, storage, and dissemination of criminal history record information. Amendments to these regulations were proposed October 24, 1975 (40 FR 49789) based upon a re-evaluation of, the dedication requirement contained in § 20.21(f). Hearings on the proposed changes were held November 17, 18, 21 and December 4, 1975. In addition, hearings were held to consider changes to the dissemination provisions of the regulations (40 FR 52846). These hearings were held December 11, 12 and 15, 1975, to consider comments from interested parties on the limitations placed on dissemination of criminal history record information to non-criminal justice agencies. The purpose of the hearings was to determine whether the regulations, as they were drafted, appropriately made the balance between the public's right to know such information with the individual's right of privacy.

As a result of these hearings modifications to the regulations have now been made to better draw this balance. The regulations are based upon section 524 (b) of the Crime Control Act of 1973 which provides in relevant part:

"All criminal history information collected, stored or disseminated through support under this title shall contain, to the maximum extent feasible, disposition as well as arrest data where arrest data is included therein. The collection, storage, and dissemination of such information shall take place under procedures reasonably designed to insure that all such information is kept current therein; the Administration shall assure that the security and privacy of all information is adequately provided for and that information shall only be used for law enforcement and criminal justice and other lawful purposes. In addition, an individual who believes that criminal history information concerning him contained in an automated system is inaccurate, incomplete, or maintained in violation of this title, shall, upon satisfactory verification of his identity, be entitled to review such information and to obtain a copy of it for the purpose of challenge or correction."

The regulations, as now amended, provide that conviction data may be disseminated without limitation; that criminal history record information relating to the offense for which an individual is currently within the criminal justice system may be disseminated without limitations. Insofar as nonconviction record information is concerned (nonconviction data is defined in § 20.20(k)), the regulations require that after December 31, 1977, most non-criminal justice access would require authorization pursuant to a statute, ordinance, executive order or court rule, decision or order. The regulations no longer require express authority, that is specific language in the authorizing statute or order requiring access to such information, but only that such dissemination is pursuant to and can be construed from the general requirement in the statute or order. Such statutes include State public record laws which have been interpreted by a State to require that criminal history record information, including nonconviction information, be made available to the public. Determinations as to the purposes for which dissemination of criminal history record information is authorized by State law, executive order, local ordinance, court rule, decision or order will be made by the appropriate State or local officials. The deadline of December 31, 1977, will permit States to obtain the authority, as they believe necessary, to disseminate nonconviction data.

The regulations, as now amended, remove the prohibition that criminal history record information in court records of public judicial proceedings can only be accessed on a chronological basis. § 20.20(b)(3) deletes the words "compiled chronologically". Therefore, court records of public judicial proceedings whether accessed on a chronological basis or on an alphabetical basis are not covered by the regulations.

In addition, the regulations would not prohibit the dissemination of criminal history record information for purposes of international travel (issuance of visas and granting of citizenship). The commentary on selected portions of the regulations have been amended to conform to the changes.

Pursuant to the authority vested in the Law Enforcement Assistance Administration by sections 501 and 524 of the Omnibus Crime Control and Safe Streets Act of 1968, as amended by the Crime Control Act of 1973, Pub. L. 93–83, 87 Stat. 197 (42 U.S.C. 3701 *et seq.*) (Aug. 6, 1973), these amendments to Chapter I of Title 28 of the Code of Federal Regulations are hereby adopted to become final on April 19, 1976. These amendments only amend subparts A and B. Subpart C remains the same.

AUTHORITY: Pub. L. 93–83, 87 Stat. 197 (42 USC 3701, *et seq;* 28 USC 534), Pub. L. 92–544, 86 Stat. 1115.

Subpart A—General Provisions

§ 20.1   Purpose.

It is the purpose of these regulations to assure that criminal history record information wherever it appears is collected, stored, and disseminated in a manner to insure the completeness, integrity, accuracy and security of such information and to protect individual privacy.

§ 20.2   Authority.

These regulations are issued pursuant to sections 501 and 524(b) of the Omnibus Crime Control and Safe Streets Act of 1968, as amended by the Crime Control Act of 1973, Pub. L. 93–83, 87 Stat. 197, 42 USC 3701, *et seq.* (Act), 28 USC 534, and Pub. L. 92–544, 86 Stat. 1115.

§ 20.3   Definitions.

As used in these regulations:

(a) "Criminal history record information system" means a system including the equipment, facilities, procedures, agreements, and organizations thereof, for the collection, processing, preservation or dissemination of criminal history record information.

(b) "Criminal history record information" means information collected by criminal justice agencies on individuals consisting of identifiable descriptions and notations of arrests, detentions, indictments, informations, or other formal criminal charges, and any disposition arising therefrom, sentencing, correctional supervision, and release. The term does not include identification information such as fingerprint records to the extent that such information does not indicate involvement of the individual in the criminal justice system.

(c) "Criminal justice agency" means:

(1) courts; (2) a government agency or any subunit thereof which performs the administration of criminal justice pursuant to a statute or executive order, and which allocates a substantial part of its annual budget to the administration of criminal justice.

(d) The "administration of criminal justice" means performance of any of the following activities: detection, apprehension, detention, pretrial release, post-trial release, prosecution, adjudication, correctional supervision, or rehabilitation of accused persons or criminal offenders. The administration of criminal justice shall include criminal identification activities and the collection, storage, and dissemination of criminal history record information.

(e) "Disposition" means information disclosing that criminal proceedings have been concluded, including information disclosing that the police have elected not to refer a matter to a prosecutor or that a prosecutor has elected not to commence criminal proceedings and also disclosing the nature of the termination in the proceedings; or information disclosing that proceedings have been indefinitely postponed and also disclosing the reason for such postponement. Dispositions shall include, but not be limited to, acquittal, acquittal by reason of insanity, acquittal by reason of mental incompetence, case continued without finding, charge dismissed, charge dismissed due to insanity, charge dismissed due to mental incompetency, charge still pending due to insanity, charge still pending due to mental incompetence, guilty plea, nolle prosequi, no paper, nolo contendere plea, convicted, youthful offender determination, deceased, deferred disposition, dismissed—civil a c t i o n, found insane, found mentally incompetent, pardoned, probation before conviction, sentence commuted, adjudication withheld, mistrial—defendant discharged, executive clemency, placed on probation, paroled, or released from correctional supervision.

(f) "Statute" means an Act of Congress or State legislature or a provision of the Constitution of the United States or of a State.

(g) "State" means any State of the United States, the District of Columbia, the Commonwealth of Puerto Rico, and any territory or possession of the United States.

(h) An "executive order" means an order of the President of the United States or the Chief Executive of a State which has the force of law and which is published in a manner permitting regular public access thereto.

(i) "Act" means the Omnibus Crime Control and Safe Streets Act, 42 USC 3701, et seq., as amended.

(j) "Department of Justice criminal history record information system" means the Identification Division and the Computerized Criminal History File systems operated by the Federal Bureau of Investigation.

(k) "Nonconviction data" means arrest information without disposition if an interval of one year has elapsed from the date of arrest and no active prosecution of the charge is pending; or information disclosing that the police have elected not to refer a matter to a prosecutor, or that a prosecutor has elected not to commence criminal proceedings, or that proceedings have been indefinitely postponed, as well as all acquittals and all dismissals.

(l) "Direct access" means having the authority to access the criminal history record data base, whether by manual or automated methods.

Subpart B—State and Local Criminal History Record Information Systems

§ 20.20 Applicability.

(a) The regulations in this subpart apply to all State and local agencies and individuals collecting, storing, or disseminating criminal history record information processed by manual or automated operations where such collection, storage, or dissemination has been funded in whole or in part with funds made available by the Law Enforcement Assistance Administration subsequent to July 1, 1973, pursuant to Title I of the Act. Use of information obtained from the FBI Identification Division or the FBI/NCIC system shall also be subject to limitations contained in Subpart C.

(b) The regulations in this subpart shall not apply to criminal history record information contained in: (1) posters, announcements, or lists for identifying or apprehending fugitives or wanted persons; (2) original records of entry such as police blotters maintained by criminal justice agencies, compiled chronologically and required by law or long standing custom to be made public, if such records are organized on a chronological basis; (3) court records of public judicial proceedings; (4) published court or administrative opinions or public judicial, administrative or legislative proceedings; (5) records of traffic offenses maintained by State departments of transportation, motor vehicles or the equivalent thereof for the purpose of regulating the issuance, suspension, revocation, or renewal of driver's, pilot's or other operators' licenses; (6) announcements of executive clemency.

(c) Nothing in these regulations prevents a criminal justice agency from disclosing to the public criminal history record information related to the offense for which an individual is currently within the criminal justice system. Nor is a criminal justice agency prohibited from confirming prior criminal history record information to members of the news media or any other person, upon specific inquiry as to whether a named individual was arrested, detained, indicted, or whether an information or other formal charge was filed, on a specified date, if the arrest record information or criminal record information disclosed is based on data excluded by paragraph (b) of this section. The regulations do not prohibit the dissemination of criminal history record information for purposes of international travel, such as issuing visas and granting of citizenship.

§ 20.21   Preparation and submission of a Criminal History Record Information Plan.

A plan shall be submitted to LEAA by each State on March 16, 1976, to set forth all operational procedures, except those portions relating to dissemination and security. A supplemental plan covering these portions shall be submitted no later than 90 days after promulgation of these amended regulations. The plan shall set forth operational procedures to—

(a) *Completeness and accuracy.* Insure that criminal history record information is complete and accurate.

(1) Complete records should be maintained at a central State repository. To be complete, a record maintained at a central State repository which contains information that an individual has been arrested, and which is available for dissemination, must contain information of any dispositions occurring within the State within 90 days after the disposition has occurred. The above shall apply to all arrests occurring subsequent to the effective date of these regulations. Procedures shall be established for criminal justice agencies to query the central repository prior to dissemination of any criminal history record information to assure that the most up-to-date disposition data is being used. Inquiries of a central State repository shall be made prior to any dissemination except in those cases where time is of the essence and the repository is technically incapable of responding within the necessary time period.

(2) To be accurate means that no record containing criminal history record information shall contain erroneous information. To accomplish this end, criminal justice agencies shall institute a process of data collection, entry, storage, and systematic audit that will minimize the possibility of recording and storing inaccurate information and upon finding inaccurate information of a material nature, shall notify all criminal justice agencies known to have received such information.

(b) *Limitations on dissemination.* By December 31, 1977, insure that dissemination of nonconviction data has been limited, whether directly or through any intermediary only to:

(1) Criminal justice agencies, for purposes of the administration of criminal justice and criminal justice agency employment;

(2) Individuals and agencies for any purpose authorized by statute, ordinance, executive order, or court rule, decision, or order, as construed by appropriate State or local officials or agencies;

(3) Individuals and agencies pursuant to a specific agreement with a criminal justice agency to provide services required for the administration of criminal justice pursuant to that agreement. The agreement shall specifically authorize access to data, limit the use of data to purposes for which given, insure the security and confidentiality of the data consistent with these regulations, and provide sanctions for violation thereof;

(4) Individuals and agencies for the express purpose of research, evaluative, or statistical activities pursuant to an agreement with a criminal justice agency. The agreement shall specifically authorize access to data, limit the use of data to research, evaluative, or statistical purposes, insure the confidentiality and security of the data consistent with these regulations and with section 524(a) of the Act and any regulations implementing section 524(a), and provide sanctions for the violation thereof.

These dissemination limitations do not apply to conviction data.

(c) *General policies on use and dissemination.* (1) Use of criminal history record information disseminated to noncriminal justice agencies shall be limited to the purpose for which it was given.

(2) No agency or individual shall confirm the existence or nonexistence of criminal history record information to any person or agency that would not be eligible to receive the information itself.

(3) Subsection (b) does not mandate dissemination of criminal history record information to any agency or individual. States and local governments will deter-

mine the purposes for which dissemination of criminal history record information is authorized by State law, executive order, local ordinance, court rule, decision or order.

(d) *Juvenile records.* Insure that dissemination of records concerning proceedings relating to the adjudication of a juvenile as delinquent or in need of supervision (or the equivalent) to non-criminal justice agencies is prohibited, unless a statute, court order, rule or court decision specifically authorizes dissemination of juvenile records, except to the same extent as criminal history records may be disseminated as provided in § 20.21(b) (3) and (4).

(e) *Audit.* Insure that annual audits of a representative sample of State and local criminal justice agencies chosen on a random basis shall be conducted by the State to verify adherence to these regulations and that appropriate records shall be retained to facilitate such audits. Such records shall include, but are not limited to, the names of all persons or agencies to whom information is disseminated and the date upon which such information is disseminated. The reporting of a criminal justice transaction to a State, local or Federal repository is not a dissemination of information.

(f) *Security.* Wherever criminal history record information is collected, stored, or disseminated, each State shall insure that the following requirements are satisfied by security standards established by State legislation, or in the absence of such legislation, by regulations approved or issued by the Governor of the State.

(1) Where computerized data processing is employed, effective and technologically advanced software and hardware designs are instituted to prevent unauthorized access to such information.

(2) Access to criminal history record information system facilities, systems operating environments, data file contents whether while in use or when stored in a media library, and system documentation is restricted to authorized organizations and personnel.

(3)(A) Computer operations, whether dedicated or shared, which support criminal justice information systems, operate in accordance with procedures developed or approved by the participating criminal justice agencies that assure that:

(i) Criminal history record information is stored by the computer in such manner that it cannot be modified, destroyed, accessed, changed, purged, or overlaid in any fashion by non-criminal justice terminals.

(ii) Operation programs are used that will prohibit inquiry, record updates, or destruction of records, from any terminal other than criminal justice system terminals which are so designated.

(iii) The destruction of records is limited to designated terminals under the direct control of the criminal justice agency responsible for creating or storing the criminal history record information.

(iv) Operational programs are used to detect and store for the output of designated criminal justice agency employees all unauthorized attempts to penetrate any criminal history record information system, program or file.

(v) The programs specified in (ii) and (iv) of this subsection are known only to criminal justice agency employees responsible for criminal history record information system control or individuals and agencies pursuant to a specific agreement with the criminal justice agency to provide such programs and the program(s) are kept continuously under maximum security conditions.

(vi) Procedures are instituted to assure that an individual or agency authorized direct access is responsible for *A* the physical security of criminal history record information under its control or in its custody and *B* the protection of such information from unauthorized access, disclosure or dissemination.

(vii) Procedures are instituted to protect any central repository of criminal history record information from unauthorized access, theft, sabotage, fire, flood, wind, or other natural or manmade disasters.

(B) A criminal justice agency shall have the right to audit, monitor and inspect procedures established above.

(4) The criminal justice agency will:

(A) Screen and have the right to reject for employment, based on good cause, all personnel to be authorized to have direct access to criminal history record information.

(B) Have the right to initiate or cause to be initiated administrative action leading to the transfer or removal of personnel authorized to have direct access to such information where such personnel violate the provisions of these regulations or other security requirements established for the collection, storage, or dissemination of criminal history record information.

(C) Institute procedures, where computer processing is not utilized, to assure that an individual or agency authorized direct access is responsible for (i) the physical security of criminal history record information under its control or in its custody and (ii) the protection of such information from unauthorized access, disclosure, or dissemination.

(D) Institute procedures, where computer processing is not utilized, to protect any central repository of criminal history record information from unauthorized access, theft, sabotage, fire, flood, wind, or other natural or man-made disasters.

(E) Provide that direct access to criminal history record information shall be available only to authorized officers or employees of a criminal justice agency and, as necessary, other authorized personnel essential to the proper operation of the criminal history record information system.

(5) Each employee working with or having access to criminal history record information shall be made familiar with the substance and intent of these regulations.

(g) *Access and review.* Insure the individual's right to access and review of criminal history information for purposes of accuracy and completeness by instituting procedures so that—

(1) Any individual shall, upon satisfactory verification of his identity, be entitled to review without undue burden to either the criminal justice agency or the individual, any criminal history record information maintained about the individual and obtain a copy thereof when necessary for the purpose of challenge or correction;

(2) Administrative review and necessary correction of any claim by the individual to whom the information relates that the information is inaccurate or incomplete is provided;

(3) The State shall establish and implement procedures for administrative appeal where a criminal justice agency refuses to correct challenged information to the satisfaction of the individual to whom the information relates;

(4) Upon request, an individual whose record has been corrected shall be given the names of all non-criminal justice agencies to whom the data has been given;

(5) The correcting agency shall notify all criminal justice recipients of corrected information; and

(6) The individual's right to access and review of criminal history record information shall not extend to data contained in intelligence, investigatory, or other related files and shall not be construed to include any other informa-

tion than that defined by § 20.3(b).

§ 20.22   Certification of Compliance.

(a) Each State to which these regulations are applicable shall with the submission of its plan provide a certification that to the maximum extent feasible action has been taken to comply with the procedures set forth in the plan. Maximum extent feasible, in this subsection, means actions which can be taken to comply with the procedures set forth in the plan that do not require additional legislative authority or involve unreasonable cost or do not exceed existing technical ability.

(b) The certification shall include—

(1) An outline of the action which has been instituted. At a minimum, the requirements of access and review under § 20.21(g) must be completely operational;

(2) A description of any legislation or executive order, or attempts to obtain such authority that has been instituted to comply with these regulations;

(3) A description of the steps taken to overcome any fiscal, technical, and administrative barriers to the development of complete and accurate criminal history record information;

(4) A description of existing system capability and steps being taken to upgrade such capability to meet the requirements of these regulations; and

(5) A listing setting forth categories of non-criminal justice dissemination. See § 20.21(b).

§ 20.23   Documentation: Approval by LEAA.

Within 90 days of the receipt of the plan, LEAA shall approve or disapprove the adequacy of the provisions of the plan and certification. Evaluation of the plan by LEAA will be based upon whether the procedures set forth will accomplish the required objectives. The evaluation of the certification(s) will be based upon whether a good faith effort has been shown to initiate and/or further compliance with the plan and regulations. All procedures in the approved plan must be fully operational and implemented by December 31, 1977. A final certification shall be submitted in December 1977.

§ 20.24   State laws on privacy and security.

Where a State originating criminal history record information provides for sealing or purging thereof, nothing in these regulations shall be construed to prevent any other State receiving such information, upon notification, from complying with the originating State's sealing or purging requirements.

§ 20.25 Penalties.

Any agency or individual violating subpart B of these regulations shall be subject to a fine not to exceed $10,000. In addition, LEAA may initiate fund cut-off procedures against recipients of LEAA assistance.

RICHARD W. VELDE,
Administrator.

APPENDIX—COMMENTARY ON SELECTED SECTIONS OF THE REGULATIONS ON CRIMINAL HISTORY RECORD INFORMATION SYSTEMS

Subpart A—§ 20.3(b). The definition of criminal history record information is intended to include the basic offender-based transaction statistics/computerized criminal history (OBTS/CCH) data elements. If notations of an arrest, disposition, or other formal criminal justice transactions occur in records other than the traditional "rap sheet" such as arrest reports, any criminal history record information contained in such reports comes under the definition of this subsection.

The definition, however, does not extend to other information contained in criminal justice agency reports. Intelligence or investigative information (e.g., suspected criminal activity, associates, hangouts, financial information, ownership of property and vehicles) is not included in the definition of criminal history information.

§ 20.3(c). The definitions of criminal justice agency and administration of criminal justice of 20.3(c) must be considered together. Included as criminal justice agencies would be traditional police, courts, and corrections agencies as well as subunits of non-criminal justice agencies performing a function of the administration of criminal justice pursuant to Federal or State statute or executive order. The above subunits of non-criminal justice agencies would include for example, the Office of Investigation of the U.S. Department of Agriculture which has as its principal function the collection of evidence for criminal prosecutions of fraud. Also included under the definition of criminal justice agency are umbrella-type administrative agencies supplying criminal history information services such as New York's Division of Criminal Justice Services.

§ 20.3(e). Disposition is a key concept in section 524(b) of the Act and in 20.21(a)(1) and 20.21(b). It, therefore, is defined in some detail. The specific dispositions listed in this subsection are examples only and are not to be construed as excluding other unspecified transactions concluding criminal proceedings within a particular agency.

§ 20.3(k). The different kinds of acquittals and dismissals as delineated in 20.3(e) are all considered examples of nonconviction data.

Subpart B—§ 20.20(a). These regulations apply to criminal justice agencies receiving funds under the Omnibus Crime Control and Safe Streets Act for manual or automated systems subsequent to July 1, 1973. In the hearings on the regulations, a number of those testifying challenged LEAA's authority to promulgate regulations for manual systems by contending that section 524(b) of the Act governs criminal history information contained in automated systems.

The intent of section 524(b), however, would be subverted by only regulating automated systems. Any agency that wished to circumvent the regulations would be able to create duplicate manual files for purposes contrary to the letter and spirit of the regulations.

Regulation of manual systems, therefore, is authorized by section 524(b) when coupled with section 501 of the Act which authorizes the Administration to establish rules and regulations "necessary to the exercise of its functions * * *."

The Act clearly applies to all criminal history record information collected, stored, or disseminated with LEAA support subsequent to July 1, 1973.

Limitations as contained in Subpart C also apply to information obtained from the FBI Identification Division or the FBI/NCIC System.

§ 20.20 (b) and (c). Section 20.20 (b) and (c) exempts from regulations certain types of records vital to the apprehension of fugitives, freedom of the press, and the public's right to know. Court records of public judicial proceedings are also exempt from the provisions of the regulations.

Section 20.20(b)(2) attempts to deal with the problem of computerized police blotters. In some local jurisdictions, it is apparently possible for private individuals and/or newsmen upon submission of a specific name to obtain through a computer search of the blotter a history of a person's arrests. Such files create a partial criminal history data bank potentially damaging to individual privacy, especially since they do not contain final dispositions. By requiring that such records be accessed solely on a chronological basis, the regulations limit inquiries to specific time periods and discourage general fishing expeditions into a person's private life.

Subsection 20.20(c) recognizes that announcements of ongoing developments in the criminal justice process should not be precluded from public disclosure. Thus, annnoucements of arrest, convictions, new developments in the course of an investigation may be made. It is also permissible for a criminal justice agency to confirm certain matters of public record information upon specific inquiry. Thus, if a question is raised: "Was X arrested by your agency on January 3, 1975" and this can be confirmed or denied by looking at one of the records enumerated in subsection (b) above, then the criminal justice agency may respond to the inquiry. Conviction data as stated in 20.21(b) may be disseminated without limitation.

§ 20.21. The regulations deliberately refrain from specifying who within a State should be responsible for preparing the plan. This specific determination should be made by the Governor. The State has 90 days from the publication of these revised regulations to submit the portion of the plan covering 20.21(b) and 20.21(f).

§ 20.21(a)(1). Section 524(b) of the Act requires that LEAA insure criminal history information be current and that, to the maximum extent feasible, it contain disposition as well as current data.

It is, however, economically and administratively impractical to maintain complete criminal histories at the local level. Arrangements for local police departments to keep track of dispositions by agencies outside of the local jurisdictions generally do not exist. It would, moreover, be bad public policy to encourage such arrangements since it would result in an expensive duplication of files.

The alternatives to locally kept criminal histories are records maintained by a central State repository. A central State repository is a State agency having the function pursuant to a statute or executive order of maintaining comprehensive statewide criminal history record information files. Ultimately, through automatic data processing the State level will have the capability to handle all requests for in-State criminal history information.

Section 20.20(a)(1) is written with a centralized State criminal history repository in mind. The first sentence of the subsection states that complete records should be retained at a central State repository. The word "should" is permissive; it suggests but does not mandate a central State repository.

The regulations do require that States establish procedures for State and local criminal justice agencies to query central State repositories wherever they exist. Such procedures are intended to insure that the most current criminal justice information is used.

As a minimum, criminal justice agencies subject to these regulations must make inquiries of central State repositories whenever the repository is capable of meeting the user's request within a reasonable time. Presently, comprehensive records of an individual's transactions within a State are maintained in manual files at the State level, if at all. It is probably unrealistic to expect manual systems to be able immediately to meet many rapid-access needs of police and prosecutors. On the other hand, queries of the State central repository for most non-criminal justice purposes probably can and should be made prior to dissemination of criminal history record information.

§ 20.21(b). The limitations on dissemination in this subsection are essential to fulfill the mandate of section 524(b) of the Act which requires the Administration to assure that the "privacy of all information is adequately provided for and that information shall only be used for law enforcement and criminal justice and other lawful purposes." The categories for dissemination established in this section reflect suggestions by hearing witnesses and respondents submitting written commentary.

The regulations distinguish between conviction and nonconviction information insofar as dissemination is concerned. Conviction information is currently made available without limitation in many jurisdictions. Under these regulations, conviction data and pending charges could continue to be disseminated routinely. No statute, ordinance, executive order, or court rule is necessary in order to authorize dissemination of conviction data. However, nothing in the regulations shall be construed to negate a State law limiting such dissemination. After December 31, 1977, dissemination of nonconviction data would be allowed, if authorized by a statute, ordinance, executive order, or court rule, decision, or order. The December 31, 1977, deadline allows the States time to review and determine the kinds of dissemination for non-criminal justice purposes to be authorized. When a State enacts comprehensive legislation in this area, such legislation will govern dissemination by local jurisdictions within the State. It is possible for a public record law which has been construed by the State to authorize access to the public of all State records, including criminal history record information, to be considered as statutory authority under this subsection. Federal legislation and executive orders can also authorize dissemination and would be relevant authority.

For example, Civil Service suitability investigations are conducted under Executive Order 10450. This is the authority for most investigations conducted by the Commission. Section 3(a) of 10450 prescribes the minimum scope of investigation and requires a check of FBI fingerprint files and written inquiries to appropriate law enforcement agencies.

§ 20.21(b)(3). This subsection would permit private agencies such as the Vera Institute to receive criminal histories where they perform a necessary administration of justice function such as pretrial release. Private consulting firms which commonly assist criminal justice agencies in information systems development would also be included here.

§ 20.21(b)(4). Under this subsection, any good faith researchers including private individuals would be permitted to use criminal history record information for research purposes. As with the agencies designated in § 20.21(b)(3) researchers would be bound by an agreement with the disseminating criminal justice agency and would, of course, be subject to the sanctions of the Act.

The drafters of the regulations expressly rejected a suggestion which would have limited access for research purposes to certified research organizations. Specifically "certification" criteria would have been extremely difficult to draft and would have inevitably led to unnecessary restrictions on legitimate research.

Section 524(a) of the Act which forms part of the requirements of this section states:

"Except as provided by Federal law other than this title, no officer or employee of the Federal Government, nor any recipient of assistance under the provisions of this title shall use or reveal any research or statistical information furnished under this title by any person and identifiable to any specific private person for any purpose other than the purpose for which it was obtained in accordance with this title. Copies of such information shall be immune from legal process, and shall not, without the consent of the person furnishing such information, be admitted as evidence or used for any purpose in any action, suit, or other judicial or administrative proceedings."

LEAA anticipates issuing regulations pursuant to Section 524(a) as soon as possible.

§ 20.21(c)(2). Presently some employers are circumventing State and local dissemination restrictions by requesting applicants to obtain an official certification of no criminal record. An employer's request under the above circumstances gives the applicant the unenviable choice of invasion of his privacy or loss of possible job opportunities. Under this subsection routine certifications of no record would no longer be permitted. In extraordinary circumstances, however, an individual could obtain a court order permitting such a certification.

§ 20.21(c)(3). The language of this subsection leaves to the States the question of who among the agencies and individuals listed in § 20.21(b) shall actually receive criminal records. Under these regulations a State could place a total ban on dissemination if it so wished. The State could, on the other hand, enact laws authorizing any member of the private sector to have access to nonconviction data.

§ 20.21(d). Non-criminal justice agencies will not be able to receive records of juveniles unless the language of a statute or court order, rule, or court decision specifies that juvenile records shall be available for dissemination. Perhaps the most controversial part of this subsection is that it denies access to records of juveniles by Federal agencies conducting background investigations for eligibility to classified information under existing legal authority.

§ 20.21(e). Since it would be too costly to audit each criminal justice agency in most States (Wisconsin, for example, has 1075 criminal justice agencies) random audits of a "representative sample" of agencies are the next best alternative. The term "representative sample" is used to insure that audits do not simply focus on certain types of agencies. Although this subsection requires that there be records kept with the names of all persons or agencies to whom information is disseminated, criminal justice agencies are not required to maintain dissemination logs for "no record" responses.

§ 20.21(f). Requirements are set forth which the States must meet in order to assure that criminal history record information is adequately protected. Automated systems may operate in shared environments and the regulations require certain minimum assurances.

§ 20.21(g)(1). A "challenge" under this section is an oral or written contention by an individual that his record is inaccurate or incomplete; it would require him to give a correct version of his record and explain why he believes his version to be correct. While an individual should have access to his record for review, a copy of the record should ordinarily only be given when it is clearly established that it is necessary for the purpose of challenge.

The drafters of the subsection expressly rejected a suggestion that would have called for a satisfactory verification of identity by fingerprint comparison. It was felt that States ought to be free to determine other means of identity verification.

§ 20.21(g)(5). Not every agency will have done this in the past, but henceforth adequate records including those required under 20.21(e) must be kept so that notification can be made.

§ 20.21(g)(6). This section emphasizes that the right to access and review extends only to criminal history record information and does not include other information such as intelligence or treatment data.

§ 20.22(a). The purpose for the certification requirement is to indicate the extent of compliance with these regulations. The term "maximum extent feasible" acknowledges that there are some areas such as the completeness requirement which create complex legislative and financial problems.

NOTE: In preparing the plans required by these regulations, States should look for guidance to the following documents: National Advisory Commission on Criminal Justice Standards and Goals, Report on the Criminal Justice System; Project SEARCH: Security and Privacy Considerations in Criminal History Information Systems, Technical Reports No. 2 and No. 13; Project SEARCH: A Model State Act for Criminal Offender Record Information, Technical Memorandum No. 3; and Project SEARCH: Model Administrative Regulations for Criminal Offender Record Information, Technical Memorandum No. 4.

[FR Doc.76-7889 Filed 3-18-76;8:45 am]

[4410-01]

Title 28—Judicial Administration

CHAPTER I—DEPARTMENT OF JUSTICE

PART 20—CRIMINAL JUSTICE INFORMATION SYSTEMS

Extension of Implementation Date

AGENCY: Department of Justice, Law Enforcement Assistance Administration (LEAA).

ACTION: Amendment to regulation.

SUMMARY: The amendment extends the date for implementation of the LEAA regulations governing Criminal History Record Information Systems from December 31, 1977, to March 1, 1978.

An LEAA examination of the ability of the States to meet the December 31 deadline has indicated that, with minimal exceptions, compliance with all or part of the regulations by the December deadline would be totally beyond the capability of many States. Further deadline extensions will be given only upon a finding that States have made a good faith effort to implement the regulations and have implemented the regulations to the maximum extent feasible.

EFFECTIVE DATE: This amendment is effective December 6, 1977.

FOR FURTHER INFORMATION CONTACT:

Thomas J. Madden, General Counsel, LEAA, 202-376-3691.

SUPPLEMENTARY INFORMATION: The regulations governing privacy and security of criminal history information systems require that States implement procedures by December 31, 1977, to insure complete and accurate records, place limitations on dissemination, require audit, and system security. The regulations also required that States prepare, and submit to LEAA, a State Privacy and Security Plan describing the operational procedures to be developed in each of these five areas.

An LEAA examination of the ability of the States to meet the December 31 deadline has indicated that, with minimal exceptions, compliance with all or part of the regulations by the December deadline would be totally beyond the capability of many States. Essentially, LEAA has determined that only those States which had been involved in criminal justice systems and/or privacy and security activity for a substantial period of time could come into significant compliance.

There are a number of reasons why full compliance cannot be achieved. Budgetary limitations at both the Federal and State levels, for example, have precluded expenditures necessary for hardware and personnel. LEAA also found that the time required for development of statewide coordination and cooperation among components of the criminal justice community exceeded initial estimates in the regulations. In addition, there were serious difficulties in many States in establishing a statewide system for reporting of court dispositions to a central repository. Furthermore, the enactment of legislation considered necessary by the States for implementation of dissemination and disposition reporting requirements has required extensive policy development and coordination and necessary legislation was not passed. This problem was compounded in those States with biennial legislative sessions that were completed in 1976. These problems have impacted on the ability of States to comply with security, audit, dissemination, and completeness and accuracy requirements.

Therefore, LEAA is extending the deadline for compliance until March 1, 1978, in order to provide an opportunity for submission of State requests for further extensions. Further extensions will be granted only upon a showing that a good faith effort has been made to implement the regulations and progress has been undertaken to the maximum extent feasible. Revised schedules for implementation will be established for individual States consistent with LEAA standards.

Recognizing that certain State compliance procedures to be effective must have explicit legislative foundation, dates for full implementation will be keyed to the legislative schedules in each State. Initial conduct of audits will be required thereafter as well.

No specific time deadline is being imposed upon complete and accurate records. To the maximum extent feasible, it is expected that all States will continuously work toward the goals set out in § 20.21(a) without undue delay.

Individual access, challenge and review requirements (§ 20.21(g)) and the ability to provide administrative security (§ 20.-21(f)) should impose no significant technical or financial hardship on States; therefore, no extension will be given. By July 31, 1978, each State will be required to submit a certificate of compliance in these two areas. Administrative security refers to administrative actions rather than physical hardware to provide system security.

LEAA determined it would be more appropriate to have individual States set their own time periods for compliance within designated outer limits rather than provide a fixed two- or three-year extension for all requirements applicable to all States regardless of prior activity or level of capability. This allows for differing State capabilities and the variations between States' legislative schedules.

Not all States may need to request an extension. However, where a State does request an extension, the State should submit a brief and succinct description of activities which have been undertaken to comply with each of the five major requirements of the regulations and of the extent to which compliance is in place at this time. The State should also submit a description of specific administrative, legislative, budgetary, or technical factors which have precluded complete implementation. The request should be accompanied by a projected schedule of full compliance and a justification for the selected dates consistent with the timetables set out in the amendment. Such documentation must be received by March 1, 1978. LEAA will approve or disapprove the request within 90 days. In addition, an amendment is being made to § 20.21(a)(1) so that where a local criminal justice agency has the most up-to-date criminal history record, it need not query the central repository before disseminating the record.

This amendment does not revise in any way the rules under Part C, the criminal history record information in the FBI's NCIC and Identification Divisions.

In view of the immediacy of the time frame which would, without this amendment, require compliance by December 31, 1977, and the necessity to allow States a sufficient period of time to submit a revised implementation schedule, LEAA has determined that notice and public procedure for comment are impracticable. Furthermore, since this amendment relieves a restriction by extending the date upon which implementation must occur, LEAA has determined that good cause exists for making the rule effective immediately.

Accordingly, pursuant to the authority vested in the Law Enforcement Assistance Administration by Sections 501 and 524 of the Omnibus Crime Control and Safe Streets Act of 1968, 42 U.S.C. § 3701, et seq., as amended (Pub. L. 90–351, as amended by Pub. L. 93–83, Pub. L. 94–

415, Pub. L. 94–430, Pub. L. 94–503, and Pub. L. 95–115), these amendments to Chapter I of Title 28 of the Code of Federal Regulations are hereby adopted:

§ 20.21   [Amended]

In § 20.21(a)(1), the fourth sentence is revised to read as follows: "Procedures shall be established for criminal justice agencies to query the central repository prior to dissemination of any criminal history record information unless it can be assured that the most up-to-date disposition data is being used."

b. In § 20.21(b), delete the words "By December 31, 1977" and begin the sentence with the word "Insure".

§ 20.23   [Amended]

a. In § 20.23, delete references to "December 31, 1977" in last two sentences and substitute "March 1, 1978" in each sentence.

b. At the end of § 20.23, add the following:

§ 20.23   Documentation: Approval by LEAA.

* * * Where a State finds it is unable to provide final certification that all required procedures as set forth in § 20.21 will be operational by March 1, 1978, a further extension of the deadline will be granted by LEAA upon a showing that the State has made a good faith effort to implement these regulations to the maximum extent feasible. Documentation justifying the request for the extension including a proposed timetable for full compliance must be submitted to LEAA by March 1, 1978. Where a State submits a request for an extension, the implementation date will be extended an additional 90 days while LEAA reviews the documentation for approval or disapproval. To be approved, such revised schedule must be consistent with the timetable and procedures set out below:

(a) July 31, 1978—Submission of certificate of compliance with:

(1) Individual access, challenge, and review requirements;

(2) Administrative security;

(3) Physical security to the maximum extent feasible.

(b) Thirty days after the end of a State's next legislative session—Submission to LEAA of a description of State policy on dissemination of criminal history record information.

(c) Six months after the end of a State's legislative session—Submission to LEAA of a brief and concise description of standards and operating procedures to be followed by all criminal justice agencies covered by LEAA regulations in complying with the State policy on dissemination.

(d) Eighteen months after the end of a State's legislative session—Submission to LEAA of a certificate attesting to the conduct of an audit of the State central repository and of a random number of other criminal justice agencies in compliance with LEAA regulations.

JAMES M. H. GREGG,
Office of Planning and Management, Law Enforcement Assistance Administration.

[FR Doc.77–34877 Filed 12–5–77; 8:45 am]

Appendix C

Comparison of
1974/1977 LEAA Privacy and
Security Surveys

ITEM	1974	1977
1. State Regulatory Authority	7	38
2. Privacy and Security Council	2	10
3. Regulation of Dissemination	24	40
4. Right to Inspect	12	40
5. Right to Challenge	10	30
6. Judicial Review of Challenged Information	10	30
7. Purging Nonconviction Information	20	23
8. Purging Conviction Information	7	13
9. Sealing Nonconviction Information	8	15
10. Sealing Conviction Information	7	20
11. Removal of Disqualifications	6	22

ITEM	1974	1977
12. Right to State Nonexistence of a Record	6	13
13. Researcher Access	6	12
14. Accuracy and Completeness	14	41
15. Dedication	2	3
16. Civil Remedies	6	22
17. Criminal Penalties	18	35
18. Public Records	9	43
19. Separation of Files	5	10
20. Regulation of Intelligence Collection	3	10
21. Regulation of Intelligence Dissemination	7	24
22. Security	12	26
23. Transaction Logs	6	11
24. Training of Employees	4	18
25. Listing of Information Systems	1	8

(Source: U.S. Department of Justice, Law Enforcement Assistance Administration. *Privacy and Security of Criminal History Information, Compendium of State Legislation.* Washington, D.C., 1978, p. 27.)

Index